STUDIES IN GERMAN LITERATURE,
LINGUISTICS, AND CULTURE
Vol. 32

STUDIES IN GERMAN LITERATURE, LINGUISTICS,
AND CULTURE

Editorial Board

Frank Banta, Donald Daviau, Gerald Gillespie, Ingeborg Glier, Michael Hamburger, Gerhart Hoffmeister, Herbert Knust, Egbert Krispyn, Victor Lange, Richard Lawson, James Lyon, Erika Metzger, Michael Metzger, Hans-Gert Roloff, John Spalek, Frank Trommler, Heinz Wetzel

Managing Editors
James Hardin and Gunther Holst
(*University of South Carolina*)

CAMDEN HOUSE
Columbia, South Carolina

Myth of a Nation

Otto W. Johnston

The Myth of a Nation —

Literature and Politics in Prussia under Napoleon

CAMDEN HOUSE

Set in Palatino and printed on acid-free paper.
Copyright © 1989 by
CAMDEN HOUSE, INC.
Drawer 2025
Columbia, SC 29202 USA

Library of Congress Catalog Card Number: 87–70864
All Rights Reserved
Printed in the United States of America

First Edition

ISBN:0–938100–53–X

Printed by Thomson-Shore, Inc.
Dexter, Michigan

For Barbara, Robby and Erik

Contents

Introduction		xiii
I	Stein and the Prussian Poets	1
II	Fichte and the Mythopoeic Process	15
III	Kleist's Philosophical Crisis	29
IV	Ernst Moritz Arndt and the New Nation	85
V	Reflections of the Myth. Presence and Absence (Schleiermacher, Süvern, Stägemann vs. Palm, Kotzebue, and Iffland)	103
VI	The Extremist Friedrich Ludwig Jahn	129
VII	Theodor Körner: The Myth Personified	143
VIII	Victory and Aftermath	159
IX	Transformations. The Little Corporal and Little Germany	177
Selected Bibliography		205
Index		227

Acknowledgments

Without the encouragement and assistance of colleagues, students, librarians and numerous other well-wishers, this book could not have been written. I am grateful to the Alexander von Humboldt Stiftung for stipends which supported two extended study trips to the Federal Republic, especially to Professor Dr. Karl Möckl at the University of Bamberg for guidance in the final stages. Günter Trumpke and others at the Bavarian State Library in Bamberg cheerfully gathered the materials I needed and pointed out a number of things I had overlooked. I have received considerable support from my own university: the Humanities Council and the Graduate School's Division of Sponsored Research at the University of Florida provided summer grants and assistance with publication costs. I am indebted to Vice President Donald R. Price in this respect and to Charles F. Sidman, Professor of German History and Dean of our College of Liberal Arts and Sciences, whose endorsement and introductions to contacts in Germany were invaluable to the completion of this study.

I wish also to acknowledge the support I received from Dr. Wulf Wülfing and his seminar students in Bochum who have assembled one of the finest collections on Napoleon in the Federal Republic. Professor Norbert Altenhofer and his doctoral seminar at Frankfurt and Professor Benjamin Gajek and his assistants in Regensburg, particularly Dr. Ernst Weber, helped me find the bibliographical and archival material I needed. I appreciate the many invitations extended by Donald Horward at Florida State University to discuss my findings in open forums and colloquia. He has been a source of constant inspiration and information. To my current and former students, especially to David Forbes, who have provided me not only with an audience but also with innumerable insights, I am much obliged. To the many friendly and helpful experts at the *Nationale Forschungs– und Gedenkstätten der klassischen deutschen Literatur* in Weimar in the German Democratic Republic I owe a special debt of gratitude. Many thanks also to Ray Jones at the University of Florida libraries who located the material I needed at the Foreign Office in London, and then acquired copies of the relevant documents. For his careful reading and perceptive suggestions, I would like to thank Wolfgang Wittkowski at SUNY-Albany. I also wish to thank Josef Herrmann and his family for making our stays in Germany so pleasant.

Without the considerable encoding skills of my typist, Annemarie Sykes, my manuscript would still be illegible and incomplete. Finally, I wish to acknowledge the debt to my wife Barbara whose patience and forbearance approached the saintly as I worked over the years piecing this puzzle together.

Introduction

THE PROFILES PRESENTED HERE do not seek simply to draw attention to such writers as Ernst Moritz Arndt, Theodor Körner and Friedrich Ludwig Jahn, all of whom enjoyed enormous popularity in Wilhelminian Germany and are all but forgotten today. The purpose is instead to study the interaction between politics and literary productivity at a significant juncture in Germany's social evolution when, for the first time, statesmen invited, even prodded, men-of-letters in Prussia to get involved in the political process. The chapters on Fichte, Heinrich von Kleist, E. M. Arndt, Jahn and Theodor Körner document each author's interest in promoting a specific view of "Germany". By adopting a distinct structure recommended by political leaders for their patriotic works, these writers sought to bring about the founding of a single German nation on the ruins of the Holy Roman Empire once Napoleon and his "Latin hordes" were driven out.

This is the story of the activist faction in the Prussian cabinet headed by the powerful Baron Heinrich Friedrich Karl vom und zum Stein and how its goals are reflected in the patriotic literature of the time. It is an analysis of a select group of authors, who, in a sense, began as propagandists but soon evolved into myth-makers, as they reached out not just to their own, but to future generations. Fearing that their socio-political vision of a single German nation would not be realized in their own day, they called upon their sons and daughters and their unborn children to complete the task of German unification. This is an account of a cultural movement dating back to at least the fifteenth century, impeded by the Reformation, then politicized three hundred years later in Prussia during the French occupation. It is the history of a literary strategy adapted from the propaganda of Royalists in France, reworked to rally bourgeois circles in Germany and repeated during a six year period in every genre from drama to poetry, philosophical discourse to political essay, sermon to soliloquy. It examines a structure found in specific works written between 1807 and 1813 and then not seen again in the nationalistic writings of authors from any other German state but Prussia before or after the Napoleonic wars.

The following nine chapters focus on individual representations of that brand of patriotism espoused by the reform faction in the Prussian government, without striving to exhaust the search for reflections of the reformers' political agenda in each work of every poet. Both Kleist and Arndt, for example, wrote political poems as well as works in other genres. In the case of Kleist, however, the play rather than the poem reflects the myth of the nation more clearly. Two volumes of Arndt's *Spirit of the Times* offer more discernible examples of political persuasion as a literary influence than do any of the poems. For that reason, the more representative works will be scrutinized and the poems neglected. In fact, once the underlying structural pattern employed by the activists' literary allies is understood, any other work of a given author, indeed any work of the period, can be examined in terms of the aims of Prussian reformers.

The works sympathetic to those aims bear a remarkably similar structure. The authors we shall investigate used comparable structural components, similar rhetorical devices; they focused on the same heroic figures and presented corresponding political perspectives in specific works written while Germany suffered under French occupation. Moreover, the general pattern was proposed by reform-oriented statesmen who blamed the defeat of Prussia at Jena and Auerstedt in 1806 as much on the political apathy or pro-French attitude of contemporaneous German writers as on the inadequacy of her army. The writers we shall examine here responded to Stein's criticism regarding their lack of patriotic fervor and sought to counteract pro-Napoleonic propaganda with a politicized myth of one German nation.

Chapter five compares specific works by Schleiermacher, Süvern and Stägemann with such anti-Napoleon pamphlets as *Germany in Her Low Abasement* and with dramas by Kotzebue and Iffland which appeared at roughly the same time. The aim here is to demonstrate that not all anti-French writers in Prussia embraced the literary strategy of activist statesmen. In fact, only a select few were privy to the literary blueprint recommended by this particular faction in the Prussian cabinet. Many other examples of anti-French literature written by Germans not aligned with the reform movement could have been cited; the ones chosen are revealing as they fictionalize Napoleon or seek to represent the heroes from Germany's past who attracted the Prussian myth-makers, but they did so without employing the activist's literary formula. Thus the differences between anti-French, pro-German writing in general, and the work of reform party sympathizers can be more readily discerned. The literary production of the nationalist myth-makers contrasts sharply, for example, with the work of so skilled a political commentator as Friedrich Gentz. But Gentz opposed Napoleon not out of any yearning for a new German nation, but out of loyalty to the Austrian crown. Achim von Arnim, Joseph von Eichendorff and Ludwig Tieck are not involved here because they were less concerned with the idea of "one German nation" in the future than with the religious unity, venerated traditions and the moral ideals that Germany had purportedly enjoyed in the past and subsequently lost. Their individual positions *vis-à-vis* the reformers' plans for German unification are less enthusiastic, more cautious, culturally rather than politically oriented. Their desire to conserve rather than tear down and rebuild is rooted in affection for what they perceived to be their German heritage handed down from the "Christian" Middle Ages and the Renaissance and since corrupted. Although often anti-Napoleon and always pro-German, their works do not exhibit the telltale pattern found in the patriotic writings of those authors aligned with Stein and the reform faction.

The last two chapters focus on events after the Wars of Liberation and the Congress of Vienna, when nationalism fell into disrepute and regional loyalties were once again the order of the day. A modest nationalistic movement outside of Prussia aspiring to German unification was stymied once specially empowered boards of inquiry established during the *Restauration* uncovered questionable, if not treasonable, machinations. Secret organizations which had likely plotted against the king were discovered, as were unauthorized contacts with British spies on the continent, covert activity between the activists and the British Foreign Office and several expressions of political aims which ran contrary to the king's wishes. These discoveries set the unification movement back for decades.

In the last chapter we shall survey the metapolitical implications of the myth of the German nation by examining the transformation of the image of Napoleon and the view of a united Germany which emerged as Bismarck succeeded in bringing the German princes together. These leaps across the decades point out some of the consequences of a dream twisted into ideology. They do not imply that the historical movement from myth to ideology proceeded in a straight line or that the myth-makers among the Romantics bear a direct responsibility for the house that Hitler built. Our rapid survey serves only to emphasize the perversions, the radical reinterpretations of a myth. Much more needs to be said about the role of political and literary historians who recast the earlier hopes for a new nation in terms of latter-day exigencies. But that is the story of how ideology is produced, not of myth-making, and I hope to deal with it in a future study.

We shall demonstrate here that Bismarck's creation did not conform to the earlier vision. The myth of the German nation, as it evolved in Prussia under French occupation, called for a unity of all people, not just of princes, a coalescence of spirit and civic-mindedness, not merely a unification of territories and power. It had presupposed a greater voice in the affairs of state for those who rushed to her defense; it had promised a more liberal constitution and more personal freedom for the citizenry; it pledged Prussia to the task of instilling moral character in all German subjects. To these ends the new nation was to commit itself to a program of national education, develop proficiency in the mother tongue in Germany's young people, dedicate itself to the arts and literature as well as to reverence for one's German forebears and one's descendants.

Prussia was not to govern by force of arms, but by the example she set for the rest of the nation. Prussia and Austria were to cooperate as parts of one whole which would also comprise five districts to be established after the dissolution of the pro-French Confederation of the Rhine. The political and literary propagators of this vision sought sacrifices from the privileged class and demanded political reform and more social equality. They continued to press for the unification of all German states even after the Congress of Vienna had decided otherwise. These German writers were united foremost in their desire for the founding of a new Germany, one nation, not seen before, but destined to endure for a millennium.

O. W. J.
Gainesville, Florida

1
Stein and the Prussian Poets

ON MARCH 27, 1807, GEORGE CANNING, Great Britain's newly appointed foreign secretary, expressed an interest in improving relations with Prussia. "His majesty will hear and attend to any proposition His Prussian majesty may have to offer," he writes, regarding the ways and means for effective resistance to French hegemony.[1] Five months earlier Prussia had suffered a crushing defeat at the battles of Jena and Auerstedt, prompting Canning to urge the Prussian government to form a common front against Napoleon together with the other states of northern Germany. Canning reasoned that any challenge to France would require more than the rebuilding of Prussia's outdated mercenary army; it would need the concerted efforts of the states in northern Germany and a broad base of popular support. Once these were assured, Prussia should seek an accord with Russia, whereupon Great Britain would dispatch an expeditionary force to northern Europe. To these ends Canning authorized a secret envoy, John Hely-Hutchinson, to place £100,000 at Prussia's disposal.

At King Frederick William III's court, Canning's recommendations were greeted coolly. Great Britain should show good intentions, the court party argued, not by merely sending a secret agent with some money, but rather by consigning arms, ammunition and even a military force to the continent in order to extract Prussia from her difficulties. Without such an initiative, Prussia's interest would best be served by seeking an accommodation with France. At least one influential statesman disagreed with this assessment: Prussia's Minister of State, Baron vom und zum Stein. Forming a loose association of those government officials and military experts sharing the same opinion, Stein's "reform party" advocated the complete reorganization of the Prussian state that would serve as a model for the rest of Germany. Stein, who had defended British policy throughout much of his career in the service of Prussia, urged the king to heed Canning's advice, to strive for unity with other German states and to turn to the peo-

---

[1] *Foreign Office. Correspondence: Prussia* 64/74. See the dispatches between George Canning and John Hely-Hutchinson, nos. 14–54.

ple rather than to the nobility (*Junker*) for support. Together with Neithardt von Gneisenau and Gerhard Scharnhorst, he agreed with the Foreign Office that both unity and popular support could be proven by the insurrection of farmers, trade workers and merchants in northern Germany aided by the Prussian army and supported by the Russian czar. As the reformers strove for this goal, they began to think less about Prussia in particular and more in terms of Germany as a whole. By 1812, Stein would state categorically in a letter to Count Münster in London: "I have but one fatherland, that is [all] Germany."[2]

In an effort to promote the spirit of insurrection in the populace of the north German states, Stein recommended a literary strategy to poets and publicists who wished to aid Prussia and to help in the creation of a united German nation which would be established once the French were ousted from the territories of the former Holy Roman Empire. To be sure, the notion of a single "Germany" was not new in 1807. As a cultural vision, promoting the German language as a worthy medium for world literature and German art as a significant contribution to the civilized world, the idea of one German nation had had a long and venerated tradition. Whether such a cultural heritage can be dated as far back as the battle in the Teutoburg Forest (9 A.D.) when Arminius defeated the Roman legions under Varus is at best questionable. Despite the insistence of Fichte, Arndt, Kleist and others, Tacitus's account of Arminius's tribe, the Cherusci, suggests that there was little "national" loyalty among the tribes, but considerable regional cohesiveness. The discovery of ancient manuscripts owned by the Medici family in 1455 is another matter. With this find, humanists turned their attention away from Livy and towards Tacitus. In later years, such cultural monuments as Conrad Celtis's edition of the *Germania illustrata* (1491) evoked curiosity and prompted scholarly inquiry into the history of the early unvanquished, "morally pure" Germans. Without delving into all the details, it may be said that by 1501 Jakob Wimpfeling, venerated as the "Praeceptor Germaniae" because of his pro-German, anti-French perspective, could edit a *Germania* with a preface containing such extravagant patriotism that it provoked the heated criticism of Thomas Murner.

However, the political tendencies inherent in such cultural developments were stymied by the Reformation which divided Germany irrevocably along confessional lines. The Thirty Years War of the next century solidified that division, and the efforts of such patriots as Martin

---

[2] *Freiherr vom Stein. Briefe und amtliche Schriften*, ed. Erich Botzenhart and Walter Hubatsch (Stuttgart: Kohlhammer, 1957–1974) 3:818. Quotes from this edition unless otherwise noted. Roman numerals in the text refer to volume number, arabic numerals to page. Noted hereafter as *Stein*.

Opitz and D. G. Morhof [*Instruction in the German Language and Poetry, 1682*] were confined to the cultural sphere with no socio-political concerns. It was difficult, if not impossible, for German poets to muster any genuine enthusiasm for the only supra-regional political entity existing, that is the Holy Roman Empire, because, as the legal scholar Samuel Pufendorf pointed out in *De statu imperii Germanici* (1667), this state had become a "monstrous political formation" incapable of providing for the common defense or of securing internal peace.

To be sure, there were even before Stein's initiatives several indications of literary commitments to the idea of a Germany. Klopstock, for example, thought of himself as a "German" rather than as a "Saxon" when he made the "Fatherland" the theme of many odes. In later life, he turned from religious topics and devoted his energies to historical and political events: the death of Maria Theresa, the French Revolution, the fate of Germany. Because they considered him to be a uniquely "German" poet, the members of the "Göttinger Hain," Hölty, Voss, the brothers Stolberg, dedicated to him their collection of poems (1773). Lessing called for a national theater and Herder bemoaned the lack of a German capital with the cultural status of Paris. However, these sentiments had neither the political backing of the regional princes nor the support of a middle class reading public whose economic interests were focused more on a unified, stable marketplace which political unification would guarantee.

By July 1807, when the disastrous Peace of Tilsit was signed, "Deutschland" had become merely a collective designation for those German states outside Prussia and Austria in which German was spoken. The Napoleonic era witnessed visions of a German "cultural identity," with and without political overtones. Hopes of a German intellectual community co-existed with retrogressive utopian representations of a united, Christian "Germany" which had existed in the distant past. Catholics and Protestants shared the glory that was Arminius (Hermann) or Theoderich (Dietrich von Bern), yet split over the issue of Frederick the Great or Luther. The idea of a single politically united German nation was either rejected outright or relegated to a purely intellectual realm. After the Tilsit Peace, however, a new current blended with the tradition of cultural identity to produce the myth of the German nation. Patriotism took a new direction as German statesmen and writers co-operated in molding citizens. Compelled to accept the humiliating terms of the treaty, Prussian reformers with increasing frequency prodded men-of-letters to counter the influence of Imperial France. While some Romantics reminisced about a Germany lost in the Middle Ages or the Renaissance, a certain group of patriots in Prussia envisioned a new nation of the future. These mythmakers did not look back, refusing to glorify Frederick the Great or other aristocratic rulers from the "glorious" past. They sought in history only those strengths and role models which would help to create a better Germany in the future — one nation in which unity was the natural outgrowth of cultural identity, with Prussia serving as guardian and archetype. As formulated between 1807 and 1813, this idea carried with it, as does any powerful social myth, the seed of ideological servitude; however, such implications could not yet be realized in practice, as they were to be in Wilhelminian Germany.

In the shadow of a treaty that cost Prussia 48% of her territory and 47% of her subjects, Stein and his fellow activists determined to establish this new nation on the ruins of the old. Stein's plans, as they developed between 1807 and 1813, called for deposing those princes who had joined the Confederation of the Rhine under Napoleon's protection, dividing their territories into five districts which would then unite with Prussia and Austria. Delegates from all the districts would form a National Assembly to draft a new constitution, granting a greater, though still limited voice in public affairs to the upper middle class. The army was to be modernized and streamlined, great centers of learning founded, the arts subsidized. But first Napoleon and his "grande armée" had to be driven out. With this goal in mind, Stein and the members of his activist party sought publicists from all spheres of German cultural life who would promote the formation of one unified German nation, and prepare the populace for a mass insurrection—the signal for a British troop landing in northern Germany.

In contrast to King Frederick William III and the Court party headed by such officials as Frederick William von Zastrow, Otto Frederick von Voss, General Karl Köckritz and Count Christian Haugwitz, who cared little about securing a broad social base for governmental policy, Stein showed an interest in molding public opinion long before the catastrophe at Jena-Auerstedt and the Treaty of Tilsit. In official papers dating back to 1805, Stein shows his willingness to inform the public and thereby gain popular support for new initiatives. Because they were practically shut out from all policy-making, poets and novelists, essayists and dramatists tended toward political apathy. Since they were not permitted a voice in the formation of public policy nor in its implementation, they tended as a group to remain aloof from politics, engaging instead in flights of the imagination far from the business of state. With the defeat of Prussia, Stein and his faction needed desperately to enlist their aid in persuading others to join the "good cause." For Stein, the defeat at Jena had proven once and for all that the aristocratic system, as practiced in Prussia, was outdated; the *Junker* were unable to provide for the common defense of the state. Therefore, banning together as a single German nation was for him the only hope of the German states. But how was he to win the support of the intellectuals who traditionally had no voice in such matters?

The reaction of Prussian men-of-letters to the humiliating defeat and dishonorable peace was discouraging. Six months after the treaty, Prussian poets and their small, yet influential reading public were still apathetic. On January 4, 1808, Barthold Georg Niebuhr complained to Stein that Prussia's scholars were not the state's best citizens, nor the king's best subjects.[3] More interested in the latest news from France, they seemed to care far too little for the consequences of the defeat and the needs of the country. In the following month, Stein wrote to Vincke that it was high time to mobilize a coalition of the best writers to off-set anticipated criticism of their plans for reorganizing the state.[4] Educated segments of the population, he wrote to Schrötter, should be allowed to participate in the business of government.[5] On August 14, 1808, he reported to Frederick William III that he was working on a plan to "preserve and strengthen the spirit of resistance in Germany."[6] Three days earlier he noted in a memorandum that the means to finance his insurrectionist strategy would have to come from the British government, which would also be called upon to safeguard the royal family if his tactics failed.[7]

During his later exile at Brünn, Stein articulated his views on the relationship between literature and public opinion more precisely. The marriage of Napoleon to the daughter of the Austrian emperor on March 11, 1810 prompted him to explain in detail why the French system would soon lead to Austria's ruin. In his "Brünn Memorandum," the former Prussian Minister of State offered his most concise pronouncement on literary matters. Noting at the outset that public opinion arrived at after a free exchange of ideas does not exist in Europe, Stein points out that even the efficient French police with all their brutality have been unable to prevent the frequent emergence of pre-eminent writers who had the courage to oppose French tyranny in speeches, literary works and in personal conduct. News of such attempts also nurtures the desire for freedom and independence in other countries under the French yoke. If liberal and noble principles are to regain their supremacy and former dignity in the German-speaking world, then, he argues, the intensity of the oppressors' deceptive art must be counteracted by government management of literature and educational institutions:

---

[3] *Stein* 2/2:611.

[4] *Stein* 2/2:655.

[5] Cf. Stein to Minister Schrötter (June 27, 1808) in: *Stein* 2/2:763–768.

[6] *Stein* 2/2:812. See also Gudrun Wilms, *Nationalgefühl und Deutschlandbild des Freiherrn vom Stein* (Diss. Stuttgart 1970).

[7] *Stein* 2/2:810–812.

> Because of their love of reading and the great numbers affected in some way by public schools, Germans are more influenced by literary works than are other people. This love of reading is a consequence of their quiet disposition, their predilection for the contemplative life as well as their governing constitution, which entrusts the country's business to a handful of public officials and not to the nation [. . . .] The number of writers is larger in Germany than in any other European country because numerous scientific institutions provide a great many scholars with pursuits and positions.[8]

After presenting supporting statistical data, he underscores the need to control literary production:

> These statistics illustrate to some degree the extent of the influence scholars and literature exert on public opinion and how important it is to take hold of such a lever and not to leave its application to chance or to the hand of the enemy.

Stein perceives writers and scholars as producers of that mythology which creates and preserves a given socio-economic structure. A government should employ those gifted citizens "who write for the good cause" to its own ends and reward those who distinguish themselves. Therefore, he recommends that Austria remove her many antiquated regulations which restrict the flow of ideas, and instead utilize literary journals and newspapers, improve her academic institutions and thwart the literary efforts of those pernicious writers who either place the present unfortunate circumstances in a charitable light, or "feign a higher position of impartiality from which to reason speciously about the catastrophe of our era with the same indifference they show toward the fate of distant races and ancient peoples."

According to Stein, it is not enough to "guide" the opinions of the *present* generation; it is more important to develop "the powers" of the *next*. To this end, he recommends combining Pestalozzi's educational methods, which "elevate the independent activity of the intellect," with an appropriate program of military training. For Stein, the pupil is the means by which the preservation of the state is ensured. Pacifistic convictions have no place in this design: the educator and the writer are instruments for eradicating nonbelligerent tendencies and for instilling in the citizen "the feeling of obligation (*Pflichtgefühl*) to give his life for the state." He concludes this exhortation by advising the regents of Germany to entrust these two powerful instruments, literature and education, to the discerning, loyal and molding hands of those who know the scholars, the conditions in the sciences, the educational institutions as well as the moral and intellectual needs of the nation.

---

[8] *Denkschrift*. Brünn (March 1810) in: *Stein* 3:296.

To his friends and political allies, he recommended Beauchamp's *History of the Vendée*.⁹ Stein perceived in the bitter struggle of the early 1790s between the last Royalist stronghold in France and the superior forces of the Republic a propaganda stratagem that would work in northern Germany. In addition, the work contained many appended examples of the Royalists' literary tactics that could be studied. Alphonse Beauchamp's *Histoire de la Guerre de la Vendée et des Chouans* appeared in three volumes at Paris in 1806; editions were also printed in 1807 and 1809. The work was well-known in British military circles: according to a "Report respecting the present state of North Germany," the Foreign Office took under advisement as early as February 1807 a plan "to organize a second Vendée," consisting of Hesse and perhaps Hanover, "should [the French] entirely be defeated in Poland."¹⁰ Stein made extensive use of the volumes in 1811 when he drafted his historical observations.¹¹ As early as 1808, however, he cited the Royalist campaign in the Vendée as prime example of a popular insurrection.¹² As we shall see, the argumentation, thought patterns and general structure of the work influenced markedly his thoughts on both public opinion and its successful management.

Perhaps the most significant contention Stein found in Beauchamp's work was that a successful insurrection depends less upon rallying the masses than upon the support of the upper classes. According to Beauchamp, secret military plans and maneuvers must be accompanied by skillfully written appeals to the educated and well-to-do; attempts at manipulating public opinion must always include a line of reasoning convincing to the upper class.¹³ Successful propaganda should be directed at the educated and should entreat petty officials in particular to join the ranks of the insurrectionists.¹⁴

Beauchamp outlines ways and means for obtaining British financial support: by opening a seaport to British ships and sending envoys to

---

⁹ See Stein to Count Arnim-Boitzenburg (April 25, 1811) in: *Stein* 2:508; Stein to Gneisenau (Aug. 17, 1811) 3:568: Memorandum to Hardenberg (Aug. 24, 1811) 3:570–572. The Memorandum is significant because it deals specifically with "awakening the public spirit." Hardenberg, however, did not share Stein's views.

¹⁰ *Foreign Office Correspondence: Prussia* 64/77, 45.

¹¹ See *Stein* 3:509.

¹² See Stein's *Immediatbericht* (To Frederick William III) of August 14, 1808 (2/2:812).

¹³ Alphonse Beauchamp, *Histoire de la Guerre de la Vendée et des Chouans* (Paris: Giguet et Michaud, 1806) 1:125. Extensive translations were made by Joseph von Hormayr, *Der Vendee-Krieg* (Vienna: Strauß, 1808).

¹⁴ *Ibid.*, 1:128.

Downing Street, those opposed to the French Revolution assure themselves of a sympathetic British ear and military aid.[15] Lack of mercy and unyielding suppression by the enemy can be used to great advantage by adept propagandists to fuel the patriotic spirit in the hearts of all people.[16] The first volume concludes with examples of Royalist propaganda, "pour propager l'esprit et les veus de l'association."[17]

The arguments contained in these *Pièces Justificatives* follow a prescribed pattern. A common image is "the blood which unites us with our brothers, our forefathers and our friends."[18] Religion, it is maintained, strengthens these bonds. Common to much of this doctrinal literature is a decidedly historical perspective. The public is prevailed upon to recognize the individual as a link in a permanent chain, connecting the past with the future. The enemy tears "from your heart the principles of your faith" and amasses the nation's "immense treasures at the price of your tears and your blood."[19] Historical figures abound in this literature; they address "the people of Clovis, Charlemagne and St. Louis."[20]

A conspicuous element is the bond of language which allegedly unites the insurrectionists against the Republicans. "Will you remain insensitive to this language?" asks the propagandist. "It is the language of your friends, brothers, of the people," he declares; it is the voice of religion. Skillfully, he points out that the Republicans have introduced a new idiom, a different jargon — they, the enemy, speak a different language. The insistence upon concerted action is uppermost in the mind of the propagandist. Neutrality is an untenable position; in times such as these no one may assume an indifferent attitude:

> Today there is no place in the state for cold and egotistical people, who, languishing in shameful laziness, affect a culpable indifference to the public interest, and standing aside become a party to personal enrichment from the leftovers of our public and private resources.[21]

---

[15] *Ibid.*, 1:278.

[16] *Ibid.*, 1:136–140.

[17] *Ibid.*, 1:373.

[18] See "Plan de l'association bretonne, le 5 decembre 1791," *Ibid.*, 1:383f.

[19] "Qu'arracher de vos coeurs les principes de votre foi, que s'amasser d'immenses trésors aux prix de vos larmes et de votre sang . . ." (1:384).

[20] *Ibid.*, 1:385.

[21] "Il n'est plus aujourd'hui de place dans l'etat pour ces êtres froids et égoistes qui, languissant dans une honteuse oisiveté, affectant une coupable indifférence pour l'intérêt général, se tiennent à l'écart prêts à s'engraisser du débris de la fortune publique et des fortunes privées." 1:385.

The parallel with Baron Stein's comments in his *Brünn Memorandum* of March 11, 1810 about political apathy is striking. He had castigated Germans who "feign a higher position of impartiality"in much the same way.[22] When Stein lashed out at the political indifference of the German intelligentsia, he was obviously following the lead of the propagandist quoted by Beauchamp. Yet the correspondence and near-quotes do not end with this critical comment: the *Brünn Memorandum* and the Royalist proclamations from the Vendée contain so many identical structural components that we discern in the latter the source of the former. A major structural unit of the "Justifications" comprises those arguments dealing with public education. The propagandists present "education and humanity" as the foremost goals of the Royalists, insisting that parochial education guaranteed the continuity of Catholic culture. Stein, in the *Brünn Memorandum*, adapts these to the political scene in the German-speaking countries: his second paragraph is devoted to the collapse of traditional values concomitant with the French takeover of Germany's educational institutions. He returns to this theme later, when he expounds upon the purpose of education. Although the Memorandum ends with a critique of ecclesiastical educational facilities, the basic arguments remain intact.

The "language bond" figuring prominently in the Royalist literature is also one of Stein's major contentions. Once again, we can observe a slight modification: "The suppression of the intellect cannot be as thorough nor as destructive today, given the present state of culture, as it was in the twelfth and thirteenth centuries, because of the various means of disseminating and obtaining information as well as the differences and peculiarities of the national languages spoken in Europe."[23] In his remarks on controlling and manipulating public debate, Stein is basing his program on the unique features of Germany's language and literature.[24]

Stein's statements regarding language lead in turn to the historical perspective which views the individual as the nexus of past and future. He not only describes the evolution of educational, political and religious institutions from the twelfth century to his own day but also deals at length with the ways and means of "managing" the "opinions and powers" of the following generations. The bond of lineage is thus the third major structural unit in Stein's political thinking as reflected in the *Brünn Memorandum*.

We see, then, that the Prussian minister in exile superimposed his own political insights upon the basic structure of the *Pièces Justificatives*. He

---

[22] *Stein* 3:297.

[23] *Stein* 3:294f.

[24] *Stein* 3:296.

modified his source to serve his own political purposes with regard to the current socio-political circumstances facing Austria and Prussia. Stein was also interested in the sections dealing with the complex network of British agents in Europe,[25] in England's political aims and military projections on the continent,[26] and in controlling the younger generation.[27] Ironically then, French propagandists served as a source for Stein's political writing, as examples for German myth-makers and hence as a cornerstone for the myth of the German nation.

Adapted by Stein from the propaganda of Catholic France to serve an insurrectionist strategy in Protestant northern Germany, the three basic components of the Vendée literature — a program of national education, a focus on the language bond uniting a national group and a portrayal of the contemporary citizen as a link between a nation's past and future development — became the blueprint for the work of those authors who cooperated with Stein's political faction. Apostrophes to historical national heroes, appeals to religious sentiment, disgust with political neutrals and pleas to the upper class to unite in sacrifice for concerted action characterize the Prussian mythogenesis as well.

There were good reasons for the positive reception of this particular pattern among Prussia's forward-looking poets, dramatists and essayists. Each set of arguments had a tradition in German-speaking territories identified for the most part with progressive thinking. A program of national education, for example, had been advocated repeatedly during the last three decades of the eighteenth century as the only means for avoiding a revolution and guaranteeing evolution to freedom and justice. As early as 1785, the *Berlinische Monatsschrift* had published an article, "New Way to Immortality for Princes," in which the author (probably Johann Erich Biester) urged monarchs to educate their subjects to freedom. As soon as the needed instructional facilities were in place, kings were to break their scepters, give the nation a constitution, and voluntarily abdicate power.[28]

However, the German princes had neither the resources nor the resolve to educate the people. Vested interests blasted the plan as dangerous and radical, the strong link between education and political freedom caused public education to be regarded as a threat to power, privilege and

---

[25] See additional examples in Beauchamp, *Histoire*, 3:77.

[26] Beauchamp, *Histoire*, 3:184.

[27] Beauchamp, *Histoire*, 3:457.

[28] "Neuer Weg zur Unsterblichkeit für Fürsten," *Berlinische Monatsschrift* 5 (1785): 239–247.

domestic tranquility. So the advocates of bourgeois progressiveness soon provoked a backlash from the ideologues of the aristocracy. By the mid-1790s the debate had become so impassioned that Frederick William II, yielding to the nobility, ordered a vigorous crackdown on writers who "encouraged ordinary people to engage in useless meditation about topics which far transcend their understanding and judgment."[29] Frederick William III followed in his father's footsteps when he commissioned his minister von Massow to draft a plan for educating the nation. Although von Massow's strategy was heralded by the nobility in 1798 as a workable program of "national education," it contained little more than recommendations for instilling loyalty to the Prussian crown in young minds.[30] After the defeat at Jena-Auerstedt, progressives saw an opportunity to re-open the discussion by addressing the entire German "nation," not just Prussia, and formulating political arguments after the Vendée propaganda which had urged citizens to revolt. After 1806 the more utopian arguments could be heard once again because, as Fichte so cogently argued, the educational system was the only social institution left to the Germans: the French controlled every other.[31]

The emphasis on the mother tongue had the support of both the German aristocracy and the bourgeoisie. Even the ideologues of Prussia's *ancien regime*, who spoke mostly French, recognized the need for developing proficiency in German. According to an atlas published in 1791,[32] the Prussian monarchy consisted of fifteen separate territories, four of which were outside the Holy Roman Empire, in which seven languages were spoken. As late as 1799, those inhabitants who spoke scant or no German showed little inclination to integrate into the Prussian mainstream nor, according to a report in the (former) Prussian Secret Archive, to learn German. The landed gentry, wishing to communicate with Polish, Lithuanian,

---

[29] Quoted by Kurt Eisner, *Das Ende des Reiches. Deutschland und Preußen im Zeitalter der großen Revolution* (Berlin: Buchhandlung Vorwärts, 1907): 44; for details, see Klaus Epstein, *The Genesis of German Conservatism* (Princeton, NJ: Princeton University Press, 1966).

[30] See "Der Nationalerziehungsplan des Ministers von Massow" in Helmut König, *Zur Geschichte der Nationalerziehung in Deutschland im letzten Drittel des achtzehnten Jahrhunderts* [Monumenta Paedagogica, ed. Kommission für Deutsche Erziehungs- und Schulgeschichte der deutschen Akademie der Wissenschaften zu Berlin] (Berlin: Akademie Verlag, 1960) 1:305ff.

[31] Johann Gottlieb Fichte, *Reden an die deutsche Nation* (Berlin: Realschulbuchhandlung, 1808): 353f.: "Möchte er [der Staat] lebendig einsehen, daß ihm durchaus kein anderer Wirkungskreis übriggelassen ist ... außer diesem, der Erziehung der kommenden Geschlechter."

[32] Friedrich Gli Leonhardi, *Erdbeschreibung der preußischen Monarchie* (Halle: Schwetschke, 1791–1798) 1:5.

Estonian, Latvian and Lusitian-speaking subjects, and the bourgeoisie, seeking to consolidate emerging markets, could unite behind Johann Friedrich Zöllner's appraisal of 1804: "Let it not be said that the German language will be introduced gradually in these provinces all by itself."[33] The Vendée propaganda offered ways to politicize the language argument to inspire resistance. After 1807 the "holy bond of language" became an integral part of "national consciousness," which Fichte molded from the philosopher's rostrum, Schleiermacher preached from his pulpit, Kleist reproduced in nationalistic dramas, Arndt promoted in poems or essays and Stägemann and Körner heralded in their "war songs."

In such works, we also find the third component from the Vendée propaganda which Stein recommended: the image of the individual as a link in a great chain. In 1790, Edmund Burke had popularized the argument in his *Reflections on the Revolution in France*:

> [The state] is a partnership in all science; a partnership in all art; a partnership in every virtue, and in all perfection. As the ends of such a partnership cannot be obtained in many generations, it becomes a partnership not only between those who are living, but between those who are living, those who are dead and those who are to be born. Each contract of each particular state is but a clause in the great primeval contract of eternal society, linking the lower with the higher natures, connecting the visible and the invisible world, according to a fixed contract sanctioned by the inviolable oath which holds all physical and moral natures, each in their appointed place.[34]

Similar thought is found in German as early as 1758 in Johann Georg Zimmermann's *On National Pride*[35] and F. E. Rambach's essay "Education to Patriotism" published in the *Yearbooks of the Prussian Monarchy* as late as 1798. However, Rambach, following the lead of several predecessors, had not used the image to advance the notion of a new, united Germany, but to further Prussian particularism; in his representation, "education" was a means to preserve the Prussian state without regard to the fate of other territories in which German was spoken. He depicted instead the Hohenzollern monarchy itself as encompassing "a great family," in which the king played the role of the loving father.[36]

---

[33] Johann Friedrich Zöllner, *Ideen über Nationalerziehung, besonders in Rücksicht auf die Königl. Preuß. Staaten* (Berlin: Reimer, 1804): 208; see also C. M. Tautte, "Plan der Schulanstalten in den neuen Kgl. Preuss. Provinzen betr. 1799" in Akten des ehemaligen preuß. Geh. Staatsarchiv. *Deutsches Zentralarchiv* 2 (Merseburg), Rep. 76, Abt. I, Nr. 41, vol. 3.

[34] *Reflections on the Revolution in France* (London: J. Dodsley, 1790): 482.

[35] Johann Georg Zimmermann, *Vom Nationalstolz* (Zurich: Orell, 1758): 67–70.

[36] *Jahrbücher der preußischen Monarchie* (1798): 2:406, 3:157.

Since each component of the Royalist propaganda also had a German tradition of its own, the presence of merely one or the other in the works of a given writer does not signal alliance with Stein's activist faction. It is rather the combination of these in an individual work, where, for example, Hermann or a similar historical figure becomes an heroic German insurgent, the symbols of blood, the oak tree and the wreath signify the evolution to a new and higher form of "Germany" and the enemy is not only the foreign soldier but also the politically neutral or disinterested individual, which distinguish the contribution of those writers who co-operated in the creation of the myth of the German nation during the age of Napoleon.

In the relative safety of his asylum at Brünn, Stein could risk formulating so confident a statement of his political strategy and literary objectives. In earlier years he had to work more subtly lest he arouse the suspicions of the king, or reveal unwittingly his often unsanctioned agenda. As the Prussian Minister of State, faced with the opposition of the king and his reactionary ministers to a large scale propaganda campaign, Stein was more prone to doubt, more given to caution, than he was during his exile years at Brünn. But even as early as 1807, when overt acts of physical and economic brutality by the French moved the German intellectuals to concern themselves with political problems, Stein was ever more tempted to follow unauthorized procedures. While official German press reports proclaimed the arrival on German soil of Napoleon, as the "great Regent, hero of all centuries, Conqueror for Peace, Founder and Protector of the Federation of the Rhine, Emperor of the French and King of Italy,"[37] the activists in Königsberg and Berlin plotted with such British agents as John Hely-Hutchinson, Lord Leveson-Gower, Jackson and Mr. Benjamin Garlike for a mass insurrection in northern Germany, to be followed by a British landing. Later, German translations of the propaganda composed by guerrilla fighters in Spain arrived from Vienna, where Archduke John had set up an Office of Public Information under the direction of Baron Joseph von Hormayr. Members of organizations, agitating far beyond the prescripts of their royal charters, set up enclaves all over Prussia and would reach out to other resistance groups in the German-speaking territories. But in 1807, Stein hesitated. He doubted. Would the propaganda strategy work? Would the people of northern Germany take up arms to defend their homeland without a direct order from the king? Would the British keep their pledge in light of Czar Alexander's fascination with Napoleon's grandiose schemes? There were still too many critics in key positions, too little organization, an abundance of spies and a scarcity of

---

[37] Quoted from the front page headlines of the official *Priviligierte Gothaische Zeitung auf das Jahr 1807* (July 23, 1807).

collaborators. The plan might fail and the king might regard the instigators as traitors.[38]

These complex concerns, coupled with existing political alliances and military weakness could well have reduced Stein, at this juncture, to a state of impotence compounded of doubt, suspicion and trepidation. Just then, however, hope appeared in the person of Johann Gottlieb Fichte. Upon ascertaining the goals of the activist party and conferring with a Stein supporter at Königsberg concerning the literary outline, the philosopher returned to Berlin to deliver a series of addresses designed to prove to the Prussian statesman once and for all that philosophers, scholars and publicists could serve the cause of Prussian rejuvenation and German nationalism valiantly and successfully. Against a backdrop of military occupation and clandestine countering, Fichte produced a metaphysical construct which corresponded to Stein's adaptation of the Vendée propaganda and prodded the youth of Germany's upper middle class to step into the political arena with a vengeance. He offered what appeared to the contemporary German intellect to be a systematic world view that demanded the expulsion of the French invaders from all the German territories. With Fichte begins a deliberate, well-organized plan to replace the heroic image of the invincible Napoleon with a myth of German homogeneity, unique potential, undaunted greatness and everlasting superiority.

---

[38] On the basis of documents found in the *Preußischer Kulturbesitz*, Rudolf Ibbeken concluded that Stein's "constant jabbing and weaving" with and without royal authorization constituted at times "highly treasonable activities." See Rudolf Ibbeken, *Preußen 1807–1813. Staat und Volk als Idee und Wirklichkeit* (Berlin and Cologne: Grote, 1970).

2
Fichte and the Mythopoeic Process

IN CONTRAST TO EARLIER SCHOLARSHIP,[1] the research after 1945 has avoided praising Fichte as a national prophet or castigating him as a Prussian chauvinist.[2] Recent studies tend to concentrate on the contradictions between the earlier speculative works and the later more popular writings.[3] These examinations have shown among other things that the *Addresses to the German Nation* (1808) represent only one, and not even the most important path of inquiry among several which remain at the conclusion of the *Science of Knowledge* (1794). Fichte's contemporaries, however, tended to regard both works as stages in the development of a philosophy which moved from the radical subjectivity of an absolute ego to the submergence of individual identity in the national state.[4] As we shall see, Fichte's involvement with Stein's initiatives helps to explain why he proceeded from strict philosophical argumentation in the Kantian vein to cultural myth-making.

In the *Science of Knowledge* (*Wissenschaftslehre*) everything in our world is perceived by the ego through the act of creative imagination. Each ego is itself an independent entity which, it would seem, is isolated and must fend for itself in arranging and interpreting the phenomena of reality.

---

[1] Hans M. Baumgartner and Wilhelm G. Jacobs, *J. G. Fichte Bibliographie* (Stuttgart-Bad Cannstatt: Frommann, 1968); also Luigi Pareyson, "Bibliografie essenziale," *Grande Antologia Filosofica*, ed. M. F. Sciacca and M. Schiavone (Milano: Mursia, 1971) 7:886–902.

[2] Walter E. Wright, "Existentialism, Ideas and Fichte's Concept of Coherence," *Journal of the History of Philosophy* 13 (1975): 37–42.

[3] Cf. *Idealistic Studies*, ed. Walter E. Wright (Worcester, Mass.: Clark University Press) vol. 6, No. 2 (May 1976).

[4] George Armstrong Kelly, *Idealism, Politics and History. Sources of Hegelian Thought* (Cambridge: Harvard, 1969): 181–285. Peter Baumanns, *Fichtes ursprüngliches System. Sein Standort zwischen Kant und Hegel* (Stuttgart: Frommann-Holzboog, 1972). John Lachs, "Fichte's Idealism," *American Philosophical Quarterly* 9 (1972): 314; also Dieter Heinrich, "Fichtes ursprüngliche Einsicht," *Subjektivität und Metaphysik*, ed. Dieter Heinrich und H. Wagner (Frankfurt: Klostermann, 1966): 188–232; Wolfgang Janke, *Fichte, Sein und Reflexion. Grundlagen der kritischen Vernunft* (Berlin: de Gruyter, 1970).

Such extreme individuation implies that the sensorial perception of each *I* processes the chaos of external reality (the Not-Me) according to its own understanding of the transcendent moral law. However, in his popular philosophy, particularly in the works written after a trip to Königsberg in 1806, Fichte does not leave matters at this subjective extreme. In his later works, he argues instead that in the mysterious depths of consciousness, the individual's ego is joined with others through language. In the fourth of his *Addresses to the German Nation*, Fichte maintains that language pervades man's innermost being, his thoughts and desires. Language is the common bond which ties people in a geographical area to a single coalescent intellect (*Verstand*).[5]

According to Fichte, language is the universal access point at which the physical and spiritual worlds converge: the German, for example, conceptualizes differently from an individual who speaks a Romance language. Language provides a unique system of prefigurations for interpreting the moral law. Hence it must never be dominated by or subjugated to another since its potential for providing mankind with insights into the differences between right and wrong will diminish under foreign influence. The prefigurations of language bind those who speak the same tongue; hence a man who thinks and chooses freely according to the dictates of moral law, thinks of his kinship and lineage. Fichte's initial affirmation of the ego and subjective idealism becomes a call for national unity. At Königsberg introversion had developed into national consciousness. Awareness of a common tie to others, to a national group, summons the individual to defend that group in its progress toward self-emendation and freedom. To do otherwise is to go against the moral law, for kinship and country support and secure eternity on earth; hence love of country must rule the state.[6]

For Fichte's contemporaries this connection between the absolute *I* and duty to the national state was an important revelation. Fichte's presentation appeared as a convincing metaphysical structure which permitted no reconciliation with foreign influences (*Ausländerei*) threatening national individuality. Fichte's point of view rejected Napoleon as a hero and agitated against him on moral grounds. His affirmation of a sociological theory that has the individual members of a society function as one being required him to oppose a foreign power which would force an incompatible system of conceptualization on another national group, thereby dis-

---

[5] *Johann Gottlieb Fichtes Sämtliche Werke*, ed. Immanuel H. Fichte (Berlin: Veit Comp., 1845), "Grundlage der gesamten Wissenschaftslehre," 2:159–178, noted hereafter as *SW*; also *Johann Gottlieb Fichtes Nachgelassene Werke*, ed. Immanuel H. Fichte (Bonn: Marcus, 1834) noted as *NW*. See here *SW*, 7:326.

[6] *SW*, 7:384.

torting the perspective capabilities of the *I*. The ego, no longer free, but confined by alien prefigurations, is unable to interpret the moral law when arranging the objects of external experience. Having submitted to an outside conceptual framework, man is no longer free; his ability to recognize his duty and choose between right and wrong is weakened.

To Fichte, then, Napoleon and the French conquerors represented not only a social and political threat but also a philosophical crisis. Under foreign domination the individual and, by association, the national group cannot realize its fullest potential. When the group's ability to think and act is no longer governed by the free will of its members in a moral as well as a political sense, the nation will succumb to a "rigid, persevering, and dead existence."[7] According to this philosophy, Napoleon menaced not only German political entities but also the German potential to understand the world, to think creatively and morally.

There are major differences between the method followed in these addresses and the procedure in the *Science of Knowledge*. In his system of "critical idealism" Fichte had used a deductive and dialectical approach, progressing from simple affirmation through negation to a higher affirmation. The method of the popular works is far less rigorous. At one point Fichte admits that his reasoning is not based upon conceptual proof but upon what he calls the "immediate experience of the individual."[8] He knows, for example, that there is such a thing as German love of Fatherland because he feels it. Moreover, whoever feels this within himself will be convinced of the correctness of his (Fichte's) assertions; whoever does not feel it, cannot be convinced. This supposition is the only proof he offers. Such a procedure represents a radical departure from the demonstrative *modus operandi* of his critical idealism. The philosopher who had attempted to deduce earlier what Kant had declared to be unknowable, postulates an argument here based not on reasoned judgment, but on feeling, intuition, insight, and pathos.

Through the *Addresses* Fichte imposes a unique social vision onto current events which reduces social reality to a simple organizational framework. It contains three basic components: a) a call for a national education program which would nurture German uniqueness (*Deutschtum*); b) a representation of the individual tied to ancestors and contemporaries by the bond of language; c) an emotive portrayal of the relationships and responsibilities of the individual to the national group. The latter is symbolized by the super-ego uniting individual personalities by a sense of duty. Once accepted on Fichte's authority, the three components, which incorporate

---

[7] *SW*, 7:372.

[8] *SW*, 7:399.

images, symbols and emotive rhetoric, account for the totality of social being. Each component is intended to propel the listener-reader farther toward a state of consciousness embracing a predetermined attitude favorable to the reform party program. Fichte draws his conclusions not from analytical thought based on a scrutiny of current events, but rather from a projection of his own vision into the contemporary social process. Such a procedure is not speculative reasoning; it is deduction within a mythopoeic process. By explaining political phenomena from the vantage point of his own social vision, Fichte takes from social reality its substance and complexity. His preconceived notion not only replaces reasoned analysis as a means for solving the problems of society but it also becomes a vehicle for promoting a state of mind, uniting and motivating the national group. In this respect, Fichte produces a modern social myth.

The creative writer is described by Fichte as revealing the innate characteristics (i.e. *Deutschtum*) of his people to future generations living in different (new) circumstances. Within a symbolic, fictional context, the poet introduces posterity to its own antecedents and illustrates the group's unique life pattern. Because the intellectual life of a people is reflected in its literature, the poet must intervene in daily affairs. By showing the old gods in new dress, the writer, according to Fichte, recreates everyday public life after the prefigurations of his own imagination already conditioned by language. If this is not his goal, then his words are wasted. There can be no literature, however, without political independence because a nation will not keep its language for long once it ceases to control its own affairs. It is "the noblest privilege and the most sacred function of the writer," argues Fichte, "to consolidate the nation and to deliberate with it about its important affairs."[9] This applied primarily to a Germany split up into separate states and held together principally by her literature. Significant affairs had traditionally been brought before the people by persuasive volunteer authors and spokesmen. In short, Fichte creates a myth and instructs the poet to spread it among the people.

Fichte himself does not address the common man. He states repeatedly that his words are intended for the educated German. He insists that the old order is dead and gone forever, that a foreign power (*die fremde Hand*) has seized control of German affairs, while an "un-German spirit" (*undeutscher Geist*) permeates the upper class where the characteristic *I* of Fichte's critical idealism has turned to egotism; his purpose, he maintains, is to destroy self-interest (*Selbstsucht*). To this end he calls upon religious leaders to reform since religion had been hitherto a servant of

---

[9] *SW*, 7:454f.

selfishness.[10] All the evil which has befallen Germany, he argues, has come from foreign countries; hence travel should be restricted. In the fifth address foreign culture, always admired by Germans, is symbolized by the sylphe, the bee or Undine, the dainty, light but soulless being inhabiting the four elements. By contrast, the German symbol is the eagle on its flight toward the sun.

A conspicuous element is Fichte's anti-Latin pronouncements. He is against the continuing preoccupation in German schools with this "dead" language. Later he relates the Latin to the Romance languages, implying that French and French culture must be repelled. German, he maintains, is by no means a language of vile, hard and raw tones as had been asserted in comparisons with the Romance languages.[11] Rome, moreover, is represented in these speeches as a symbol of what Germans have already overcome. The German forefathers bravely resisted domination by Rome which would have reduced them to slavery. They fought with valor for the preservation and development of their German character which led them to greatness. Fichte claims indebtedness for everything Germany has been and will be to Arminius and his people. "To them we must look back with gratitude, from them we have inherited our land, our customs, our language and national convictions, because of them we are today free and independent Germans."[12]

Fichte's thoughts on national education are stressed particularly in Addresses II, III, IX, X, XI. At first, Fichte accentuates each component, mentioned earlier, in a given set of speeches, and in a later address he returns to them. Interspersed throughout this general progression are observations, allusions, symbols and emotive rhetoric designed to arouse nationalistic passions and to silence critics.[13] The structural parallel with the propaganda reprinted by Beauchamp as emended by Stein is conspicuous: the same three components found in the Vendée literature, which attracted the Prussian Minister of State, re-appear in more detail in Fichte's *Addresses*.

As the Royalists had advocated a process of national education for the Vendée, Fichte demands such a program for Germany also. However, he does not suggest public support for parochial schools; instead, he integrates some of the proposals made by Republicans in France into his ideas. His agenda then contains a strange mixture of Republican reform

---

[10] *SW*, 7:298f.

[11] See Fichte's note *SW*, 7:344.

[12] *SW*, 7:390.

[13] For example, see *SW*, 7:455ff.

and Royalist rigidity; this is the case with Stein as well. Furthermore, the plans for national education outlined in the *Addresses* are not original with Fichte. In a speech to the French National Assembly on public education published in 1791, the senior statesman of the French republic, Count Mirabeau, had already articulated many of these arguments.[14] He too had maintained that education is the only foundation on which a state can build the principles of reason and had pointed out that students needed to be motivated, their initiative encouraged and guided toward good citizenship. Both denounced public expenditures for standing armies,[15] and Fichte also subscribed to Mirabeau's notion of a national militia comprised of pupils educated to love the aggregate and to defend it at a moment's notice. Unlike Mirabeau, however, Fichte insisted on rigid control of every hour of the pupil's life and offered him virtually no choice of instructors or of subjects. Thus the philosopher's proposal combines the discipline demanded by the Vendée Royalists with the liberal civic-mindedness championed by French Republicans. To this he appends his own ideas of what is good for German youth.

From Pestalozzi, Fichte learned of the need to prepare a mother for the preliminary education of her child. An analysis of Pestalozzi's work takes up much of the ninth address. The Swiss educator had argued in favor of a gradual development of the child's potential for registering sensation and had advocated the establishment of training schools for teachers and educators. To these borrowed elements Fichte affixed his own mystic impression of innate German potentials. In his vision he sees national education as preserving and unfolding the unique characteristics of the German people. As we shall see later, Kleist dramatized these unique features and their potential. Whereas Mirabeau's platform was intended to safeguard the principles of the French Revolution by implanting the ideas and philosophy of its supporters in young minds, Fichte's purpose is to rescue German national independence by instructing the young in sacrifice stimulated by love of a national heritage. He would impose upon all young Germans a new outlook on national life, a revised ethical code, a specific character development in the interest of the state. This new attitude toward compulsory education represents a striking reversal of Fichte's earli-

---

[14] See *Travail sur l'éducation publique trouvé dans les papiers de Mirabeau l'aîné*; publié par P. J. G. Cabanis (Paris: de l'imprimairie nationale, 1791). The work was probably outlined as early as 1789. It was translated into German by Eberhard von Rochow, *Herrn Mirabeau des älteren Diskurs über die Nationalerziehung*, in 1792 and widely read in Germany.

[15] Cf. *SW*, 7:431. In the essay, *Zum ewigen Frieden*, Kant put forth the same argument, which he too probably found in Mirabeau's work.

er stand, for as late as 1796 he had staunchly opposed public education.[16] After 1806 he had changed his attitude completely.

The central role ascribed to the native tongue may be seen as maximizing the potential in the contemporary debate about language. Fichte's initial contribution was an essay for the *Philosophical Journal* in 1795,[17] in which he described how language must have originated. By correcting earlier postulates and by modifying Herder's contentions, Fichte made a modest contribution to the discussion. But the view of language outlined in the *Addresses to the German Nation* represents a radical departure from these theories. Here language becomes a bond mystically uniting all those who speak it. Although his essay of 1795 did not incorporate the results of the inquiry into the *Science of Knowledge*, Fichte appeared in his *Addresses* to move systematically to a representation of the individual ego in its social environment. In his essay on language, he was concerned with arbitrary oral signs as an expression of thought;[18] within the framework of the *Addresses*, however, language is not a vehicle for expressing cognition, rather cognition is pre-determined by language.[19] Language is postulated as bringing a national character into being; it is not molded by man, but instead it molds men. At one point, language is placed on a par with sensorial perception and thus becomes an absolute.[20] These examples may serve to illustrate Fichte's inversion of his earlier arguments.

There are other essential differences, if not outright contradictions, between the essay of 1795 and his *Addresses* of 1807–08. In the latter, Fichte posits an original people, an archetypal tribe, the typical German. He has preserved his original language. This is the bond between contemporaries and their ancestors because it assures one permanent set of conceptualizations. Prefigurations, archetypal thought patterns, the organizational framework for ordering nature is handed down from father to child through language. Yet in his essay he had insisted that in the evolution of the original language (*Ursprache*) the archetypal sounds (*Urtöne*) are crowded out. With the development of culture, Fichte had argued, the language of nature once spoken by the people begins a process of decay because new forms are needed to express new ideas. Thus with each succeeding generation the ties to the ancestral tribe *diminish*. This loosening of

---

[16] Cf. "Grundlage des Naturrechts" (1796), SW, 3:358–365.

[17] "Von der Sprachfähigkeit und dem Ursprung der Sprache," *Philosophisches Journal einer Gesellschaft Teutscher Gelehrten* 1 (1795) Heft 3, 255–273 and Heft 4, 287–326.

[18] SW, 8:302.

[19] SW, 7:314.

[20] SW, 7:316.

the pre-supposed bond will take place, he had maintained in 1795, even if the people remain free of outside influences, never mix with other national groups and never change their place of residence. Another and ever-changing language will emerge, having not the least resemblance to the original tongue.[21] The arguments presented in the essay and those in the *Addresses* are mutually exclusive. Fichte has done a complete *volte-face*.

Just as Fichte's notion of national education and his image of a people bound together by language had certain antecedents, so did his description of the individual's relationship to the state. Social thinking at the beginning of the nineteenth century is marked by a specific recoil from the atomistic, individualistic, and mechanistic social concepts of earlier decades. Rousseau's social contract theory, Pascal's "artificial man" and Hobbes's machine gave way to the contention that society is a living unity, originating spontaneously, that it has super-individual reality governed by laws.[22] Lessing, Kant and especially Edmund Burke in his *Reflections on the Revolution in France*, popularized in Germany in the translation by Friedrich Gentz, laid down various characteristics of the organic conception of society.[23] A model for organic analogies was found in Plato's *Republic*, and in other works of classical antiquity.[24] As early as 1767, Herder, in his *Fragments concerning Recent Literature* (*Fragmente über die neuere Literatur*), had called for original German literary works which should derive from German history, customs, religion and climatic conditions. In his essay, *On German Style and Art* (*Von deutscher Art und Kunst*) (1773), he had argued that art forms are predicated upon the spatiotemporal conditions under which a given society exists.

Fichte revamps many of these theories into an emotional and arousing appeal to German youth. His exaggerations were overlooked not only because of the contemporary historical circumstances but also because of their apparent emergence from a more complex metaphysical system. His solicitation of national sentiment coincided with the socio-economics of defeat. The strength of his personality, in view of the personal risk involved in making such statements in an occupied city, added persuasive power to his words. In an earlier essay on the *Closed Commercial State*

---

[21] *SW*, 8:340f.

[22] Ezra Thayler Towne, *Die Auffassung der Gesellschaft als Organismus* (Halle: Kaemmerer, 1903): 15–54.

[23] See Francis William Coker, *Organismic Theories of the State* (New York: Columbia University Press, 1910): 4–31.

[24] For a survey of the "organic" citations from Aristotle, Cicero, Livy, Seneca and others, see Albert Th. von Krieken, *Über die sogenannte organische Staatstheorie* (Leipzig: Duncker and Humblot, 1873): 19–26.

(1800), he had described the nation-state strictly as an economic entity in which every man had the right to a livelihood. In his *Characteristics of the Present Age* (1804–05), he initially presented the case for the submission of the citizen to national goals; in the *Addresses* (1807–08), he carries this line of reasoning even farther. Under the guise of an appeal to the public to deliberate its future, Fichte sought to implant a political attitude in the mind of the listener. He was calling for popular support of a social program already on the drawing boards in Königsberg. His purpose was to prepare public opinion for those proposals.

The link between Fichte's critical idealism and his popular philosophy is the search for the similarities and differences among various egos in the stream of life. But Fichte embarked on this path of inquiry before several pertinent questions about the ego as an entity had been answered. From the standpoint of speculative metaphysics, there was no compelling need to deal exclusively and at such lengths with a supplemental problem, while intrinsic questions were left unanswered. The inquiry was prompted by social and political influences, not by the necessities of logic. When he did occupy himself with the interdependence of individualities, his method changed drastically. Forsaking the deductive, dialectic approach of his critical idealism, he resorted to an emotional portrayal of his own social vision, which reduced the complex of reality to simple principles. The tripartite structure of the vision consists of a national educational movement designed to distinguish and nurture "authentic" German characteristics, an image of individuals bound to each other by a common language, and finally an impassioned account of why and how the individual must be absorbed into the superindividual nation-state. The first two components contained contradictions to earlier positions, while the third carried an earlier argument to extremes. This 'metaphysical' structure comprises instruments for solving social, political and economic problems. Solutions manifest themselves in rhetoric, images and symbols; deductive thought is abandoned. As his symbols expand to a state of consciousness which induces a desired behavioral response in a large segment of the population, Fichte creates a myth.

What induced Fichte to forsake his "individualistic" speculations in order to glamorize the aggregate? On the one hand, his references to his own earlier work and the testimony of contemporaries suggest that Fichte derived these social imperatives from his system of critical idealism. On the other hand, several contradictions to earlier statements attest to a motivating force outside the dictates of his metaphysical system. While working on the *Science of Knowledge* in April 1795, Fichte wrote a revealing letter to Jens Baggesen, an ardent admirer of the French Revolution, who collaborated with highly placed French officials in Germany. Fichte asked Baggesen to arrange an administrative position for him writing French propaganda.[25] He was turned down: the French had enough German writers espousing the ideals of the Revolution.[26] The request itself is generally seen against the background of Fichte's *Beiträge zur Berichtigung der Urteile des Publikums über die französische Revolution* written in 1793; it is cited as another example of the philosopher's enthusiasm for the French upheaval and as a testament to his dire lack of money.[27] But Fichte's sympathies for French ideals are not as important here as his willingness to write propaganda. A decade later he will ask Prussian officials for a post writing in favor of the Prussian cause. This biographical parallel confirms Fichte's eagerness to write in favor of change.

The Prussian king, however, was less than receptive to the philosopher's formula for "educating" the public in matters of state. He and such trusted advisors as Wilhelm von Humboldt and Karl August von Hardenberg remained unconvinced that a massive anti-French campaign was desirable; nor did they believe it would be effective.[28] But Fichte persisted. His letters to government officials during this period abound in appeals both for support of his proposal and financial help. Even before the Prussian disaster at Jena, Fichte had outlined his strategy to the privy councilor Karl Friedrich Beyme. On September 20, 1806, Beyme informed him that his plan though honorable would have to wait — the king had decided to settle his differences with the French emperor on the battlefield, not in the press.[29] Fichte thereupon offered to serve as an orator to the Prussian soldiers. The government declined.[30]

As French forces advanced on the capital after the rout of the Prussian army, Fichte, abandoning his family in Berlin, climbed into the coach of the king's physician bound for the provisional court at Königsberg, where he pleaded relentlessly for his propaganda stratagy. On October 18, 1806, for example, he wrote Hardenberg about his plans for instilling patriotic fervor in the public: he would write for the "German heart" and, if he

---

[25] *J. G. Fichte Briefwechsel. Kritische Gesamtausgabe*, ed. Hans Schulz (Leipzig: Haessel, 1930) 1:449f.

[26] For a discussion, see Eugene N. Anderson, *Nationalism and the Cultural Crisis in Prussia 1806–1815* (New York: Farrar and Rhinehart, 1939): 26ff.

[27] *Ibid.*, see also John R. Seeley, *The Life and Times of Stein* (London: Cambridge University Press, 1878) 1:30f.

[28] See [Wilhelm von Humboldt] William Humboldt, *The Sphere and Duties of Government*, trans. Joseph Coulthard (London: Chapman, 1854), also Reinhold Aris, *A History of Political Thought in Germany from 1789 to 1815* (London: Allen and Unwin, 1936).

[29] *Briefwechsel*, II, 421.

[30] Anderson [Note 26], 37.

could, would deliver a series of patriotic speeches.³¹ He was offered a position at the University of Königsberg instead. In addition, for two hundred *Reichstaler* a year, he was to oversee the censorship of the Königsberg newspapers. But the task proved so demeaning that Fichte quit in February, 1807.³²

On July 10, 1807, he left Königsberg for Copenhagen, returning in August. He wrote to his wife that he had made several important political contacts there and, more significantly, the trip had revealed to him the inner workings of government.³³ Later he sat on the Education Reform Committee, and helped plan the new university of Berlin, where he was promised a position — at no more salary than he was making.³⁴ His financial position deteriorated rapidly. Since there was simply no money to be made in Königsberg,³⁵ he not only asked his wife to send funds but also, as late as November, 1807, found it necessary to borrow one hundred *Taler* from Beyme.³⁶

Meanwhile sweeping reforms affecting the entire social order were being planned. Considerable resistance to Stein's reform policies was to be expected from the large estate owners. The most urgent problem facing the new cabinet was to win over the upper-middle class to the idea of sacrifice for the common good. But the attitude prevalent among educated upper-class Prussians is typified by the observations of Varnhagen von Ense, who at the time of the Battle of Jena was more concerned with aesthetics than with the fate of the country. Watching the king depart from Berlin after the ill-fated campaign, Varnhagen feels pity for the unfortunate ruler; yet he and his friends are not particularly alarmed:

> ... we were simply unable to muster any genuine political zeal that might include an exclusive pre-occupation with political reports and communiqués all day long. General discussions of nothing but politics bored us to tears ...

---

³¹ *Briefwechsel* II, 422.

³² See *Briefwechsel*, II, 428, 457ff., also Robert Prutz, "Fichte in Königsberg," *Allgemeine Zeitung* Beilage 181. Nr. 218. Munich, August 8, 1893; Paul Czygan, *Zur Geschichte der Tagesliteratur während der Freiheitskriege* (Leipzig: Duncker and Humblot, 1909) 1:7ff.

³³ *Briefwechsel*, 2:474.

³⁴ See Beyme's letter of September 5, 1807 in *Briefwechsel*, 2:480.

³⁵ *Briefwechsel*, 2:428; also 419, 471f.

³⁶ *Briefwechsel*, 2:496.

there was no place for ardor and sentimentality: everything in our lives was detached and disassociated, pushing on into the wide world outside.[37]

This report of the contemporaneous political attitude among members of the upper class is corroborated by Henriette Herz, who noted also that no trace of political interest could be found in her Berlin salon.[38]

Nevertheless, without the support of the educated, the government could not extricate itself from the autocratic French system. In their own vital interests, Prussian administrators had to rally public opinion to their cause or they would cease to rule entirely. At this historical juncture Fichte begged for the chance to manipulate the intelligentsia by countering the image of the heroic Napoleon presented in French propaganda with the myth of a German nation. In December, 1807, the philosopher returned to French-occupied Berlin and demonstrated the power of modern myth-making when he held his *Addresses to the German Nation*.

As Fichte negotiated the financial aspects of his project with government officials, he was quick to point out the personal risks involved and the great sacrifices he would have to make. Foremost among these, he wrote to Hardenberg, was interrupting work on his *Science of Knowledge*! His life's ambition, he tells the Prussian minister, was to complete his philosophical investigations; but Prussia's political fortune had compelled him to abandon this project in favor of patriotic essays and speeches.[39] A little later, when requesting more money from the ministry of finance, he calls Karl von Altenstein's attention to his patriotic activities, which included stopping his work on the *Science of Knowledge*. He then requests permission to return to it.[40] Despite his attempts publicly to reconcile the patriotism of the popular works with the metaphysics of his earlier tracts, Fichte acknowledged privately that the two directions were not quite part of the same metaphysical system. His appeal to the intelligentsia was predicated on a systematic transition from critical idealism to social involvement — and in upper and upper-middle class circles his arguments were persuasive. However, to the government officials in whose service

---

[37] See *Ausgewählte Schriften von K. A. Varnhagen von Ense*. Part 1: "Denkwürdigkeiten des eigenen Lebens," 3rd edition (Leipzig: Brockhaus, 1871) 1:314. For a detailed description of the intellectual climate in Berlin and the political upheavals of 1806, see 1:358–385. A year later Varnhagen reported that he and his friends experienced "den gewaltigen Drang des politischen Zwiespalts" intensely, yet still attempted to keep politics out of their personal lives; see 2:126.

[38] *Henriette Herz. Ihr Leben und ihre Erinnerungen*, ed. J[ulius] Fürst (Berlin: Hertz, 1850): 125ff.

[39] *Briefwechsel*, 2:422.

[40] *Briefwechsel*, 2:452.

he labored Fichte emphasized he had taken the new path for their sake and the nation's.

Fichte also succeeded in winning a new and powerful ally: Baron Stein. Beyme writes Fichte in February 1808: "You have even won over the Minister of State, Baron vom Stein, and I can only offer you our profoundest thanks."[41] Nor did Stein and his party of patriots neglect to reward *their* philosopher. To be sure, he would have been of more service to them, had he been able to read English: the British were secretly financing the reform faction. But Fichte was fluent neither in English nor Russian, the other language they had need of.[42] Nevertheless, when England supplied £30,000 to the activists in the Spring of 1809, they presented Fichte with 700 *Reichstaler* — three and a half times his salary as a censor in Königsberg.[43]. On June 10, 1809, he tells Altenstein that the amount received with the latter's assistance had taken care of his financial needs completely.[44] But still the monetary awards continued: Wilhelm von Humboldt reports to Caroline that he had encountered no objections from cabinet members when he suggested that the Prussian government pay Fichte a pension. Thus the philosopher received an additional 800 *Taler*.[45] For years Fichte had labored to obtain this pension which, he argued, was rightfully his from his tenure at Jena. He had been turned down repeatedly by the Prussian cabinet. After he delivered his *Addresses*, however, the pension was granted virtually without a request.

The influence of these *Addresses* has been underestimated. Reference is made to the inconvenient time, Sunday from 12:00 to 1:00 p.m., chosen for their delivery, to the resulting sparse attendance and to the limited first printing of the collected lectures; a new edition was not prepared until six-

---

[41] *Briefwechsel*, 2:503.

[42] In a letter to Altenstein (June 3, 1807), Fichte laments that he cannot do a good job with the Königsberg newspaper because he cannot read English. Reports supplied by the Foreign Office were intended for publication in Königsberg; see *Briefwechsel*, 2:458: "Noch muss ich bei diesem Artikel bemerken, dass ich nicht Englisch lese (Russisch oder Polnisch wird man nicht erwarten)." Lord Hely-Hutchinson was bound for St. Petersburg after consulting with Stein and the activists. After Prague, the Russian city became their base of operations when Napoleon ordered them out of the Prussian cabinet once Stein's letter to Wittgenstein was intercepted by French agents.

[43] Fichte received his full salary of 200 *Reichstaler* in March 1808. At that time, Beyme comments that Fichte ought to be glad he was paid so promptly by the king where others did not receive their money. In January 1809, Friedrich Stägemann, the activists' financial wizard, lent Fichte 700 *Reichstaler*, which he paid back in April. See *Briefwechsel*, 2:531.

[44] *Briefwechsel*, 2:532.

[45] *Wilhelm und Caroline von Humboldt in ihren Briefen*, ed. Anna von Sydow (Berlin: Mittler, 1909) 3:167.

teen years later.[46] Nevertheless, in view of the fate of the publisher, Johann Philipp Palm, who one year earlier had been executed on Napoleon's orders for printing an anti-French pamphlet, the courage Fichte showed by making such speeches inspired and motivated educated Germans of the period. The philosophy professor so totally committed himself to social action that he soon became a hero for the youth of Prussia. Wilhelm von Humboldt wrote to Caroline that Fichte's *Addresses* were rapidly assuming the role of a prayer book among the young people.[47] Fichte's proposals were not carried out in complete accordance with his wishes; however, his arguments made a lasting impression on the minds of the younger generation of writers, artists and commentators. The myth of the nation as it was disseminated in Prussia took root as more young people heard of Fichte's outspokenness. The results of a campaign to depose the image of the heroic Napoleon influenced German social thought for the next half-decade and became a potent instrument for reform, delivered into the hands of Prussian statesmen by their literary ally, the philosopher from Lausitz.

---

[46] See Daniel Jacoby, "Fichte und sein Verhältnis zu Preußen," *Euphorion* 21 (1914): 237–251; Max Wundt, *Fichte* (Stuttgart: Frommann, 1927): 68f. and George Armstrong Kelly's introduction to a recent edition of the English translation by R. F. Jones and G. H. Tunstall, *Johann Gottlieb Fichte. Addresses to the German Nation* (New York: Harper, 1968), p. xxvii.

[47] *Wilhelm und Caroline von Humboldt in ihren Briefen*, 3:93.

3
Kleist's Philosophical Crisis and the Origin of the Prussian Myth

WAS KLEIST'S "KANT-CRISIS" PRECIPITATED by his readings of Fichte? Despite the reservations of such noted scholars as Gerhard Fricke[1] and Israel Soliman Stamm,[2] considerable evidence suggests that Kleist saw Kant through Fichte's eyes. At any rate, Kleist's "misinterpretations" of Kant correspond closely to those of Fichte.[3] Kant made no attempt to take from cognition its objective character and give it a subjective one; he intended instead to define "objectivity" in its relation to cognition. Kleist, however, came to regard all knowledge as so clouded by subjectivity that cognition of absolute truth is impossible. The subjective element so characteristic of Fichte's system dominates Kleist's thinking: just as man's feelings are determined by physiological organization, so too do man's thinking and knowing originate in the structure of the intellect. Both feeling and conceptualization remain inside the circle of subjectivity. Hence, through the medium of the "new so-called Kantian philosophy" — as he calls this system in his famous letter to Wilhelmine von Zenge of March 22, 1801 — Kleist arrived at the same position as Fichte, who had described his own philosophy in the same words.[4]

---

[1] Gerhard Fricke, *Gefühl und Schicksal bei Heinrich von Kleist* (Berlin: Junker and Dünnhaupt, 1929). Fricke regards the Fichte-theory as unnecessary. For Fricke the Kant-crisis developed from Kleist's lack of distinction between "real" and "transcendental." He was unable to see an "Ich" as an idea and thought that the ideal ego must correspond to his real one. The cause of the crisis, according to Fricke, is Kleist's confusion of the transcendental world with reality. This led him to draw false conclusions.

[2] "Note on Kleist und Kant," *Studies in Honor of John Albrecht Walz* (Lancaster, Pa.: Prince and Lemon, 1941): 31–40.

[3] See Eugen Kühnemann, "Kleist und Kant," *Schriften der Kleist-Gesellschaft* 2 (1922): 1–30.

[4] In his *Sonnenklarer Bericht an das größere Publikum über das Wesen der neuesten Philosophie. Ein Versuch, die Leser zum Verstehen zu zwingen* (Berlin: Realschulbuchhandlung, 1801), Fichte insists that his philosophical system is identical to Kant's: "Ich nehme hier das Kantische und das neueste für Eins" (viii) and goes on to speak of "die sogenannte

Kleist's image of humans with green glasses instead of eyes suggests a more than casual acquaintance with Fichte, who had used a similar metaphor to refute accusations that his philosophy was atheistic. In his widely read legal defense published in 1799, Fichte had described sensorial perception as "an instrument like a colored glass through which we are able to perceive [our call to duty] under certain conditions . . . and whatever we do perceive in this colored glass undergoes a change in appearance."[5] Fichte, in turn, may have borrowed his simile from the introduction to Christian Ernst Wünsch's *Cosmological Conversations* [*Kosmologische Unterhaltungen* (1791–94)], which Kleist sent to Wilhelmine in 1801. The image appears again in Klinger's *The Chain Bearer* [*Der Kettenträger* (1797)] read by Kleist during this period. Thus the attempt to clarify and consolidate the complex problem of absolute knowledge in the letter to Wilhelmine suggests that Kleist's acquaintance with Kant was made, at least initially, not through the *Critiques* themselves, but rather via Fichte and other interpreters.

In 1954 Ludwig Muth joined the opponents of such theories. Muth argued that Kleist's reading of Kant's *Critique of the Power of Judgment* had brought on the "crisis" because here, especially in the second part, Kant had destroyed all hope for attaining true knowledge on earth, the source of Kleist's despair.[6] However, Muth fails to explain why Kleist experienced this crisis suddenly, when, allegedly, he had been studying Kant for months. Moreover, Kant presents a profound message of hope in this work, which would have allayed Kleist's worst fears had he known it firsthand. Fichte, on the other hand, interpreted Kant's postulates without exploring their more optimistic implications, when he penned his explanations in such works as the "Sonnenklarer Bericht." Kleist came to understand Kant's contentions regarding man's inability to obtain absolute truth abruptly, thereby suggesting that an interpretation precipitated the crisis, not Kant's writings themselves. Moreover, Kant's *Critique of the Power of Judgment* served as the starting point for Fichte's exposition.

---

neuere Philosophie." See D. F. S. Scott, "Kleist's Kant Crisis," *Modern Language Review* 42 (1947): 474–485.

[5] See the "Verantwortungsschrift" in *J. G. Fichte. Gesamtausgabe der bayerischen Akademie der Wissenschaften*, ed. R. Lauth and H. Gliwitzky (Stuttgart: Frommann, 1981), 1, part 6:45; also Hanna Hellmann, *Heinrich von Kleist. Darstellungen des Problems* (Heidelberg: Winter, 1911): 71; "Heinrich von Kleist und der Kettenträger," *Germanisch-Romanische Monatsschrift* 13 (1925): 350–363; here Hellmann points out parallels between Klinger's novel of 1796 and Kleist's letter to Wilhelmine.

[6] Ludwig Muth, *Kleist und Kant. Kantstudien*. Supplement No. 68 (Cologne: Cologne University Press, 1954): 54.

Ernst Cassirer was the first noted scholar to advocate that Fichte's exegesis had brought about Kleist's "Kantkrise."[7] Pointing out that Kleist and Fichte had been introduced by their mutual friends Dorothea Veit and Friedrich Schlegel, Cassirer argued that Fichte's *Vocation of Man* (1800) had deeply affected Kleist. Later research has established that Kleist, who makes no reference to Fichte in any of his extant letters, was also familiar with other works of the philosopher.[8] Rudolf Unger discovered that Kleist's concept of death closely parallels that of Fichte.[9]

This "Fichte-crisis" takes on a new dimension when seen in the light of Kleist's philosophical and political development. Kleist, like Fichte, was preoccupied initially with the individual as a distinct and separate entity or, in the words of Günther Blöcker, as an absolute *Ich*.[10] Later he moved to a more liberal individualism which recognized a collective spirit; from there he proceeded to a nationalistic stance, justifying limitations imposed on the individual by the state. Both men found morality's purest form in service and commitment to the nation. Both were in Königsberg when the Stein-Hardenberg reforms were drafted and both were close to the same government officials, particularly Baron Karl von Altenstein. Fichte and Kleist not only experienced identical metaphysical conversions during their stay at Königsberg but also expressed the same political viewpoints after the Peace of Tilsit. If Kleist was not influenced by Fichte's *Addresses to the German Nation*, then both men must have drawn from the same philosophical-political sources for them to have undergone such an abrupt and profound change. It would appear to be more than mere coincidence that two keen intellects went through a transformation along identical lines, in the same place, during the same time period. As Fichte delivered his speeches in Berlin, Kleist was working on his dramas in Dresden. Kleist either had knowledge of and access to those lectures or he and Fichte structured their compositions on a framework prepared at Königsberg. As we shall see, *Hermann's Battle* (*Die Hermannsschlacht*) and *Prinz Friedrich von Homburg* contain striking parallels to Fichte's work.

Michael Kohlhaas reflects changes in Kleist's political point of view. Sembdner's contention that Kleist began *Kohlhaas* in Königsberg in 1804 is

---

[7] Ernst Cassirer, "Heinrich von Kleist und die Kantische Philosophie," in: *Idee und Gestalt. Fünf Aufsätze* (Berlin: Bruno Cassirer, 1921).

[8] See D. F. S. Scott [Note 4], 475–478.

[9] Rudolf Unger, *Herder, Novalis, Kleist. Studien zum Todesproblem* (Berlin: Diesterweg, 1922): 10.

[10] Günther Blöcker, *Heinrich von Kleist oder das absolute Ich* (Berlin: Argon, 1960).

an oversight;[11] Kleist did not arrive in that city until May 6, 1805. It is more likely that the original version, probably just a part of the story, was written in 1806–1807; it illustrates thematically the self-destruction of a character who carries a virtue to excess. After publishing roughly the first quarter of the story in *Phöbus* for June 1808 (published in November), Kleist changed his evaluation of the hero's absolute demand for justice. Between 1808 and the book version of 1810, Kleist focused on the conflict between the individual and the rights and needs of society. This shift in emphasis brought with it structural incongruities, contradictions in character development and incompatible perspectives.[12]

Among the outstanding contradictions is the transformation of Kohlhaas's demand for compensation from the Junker Tronka to an all-consuming desire for revenge upon the Elector of Saxony, who has committed no crime against the horse-dealer. Heinrich Meyer-Benfey argues convincingly that Kohlhaas's prejudice against the Saxon Elector has no justification within the structure of the story. He points out also that the Elector of Brandenburg, who is very much a party to the obstruction of justice which fired Kohlhaas's revenge, is a completely different personality at the end of the story than he was at the beginning. The original plan most likely called for only one sovereign in the story. Considerations external to the artistic structure induced Kleist to involve a second ruler from whom Kohlhaas would obtain justice. Nevertheless, it is a structural inconsistency that in the end this prince should be the Elector of Brandenburg. Political reasons, Meyer-Benfey maintained, must have prompted Kleist's attempt to place the Brandenburg prince in a very positive light after the *Phöbus* fragment was published. Meyer-Benfey concluded that the artistic stages in the development of *Michael Kohlhaas* reflected Kleist's political maturation from the subjective, psychological viewpoint of the individual (1806) through the recognition of the nation-state and its urgent needs (1808) to a patriotic faith in the Prussian fatherland (1810).[13]

---

[11] *Heinrich von Kleist. Sämtliche Werke und Briefe*, ed. Helmut Sembdner. 4th edition (Munich: Hanser, 1965) 2:895. All quotes from this edition; numbers in parenthesis correspond to line numbers in Sembdner's text. Translations are mine except for *Prinz Friedrich von Homburg* which are taken from the English version by Diana Stone Peters and Frederick G. Peters, *Prince Friedrich of Homburg. A Drama by Heinrich von Kleist* (New York: New Directions Books, 1978).

[12] Three scholars in particular have compiled a lengthy catalogue of Kleist's inconsistencies in connection with Kohlhaas; see Karl Wachter, *Kleists Michael Kohlhaas* (Weimar: Duncker, 1918), Joseph Körner, *Recht und Pflicht* (Leipzig: Teubner, 1926) and Hans M. Wolff, *Heinrich von Kleist als politischer Dichter*. University of California Publications in Modern Philology, vol. 27, No. 6 (Berkeley, 1947).

[13] Heinrich Meyer-Benfey, "Die innere Geschichte des 'Michael Kohlhaas'," *Euphorion*. 15 (1908): 99–140.

Why were political and not aesthetic concerns responsible for the structural mutations in *Michael Kohlhaas*? In 1807, Kleist entered the service of the Prussian government. Saxony had recently joined the Confederation of the Rhine and was aligned, therefore, with Napoleon against Brandenburg. By reworking the plot, Kleist accentuated the historical parallel with 1540 when the two German states had been adversaries. The Kohlhaas (or Kohlhasen) of the annals was a subject of Brandenburg who, after many unsuccessful civil suits against a Saxon family over two horses, led raiding parties into Saxony with the knowledge and support of Brandenburg authorities.[14] Therefore, when he altered his original plan, Kleist not only paid homage to his employer-sovereign but also castigated the Saxon ruler for renewing an adversary relationship to Brandenburg-Prussia.

The similarity between Fichte's and Kleist's political development is striking. In his early works, Kleist constructs a detailed psychological portrait of the individual struggling with the problem of external encroachment upon his well-being. Wolff even labels the individual in *Die Familie Schroffenstein* and *Robert Guiskard* as "anti-social."[15] Kleist's point of view here corresponds to the *Ich* of Fichte's *Science of Knowledge*, where no references to external bonds are made. The world from the vantage point of the individual consciousness is fundamental to the early work of both men. Fichte subsequently moved to the problem of restricting the individual and to reforms which would foster the economic prosperity and welfare of the citizen. Kleist's initial representation of Kohlhaas as an unfairly treated businessman, who sees his duty in correcting such official wrong-doing runs parallel to this shift in Fichte's thinking. However, after visiting Königsberg and conferring with Prussian political leaders, Fichte took up the banner of German nationalism. A similar change is reflected in Kleist's attitude when he reworked *Michael Kohlhaas* in order to enhance the historical image of the Brandenburg rulers and to stress communal rights over the individual. In his *Addresses to the German Nation*, Fichte promulgated a myth of German homogeneity, superiority and strength founded on public education, language and national heritage. From June to December 1808, Kleist dramatized the same myth in his *Hermann's Battle*.

---

[14] Not until Kohlhaas and his accomplice Nagelschmidt attempted to steal a silver shipment under the protection of Brandenburg did state officials apprehend him; see Kleist's source: Peter Hafftitz, "Nachricht von Hans Kohlhasen, einem Befehder derer Chur-Sächsischen Lande" in: Christian Schöttgen und Georg Christoph Kreysig, *Diplomatische und curieuse Nachlese der Historie von Obersachsen und angrentzenden Ländern* 3rd. Part. (Dresden and Leipzig, 1731).

[15] Hans M. Wolff [Note 12], 347–391, 489.

In dealing with Kleist in his history of nineteenth century Germany, Heinrich von Treitschke uttered a curious exclamation: "And how often did Lt. Hüser ride from Berlin to Baruth in order to commit to the Saxon post letters to the fellow conspirator Heinrich von Kleist!"[16] The phantom Lt. Hüser returned in the next century to haunt Kleist scholarship when Richard Samuel discovered the memoirs of General Johann Hans Gustav Heinrich Hüser (also: Huesser), edited by Mathilde Quednow and published by Reimer in 1877.[17] Here we find remarkable evidence that Kleist, as early as 1808, was involved in a broadly-based political conspiracy:

> Various little trips became necessary, not only to speak with people but also to mail letters from inconspicuous places which were not under surveillance. Since the post office in Berlin was in French hands, we couldn't send letters from there. For this reason, I had to ride several times to Baruth, for example, in order to mail dispatches to Heinrich von Kleist who was known as a poet (*Dichter*), lived in Dresden and shared our convictions ("... der unser Gesinnungsgenosse war...")[18]

Hüser goes on to describe the group which promoted these opinions: at the center stood Gneisenau,[19] Stein and Scharnhorst.[20] Based on this evidence, Richard Samuel wrote two Kleist studies — one examined the relationship to Stein, the other to Gneisenau[21] — which showed that Kleist's pen had been enlisted in their crusade. Samuel's interpretation of *Die Hermannsschlacht* posited a direct relationship between Hermann-Stein and Marbod-Francis II. At the conclusion he pointed out, as had Meyer-Benfey, that contemporaries would have easily recognized the allusions and could have identified among Kleist's characters those German princes who had joined the Confederation of the Rhine.

---

[16] Heinrich von Treitschke, *Deutsche Geschichte im neunzehnten Jahrhundert*. 10th edition (Leipzig: Hirzel, 1918); the first edition appeared in 1879. I have consulted the translation by Eden and Cedar Paul (New York: McBride and Nast, 1915) 1:354.

[17] See Richard Samuel, "Kleists 'Hermannsschlacht' und der Freiherr vom Stein," *Jahrbuch der Schillergesellschaft* 5 (1961): 64–101. Reprinted in *Heinrich von Kleist. Aufsätze und Essays*, ed. Walter Müller-Seidel (Darmstadt: Wissenschaftliche Buchgesellschaft, 1967): 412–458. See Samuel's footnote 26. I have found copies in the Geheim Archiv (Berlin-Dahlem) and the British Museum.

[18] *Denkwürdigkeiten aus dem Leben des Generals der Infanterie von Hüser grösstenteils nach dessen hinterlassenen Papieren zusammengestellt und herausgegeben von M. Q.*. Mit einem Vorwort von Professor Dr. Maurenbrecher (Berlin: Reimer, 1877): 72.

[19] *Ibid.*, 73.

[20] *Ibid.*, 74.

[21] Richard Samuel, "Heinrich von Kleist und Neithardt von Gneisenau," *Jahrbuch der deutschen Schillergesellschaft* 7 (1963): 352–370.

Other scholars tend to avoid the question of Kleist's political involvement or dismiss Hüser's assertions as too vague. Joachim Maaß, for example, advised caution in his study of Kleist because "we don't know what those dispatches contained."[22] It is not enough, however, to pass over Hüser's immediate reference to Kleist and conclude that nothing may be added. When seen in the larger context of Hüser's memoirs, the reference to Kleist sheds a good deal of light on the political activities of the playwright/journalist, for Hüser paints a picture of a far-reaching political operation, involving surveillance, arms shipments, communications and propaganda. Especially illuminating is Hüser's record of various politically active groups directed by the Königsberg triumvirate, but unknown to each other. Specially named as literary collaborators are, in addition to Kleist, Ernst Moritz Arndt, Friedrich Schleiermacher and the book dealer Georg Reimer.[23] As we shall see, the structural components found in Arndt's *Spirit of the Times* and Schleiermacher's sermons from this period correspond to the framework found in Kleist's *Hermannsschlacht* and, in part, *Prinz Friedrich von Homburg*.

Phoebus also figured in Kleist's plans to promote nationalism. He and Adam Müller came upon the idea of uniting Germany culturally through an art journal dedicated to outstanding literary achievement. In their announcement for the journal, they declared Dresden the artists' "home away from home" ("unsere zweite Vaterstadt"), for the city was, on the one hand, the residence of the "most eminent artists and connoisseurs" (2:447), and on the other, a base from which to launch a campaign against the French satellite system. Once Saxony aligned with France by joining the Confederation of the Rhine, Dresden became a major observation and communication post between Prussia and Austria. The Austrian embassy served as the meeting place for patriotic organizations in Saxony, where the strategies of north and south were coordinated with the policies of England and Russia. Kleist's benefactor in Dresden, Joseph Baron von Buol-Mühlingen, Austrian chargé d'affaires since 1803, belonged to Johann Philipp Stadion's war party. Kleist was also an intimate friend of Philipp's brother, Frederick, who was not only a member of the Austrian activists but also the head of the Franconian church seated at Mainz and Würzburg.[24] Stadion, Buol, and Gentz corresponded regularly and were

---

[22] Joachim Maaß, *Heinrich von Kleist* (Berlin and Munich: Scherz, 1977): 232. The original text, *Die Fackel Preußens* (Vienna, 1957), was revised by Scherz Verlag twenty years later.

[23] Hüser [Note 18], 73; see also Beda Allemann, "Der Nationalismus Heinrich von Kleists," *Nationalismus in Germanistik und Dichtung*, ed. B. von Wiese and R. Henß (Berlin: Schmidt, 1967): 305–311.

[24] Hellmuth Rössler, "Buol," *Schriften der Kleist-Gesellschaft* 18 (1938): 98–109.

no doubt aware of Altenstein's memorandum of 1807 about Bayreuth drafted with Kleist's help. It is likely that Frederick Stadion alerted Buol to Kleist's arrival in Dresden, which helps to explain Buol's enthusiastic welcome and patronage of the author whom he had never met.[25]

Moreover, the initial costs for *Phoebus* were underwritten by Buol and Karl Adolf von Carlowitz, a friend of Gentz. They, in turn, prevailed upon the Russian ambassador, Baron Vassily Kanikov to assume responsibility for *Phoebus'* subscription lists. The Bohemian circle headed by Gentz established communications with the Dresden group and exchanged military information regarding the troop movements of the Rhine confederation via Ludwig von Ompteda. Prague and Dresden became relay stations for agents traveling between Königsberg/Berlin and Vienna. As Rössler has pointed out, the primary objective for Kleist and the Dresden patriots was to act as go-between for Vienna and Berlin.[26]

Recently, Hermann F. Weiss discovered in the Statni Oblastni Archive at Brno in Czechoslovakia an unpublished Kleist manuscript which suggests that Kleist mitigated his sharp criticism of the Saxon king. The essay "The King of Saxony's Departure from Dresden"[27] which, as Weiss shows, dates from the spring of 1809, depicts Frederick August I (1750–1827) in a predicament. Because Napoleon wanted to use Saxon troops for an offensive outside of Saxony, he instructed Marshall Bernadotte to "evacuate" the king for his own safety. In his essay, Kleist presents the king as a reluctant victim of powers beyond his control. He did not fear an Austrian invasion because Emperor Francis II had declared that his only enemy was Napoleon. Nevertheless, according to Kleist, the king had to do Napoleon's bidding or face his wrath.

As Weiss points out,[28] Kleist wrote several "secret" essays for the Austrian embassy occasioned by political circumstance in early 1809. *The King of Saxony's Departure from Dresden,* probably commissioned by Buol, reflects more of Austria's conciliatory policy toward Saxony than Kleist's view expressed in such other works of the period as Die Hermannsschlacht or the Catechism for the Germans. As Weiss surmises, the essay was probably intended for publication in the proposed journal *Germania* planned under the spell of Austria's victory over Napoleon at Aspern on 21/22 May 1809. But later events, culminating in the defeat of Archduke Charles's

---

[25] *Ibid.*, 98.

[26] *Ibid.*, 100.

[27] Herman F. Weiss, *Funde und Studien zu Heinrich von Kleist* (Tübingen: Niemeyer, 1984): 244–266.

[28] *Ibid.*, 241.

forces at Wagram on 6 July 1809, moved so rapidly that the essay for Buol never appeared.

However, it is unlikely that Kleist pushed very hard for its publication since the perspective of the piece was Austrian, not that of Kleist, Stein, or his faction. In his major political works of this period, Kleist often deliberates the strategy of Austria's war party, yet, for the most part, decides in favor of the plans drafted at Königsberg, not at Vienna. Despite Weiss' detailed account of Kleist's close ties to the Austrian embassy at Dresden, a letter in December 1807 to his mentor Altenstein testifies to Kleist's first loyalty: "May we meet again in Berlin very soon. Because never, regardless of where circumstances may force me to turn, will my heart choose any other Fatherland than the one in which I was born" (2:803). To be sure, both *Die Hermannsschlacht* and the *Catechism for the Germans* reflect Austria's strategy for the war and its aftermath. Nevertheless, as we shall see, both favor the Prussian rather than the Austrian agenda. In fact, *Die Hermannsschlacht* contains all the components of the Prussian activists' myth of the German nation.

As we have seen, Fichte claims in his *Addresses* that the contemporary Germans owed a great debt of gratitude to Arminius and his Germanic clansmen for preserving German national identity in the face of the Roman onslaught. Rome thus became a symbol of German triumph and strength. Kleist began illustrating this victory in a play only weeks after Fichte concluded his speeches. The structure of his mythic vision is similar to that of Fichte in the *Addresses*. Hermann's first response to Roman aggression is neither an appeal for immediate tactical support from German leaders, nor for armed resistance by his own people. Instead, Hermann proceeds to teach his fellow Cherusci, other German princes, Marbod and, on the personal level, his own wife the essence of the struggle against Rome. He begins by showing other tribal leaders the extent of their disunity. Aware of their petty disagreements over land, Hermann tells the German princes (in the third scene of the first act) that he must join forces with Rome because there is no unity among Germans. Turning to Dagobert and Segler, who have urged him to head a tribal coalition, Hermann predicts: "The Roman you would leave in the lurch and attack each other like two spiders" (243). Hard times have put men's dispositions to the test, he says, but German princes are bent on losing everything ("... since losing everything is the only purpose ..."). They have no plan for defending their borders; nonetheless, they reject Hermann's scorched earth policy immediately. By forcing the princes to deliberate the real state of affairs, Hermann attempts to overcome their particularistic thinking. In this way, he initiates a process of national education.

By the fourth act, the princes have yet to see the error of their ways. Hermann sums up all that the German leaders do wrong: "To free Germany they write to each other in code and, at mortal risk, send messengers, whom the Romans hang. They meet in twilight — eat, drink and, when night comes, sleep with their wives... The hope that Augustus will die tomorrow lures them, covered with disgrace and shame, from one week to the other. We need action not conspiracies" (1498ff). By his own conduct he teaches tribal leaders how to preserve the national identity. To these ends he also uses propaganda, arranges a secret alliance and plans a careful military strategy. The results of this educational process are stated in Komar's description of the battle in act five. Komar informs Marbod that before the troops arrived: "The German people had risen screaming and ripped off their chain..." (2447). Brunhold did not begin the battle: the German people had already revolted; Marbod's army came to their aid. Under Hermann's guidance, the German people had united in insurrection. The fruition of Hermann's efforts to instruct tribal leaders is reflected in the words of Fust, Prince of Cimber, who claims the right of combat with Varus: "He [Varus] hurled me into disgrace and shame, making me an assassin and traitor to Germany, my Fatherland. I'll wash off this infamous blemish in his blood" (2494). The warriors also mirror the progress of the national education program when they proclaim: "Triumph! Triumph! Germany's deadly enemy is crashing down" (2524). The enemy is seen from a nationalistic rather than a particularistic perspective. Rome is not the enemy of one tribe, but of all Germany. Similarly, all the important princes except Aristan contribute to the victory. Komar, Fust and the soldiers give concrete expression to the success of Hermann's attempts to enlighten his countrymen.

Aristan, on the other hand, learns the fate of traitors. When the death sentence is pronounced, Aristan calls Hermann a tyrant. But Marbod remarks to Wolf: "The lesson is a good one" (2619). A more emphatic statement is made by Marbod in a variant corrected in Kleist's own hand. Here Marbod comments: "By the river Styx! The lesson is well devised for guiding minds in Germany to think about such matters" (1:906). In the manuscript of the play published by Tieck in 1821, Marbod's allusion is simple; the variant accentuates the educational process. By reflecting contemporary politics in a portrayal of the past, the dramatist illustrates that victory can be achieved through unified action. Hermann becomes a spokesman for the activists' concept of national education; through Hermann's words and deeds the audience is initiated into their plans for extricating the country from its current difficulties. In the concluding scenes, the German princes also learn that Germany's destiny lies in her political unification.

The fate of Aristan is significant not only because it represents one of the lessons to be learned in the national education program but also because it contradicts Austrian policy as formulated by Gentz, Stadion and the Empress Maria Ludovica. Their goal was above all else to re-establish the principle of dynastic sovereignty by restoring all European thrones to their rightful heirs — even if a prince refused to join Austria and remained loyal to Napoleon. In such an event, his dominion would be severely limited, or he might be induced to abdicate in favor of another family member. Under no circumstances was he to be deposed, much less executed.[29]

Baron Stein, on the other hand, considered such indulgence of the "Rhine Confederation traitors" or, as he described them on another occasion, "that riff-raff of German princes" ["das Lumpengesindel der deutschen Fürsten" (3:771)], unjust and politically unwise. After conferring with him in Prague, General Westphalen wrote to General Fassbender: "[Stein] agrees completely that mild treatment of those miserable German princes would be anathema both to justice and good politics."[30] Nevertheless, Austrian government spokesmen reiterated that the war against Napoleon was being fought to defend the basic rule of legitimacy. On 21 March 1809, Johann Philipp Stadion wrote, "There must be no talk of operating through the people, but, on the contrary, through those legitimate regents we shall give back to the people ... for this single purpose: restoration of the prior governments and with that law and order."[31] Regarding insurrectionist activities, the Empress asked: "With what right do we encourage ... disloyalty to legitimate rulers? ... secret betrayals must not be permitted!"[32] Thus Kleist's representation of Aristan's punishment rejects the official Austrian position in favor of the platform advocated by Stein and those among the Austrians who embraced this position. Although it is unlikely that Stein would have executed those princes who failed to revolt against Napoleon, he would surely have deposed and exiled them. (There can be little doubt that Gneisenau and Blücher would have executed Napoleon had he fallen into their hands after the Battle at Waterloo).[33]

---

[29] See, for example, Friedrich Gentz' memorandum "Gedanken über die Frage: was würde das Haus Habsburg unter den jetzigen Umständen zu beschließen haben, um Deutschland auf eine dauerhafte Weise von fremder Gewalt zu befreien?" In: *Friedrich von Gentz. Memoirs et lettres inedites*, ed. Gustav Schlesier (Stuttgart: Hallberger, 1841): 124ff.

[30] Österreichisches Staatsarchiv. Abt. I: Haus-, Hof-, und Staatsarchiv. Vienna. Fassbender Akten. Faszikel XXVIII.

[31] *Ibid.*, Faszikel 486.

[32] The text of these remarks made by Maria Ludovica in a letter (16 April 1809) to her brother-in-law, Archduke Johann is quoted in Karl Paulin, *Andreas Hofer*. 4th edition (Innsbruck: Tyrolia, 1970): 27.

[33] See Hans Otto, *Gneisenau: Preußens unbequemer Patriot* (Bonn: Keil Verlag, 1979): 362–364. For a study of Kleist's sympathies for Prussia, see Sigurd Burckhardt, "Heinrich von Kleist: The Poet as Prussian," *Centennial Review of Arts and Sciences* 8 (1964): 435–452.

Furthermore, the program of national education reflected in *Die Hermannsschlacht* corresponds to Prussian initiatives not to those of Austria. Hermann teaches the other German princes as well as his own people. All the tribes must learn what Hermann has perceived: the real aim of Rome is the destruction of all Germany.[34] He teaches Luitgar, for example, that he must be willing to subjugate particularist interests to those of the collective in order to repel foreign invaders. In the third act, he reveals his goal to Einhardt in the following words: "If I can't kindle hatred of Rome in Cheruscan hearts before I break camp, so that it beats through all Germany, then my plan will fail" (1486). Here again, Kleist, speaking through Hermann, agitates for Stein's plan and against Austrian strategy. Whereas Stein sought every avenue to spread nationalistic propaganda all over Germany, Stadion refused to permit the circulation of anti-French literature in those German states not under Austria's immediate control. He proposed invading those territories first, and then demanding that the prince decide for or against Austria while Austrian troops occupied his lands. Propaganda was not to be spread to the people before an Austrian offensive because it could incite the people to a revolution even Austrian soldiers might not be able to put down.[35] Moreover, Hermann like the Prussian activists embarks on a course of military reform, which is made exceedingly difficult because of the Roman military leader, Septimius Nerva. This corresponds much more to the Prussian dilemma than to the Austrian. Just as in Prussia, where pro-French spies prevented vital reforms, so too, Hermann's reforms can not always be effectively implemented (1631ff).

Hermann's efforts to educate the people are given religious significance when he orders Hally's body cut into fifteen pieces, one for each of the Germanic tribes. In this scene (act four, scene six) Kleist uses the biblical motif of the Levite who dismembered the concubine, sending her twelve parts to the twelve tribes of Israel (Judges 19–21). Thus the Levite corroborated his testimony of what had befallen him in the land of the Benjamites. Just as the tribes of Israel send envoys and troops to avenge the horrible crime, so do the German tribes come faithfully to the aid of their compatriots. At the conclusion, Hermann also teaches the Cherusci that the losses incurred in a War of Liberation can be regained after the final victory (2565).

---

[34] "Germany's fate teaches me all too clearly that Augustus' final goal is to destroy us both, him and me. And once he, Marbod the Sueven prince is destroyed, then I feel it vividly, Hermann's turn will come" (559f).

[35] Details in Hellmuth Rössler, *Österreichs Kampf um Deutschlands Befreiung* (Hamburg: Hanseat. Verlag, 1940) 1:480ff.

The process of national education proceeds from the personal level. Hermann enlightens his wife regarding the true nature of the Romans. Thusnelda mistakenly applies her German notion of love to Ventidius. Hermann points out the differences in national characteristics when he asks her: "No, tell me earnestly, you believe that? Something a German would call love, with respect and longing, as I [love] you?" (667). Kleist regards national education as an all-encompassing movement. The learning process takes place not only between the national leader and his people but also on a one-to-one basis. In his drama it pervades the national group from military strategists to fighting men, from the family to the husband and wife relationship, uniting all those who share the same language and national heritage. Kleist shows that a public instruction program of such dimensions can prepare the nation for a successful insurrection. Thusnelda is taught that group membership must also determine the personal response to another individual regardless of his or her own personality. Insisting that no enemy of the national group may be spared, Hermann explains to Thusnelda what will befall her if the invaders conquer the land. In this way, Kleist illustrates a method for assuring unrelenting resistance by all the people.

After Marbod is reminded by Rinold of his pledge to rid all Germany of the Roman legions, Hermann instructs Marbod in a plan to defeat Varus. Komar's report of victory emphasizes the success of Hermann's strategy: "We took the field against the legions at the first ray of sun, as you know, according to Hermann's plan..." (2445). Marbod learns foremost that this is not an isolated conflict between his people and the Romans, but a battle for the survival of the German race (2459ff). By personal example, Hermann shows Marbod his willingness to serve his countrymen. In the end their roles are reversed: Marbod kneels before Hermann, a sign that Hermann's program of national reorientation has succeeded. It is complete when he defeats Varus who realizes that the times can be turned about like a glove. Varus envisions the Rome of the future: "And over us I see ruling the world every horde that has the urge"(2471). He then adds that Hermann has taught him to think this way: "Over there approaches the dervish Armin, who taught me these bywords" (2473). His reference to the Muslim ascetic order reveals that, as far as Varus is concerned, Hermann has engaged in little more than an ecstatic observance accompanied by vociferous chanting and shouting. Although he cannot deny Hermann's success, Varus fails to understand such zeal. From his point of view, Rome is brought down by the cunning of a savage. Hermann shows him patriotism fired by religious fervor; but Varus is unable to grasp its significance. Left with defeat and shame, he attempts suicide. By consistently showing Hermann in his role as the nation's preceptor and liberator, Kleist presents that component of Fichte's mythic vision.

Language, which is a key ingredient in Fichte's myth, also plays a role in *Die Hermannsschlacht*. Here, however, Kleist gives this component a humorous turn. Varus and his legions march in a circle through the woods because Hermann has instructed their German guides to lead them to a location with a name similar to that of the military target: instead of to Iphikon, the Cheruscan guides take the Romans on a bewildering march to Pfiffikon. In the midst of the confusion, the third Roman General makes the following remark:

> Pfiffikon! Iphikon! –Was das, beim Jupiter! Für eine Sprache ist! Als schlüg ein Stecken
> An einen alten, rostzerfressenen Helm!
> Ein Greuelsystem von Worten, nicht geschickt,
> Zwei solche Dinge, wie Tag und Nacht,
> Durch einen eignen Laut zu unterscheiden.
> Ich glaub, ein Tauber wars, der das Geheul erfunden,
> Und an den Mäulern sehen sie sichs ab.

> Pfiffikon! Iphikon! By Jove, what a language that is! As if a stick were striking an old rust-eaten helmet!
> An abominable system of words not capable of distinguishing two such things as day and night by a single sound.
> I believe the man was deaf who invented this howling, and they read it from each other's snouts (1898ff).

The Romans are led astray by the mispronunciation of a camp name. Kleist found this motif in the historical writings of Livy (XII, 13); yet he reworked it in his play to emphasize the difference in the Roman and German conceptual framework. The humorous befuddlement heightened by Varus's helpless questioning of the guides, had its serious side in the inability of the foreign invaders to comprehend another system of thoughts. The Roman can only negate or belittle an intellectual process alien to his own. Because their respective languages cause them to think differently, the Cheruscan remains totally incomprehensible to the Roman. Therefore, when the Germanic tribes take up arms against the Roman intruders, they not only defend home and hearth but also preserve a frame of mind for arranging and analyzing the external objects of experience.

Die Hermannsschlacht also dramatizes the third component in the myth outlined by Fichte: the relationship of the individual to his lineage and national group. When Wolf asks Hermann whether he considers the Latins superior people, Hermann answers in Fichtean terms: "I believe the Germans enjoy a superior disposition (*Anlage*); the Italian, however, has developed his inferior talents more at the moment" (304ff). Thus German preeminence is upheld despite contemporaneous appearances.

Ventidius's answer to Varus also exemplifies the philosopher's influence. Regarding Hermann, he tells Varus: "He is a German" (1250), and proceeds to characterize the individual according to what he perceives as national characteristics. Kleist expresses here his own reservations about the desirability and practicality of certain virtues in the German people. If the Germans remain steadfast in their honesty and candor, he argues, they will forever be victimized by foreign blackguards and schemers.

At the conclusion of act four, Hermann asks Eginhardt: "Do I fight for the sand I walk on too? Do I fight for myself? Protect Cheruscia! What! Where Hermann stands, he conquers and hence Cheruscia is there" (1852ff). He is not concerned with his own life, ambition or pride, but with the symbol of the nation which he has become. Therefore, he can tell Egbert to forgive, forget the past and love Germany's children. Yet he will not spare the enemy and thinks only of revenge since any other feeling goes against the "national instinct" (2256). Hermann's argument implies that a nation is not a geographical, but rather, as Fichte had argued, a living entity. In giving himself wholly to the service of the nation, the individual assumes the group's characteristics — he becomes one with the organism which is the nation. We see then that the myth proclaimed in Fichte's *Addresses* is rendered in its entirety in a stage adaptation.

This is not to suggest that socio-political myth-making was Kleist's only concern. On the contrary, Kleist added to the components of the myth his own poetic devices. *Die Hermannsschlacht* is not simply a propaganda play. It has been shown that the play is concerned with both the propagandist and literary productivity.[36] Beyond Fichte's myth, the drama bears the imprint of Kleist's artistry. This may be illustrated by examining the many images from the animal world which function within the play as characterizations and symbols of the places, personalities and events Kleist regarded as significant in his own day.

The second scene focuses on the killing of an aurochs. A joke is made at Ventidius's expense: by felling the crazed animal he mistakenly believes that he has saved Thusnelda's life. In fact, by standing in a thicket, Thusnelda had avoided any real danger. Historically, however, the Teutoburg Forest had never known the wild ox. According to an encyclopedia published in 1821, which reflects the extent of scientific knowledge in Kleist's day, the *Ur*, extinct since the seventeenth century, was not found in any part of Germany other than northern Prussia.[37] It had not

---

[36] Ruth K. Angress, "Kleist's Treatment of Imperialism: *Die Hermannsschlacht* and 'Die Verlobung in St. Domingo'," *Monatshefte* 69 (1977): 17–33.

[37] Cf. J. S. Esch and J. G. Gruber, *Allgemeine Enzyclopädie der Wissenschaften und Künste* (Leipzig: Gleditsch, 1821) Sec. 1, 6:286.

roamed the historical land of the Cherusci. Yet it is not difficult to recognize Kleist's motive for interjecting this animal into an area in which it historically did not belong. The aurochs is a symbol through which Kleist, at the beginning of his play, makes a veiled reference to Prussia, where the significant battles of the day are to be fought. Moreover, the introduction of this animal into an unnatural habitat ties in with Kleist's general descriptions of the Cheruscan domain: a country of sand, swamp, mud and murderous terrain which, when wet, becomes "slippery as bird-lime" (1893f) — all of this characterizes the Brandenburg Marches and to a much lesser extent the Teutoburg Forest.

The aurochs was hunted by stalking, not with bow and arrow. Woodsmen lured the animal into a wooden area where it fell into a trap dug in the ground. (Only then was it killed with spear and shaft). At the end of the play, Ventidius will be lured into a death trap by the person he believes he has saved. Having hunted the *Ur*, he will become Thusnelda's prey, which she entices into the snare. This reversal of roles between the hunters and the hunted also takes place between the Romans and the Cherusci. A similar death trap in the woods awaits Varus and his legions as they break camp to fight Marbod and the Suevians. Kleist uses another foreshadowing technique in this scene: Ventidius is led to believe that he has saved Thusnelda, which is false as shown in the interchange between Wolf and Thuiskomar (110ff). Hermann, by creating similar illusions in their minds, will later lure the Romans into the woods and destroy them.

Two animal images in particular are associated with the Romans: the wild boar (*Eber*) and the wolf. When he realizes he is trapped, Varus takes sword and shield in hand and, comparing himself to a wild boar, explains he will fight to the death (2110ff). Recounting the battle to Marbod, Komar describes Varus as a wild boar (2450). In Roman history,[38] this animal symbolized Roman luxury and pomposity. Plinius calls it "animal propter convivia natum,"[39] pointing out that a boar's head was often the main course served at the table of wealthy and haughty Romans (*caput coennae*). Thus, apart from his immediate affiliation with swine, Varus, as soon as he "becomes" a wild boar, personifies the arrogant Roman, living sumptuously at the expense of the oppressed peoples. This is Kleist's assessment of the French in Germany.

---

[38] Tacitus notes in the *Germania* that certain Germanic tribesmen (e.g. the Astrys) wore figures of the wild boar for protection in battle. Among the Suevians, it was a symbol of fertility. In Norse mythology, Freya turns her suitor Otlar into a wild boar (Hyndlu-Lioth), which is figuratively what the Germanic tribes united under Hermann do to Varus.

[39] N. N. 8:5.

The wolf is employed as a symbol at key points in the play. The first scene ends with the character Wolf, Prince of the Catts, proclaiming: "The wolf, O Germany, raids your herds and your herdsmen quarrel over a handful of wool" (72ff). Thuiskomar characterizes Varus in the third scene as a "wolf of the desert" (203); in scene twenty-two of act five Gueltar commands Varus: "Stand [and fight], you wolf from the Tiber" (284). In these three instances the wolf represents Napoleon as is evidenced not only in other anti-French literature of the period in which the emperor is consistently depicted as a wolf but also in Kleist's other writings. The wolf is one of his favorite images for Bonaparte. In his ode, *Germania and her Children*, the choir sings: "A sporting hunt, as when marksmen are on the track of the wolf!" (1:27). Here Kleist calls upon all Germany, not simply Prussia, to build a pyramid of glory or go to the grave in the fight for freedom. The *Germans' War Song* contains the lines: "For the wolf, as far as I know, a reward is offered" (1:28). The symbol's meaning becomes apparent in the last verse when Kleist tells his German brothers to take up the cudgel and force the French out of Germany. This poem written at Dresden in 1809 begins with a reference to the shaggy bear ("Zottelbär"), which will reappear as she-bear in *Die Hermannsschlacht*. The interplay between the wolf and the bear in both works has an historical root in Napoleon's fascination with pitched battles between wolves and bears, a spectacle he attended often in Paris.

The most significant symbol in the play is the bear Thusnelda uses in her revenge upon Ventidius. Hermann had informed his wife that Roman women preferred the dry blond hair of Germanic tribeswomen to their own dark oily hair. She had subsequently discovered Ventidius's intention of shearing all her tresses after Hermann's demise and presenting them to his beloved Livia as a gift. Having told her deceitfully that he loved her and promising never to part with the single lock he had stolen from her, Ventidius enraged Thusnelda by covertly sending his plunder to Livia as a sample of his forthcoming tribute. Historically, Germanic tribeswomen wore amulets of bear teeth and claws. Here Ventidius is to feel the cutting fangs and slashing nails of a hungry she-bear. "Tell her you love her," Thusnelda calls to Ventidius through the gate as she throws the key away, "then she [the bear] will stand still and give you her curls" (2422). At one level of meaning, the bear is a personification of Thusnelda's rage. "Out of my way," she says to Gertrud, "he [Ventidius] has made me into a bear" (2312). The she-bear is, at this point, a symbol of a woman's strength and unleashed fury. On another level, however, the bear may be seen as representing the unfettered vengeance of Prussia. As a symbol, the bear has been associated with Brandenburg since Albrecht the Bear founded Berlin and other Prussian cities in the middle of the twelfth century. When the bear crushes Ventidius, she symbolizes Kleist's hope for the outcome of Prussia's struggle with France. On yet another level, the bear may be regarded perhaps as a subtle reference to Prussia-Anhalt. It will be remembered that Napoleon's march through that territory in flagrant violation of Prussian sovereignty precipitated the tragic conflict which ended at Jena and Auerstedt in 1806. Historically the bear is found at various times in the coat-of-arms of that region. Thus Kleist may have intended his bear as an animated symbol of the territory violated by Napoleon, which has come to life here to avenge the crime. Furthermore, the house of Anhalt had sworn allegiance to the Confederation of the Rhine on April 17, 1807. Ventidius's fate can be seen perhaps as Kleist's projection of the revenge taken by Anhalt's heraldic bear upon those who serve Germany's oppressors.

Kleist also included other allusions to contemporary events and personalities. It has been shown that *Die Hermannsschlacht* reflects in considerable detail the plans made in the summer of 1808 for an insurrection in northern Germany supporting Austria's efforts against Napoleon,[40] which was to begin in the Spring of the following year. In his essay, "Kleists 'Hermannsschlacht' und der Freiherr vom Stein," Richard Samuel argues cogently that Kleist had access to considerable information, which he incorporated into *Die Hermannsschlacht*, about the strategy of the Königsberg triumvirate for the anti-Napoleon campaign. Dating the play from as late as October-December 1808, Samuel points out such reflections of contemporary politics as the provocation of the German populace through secretly distributed propaganda, the arguments concerning an alliance with Austria, the influence of the Spanish guerrilla war, and the indecisiveness at the court in Königsberg. A striking example overlooked by Samuel deserves special mention here. It is not by chance that Hermann's allies in the play are the Suevians. This Germanic tribe had conquered large territories in Spain and had remained behind to rule Spanish lands after the Vandals and Alans crossed over to Africa (ca. 429 A.D.). They were later vanquished by the Visigoths. Thus, independently from Marbod's symbolic role in the play, the Suevians are a reminder of the German heritage in Spain. In 1808 the Spanish guerrilla war against Napoleon inspired Prussian political leaders to plan an uprising in northern Germany; for this reason, the Spaniards were regarded as allies. Kleist was assured that his audience would understand his allusion to Spain since the first volume of Ernst Moritz Arndt's *Geist der Zeit* ("Spirit of the Times") had appeared only two years earlier and had found a large enthu-

---

[40] Cf. Hermann Schneider, *Studien zu Kleist* (Berlin: Weidmann, 1915): 14f. and Max Fischer, *Kleist. Der Dichter des Preußentums* (Stuttgart: Cotta, 1916): 55.

siastic audience. Here Arndt had detailed the Suevian rule in Spain.[41] According to Samuel, Kleist refers in the play to Stein's letter to Wittgenstein (which prompted Frederick William III to dismiss his Minister of State), to Prussian overtures to Austria, the attempts of Prince William in Paris to secure better conditions for Prussia and the secret mission of Count Götzen, governor of Silesia. Such advertences document Kleist's firsthand knowledge of the happenings and proposals deliberated at Königsberg. Moreover, little of this information had been disseminated in the newspapers and journals at the time. Samuel concluded that Hermann, despite exhibiting certain characteristics of Frederick William III later in the play, is a representation of Baron Stein in his efforts against the French.[42]

In adopting Fichte's myth and incorporating it in his drama, Kleist abandoned his former position. In his early works generally, Kleist dealt with the problem of how the individual might protect himself from the encroachment of the social order. In *Die Hermannsschlacht* his perspective is the opposite: here the aggregate is threatened by the egotistical attitude of single members; the nation, now seen as more than the sum of those united by language and lineage — as a "living" organism — must be protected from the individual. As we shall see, this point of view also permeates *Prinz Friedrich von Homburg*. Before turning our attention to that play, we shall look first at Kleist's other political writings in 1808 and 1809.

Although *Die Hermannsschlacht* illustrates the activists' myth of the nation, it does not represent the total extent of Kleist's anti-Napoleon activity at this time. From April 23 to May 22, 1809, Kleist fashioned the sixteen chapters of his *Catechism for the Germans* from the *Citizen's Catechism and Short Embodiment of a Spaniard* which had been translated from Spanish into German at Vienna.[43] With a simple question-and-answer technique, Kleist attempts to reach readers in all walks of life, particularly soldiers in

---

[41] See *Arndts Werke*, ed. August Leffson and Wilhelm Steffens (Berlin: Bong, n. d.) 6:115. Concerning the popular response to Arndt's first volume, see Steffen's introduction, 9f. The significance of such allusions to contemporaneous events has been called into question by Hans-Dieter Loose, *Kleists 'Hermannsschlacht'. Kein Krieg für Hermann und seine Cherusker* (Karlsruhe: von Loeper, 1984).

[42] The difficulties in determining whether Hermann represents the king of Prussia, the emperor of Austria, Stein or another stateman was noted earlier by Meyer-Benfey, who contended that this obfuscation was intended by Kleist. The main concern was Germany's liberation, not the first one to initiate the action. See Heinrich von Meyer-Benfey, "Kleists politische Anschauungen," *Schriften der Kleist-Gesellschaft, Jahrbuch* 1931, 13 (1932): 14f.

[43] See Johann Bethke, *Heinrich von Kleist und Österreich* (Diss. Vienna, 1932); also Rainer Wohlfeil, *Spanien und die deutsche Erhebung* (Wiesbaden: Steiner, 1965). For details of Kleist's political connections at this time, see Hermann F. Weiss [Note 27], 187–225.

the service of Saxony. The difference here is that Francis II of Austria is portrayed as the mighty avenger, the restorer of the German nation, the liberator and guardian. However, such a representation did not run counter to Stein's assessment. He even advocated the temporary restoration of the Holy Roman Empire the better to fight Napoleon and the French. Stein doubted that such a restoration could be achieved (3:744). Napoleon personifies the spirit of patricide which has risen from hell. In the fourth chapter, the father questions his son:

> Question: Who are your enemies, my son?
> Answer: Napoleon and as long as he is their emperor, the French.
> Question: Do you hate anyone else?
> Answer: No one else in the world (2:352).

Francis II is by contrast a brave and honest ruler:

> Question: How do you know that the struggle waged by the Germans is justified?
> Answer: Because the emperor Francis of Austria has assured us that it is.
> Question: Where did he assure this?
> Answer: In an appeal his brother the Arch-duke Charles, made to the nation.
> Question: So, if two reports are presented, one from Napoleon the Corsican emperor, the other from Francis, the emperor of Austria, which one will you believe?
> Answer: The report of Francis, emperor of Austria.
> Question: Why?
> Answer: Because he is more honest (*Ibid.*).

The king of Saxony is shown to be a more undeserving monarch, as Kleist presents the justification for that disdain which, a short time earlier, had motivated him to rework *Michael Kohlhaas*:

> Question: Your own ruler, for example, is the king of Saxony.
> Answer: The king of Saxony?
> Question: Yes, the king of Saxony.
> Answer: This noble lord *was*, my father, when he still served the Fatherland. He will be again as surely as he returns to his duty which commands him to dedicate himself to the Fatherland. But now that he, lured by bribed and terrible advisors, has aligned with the enemies of the land, now the stout-hearted among the Saxons can no longer regard him as their ruler, and your son, as much as it pains him, owes him no obedience! (2:357)

This was not the official Austrian position. As we have seen, Stadion and, especially the Empress, completely rejected the notion that subjects may disobey legitimate rulers under certain circumstances. This is not to deny that Kleist wrote occasional pieces which furthered Austrian interests;

however, in most cases, he did so when those interests corresponded to the goals of the Prussian activists. Even the chapter headings of the *Catechism* — "About the Education of Germans," "About Love of the Fatherland," "About Germany in General" — mirror the structure of the Prussian myth. In both the *Catechism* and *Die Hermannsschlacht* the protection of land and chattel provide at most secondary motivation for repelling foreign invaders. More important is the preservation of such ideals as God, Fatherland, Freedom and Loyalty. In his aphorisms *On the Liberation of Austria*, Kleist lists God, freedom, law and morality as those German ideals prompting insurrection against the French. The play, the ode, the *Catechism* and the aphorisms are marked by a high degree of consistency in the presentation of arguments; they complement each other in the effort to promote a myth intended to counteract French propaganda in Germany.

There are additional compositions in which Kleist opposes French hegemony. His *Textbook of French Journalism* offers an exposé of Napoleon's manipulation of the French press for his own advantage. Kleist reveals how statistics are altered, setbacks covered up, and editors critical of the French government silenced. His four *Satirical Letters* illustrate the hypocritical German army officer, who plays lip service to the cause of German liberation, but draws his pay from the French military command; the unscrupulous French officer who takes advantage of a German woman's weaknesses in order to gain her inheritance; a mayor's ironic instructions which serve to protect his own property while others sacrifice, and the astonishment of a South American at the report in a Nuremberg newspaper about German participation in the defeat of Austria. In contrast to his *Catechism* which addresses the common man, particularly the soldier, Kleist's *Satirical Letters* are directed to the more discriminating reader. Here Kleist turns to the intelligentsia with all the refined subtleties in his poetic arsenal in an effort to arouse widespread indignation.

In his play, political writings and *Satirical Letters*, Kleist called for concerted action against the French enemy without and the egocentric enemy within. Representing artistically the plans of the Königsberg triumvirate, he spoke to the common man as well as to the intelligentsia. He incorporated into his writings those elements of the Fichtian myth that served to arouse anger and to unite factions. On the one hand, he exposed what he considered to be the fundamental weakness in the French character; on the other, he glorified inherent German traits. In Kleist's thinking the national heritage, German lineage and the German language were threatened with extinction under Napoleon's despotic rule. All over Germany the efficient bureaucracy, following on the heels of Napoleon's armies, was streamlining and homogenizing national life along lines dictated in

Paris. The enforced political uniformity made gifted Germans more and more aware of inherent differences in their country's own cultural, economic and political development. Kleist, like Fichte, insisted on the preservation of the uniquely German intellectual framework for organizing and understanding the chaos of sensations which constitutes "reality." With this, Kleist became a collaborator in the creation and illustration of a powerful Napoleonic anti-myth: the myth of German superiority overshadowed temporarily by historical appearances, but destined nonetheless to rescue Europe from the French conquerors.

Much of this found its way into *Prinz Friedrich von Homburg*. There was, however, a decided difference. Having illustrated the activist's myth upon the background of the Austrian war initiatives in *Die Hermannsschlacht*, he felt no compulsion to reproduce the myth with all its components once again. Instead, Kleist represented in this, his greatest drama, the results of accepting and living according to the myth of the nation. Here Kleist worked out the implications of German unification with Prussia serving as a model for the realization of transcendent moral goals. How could Prussia lead the way? What was so unique about this particular state that she should serve as an example for the other German states? What transformations were necessary in the current state of affairs in Prussia and in the behavior of her government before she could play such a role? Moreover, when Kleist began this play, the activists were in total disarray. In the spring of 1809 they had put their plans into action: Major Ferdinand von Schill had led the troops under his command out of their garrison and across the flatlands of northern Germany, urging others to join him, the peasants, workers and bourgeois merchants to revolt against the despotic French rule. His maneuver was to signal the British who had pledged an expeditionary force to the continent and to start a war in the north co-ordinated with an Austrian offensive in the south. But the plan fell through. The peasants and the middle class failed to rally; the British expeditionary force bogged down in the mud along the banks of the river Scheldt; Schill was killed in street fighting in the seaport city of Stralsund, and Napoleon crushed the Austrians at Wagram. Incensed at such unauthorized activity, King Frederick William III denounced Schill's insubordination and turned his back on all advisors with activist leanings.

What could be saved? How could the activists regain the king's confidence? What could they offer by the way of apology? Against this background Kleist illustrated Kant's idea of the moral law as interpreted in Fichte's popular philosophy. In *Prinz Friedrich von Homburg* the absolute *Ich* comes to recognize the needs of the state to which he belongs and his own responsibilities to the nation. Inasmuch as Kleist equates the moral law with service and loyalty to that nation, he offers an apology to the king for the faction in whose services he labored. When he justifies the act of disobedience in order to prompt forgiveness, he strives for reconciliation with the court. Above all, he sought to rescue from extinction those unique aspects of the Prussian character, which the activists had fostered. The play portrays the personal development of the prince to an awareness of the moral obligations engendered by membership in the national group. In agreement with Fichte's popular philosophy he subjugates egocentric desires to the imperatives of national life in an expression of ideal morality. The prince becomes a man when he discovers the state as a superindividual entity and willingly commits himself to its service and preservation according to its laws. But these laws cannot be obeyed without question, administered without compassion, adhered to in every circumstance. The danger, as Kleist perceived it, was the stifling of individual initiative to the point of slavery. In his play, it is precisely the impulsive summons to personal action in the midst of a national crisis which characterizes the Brandenburger, the Prussian. Neither the king nor his counterpart in the play, the elector, can insist on the letter of the law to the detriment of innate national characteristics. The distinguishing feature of the margraviate's inhabitants is their willingness to follow the "order of the heart," to do what they feel must be done, to ensure the victory and secure the country. Not the will of the ruler, but the inner law which compels personal initiatives in times of war is the essence of the Prussian spirit which must be saved so that it may serve as the corner stone of the united German nation. Thus the play apologizes for those activist initiatives not sanctioned by the king, but also explains why they were necessary and how, from what source, they were prompted. The purpose is to get Frederick William III to recognize this and move towards reconciliation.

When the prince concludes the second scene of act two with the words: "Let it [disobeying orders] be upon my head. Follow me, my brothers" (496), the absolute ego has reached its zenith. This command is an expression of the will to personal glory. The prince disobeys orders which were to serve the total effort against the enemy because, at this point, he considers only the *Ich*, not others. His ego is sovereign and persists in an attitude which fails to consider total needs. The famous fear-of-death scene in the third act illustrates the nadir of egocentric behavior. The absolute *Ich* shuns nothing in an effort to negate the encroachment of the nation's law. However, the elector's letter establishes the individual's obligations by forcing the prince to recognize his own role in meeting them. The totality of the prince's experiences constitutes the educational process both for him as an individual and for the audience which becomes a participant in self-edification. Inasmuch as the audience identifies with Kleist's protagonist, the public is led from an egocentric to a nationalistic viewpoint.

It has been argued that *Prinz Friedrich von Homburg* is not an educational drama (*Erziehungsdrama*).[44] The elector does not educate the prince, according to this hypothesis, because he does not stand above the action. He experiences himself a weakening of his belief in the principles of autocratic rule. Hence, as a teacher he misses the mark. This contention, however, fails to see the drama as a total structure. The elector does contribute to the prince's education along nationalistic lines whether he intended to teach the prince or not. The sum of his tribulations produce the edification process for him and for the public. Kleist gives concrete expression to a mythic vision in which national education plays a key role. His purpose is to instruct the audience. When the elector sends the prince the letter, requesting he state categorically that he has been treated unfairly, the elector is pursuing a pedagogical goal. He forces the prince to decide his own fate, and consider his status as upholder of the law. The prince does not obey until given the opportunity to make the order his own law by his own creative action. The law becomes an imperative only by virtue of his free and active positing of it. That which initially threatened him from without now begins to grow out of the creative depths of his own being. With this process he experiences the expansion of the *Ich* towards infinity ("nun, o Unsterblichkeit, bist du ganz mein!"). This is the basic element of the Fichtean system.[45]

Before the fear-of-death scene, the prince takes for granted that others too are governed by egocentricity. He asks Hohenzollern how the elector could bring him before judges who sing only the song of death unless he was preparing to appear "like a God within their circle" (856) and free him. The prince has not yet learned that the organism of the nation demands that all men subjugate personal desires to its needs. Therefore, once the elector posits the law, he is bound to uphold it himself. It becomes greater than he. The prince recognizes this when he answers the elector's letter. He has reached a clear understanding of the superindividual prerogative when he states that a triumph over the Swedish General Wrangel is not nearly as important as a victory over "the most destructive enemy which we harbor in ourselves: defiance and arrogance" (1757). Furthermore, Kleist relates this problem to national characteristics by having the prince comment about himself after his arrest: "I have a German heart of the old fashioned kind which is used to generosity and love"(784). With these words, the dramatist suggests that the German people will have to forsake antiquated notions of the law and

---

[44] Hans M. Wolff [Note 12], 504–510.

[45] See F. W. Kaufmann, "Kleist and Fichte," *GR* 9 (1934): 1–8. Kaufmann points out several links between the drama and Fichte's *Wissenschaftslehre*.

alter some ingrained behavioral patterns in the interest of the nation. It is not only the prince who must learn to control impulsive action but also all Germans who desire national salvation.

In the last act we are reminded that the play illustrates a national educational process. After the elector orders the prince brought from his cell, he remarks: "He will teach you, I am certain, what military discipline and obedience are!" (1616). The prince's progress moves the elector to elevate him to an example of what must occur in Germany. At this point in *Prinz Friedrich von Homburg*, the instructional component combines with the complex of nationalist arguments to reflect the Fichtean myth. Only the language element is absent from Kleist's dramatic illustration. However, this omission suggests that Kleist, having completed *Die Hermannsschlacht*, was not simply re-illustrating the myth promulgated by Fichte. He wrote *Prinz Friedrich von Homburg* in order to draw the metasocial consequences of accepting the myth. Patriotism does not derive simply from carrying out orders: it is a state of mind arrived at through the suppression of egotistical desires and self-aggrandizement in the interests of the national group. By positing the law through an act of free will, the individual becomes one with the national super-personality. In this play, then, Kleist reproduces key components of the myth envisioned in the *Addresses*, explores the commitment resulting from a widespread popular response and in so doing promotes the socio-political point of view advocated by Fichte. This is not to deny the influence of other popular political philosophies of the time. It has been proven, for example, that Adam Müller's lectures *Elemente der Staatskunst*, given at Dresden in 1808–09, had made a profound impact on Kleist and are also reflected in *Prinz Friedrich von Homburg*.[46] Other political and social commentaries helped him to draw logical conclusions from a positive reception of Fichte's myth. With *Prinz Friedrich von Homburg*, Kleist goes beyond the social vision contained in Fichte's popular philosophy by illustrating how such structures would operate in the real world and the consequences they bear for individual behavior.

Hüser's remarks may also serve as grounds for speculation that *Prinz Friedrich* is not a play about the historical Homburg at all, but instead an attempt at vindicating Major von Schill. But even if this contention is correct, Kleist's prince is not simply a carbon copy of Schill. The dramatist also incorporated in his characterization of Homburg the dashing, audacious and, in some ways, reckless behavior of Frederick William's brother,

---

[46] See Hans M. Wolff [Note 12], 493–519; also Bernhard Luther, "Kleists *Prinz von Homburg* und Adam Müllers *Elemente der Staatskunst*," *Zeitschrift für deutschen Unterricht* 30 (1916): 171–183; also Siegfried Streller, *Das dramatische Werk Heinrich von Kleist* (Berlin: Rütten and Loening, 1966).

Prince Louis, who had disobeyed orders four days before the battle at Jena and, as a result, paid with his life. Like Kleist's prince, Louis was ordered to gather his forces opposite the enemy's left flank and await the arrival of the rest of the army before crossing the river Saale.[47] In the night of the 9th to the 10th of October 1806, Louis received a direct command not to attack. But, wishing to secure the river crossing, he disobeyed the order and, cut-off from the main force, was killed during a French cavalry charge. Despite his reasoned, yet nonetheless bold, insubordination, Louis was celebrated as the "hero of Saalfeld."[48] In his portrayal of Prince Friedrich, Kleist reminded Frederick William of his brother's heroic display of reckless abandon, which the king had "forgiven" at once.

Kleist then went farther. He patterned the execution-clemency scene at the end of his play after an actual event in which the king had, in fact, pardoned an officer for insubordination. Carl von François, in a fit of temper, had drawn his sword against a superior officer, was court-martialed and sentenced to death before a firing squad. After the errant officer had been blindfolded, the king, acting at the behest of his son, Crown Prince William, the latter day German emperor, issued a last minute pardon.[49] Kleist alludes to Louis and François both in the characterization and fate of his prince. Through allusion and illusion, he hoped to effect a reconciliation between the king and those activists who had likewise disobeyed orders. For our purposes, the insubordination of Major Schill is of greater significance because with its many ramifications this act, more than any other, provided the background for Kleist's apologetic intention.

According to Kleist's sources, especially K. H. Krause's reader with its accounts of the battle at Fehrbellin in 1675, the Elector of Brandenburg forgave the prince immediately for his "error in judgment, embraced him on the battlefield and assured him of his great respect and friendship."[50] Conversely, Kleist's protagonist must endure an agonizing ordeal, leading to the edge of the grave, before the elector is moved to forgiveness. The prince's insubordination corresponds to Schill's unsanctioned initiatives which, orchestrated by Stein, were intended to launch the north German

---

[47] For details relating to the play, see Klaus Kanzog, *Heinrich von Kleist. Prinz Friedrich von Homburg. Text, Kontexte, Kommentar* (Munich: Hanser, 1977): 151–157. Kanzog traces the "codes" reflected in the play.

[48] As Kanzog points out, Prince Louis became the central figure in Fritz von Unruh's drama *Louis Ferdinand* (1913) and Friedrich Bethge's *Rebellion in Preußen* (1939).

[49] Kanzog, *Homburg* 212–214.

[50] K. H. Krause, *Mein Vaterland unter den hohenzollerischen Regenten* (Halle: Schwetschke, 1803): 181–184; reprinted by Kanzog, 115–116.

insurrection and prompt a British troop landing.[51] The beginning of a Schill biography had already appeared in the first issue of the *People's Friend* (*Der Volksfreund*), the literary organ of the "Moral Scientific Union" (*Tugendbund*), a semi-secret society dedicated to driving the French from Germany and spreading anti-Napoleon propaganda.[52] Here it had been reported that Schill's considerable personal popularity would gain him thousands of recruits once he decided to march. This proved to be a grave miscalculation. Angered at the unauthorized troop movement, the king resolved to court-martial those officers who survived the fighting.

The first act lays the dramatic framework for insubordination with parallels to historical events from the Fall of 1808 to March 12, 1809, culminating in Schill's march of April 28, 1809. Homburg, like Schill, is an impatient young cavalry leader, who has already determined his plan of action before the conflict. Schill was led by the patriots to believe that his popularity among the people would guarantee the success of the project designed at Königsberg. Homburg, too, is motivated by a desire for fame. When he led a north German insurrection intended to liberate Germany, Schill responded to the Fatherland's call for loyalty and service which transcended even the obedience demanded by Frederick William III. The figure of Homburg also represents the individual from Prussia's intelligentsia, who heeds his personal calling; his disobedient behavior is prompted by his own aspirations. The Prince's loyalty is to his own patriotically inspired desire to free his homeland; therefore, he disregards commands from his sovereign for restraint.

On the one hand, the elector embodies the law; on the other, he represents King Frederick William III, who, having commanded Count Götzen, governor of Silesia, and all other patriots to cease agitating for war against France, insisted upon obedience. In response to the rumors of anti-loyalist machinations, he warned the activists, in language employed by Kleist's elector, that they would answer with their heads if they disobeyed royal instructions and engaged in caprices (*Willensmeinungen*) of their own. When a report of insurgence, brewing in the garrison at Berlin, reached him late in April, 1809, Frederick William III cancelled all military leaves west of the Elbe river to insure compliance with his commands. Two unsuccessful popular uprisings before Schill's maneuver had already taken

---

[51] Concerning Schill, see Georg Baersch, *Ferdinand von Schills Zug und Tod im Jahre 1809* (Leipzig: Brockhaus, 1860), Hüser, 77ff. and George Heinrich Pertz, *Das Leben des Feldmarschalls Grafen Neithardt von Gneisenau* (Berlin: Reimer, 1869) 1:452–459, 677ff. and (the Memorandum of Count Götzen) 691–693; Kanzog, 138–153. From these sources many parallels with Schill's maneuver may be drawn.

[52] For the role of this organization and the links between the Prussian activists and Great Britain, see my forthcoming study, *British Pounds and Prussian Patriots*.

place: Wilhelm Caspar von Dörnberg had initiated a short-lived revolt in Westphalia and Hesse; Friedrich von Katte sought to incite a riot in Magdeburg and take control of the fortress. The Prussian regent could well caution, even warn, the patriots with the elector's phrase, "control yourself" ("regier dich wohl"), because a third insurrection would antagonize the French and perhaps cost him both "throne and country." This is reflected in *Prinz Friedrich von Homburg* when the elector admonishes the prince before the battle to be patient and obedient.

The second act deals with Homburg's actual insubordination. Prince Friedrich is deaf to Hohenzollern's recitation of the royal battle plans. Instead, he commits what Frederick William III, referring to Schill, decried as the "unbelievable act" (*unglaubliche Tat*). Homburg first strips the sword from a subordinate unwilling to follow "the Margraviate's ten commandments" ("Zehn märkische Gebote") then, with an appeal to the "dictates of the heart," ("Ordre des Herzens,") persuades Kottwitz and the others to follow him into battle. The old fighter submits to his young protégé's will with the proviso that the Prince take full responsibility for the insubordinate action: "I'll follow you, but be it on your head" ["Auf deine Kappe nimms. Ich folge dir." (496)]. Roused by such loyalty, Prince Friedrich accepts the responsibility: "Let it be upon my head. Follow me, my brothers!" ["Ich nehms auf meine Kappe. Folgt mir Brüder!" (497)]

Major von Schill rallied his hussars outside Berlin with patriotic speeches in support of the national cause. Producing a letter and a handbag from the queen as evidence to suggest that he acted with royal approval, he promised glory in return for self-sacrifice. Had their offensive been successful, national prominence would be but one of many honors for each participant. For Homburg, satisfaction of the ego is synonymous with dictates of the heart. He persuades the unquestionably loyal Kottwitz that his "Ordre" is patriotically inspired, which permits him impulsively to enter the fray in order to acquire his pre-ordained honors. As the cavalry overlooking the battle claims victory, the prince commands: "Let's go! Sound the fanfare! Follow me!" ["Auf! Laß Fanfare blasen! Folge mir!" (468)] Since his nocturnal vision suggested that the day's victory belonged also to him, Homburg induces the men to follow his personal imperatives. They believe the prince's desire to fight is a manifestation of selfless patriotism. Thus both Schill's and Homburg's squadrons follow the leader's individual impulses. Homburg rallies his men with the words: "Follow me, brothers!", ("Folgt mir, Brüder!") the same command spoken by Schill.[53]

---

[53] Ferdinand von Schill, Proclamation: "An die Deutschen":
Meine in den Ketten eines fremden Volkes schmachtenden Brüder! Der Augenblick ist erschienen, wo ihr die Fesseln abwerfen [...] könnt [...] Ermannt euch, folgt meinem Wink, und wir sind, was wir ehmals waren. Ziehet die Sturmglocken! Dies schreckliche

In act 2 (5–6) we learn of the elector's alleged death while aiding the beleaguered cavalry, which had charged the foe's artillery (545f). Believing his ruler had fallen, Prince Friedrich renewed the attack with vengeance, "like a wild bear driven by revenge" ["dem Bären gleich, von Wut gespornt und Rache"(552)]. Here the bear is a link between *Prinz Friedrich von Homburg* and *Die Hermannsschlacht*. The scene also reflects Schill's impassioned oratory before Berlin's city gate, where he claimed that Napoleon intended to dethrone Frederick William III and denigrate the Germans. Schill convinced his troops that they had been chosen to avenge the insult. In similar fashion, the Prince and cavalry retaliate for the "death" of their monarch.

With scene 6 of the second act, Prince Friedrich arrives to console Princess Natalie over the loss of her uncle and to win her hand. The prince is consumed as much by love for Natalie as by the idea of protecting the state. He now wishes to champion Brandenburg's cause "against this world full of enemies" ("vor dieser Welt von Feinden") (579). Commissioned by Natalie and in command of the state's armed forces, the prince envisions undertaking a mission to secure Brandenburg's borders:

> Ich, Fräulein, übernehme eure Sache!
> Ein Engel will ich, mit dem Flammenschwert,
> An eures Throns verwaisten Stufen stehn!
> Der Kurfürst wollte, eh das
> Jahr noch wechselt,
> Befreit die Marken sehn;
> Wohlan! Ich will der
> Vollstrecker solchen letzten
> Willens sein! (581ff.)
>
> I, dear lady, will take on the responsibility.
> Like an angel with a flaming sword,
> I will stand beside your throne now deserted by His Majesty's death.
> The Elector intended to free Brandenburg before the end of the year.
> Very well! I shall be the executor of his last wish.

The significance of the scene lies in the action proposed and taken by Homburg and Natalie under the assumption that the elector had been

---

Zeichen des Brandes fache in euren Herzen die reine Flamme der Vaterlandsliebe an und sei für eure Unterdrücker das Zeichen des Untergangs [...] Jeder greife zu den Waffen und nehme teil an dem Ruhme des Befreier des Vaterlandes, erkämpfe für sich und seine Enkel Ruhe und Zufriedenheit. Wer feige genug ist, sich der ehrenvollen Aufforderung zu entziehen, den treffe Schmach und Verachtung, der sei zeitlebens gebrandmarkt. Ein edles deutsches Mädchen reiche nie einem solchen Verräter die Hand [...] Auf zu den Waffen!
As quoted in *Die deutschen Romantiker*, ed. Gerhard Stenzel (Salzburg: Bergland, 1954) 1:118f.

killed. The activists proceeded with their plan for national liberation in much the same way — under the assumption that Frederick William III was non-existent. It was even rumored that they planned to overthrow him if necessary to implement their strategy.[54] Chief among those opposing the king's appeasement policy towards Napoleon were Prince and Princess William, who used their influence at court to promote the *levée en masse*.

Kleist's dedication of the play to Marianne of Hesse-Homburg, known at court as Princess William, must be seen in this light. To be sure, the hero of Fehrbellin had a place in her family chronicle; however, it is equally significant that Marianne was an active supporter of the reform party. When Stein left Königsberg, she wrote to him on Nov. 26, 1808: "You will live in my heart (*Seele*) forever."[55] In July 1810 she writes to him of her desire to resist all that is mean and base in her era and assist in directing public opinion against Napoleon's dictatorship.[56] As early as 1808, Stein instructed Nagler to initiate Princess William into their plans.[57] In September 1808 she writes two letters in which she outlines to her husband the role he might play in a north German insurrection.[58] Thus when Kleist dedicated his play to her, he emphasized the link not only with the Homburg family but also with the reform faction which had encouraged and controlled Schill's maneuver.

Allusions to Princess William are contained in Natalie's description of her background

> Ja, was soll ich, nach diesem Wetterschlag,
> Der unter mir den Grund zerreißt, beginnen?
> Mir ruht der Vater, mir die Mutter,
> Im Grab zu Amsterdam; in Schutt und Asche
> Liegt Dortrecht, meines Hauses Erbe, da;
> Gedrängt von Spaniens Tyrannenheeren,
> Weiß Moritz kaum, mein Vetter von Oranien,
> Wo er die eignen Kinder retten soll:
> Und jetzt sinkt mir die letzte Stütze nieder,
> Die meines Glückes Rebe aufrecht hielt.

---

[54] Whether or not the activists informed the king of all their initiatives is a matter of considerable controversy, see my forthcoming study, *British Pounds and Prussian Patriots*.

[55] *Stein* 2/2:994.

[56] *Stein* 3:329.

[57] See Leonie Wuppermann, *Prinzessin Marianne von Preußen, geborene Prinzessin von Hessen-Homburg in den Jahren 1804–1808* (Diss. Bonn, 1942) 146f. See her letter to Prince William, 14 September 1808.

[58] *Ibid.*, 164f. Letter to Prince William 14 September 1808.

> Ich war zum Zweitenmale heut verwaist. (589ff)
>
> Oh, what am I to do now that this storm has destroyed the ground beneath my feet?
> My father and my dearest mother are resting in their graves in Amsterdam while Dortrecht, my ancestral home, lies destroyed in ashes and in ruins.
> Maurice of Orange, my cousin, who is himself hard pressed by the Spanish tyrant's armies, scarcely knows how he is to rescue his own children from destruction. And now, the last support to my flowering hope has crumbled.
> Today I have been orphaned for the second time.

Natalie is related, as was Princess William, to the House of Orange, whose original estate was in Hesse-Homburg. The Prince of Orange was also assigned a major role in the insurrection planned for the summer of 1809; this attempt was organized by Stein, another native of the area Hesse-Homburg. Moreover, in Ludwig Tieck's edition of 1846 the line, "Gedrängt von Spaniens Tyrannenheeren," reads "Gedrängt von den Tyrannenheeren Frankreichs"; according to Tieck, Kleist was forced to change the wording to accommodate the censors.[59] With this passage Kleist refers directly to the crisis facing Prussia; the censored phrase alludes to the Prince of Orange's qualities which made him the suitable choice to lead an insurrection in Germany. With the House of Orange's ties to Britain and the prince's respected image in Germany, the pro-insurrectionists expected widespread support for the offensive.

Finally, Natalie's reference to a "world full of enemies" reflects Prussia's political position after 1809. To the West sprawled the Confederation of the Rhine; in the Southeast, Austria, after Marie Louise's marriage to Napoleon in 1810 and the Vienna Peace Treaty had become an ally of France. On Prussia's eastern border lay the Duchy of Warsaw, established by Napoleon from large parts of East Prussia and Poland. In the north, Denmark was unfriendly and Sweden unaligned. Thus, Natalie's assessment of "surrounded Brandenburg" depicts the geographic isolation of the Prussian state: the statement expresses the dramatist's sympathy for his country's political predicament and accents the reformers' nationalist objectives. Prussia can rely on no other nation for its political survival. Scene 6 offers additional arguments in support of the insurrection. However, the Prussian king had denounced Schill immediately, and thereby doomed the popular revolt. The parallel in the play is Homburg's punishment after the victory by an angry regent, whose rumored death had been a false report.

---

[59] See Sembdner 1:950 for Tieck's letter to Reimer (23 June 1846).

The elector's first action in asserting his authority is to place the leader of the cavalry before a military tribunal:

> Wer immer auch die Reuterei geführt,
> Am Tag der Schlacht, und, eh der Obrist Hennings
> Des Feindes Brücken hat zerstören können
> Damit ist aufgebrochen, eigenmächtig,
> Zur Flucht, bevor ich Order gab, ihn zwingend,
> Der ist des Todes schuldig, das erklär ich,
> Und vor ein Kriegsgericht bestell ich ihn.
> Der Prinz von Homburg hat sie nicht geführt? (715ff)

> Whoever it was who led the cavalry on the day
> of the battle and arbitrarily advanced before I gave
> him orders to attack, forcing the enemy to retreat
> before Colonel Hennings was able to destroy the bridges . . .
> whoever it may be, I say he has incurred the penalty
> of death, and I command that he appear before
> a court martial.
> The Prince of Homburg did not lead the troops, you say?

At this point, Kleist departs from the legendary insubordination at Fehrbellin to include aspects of the court martial ordered for Schill's officers who were sentenced to terms in prison by Prussian military courts. Those officers captured at Stralsund were shot on Napoleon's orders. In scene 10 of act 2, Prince Friedrich appears with war trophies, only to be arrested promptly for insubordination (750). Although the battle had been a brilliant victory, the law must be upheld:

> Der Sieg ist glänzend dieses Tages,
> Und vor dem Altar morgen dank ich Gott.
> Doch wär er zehnmal größer, das entschuldigt
> Den nicht, durch den der Zufall mir ihn schenkt:
> Mehr Schlachten noch, als die hab ich zu kämpfen,
> Und will, dass dem Gesetz Gehorsam sei.
> Wers immer war, der sie zur Schlacht geführt,
> Ich wiederhole, hat seinen Kopf verwirkt,
> Und vor ein Kriegsgericht hiemit lad ich ihn.
> — Folgt, meine Freunde, in die Kirche mir! (729ff)

> Today's victory was brilliant, and I will
> thank God for it tomorrow at the altar.
> But even if it had been ten times greater, it
> would not exonerate the person who procured it
> by mere chance. I have many more battles than this one
> to win and demand obedience to the law.
> Whoever it was who led the troops into battle,
> I repeat it once again, has forfeited his head,
> and I hereby summon him to appear before a military court.
> Now, my friends, follow me into the church.

The elector's words parallel those of Frederick William's royal decree of March 12, 1809, in which the Prussian ruler emphasized the need to avoid risky military offensives, threatened harsh repercussions for disobedience, and declared that maintaining the law's integrity was a patriot's foremost duty. Private opinions and actions, he stated, must bow to royal prerogatives:

> Kraft, Mut und aber ebenso wesentlich Gehorsam bezeichnen den wahren Patrioten, der seine Privatmeinung und Ansicht stets dem letzteren aufzuopfern gewillt sein muß.[60]
>
> Strength, courage, but just as essentially, obedience mark the true patriot, who must be ready at all times to sacrifice his private opinions to the latter.

When Frederick William III charged Schill and his officers with insubordination, the activists were shocked, outraged and embarrassed. General Blücher was especially irritated and voiced his complaint to the king, while lauding Schill's heroism. Likewise, the dramatic figure of Kottwitz, a loyal old soldier representing Blücher, feels affronted as the elector usurps Homburg's honors (760 ff). He expresses his anger with the sentence, "By the living God, he's pushing this a little too far!" ["Das, beim lebendigen Gott, ist mir zu stark!"(763)] Prince Friedrich becomes confused, then angry at his treatment and the sudden change of fortune: "Am I dreaming? Am I awake? Do I live? Am I in my right mind? ... I, a prisoner?" ["Träum ich? Wach ich? Leb ich? Bin ich bei Sinnen? ... Ich, ein Gefangener?" (766f.)] Feeling betrayed, he criticizes the monarch's conduct: "My cousin Frederick wants to play Brutus." ["Mein Vetter Friedrich will den Brutus spielen." (777)]. The Roman Consul Lucius Junius Brutus had his two sons executed for conspiring to establish a republic.[61] Analogously, Homburg, inasmuch as he represents the activists responsible for the 1809 insurrection, is to be executed for disobeying the elector, whom he regards as a father. The party's strategy smacking of disloyalty was disclosed to Frederick William III in June, 1809, in the wake of Schill's demise: Stein and the activists were suspected of conspiring to bring about a popular revolt and possibly place Prince William on the throne. However, Schill's maneuver failed and their project, whenever renewed, was mistrusted by Frederick William, although he agreed that aspects of the insurrectionist scheme were indispensable for the liberation of Prussia.

Act 3 delineated the crisis looming before Prussia's intelligentsia. Kleist saw the spiritual affliction permeating Prussian society as the absence of will to fight either for ideals, the state's political independence, or

---

[60] As quoted by Kanzog, *Homburg* [Note 47], 150.

[61] Cf. Sembdner 1:951.

for individual pride as a German. Prussia lacked the willpower to accomplish the reform objectives because of the regent's indecision and the citizenry's high regard for personal safety. Once Frederick William III denounced the maneuver, Schill and those who engineered and participated in the insurrection could not generate the needed popular support. This is not to suggest that the king had no sympathy for the patriotic intentions of Schill and his squadron. However, he was reluctant to risk the Hohenzollern crown on the hope of a *levée en masse*. This, in turn, cost the activists the required popular base.

From Kleist's point of view, the monarch had to be persuaded that a future military operation, similar to Schill's and including popular resistance, could be successful; the people would respond to a royal appeal. The intelligentsia needed inspiration from "perceptive, trustworthy, and powerful men familiar with the state's moral and spiritual needs" (Stein 3:297). According to Kleist, the upper-class must realize that since Schill's campaign all Prussians were caught in a life and death conflict with an insidious enemy. To unite all sectors of Prussian society, the patriots must apologize to Frederick William III for Schill's insubordination, yet encourage the monarch to help prepare a similar military venture. As the reformers sought to impress upon each individual the need to harness the state's available resources for the goal of liberation, the enthusiasm for the reorganization efforts found renewed expression in *Prinz Friedrich von Homburg*. The Prussian state envisioned by Kleist and the activists was a "living" community, an organism, whose welfare must remain paramount for each member. Kleist illustrated how such a community could be created by developing aesthetically the key principles of Fichte's popular philosophy.

But if Fichte provided the metaphysical postulates, Adam Müller furnished the social theory, while Gotthilf Heinrich Schubert supplied scientific discoveries which supported Kleist's view of a "fatherland of love"[62] somewhere in the offing. The prince was characterized, after all, as a somnambulist, who during a dream-like state grabs at the victory wreath and at the people he loves. He calls the elector, "my father" (67), the elector's wife, "my mother"(69) and Natalie, "my bride" (65) during a trance, thereby suggesting that the preconscious nation is in essence an extended family, in which the regents are loving parents. This is precisely the metaphor Adam Müller used to describe the "true fatherland" in a series of lectures delivered at Dresden in the winter of 1808/1809. Müller, who later published these lectures under the title *Elemente der Staatskunst*, de-

---

[62] The drama is interpreted under this caption by Rolf Dürst, *Heinrich von Kleist, Dichter zwischen Ursprung und Endzeit* (Berne: Francke, 1965). second, expanded edition, 1977, 147–165.

scribed in detail the problems which arise in "the family" when rulers insist on strict adherence to the letter of the law; the result is inertia, the stifling of all initiatives and eventually contempt for the legal process. The "dead letter of the law" is, according to Müller, the surest way to doom the family/nation.[63] The antonyms "self-determination vs. alien authority," "monarch vs. the nobility," "insubordination vs. equality before the law" which provide the social dialectic of the play are prefigured in Müller's talks.

Kleist also heard the series of lectures at Dresden later called *Views From the Nightside of Science* [*Ansichten von der Nachtseite der Naturwissenschaft* (Dresden: Arnold, 1808)] delivered by Gotthilf Heinrich Schubert a year before Müller presented his social theory. Schubert had attempted in lectures which paralleled Müller's talks on the notion of beauty [*Von der Idee der Schönheit*] to summarize for the audience, the *haut monde* of Dresden, the current state of research in the natural sciences, describing what was known and what needed to be ascertained. Among the psychological phenomena Schubert discussed were sleepwalking, hypnosis and dreams. Despite some critical remarks about each,[64] Schubert depicted the somnambulist as one who is not necessarily ill, but one who under great stress obtains by some unknown process a "sense" of the future.[65] In a trance, the sleepwalker perceives aspects of what will be and is momentarily projected into this "higher" state that is to come. More importantly, Schubert, under the heading, "Concerning those powers of the future which lie dormant in our lives today," combined elements of somnambulism, patriotism and art, when he described a painting, since lost, by Caspar David Friedrich entitled *Autumn* (1808) which he (and Kleist) had seen in Friedrich's Dresden studio. According to Schubert, this

---

[63] See Adam H. Müller, *Elemente der Staatskunst 1809*, ed. Jacob Baxa (Jena: Fischer, 1922) 1:145f. Müller argues that individuals are linked "in der einen unsterblichen Familie, welche in der Mitte des Staates steht, in der Regentenfamilie und [...] in dem Majoratsherrn dieser Familie." Earlier he writes: "Der Buchstabe des Gesetzes allein kann, und der Souverän allein soll nicht zwingen. Die Idee des Rechts allein darf zwingen" (59).

[64] A good deal has been made of somnambulism as a "sickness" (see Kanzog [Note 47], 200–208, including bibliography); yet Schubert did not treat the phenomenon as a psychological disorder, but rather as a "gift" to deal with stress. This is not to suggest that Schubert is Kleist's only source of knowledge regarding sleepwalking. See also, Maria M. Tatar, "Psychology and Poetics: J. C. Reil and Kleist's *Prinz Friedrich von Homburg*," *Germanic Review* 48 (1973): 21–34.

[65] Schubert categorizes somnambulism as a "Grundform" which affords glimpses of "die nächste Stufe der Geschichte des Lebens" (see the Introduction); later he describes the phenomenon as "nichts anders als derjenige Zustand des Einzelnen, wo dasselbe auf den höchsten Gipfel der [...] Empfänglichkeit für höhere Einflüsse, mit dem Ganzen wieder am innigsten vereint ist" (21). He regards such a gift as "jenes dunkle Gebiet der Vorahnungen" (352).

painting showed a ramp, leading to a temple-castle in the background. Upon this lighted ramp climbed a young warrior, wearing a wreath of oak leaves:

> Wenn nun der schöne Jüngling mit deutschem Eichenlaube bekränzt, wenn der Geist jenes edlen Landes, dem jetzt die inneren Kräfte gelähmt scheinen, und durch die Hand der Schönen Lilie, der er vor allen treu gewesen in Schlummer versenkt ist, dann wird die Zeit näher kommen, wo der Tempel, welcher das Eigentum einer anderen Welt geschienen, über den Strom herüber, in das jetzige Dasein eintreten wird. Dann werden beyde Welten tief im inneren Wesen sich vereinen [. . .] Dann erwacht der schöne Jüngling und wird herrschen (324).

> Now when this beautiful young man adorned in a wreath of German oak leaves, when the spirit of that noble land whose inner powers seem paralyzed at the moment, whose own lofty striving seems exhausted, are submerged in slumber by the hand of the beautiful lily to which he had above all remained true, then the time will draw near when the temple, having appeared as part of another world, will cross over the stream and enter into this life. Then both worlds will merge into inner being [. . .] Then the beautiful youth will awaken and will rule.

It is obvious that Kleist worked such requisites as the wreath, the ramp, the castle in the background, the slumbering youthful warrior under considerable duress who awakens to rule, into his play, which, as we can deduce from this passage in Schubert's *Views*, is concerned with the spirit of that noble land which one day will come to life. Schubert interprets the symbols in this painting as belonging to the patriotic vision of a noctambulist who "under the spell" ("im Magnetismus") catches the "first glimmer of a higher world" (380). Likewise, the young warrior-prince of Kleist's play is afforded glimpses of the "higher fatherland of love," which he, out of the depths of his own subconscious, is summoned to serve.

Moreover, Schubert's lectures prompted two other central motives of *Prinz Friedrich von Homburg*: the compulsive obedience of an entranced sleepwalker to commands issued by a strong personality and the detriment to the individual of his own personal initiatives intended for what he perceives to be the common good. When, at the end of the first scene, the elector orders the somnolent prince back into oblivion because what he seeks cannot be gained in a dream but must be earned on the battlefield, he has, according to Schubert, placed a command so deeply into the subconscious mind that it must be heeded. According to theories current in the natural sciences of Kleist's day, Hohenzollern's arguments (act 5, scene 5), blaming the elector for the prince's unsanctioned initiatives on the field of battle, had considerable merit.

The notion that such actions are detrimental, even fatal, to the individual was also presupposed by Schubert. Whatever one does to bring about the "higher world," tends to destroy one's existence in this one: "In this way, the highest moments and motivating features in a person's life work consume that life because in it a future, higher state is infringing upon that condition preceding it."[66] Thus when the prince's personal initiatives lead him to the edge of the grave and to that moment of execution at which presentiment begins to pass into the next world, he illustrates what Schubert had declared to be the seer's way of bringing about a future, "higher," more noble world, a truly exalted fatherland, in short, a nation ruled by naught but the sublime. In this way, Kleist adapted the latest theories in the natural sciences for the activists' purposes, as he sought to dramatize their vision of a fatherland of love whose preservation was guaranteed by the strength of Prussian devotion and virtue.

How then are we to interpret Kottwitz's statement toward the end of the play? After what has happened, he says, the prince, regardless of future exigencies, will not draw his sword to save the elector unless specially called upon to do so ("Du könntest an Verderbens Abgrund stehen/ Daß er, um dir zu helfen, dich zu retten,/ Auch nicht das Schwert mehr zücktest, ungerufen!" lines 1826–1829). Is this Kleist's last-minute, cynical appraisal of what has occurred on the stage, an indication perhaps of some intuitive feeling that everything in Prussia will simply continue in the military tradition? Is Kleist expressing through Kottwitz, who had stated earlier he would act, given similar circumstances, exactly as the prince had, that Arthur has been totally "re-programmed" to be the "good" Prussian soldier who will obey without question the letter of the law? Our interpretation suggests that Kleist had something else in mind. As we have seen, the play is, among other things, an apology for the willful acts of disobedience committed by the activists. Kottwitz's statement is part of that apology: it is a promise that, having taken the law into their own hands unsuccessfully on three occasions—insurrections led by Wilhelm Caspar von Dörnberg in Westphalia and Hesse, Friedrich von Katte at Magdeburg and Ferdinand von Schill in northern Germany—the activists now pledge to act in the future only upon specific orders from Frederick William III.

We must bear in mind that a process of ennoblement was illustrated in the preceding scenes: having critically examined the law and found it just, the prince embraced it. The elector discovered that rebellion is imminent whenever the law is defined according to the letter rather than the spirit. Through Kottwitz's words the prince pledges obedience to a Prussia which combines the principles of willing sacrifice and self denial with

---

[66] "Auf solche Weise wirken die höchsten Momente des individuellen Daseyns für dieses selber zerstörend, weil in ihnen ein künftiger höherer Zustand in dem vorhergehenden eingreift" (250).

forgiveness and reconciliation. This synthesis is to serve as the cornerstone of that new German nation for which Brandenburg-Prussia was to be the model.

The concluding lines, "Into the dust with the enemies of Brandenburg" ["In Staub mit allen Feinden Brandenburgs"] is, therefore, not an expression of rabid particularism. Such a reading runs counter to the structure of the play. The lines are instead a confession of faith in the innate characteristics of Brandenburg-Prussians who were to serve as the model for the rest of the German nation. These lines are also a warning to those enemies of Prussia who agitated against the founding of a unified German nation to be grounded in obedience to self-imposed laws, to be established by the dictates of the heart and to be secured through the personal initiatives and self-sacrifice of all her citizens. In Kleist's day the enemies were the French who enslaved the nation and the particularists who impeded her political evolution. Kleist's play heralds the realization of the activists' vision of that "higher" state of the future and pronounces sentence on those who stand in the way.

But the court would have none of Kleist's fatherland of love. If Egon-Erich Albrecht's interpretation of a negative comment uttered by Duke Charles of Mecklenburg is correct,[67] then a performance of *Prinz Friedrich von Homburg* was arranged for the private theater of Prince Radziwill sometime in 1810 or 1811, where it was ridiculed and rejected. Even a decade later, the Austrians spurned it. Because of Archduke Charles's objections, the play was cancelled after four performances in Vienna in October of 1821. Seven years later, an attempt was made to perform the play in Berlin. However, after the third performance during the summer of 1828, Frederick William III ordered it cancelled and "never played again."[68] The "cowardly" fear-of-death-scene, the problem of insubordination, and the re-opening of all the old wounds from two decades ago, kept Kleist's prince off the Berlin stage for another thirteen years. On 15 October 1841, *Prinz Friedrich von Homburg* received the royal recognition Kleist yearned for, when it was performed for the next monarch's birthday. But it was not received in the manner Kleist had hoped. Thirty years after his death, it was celebrated as a "great national drama" — that is, once the "fatal cowardice scene" was removed by order of Frederick William IV.

From that point on, *Prinz Friedrich von Homburg*, at times with and at times without that fear-of-death scene, was open to the most diverse interpretations. Critics like Wilhelm Hausenstein regarded the play as "a

---

[67] Egon-Erich Albrecht, *Heinrich von Kleists 'Prinz Friedrich von Homburg' auf der deutschen Bühne* (Diss. Kiel, 1921): 11–12.

[68] Kanzog, *Homburg* [Note 47], 255.

bloody satire on the traditions of the Prussian state."[69] Georg Lukács saw the exact opposite: a drama glorifying "old-fashioned Prussianism" as an "objectified social force."[70] For others, among them such connoisseurs of German literature as Constantine Grunwald, the play remained an enigma, an interpreter's nightmare: "Ce 'conflit tragique' reste incomprehensible à tout lecteur non prussien"[71] As we have seen, the reason for the difficulties encountered by Grunwald and others in coming to grips with the text is that Kleist is pre-occupied with what he perceived to be the unique characteristics and potentials of those who inhabit the Brandenburg margraviate. The confusion experienced by non-Prussians is caused by Kleist's insistence that specific traits others do not normally think of as "Prussian" are the genuinely innate features of the Brandenburgers. He argues, furthermore, that historical expression of these attributes can be found at least as far back as the battle at Fehrbellin when Prussia emerged as a European power. Kleist rejected the notion of Prussians as one-sidedly militaristic, cold and haughty, subservient and unforgiving. He recognized that they were becoming such people the more Frederick William III subjugated all personal initiatives to his own will. For that reason, Kleist satirized blind subordination to the letter of the law and exalted the character who initiates action. Self-determination, self-discipline, love and mercy are, according to Kleist, the personality traits which set the genuinely patriotic Prussian apart from other Germans down through the centuries. If his dramatic intention is often overlooked, it is because he regarded these qualities as innately Prussian, as those which must be nurtured in that "higher" German nation of the future to which the somnambulist reaches out in his trance,

Prinz Friedrich von Homburg did not find a receptive audience for three decades after the author's death: the *Hermannsschlacht* did not fare much better. Completed in the last weeks of 1808, the *Hermannsschlacht* could not be performed in Berlin because the capital was occupied by French troops. Moreover, Iffland had just staged Karl Wohlfahrt's mediocre *Hermann* there with great pomp and circumstance. On January 1, 1809, Kleist sent the drama "geared to the moment" to his friend Heinrich von Collin in Vienna. But he couldn't arrange for a performance there either. The premier performance was not to come for two more decades. On August 29, 1839, the Court theater at Detmold included the play among its more

---

[69] Wilhelm Hausenstein, "Heinrich von Kleist. Gestorben am 21. November 1811," *Mannheimer Volksstimme* (22 November 1911).

[70] Georg Lukács, "Die Tragödie Heinrich von Kleists" (1936), *Deutsche Realisten des Neunzehnten Jahrhunderts* (Berlin: de Gruyter, 1951): 37.

[71] Constantine Grunwald, *Stein. L'ennemi de Napoléon* (Paris, 1936): 220.

avant-garde offerings. Thus neither play was staged during Kleist's lifetime. Vienna wanted no part of the Prussian activists' strategy for uniting the German nation; the Hohenzollern court at Berlin rejected Kleist's fatherland where a military officer might exhibit an unrestrained fear of death. Despite these major setbacks with his plays, Kleist did not give up. He seized upon one more opportunity to participate as a creative artist, editor, journalist in the political process. He had departed Dresden in 1809 when a journalistic pamphlet, *Materialien zur Geschichte des österreichischen Revolutionierungssystems* (Nuremberg: Stein, April 1809), published an exposé of the machinations of "Gentz and cohorts in Dresden." According to these disclosures, Adam Müller and his "collaborators" had spread "revolutionary," "democratic," "national" ideas among the citizenry and had completely "twisted the true state of affairs" in Saxony. With this intimidating report, Kleist's political activities and his usefulness to the Prussian activists or the Austrian war party ended. Following Müller to Berlin, he left on a roundabout route, arriving late in November. In the following year, he edited an unusual and, at least initially, successful newspaper.

The notion that Kleist collaborated with a political faction in Prussia is not new to Kleist scholarship. In 1901 Reinhold Steig postulated that Kleist's *Berlin Evening News* (*Berliner Abendblätter*) was an instrument for disseminating political propaganda.[72] However, Steig perceived in Kleist a spokesman for the more reactionary *Junker* who opposed the Stein-Hardenberg reforms. According to this theory, Kleist's newspaper was the journalistic organ of the Christian German Table Society — a notoriously anti-Semitic, reactionary clique.[73] With a multifaceted panorama of Berlin in 1810/11, Steig therefore, portrayed Kleist as "a poet of the Margraviate," whose anti-reform convictions, as expressed in the *Berliner Abendblätter*, were rebuffed by Chancellor Hardenberg's office which subsequently sought to suppress the newspaper. This censorship and the loss of its political character led to the demise of Kleist's journal. With Steig's book, the hypothesis that Kleist was in some way an artist-collaborator with Prussian statesmen and politicians gained credence in literary scholarship.

In the following year, Steig reiterated his contention and insisted that Kleist's *Warsong of the Germans* (*Kriegslied der Deutschen*) was intended to

---

[72] Reinhold Steig, *Heinrich von Kleists Berliner Kämpfe* (Berlin and Stuttgart, 1901; reprinted Berne: Lang, 1971). See the Introduction.

[73] Ibid., 40–48.

instill the "courage of the Prussian Margraviate" in the hearts of Germans.[74] Steig also acknowledged that Kleist had borrowed several articles from the Hamburg-based *Gemeinnützige Unterhaltungsblätter* and had lent a few to that weekly. With reference to England's influence in this connection, Steig observed that "quiet arrangements, secretly conducted, were underfoot between Hamburg and Berlin."[75]

Two decades later, the archivist Helmut Rogge[76] discovered some posthumous papers of Julius Hitzig, the publisher of the *Berliner Abendblätter* (Nos. 1–72) from October 1 to December 22, 1810, which undermined Steig's position. Rogge pointed out first that Kleist was not anti-Semitic and had distanced himself from the "eating society's" more rabid anti-Semitic pronouncements. Second, the fact that Hitzig, a Jew, had published the newspaper for a length of time (the first quarter) constituted proof that the *Berliner Abendblätter* was never an organ of the organization. Third, Hitzig's papers indicated that sales had declined before the government sought to suppress the newspaper. According to Hitzig, Kleist's mistake was to have filled his columns with a mixture of major and minor articles which pleased neither his contributors nor the public. Rogge concluded that Steig's argument was untenable: the *Berliner Abendblätter* could not be regarded as the publication of a specific, unified political party.

Heinrich Meyer-Benfey continued the assault by asserting that Steig had re-cast Kleist in his own image.[77] Steig had found a reflection of his own political opinions in the columns of Kleist's newspaper. Pointing to various disparaging remarks about the nobility which Kleist had made throughout his life, Meyer-Benfey rejected the attempt to align Kleist with Prussia's conservatives. Instead, he contended, Kleist's position was nationalistic, whereas the conservative politicians, even those who favored continued hostilities with France, were decidedly particularists. Meyer-Benfey concluded that Kleist, who was after all not a political expert, regarded his newspaper as a forum for both conservatives and progressives.

The death-knell for Steig's theory sounded in 1939 when Helmut Sembdner published a penetrating study of the source material and edito-

---

[74] *Neue Kunde zu Heinrich von Kleist* (Berlin: Reimer, 1902): 67.

[75] *Ibid.*, 111f.

[76] Helmut Rogge, "Heinrich von Kleists letzte Leiden. Nach unveröffentlichten Zeugnissen aus dem Nachlaß Julius Eduard Hitzigs," *Schriften der Kleistgesellschaft* 2 (1922/23): 31–74.

[77] "Kleists politische Anschauungen" [Note 42], 9–37.

rial policy of the *Berliner Abendblätter*.[78] His careful analysis proved that contributions expressing regressive viewpoints were published on one day, only to be refuted the next. He outlined Kleist's three-pronged plan: 1) to inform his readers of Europe's true state of affairs, 2) to disclose the brutal methods with which the French maintained power, and 3) to give Germans the courage to fight for the liberation of their country. "In order to smuggle reports of this kind through censorship," Sembdner stated, "highly differentiated editorial tricks were necessary, which Kleist employed masterfully. Later, when Kuhn became the publisher, this kind of reporting ceased almost entirely."[79]

We see, then, that the political portrait of Kleist changed from conservative to progressive as literary scholars examined the substance of Kleist's journalistic essays. Yet the underlying impression that Kleist was involved with political leaders was not dispelled. Since Sembdner's account, scholarship concerned with the *Berliner Abendblätter* has vacillated between resurrecting Steig's picture of Kleist as a spokesman for the *ancien regime* and confirming Sembdner's portrayal of Kleist as a champion of progressive thought. In the three volumes on Kleist written by Kurt Gerlach (1971, 1972, 1977), for example, Steig's thesis is revived and Kleist is depicted as a true disciple of the "margraviate's nobility."[80] But Gerlach's second volume had scarcely made it to the book stores when Dirk Grathoff denounced as totally unacceptable all such attempts to reinterpret individual articles which had been favorable to reform "into essays in support of the opposition."[81] No sooner was Gerlach's third volume in print than Eberhard Scheibner held up two articles from the newspaper which, he claimed, "totally refute" any attempt to "misrepresent" Kleist as a *Junker*.[82] These two articles, asserted Scheibner, offered "irrefutable proof" of Kleist's pro-reform attitude. But in the same issue of the journal which published Scheibner's "irrefutable proof," Heinz Härtel entered the debate, claiming that hitherto "unknown statements about Kleist

---

[78] Helmut Sembdner, *Die Berliner Abendblätter Heinrich von Kleist, ihre Quellen und ihre Redaktion* (Berlin: Weidmann, 1939).

[79] *Ibid.*, 378.

[80] Kurt Gerlach, *Heinrich von Kleist. Sein Leben und Schaffen in neuer Sicht* (Dortmund: Ostohe. Forschungsstelle, [vol. 1] 1971, [vol. 2] 1972, [vol. 3] 1977).

[81] Dirk Grathoff, "Die Zensurkonflikte der *Berliner Abendblätter*," in *Ideologiekritische Studien zur Literatur*, ed. Volkmar Sander (Frankfurt: Athenäum, 1972): 35–168.

[82] Eberhard Scheibner, "Zu Kleists politischen Ansichten zur Zeit der *Berliner Abendblätter*," *Weimarer Beiträge* 23 (1977): 144–165.

uttered by Achim von Arnim," totally undermined such evidence.[83] Thus Härtel concurred with Heinz Günther Thalheim, who had described Kleist's ideological position as firmly entrenched in the *ancien regime*.[84] Günther Rudolf not only agreed but also pinpointed Kleist's political convictions on the ultra-right, much closer to the "most reactionary representatives of the feudal order."[85]

As the battle over Kleist's rightful place on the ideological spectrum raged, J. M. Lindsay looked at the problem from a different angle. In 1972 he sought to "relativize" Kleist's mutually exclusive positions as expressed in the *Berliner Abendblätter* within the historical context and Kleist's own personality. Arguing that Kleist took either a pro- or contraposition regarding reform on an issue by issue basis, Lindsay regarded some of the more obvious contradictions in the articles as symptomatic of a deep-seated psychological problem.[86] But less than a decade later Wolfgang Wittkowski firmly rejected the entire approach. Emphasizing the "transcendent" (*überzeitlich*) and, for that very reason, topical essence of Kleist's attitude, Wittkowski pointed out the many places where Kleist articulated "an anti-authoritarian viewpoint" which "along with his criticisms of the material opportunism motivating all the parties constitutes Kleist's position in the *Abendblätter*."[87]

With Wittkowski's refutation of the psychological approach, scholarship has turned, once again, from Kleist, the intransigent, to Kleist, the progressive. To be sure, these studies have contributed a wealth of detail to our picture of Kleist and his newspaper, especially in the eyes of contemporaries. However, at least a few significant questions generated in the earliest debates have remained unresolved: first, what role was played by Adam Müller and where does Justus Gruner figure in the ascent and decline of the *Abendblätter*? Second, why did Kleist publish so many articles sympathetic to England at a time when the Prussian court regarded Great Britain as an unfriendly power? The answer to these questions will provide, perhaps, a deeper insight into the forces which helped mold the *Ber-*

---

[83] Heinz Härtel, "Unbekannte Äußerungen Arnims über Kleist," *Weimarer Beiträge* 23 (1977): 178–181.

[84] Heinz-Günther Thalheim, "Kleists *Prinz Friedrich von Homburg*," *Weimarer Beiträge* 11 (1965): 483–550.

[85] Günther Rudolph, "Adam Müller und Kleist," *Weimarer Beiträge* 24 (1978): 121–135.

[86] John M. Lindsay, "Figures of Authority in the Works of Heinrich von Kleist," *Forum of Modern Language Studies* 8 (1972): 107–119.

[87] Wolfgang Wittkowski, "Schrieb Kleist regierungsfreundliche Artikel? Über den Umgang mit politischen Texten," *Literaturwissenschaftliches Jahrbuch im Auftrage der Görres-Gesellschaft* 32 (1982): 95–116.

liner Abendblätter. As we shall see, the "self-contradictions" uncovered by literary scholars were not symptoms of a psychological disorder, but part of a master plan devised by Müller and adopted by Gruner.

But, to start with the second question, it was Sembdner who discovered a remarkably high percentage of articles in Kleist's newspaper dealing with England when very little news from London was disseminated on the continent. Napoleon did permit *Le moniteur* to publish translations of highly critical speeches delivered to the House of Commons by opposition leaders; yet reports sympathetic to England's cause were squelched. Nevertheless, Kleist sought out pro-British sources for his articles. Why? An analysis of a prime example can help resolve the mystery and clarify Kleist's political allegiance.

On December 4, 1810 Kleist published a "Geographical Report on the Island of Heligoland," reworked from an article printed on 22 September in the *Hamburger Gemeinnützige Unterhaltungsblätter*. Steig interpreted the story in light of the continental blockade in effect since the beginning of September 1810 and the concomitant burning of colonial goods found on the continent. Heligoland, he argued, had become an important supply depot for the economic struggle against the Napoleonic system. These conditions gave Kleist the background for both his introduction and his conclusion.[88] Sembdner disagreed. The "strange" and the "unusual" attracted the writer's attention to this story. Kleist's goal was to work out the contrast between the political significance of an island housing British goods valued at 20 million Pounds Sterling and the totally wrecked environment in which the inhabitants were forced to live. According to Sembdner, Kleist sought to arouse sympathy for the islanders who, although sitting on a fortune, were suffering nonetheless from Napoleon's blockade.[89]

Neither interpreter took the negotiations into account which were underway between the Foreign Office and the insurrectionist "committees" aligned with Stein. In the summer of 1809, Downing Street had agreed to ship arms for the planned insurrection; these were to be stored on Heligoland. A major shipment arrived the following year.[90] The article in the Hamburg weekly was a signal to the activists that arms had arrived safely and should be picked up as soon as possible. Kleist amended and republished the article six weeks later after the Foreign Office complained

---

[88] Steig [Note 72], 571–573.

[89] Sembdner, *Die Berliner Abendblätter*, 237–239.

[90] Cf. John Sherwig, *Guineas and Gunpowder. British Foreign Aid in the Wars with France 1793–1815* (Cambridge: Harvard University Press, 1969): 174 and 211. Sherwig traces the events, leading to the establishment of an arms stockpile on Heligoland.

that the Prussians had been much too slow in taking possession of the weapons.[91] Christian Ompteda sent copies of Kleist's article back to the Foreign Office in order to show that the Prussians were doing all they could, including circulating the news.[92]

Christian Ompteda's contribution to the *Abendblätter* confirms Kleist's pro-British attitude, while revealing his goal as editor. On 20 November 1810 the *Abendblätter* had published an article "Concerning England's Desperate Situation." Four days later, Kleist attempted to publish Ompteda's essay: "Concerning Great Britain's Current Situation." But the censors prohibited the publication of such a positive description of England's position. Kleist returned the manuscript to Ompteda with the following comment:

> The two crosses across the paper are like two swords cutting across our dearest and most holy interests. It would be impossible for me to describe to you the state of triumphant joy and sentiment in which reading this masterful essay, especially the conclusion, has put me and those around me (there are already several copies in circulation) (2:841).

This statement suggests that Kleist was publishing opinions opposed to the activist's program on one day in order to refute them a few days later. This is confirmed by the way Kleist handled this particular setback. On the night of 24 November he published the following announcement in his newspaper:

> The author of an essay, "Concerning Great Britain's Current Situation," which could not be accepted for reasons too complex to be recounted here, is asked to ... pick up ... a letter to him in the delivery office of the *Abendblätter* (2:456).

Why would Kleist act as if he did not know who authored the piece after having returned the essay that very afternoon? The answer is that he was alerting the activists to its existence and availability. Patriots, reading this announcement, would know immediately why such an analysis could not be published. Since, as Kleist remarked to Ompteda in the cover letter, there were several copies in circulation, he sought to let those who were interested know that such an essay could be found. Four days later, Ompteda writes to Kleist about the dangers any meeting between them

---

[91] The Prussian Correspondence in the Foreign Office (64/84) attests to the stockpiling of arms on Heligoland for insurrectionist activities in northern Germany. Several dispatches emphasize the necessity of announcing the arrival of arms shipments in subtle ways in the Hamburg newspaper. The complaint regarding Prussian hesitancy in removing the weapons is dated October 1810.

[92] Ompteda's reference to Kleist's newspaper are found in FO 64/84 (1810); see also Steig [Note 72], 574.

poses for both, and how they would be able, if such a meeting were possible, "to clasp each other's hand in more than one confidence" (2:842). Moreover, Müller is described as an "esteemed" friend, a "scholar with whom we are on the friendliest of terms." It is, therefore, apparent that Kleist was pro-British and that he printed unsympathetic articles in one issue in order to refute the underlying arguments in a later one. As we shall see, this corresponds to a plan Müller had outlined to Hardenberg several months earlier.

By re-publishing and re-working the Heligoland article from the Hamburg weekly Kleist was reporting the arrival of British goods and munitions on Heligoland in a disguised account of the island and its inhabitants. Hence Steig was correct when he emphasized the political situation and the behind-the-scenes motivation for Kleist's interest in the original article. Sembdner, however, was not mistaken in suggesting the "strange and unusual" attracted Kleist, for that was the cloak in which his reconnaissance report was wrapped. Nevertheless, it is a bit difficult to conceive of continentals pitying islanders who are sitting on twenty million pounds worth of desperately needed goods the continentals wished they had!

How and why did such articles find their way into Kleist's newspaper? The key to this puzzle is Justus Gruner. In a half dozen letters about the *Berliner Abendblätter*,[93] the journalist-editor points directly to the Berlin Police Chief as his contact. Kleist had received *his* assurances that "subsidies" would be forthcoming for what was published. Therefore, we must look at the activities of this middleman more closely. Gruner was not a Prussian. He was born in 1777 in Osnabrück, where his father served in the chancellory. For service rendered by the senior Gruner, King George of England had given the family a tract of land and, upon the early death of her husband, had provided the mother with a pension later confiscated by Napoleon. In 1802 Gruner, who had been assured a prominent post at the court of St. James, opted instead for a position in the Prussian government. In 1805 he carried out clandestine missions to France, where he reconnoitered military installations.[94] In 1806 he was Director of the War

---

[93] In an extra section to the first number of the *Berliner Abendblätter*, Gruner is named as a contributing patron; see Sembdner 2:423. Kleist names Gruner as his political contact in virtually all correspondences regarding his newspaper; see Sembdner 2:844, 846ff, 851, 863f, 866. In a letter to Hardenberg (6 June 1811), Kleist asserts that Gruner had approached him "in the name of your excellency." Yet Hardenberg insisted that this was not so. It appears likely that Gruner did what Kleist claimed, however, not for Hardenberg's sake, but to favor Stein's initiatives; see Sembdner 2:868.

[94] The main sources for information about Gruner are the *Allgemeine Deutsche Biographie*; G. Volz, ed. "Aus dem Briefwechsel zwischen dem Freiherrn vom Stein und Justus Gruner," *Annales Universitatis Saraviensis* (Saarbrücken, 1958) and August Fournier,

and Domain Chamber at Posen. But when the French occupation put an end to that career, he went to Königsberg where he met Stein, Gneisenau and Scharnhorst as well as other members of their faction, who arranged his appointment as chief of police in Berlin.

Gruner's prime objective between 1809 and 1811 was to hold the French agents in check and to deepen patriotic and nationalistic convictions in the capital by skillfully producing propaganda. Varnhagen von Ense noted that Gruner stood at the center of a broad and firmly rooted conspiracy; according to his account, Gruner had impressive financial resources and excellent reconnaissance agents.[95] Another contemporary, Henrik Steffens remarked about Gruner: "He had a natural talent for intrigue ... and spun his secret threads all around Germany .... It was truly remarkable how he was able to play his deceptive role in the midst of the enemy during those years."[96] Gruner's hatred of the French, who had taken his family possessions, his zeal in support of the "British-Russian" policy and his collaboration with Stein caused problems with Hardenberg, Sack and other members of the Internal Affairs Ministry. Because he so overtly favored the views of Stein and his party, the Berlin censors, particularly Himly and Küster, who had jurisdiction in political matters, castigated Gruner constantly. According to them, the chief of police was allowing pro-British articles to appear in the press and was distributing the imprimatur much too freely to the authors he favored. At this point, Hardenberg stepped in. The fortunes of Kleist and his newspaper were determined from this point on, at least in part, by Gruner's covert activity, unknown to Hardenberg, in support of Stein's strategy. Kleist's fate was sealed when Gruner sought to use the *Berliner Abendblätter* for Stein's purposes, keeping Hardenberg in the dark. Kleist fell victim to those intrigues made necessary by the major differences separating Hardenberg and Stein. Foremost among these was Stein's co-operation with British agents who, as we shall see, had reason to avoid Hardenberg.

Although it has become commonplace in accounts of Prussia under Napoleon to talk of the "Stein-Hardenberg reforms," major disagreements marred their working relationship. Stein was a nationalist who saw the future of all Germany tied to the fate of the Prussian crown. Hardenberg was a particularist bent on strengthening and enlarging the Hohenzollern domain. Stein rejected anything other than a pseudo-alliance with France which might placate Bonaparte for a time, thus gaining Prussia those pre-

"Stein und Gruner in Österreich," *Deutsche Rundschau* 53 (1887): 120–1142, 214–247, 348–362.

[95] Varnhagen von Ense, *Denkwürdigkeiten und Vermischte Schriften* (Mannheim and Leipzig: Hoff, 1837–1859) 2:360.

[96] Heinrich [also Henrik] Steffens, *Was ich erlebte* (Breslau: Max, 1842) 7:53.

cious weeks to reform and rearm. Hardenberg, on the other hand, accepted a treaty with France whenever Prussian interests were served without regard to the rest of Germany. Stein favored armed resistance to Napoleon on the side of England, Austria and Russia; Hardenberg argued for neutrality.[97] Stein wanted also to harness the energies of the German people by including the owners of large estates in the business of government. With propaganda he wished to revitalize the "national sentiment" which, he believed, lay dormant in the educated and well-to-do. Hardenberg questioned the value of a massive anti-French writing campaign and feared Napoleon's wrath if such enterprises were traced back to the throne.[98] He was closer to Frederick William III and more responsive to his wishes. Stein found the monarch's indecisiveness unacceptable and was prepared to act without the king's sanction. In the years after the Congress of Vienna, Stein refused to receive Hardenberg, or to speak to him, because he believed that Hardenberg had sabotaged the work of Prussian reform.[99] What united Stein and Hardenberg was the conviction that Prussia was in need of reform; what divided them was their views on the ways, means and goals of reconstruction. Moreover, Stein took offense at what he called Hardenberg's "intimate relationships with worthless females."[100] This aspect of Hardenberg's personality had already occasioned embarrassment to the British crown.

In 1774 Hardenberg married the fifteen year old Countess Juliane von Reventlow, who accompanied him on a diplomatic mission to England. The doors to the best homes in London were opened to the couple who, as warmly received guests, were soon involved in the intrigues concomitant with a life of pleasure, frivolity and passion. Within a short time, British tabloids filled their gossip columns with the details of the Countess's intimacies with the Prince of Wales. Their affair was soon a full-blown scandal. The enraged Hardenberg went after the heir to the British throne with a dagger — only the authority and personal intervention of the king pre-

---

[97] Hans Hausherr, "Stein und Hardenberg," *Historische Zeitschrift* 190 (1960): 267–289. A good example of Stein's strategy of "double alliance" is found in his Memorandum of 11 August 1808; see *Stein* 2/2:808–812.

[98] See Wilhelm Dilthey, "Karl August Hardenberg," *Diltheys Gesammelte Schriften*, ed. Erich Weniger (Stuttgart and Göttingen: Teubner and Vandenhoeck & Ruprecht, 1960) 12:53–64.

[99] Hausherr [Note 97], 284–289; see also Georg Holmsten, *Freiherr vom Stein* (Hamburg: Rowohlt, 1975): 95, 108–112.

[100] *Die Autobiographie des Freiherrn vom Stein*, ed. Kurt von Raumer. second edition (Münster and Cologne: Böhlau, 1955): 40. See also Raumer's excellent study, *Deutschland um 1800. Krise und Neugestaltung 1789–1815* (Constance: Hatchfeld, 1958).

vented a duel.[101] The British crown subsequently severed what had been close ties to Hardenberg, who resigned from the service of Hanover in 1782. He was still consulted by British diplomats once he gained high office in the Prussian government; yet, he was, for the most part, kept in the dark regarding British objectives and activities in northern Germany. He was never again to enjoy the confidence of British negotiators who turned increasingly to the more trustworthy Stein. The latter shared few of his secrets with Hardenberg, even after he had recommended him to the Prussian king as a possible successor to the office of Minister of State. The scandalous rift with the British throne and Stein's reticence toward Hardenburg regarding British initiatives in northern Germany and his collaboration with British emissaries had serious repercussions among writers in the service of the Prussian activists since many believed Stein and Hardenberg were, at the very least, working together. Hardenberg's ignorance of Stein's joint operation with British agents[102] had a devastating effect on the life and fortune of Heinrich von Kleist.

Because of his difficulties with Hardenberg, Gruner tried, as of January 1, 1811, to keep some of the more controversial items, particularly pro-British articles, out of the newspapers. He succeeded in appeasing his superiors, for despite his covert operations he was promoted on February 5, 1811 to a position in Hardenberg's cabinet with influence in censorship matters greater than that of either Himly or Küster. Nevertheless, by March 1812 Prussia was moving ever more rapidly into the French camp. Gruner, sensing the impending exposure of his clandestine activities, abandoned Berlin and hurried to Prague, where he joined Baron Stein. Once there neither Gruner nor Stein could move undetected. They were observed by Prussian undercover agents, who in turn were watched by French spies. Stein met with Gentz, with the British charge d'affairs, Alexander Horn, who supplied him with a British passport, and with such operatives as Peter Maurus von Regensburg, who worked for Johnson, a Foreign Office intelligence specialist assigned to Austria. This surveillance system was itself carefully monitored by the Austrian police, who were especially conscientious. Within a few months Austrian intelligence had uncovered not only the British connection but also the route by which British financial support was reaching Stein and Gruner: the Foreign Of-

---

[101] Wilhelm Dilthey, "Die Reorganisatoren des Preußischen Staates (1807–1813)," *Gesammelte Schriften* [Note 98], 12:55.

[102] Hardenberg did not become suspicious of Gruner's motives until 1812 when his spy J. E. Th. Janke reported that Gruner had ties to the remnants of a supposedly disbanded organization, the *Tugendbund*. It is likely that Hardenberg asked the Austrian police to take Gruner into protective custody; for details see my article, "Der Freiherr vom Stein und die patriotische Literatur," *IASL* 9 (1984): 65f.

fice deposited monies into accounts with the banking house Marten & Gower in Hamburg, which transferred the funds to the banker Schickler in Berlin, who turned over the balance to Stein. When Napoleon annexed the Hanseatic cities, the channel through Hamburg was blocked. Therefore, London placed the sums into the account of Mötler, Berend and Sons in Göteborg, Sweden, who forwarded them to the bankers Osilvio in Memel. Schickler simply drew the balance from Osilvio's account.[103] After Stein left for Prague, Schickler transmitted the British receipts to the Prague branch of Thun and family. Swedish couriers and British officers delivered additional sums in person. The activists also maintained accounts with the merchant Schroeder in Berlin, Gibson in Danzig and Phillips in Königsberg. Less than twelve weeks after Heinrich von Kleist's suicide, Austrian agents took Gruner into protective custody: on his person, they discovered 5,000 *Taler*, 1,394 Ducats and a quantity of British pound Sterling.[104] In a confidential memo to Stein dated May 27, 1812, Gruner listed as "money depots" (Gelddepots) "various points in Vienna, Hering in the city of Brünn, Tenel, Balbene & co. in Prague" (Stein 3:648). With assets of this kind, Gruner could make very attractive promises to such literary allies as Heinrich von Kleist.

Of course, the fact that Gruner controlled or at least had considerable access to the purse strings, does not mean that he paid Kleist anything at all. Kleist's complaint is that subsidies had been pledged which he never received. He thought Gruner had enlisted his support for the Ministry of State under Hardenberg. However, the police chief was working for Stein. Thus Friedrich Raumer was undoubtedly telling the truth when he wrote that Hardenberg had no knowledge of the reasons for Gruner's financial "assurances."[105] And Hardenberg was justified in rejecting Kleist's requests for subsidies because he had not promised any.[106] The point is that Gruner *did* — he expected to pay Kleist from the money he had access to because of his collaboration with Stein. As we shall see, Adam Müller had approached Hardenberg with an offer to produce both an "official" and a mass-circulation newspaper favoring reform. However, the "official" journal never got beyond the planning stage, so he tried to realize his plan in the newspaper edited by Kleist. But Hardenberg was not privy to Gruner's machinations in collaboration with Stein, thus creating an unfor-

---

[103] See the "Bericht der Prager Stadthauptmannschaft an Kolowrat," *Stein* 3:864–873.

[104] See August Fournier [Note 94], 224.

[105] "Since the Chancellor [Hardenberg] does not know the reason that Chief Gruner made such unpleasant overtures to you [...]" Sembdner, *Die Berliner Abendblätter*, 2:846.

[106] See Hardenberg's letter (18 February 1811), Sembdner, *Dier Berliner Abendblätter*, 2:852f.

tunate constellation of events ultimately responsible for Kleist's mistaken belief that Hardenberg had "guaranteed" subsidies for the *Berliner Abendblätter*.

There was yet another reason for Kleist's confidence that subsidies would be paid: his cousin, Ludwig, son of General Kleist von Nollendorf, who had surrendered the Prussian fortress at Magdeburg to the French without firing as much as a shot, was deeply involved with activist attempts to secure financial backing from England. Moreover, these initiatives went on behind King Frederick William III's back, as illustrated in the following example: On April 7, 1809, Thomas Grenville wrote to his father, "Kleist, the son of the Magdeburg General, is come here as a private agent to Canning from several leading men in Prussia and Saxony to ask for arms to assist a general insurrection in the North of Germany; but I do not believe that the King of Prussia is any party to this mission."[107] Since Canning could not be certain of Kleist's credentials, he agreed to an arms depot to be established on the island of Heligoland and a letter of credit for 20,000 pounds; he insisted that Ludwig von Kleist be accompanied by a British agent, Lt. Maimburg, who was to ascertain the status of Kleist and his confederates with the Prussian government. Maimburg's favorable reports prompted Canning to continue supporting the "secret" movement.[108] Only a few months later, Ludwig and Heinrich met in Berlin. It is, therefore, highly unlikely that Heinrich knew nothing of the cooperation between the Prussian activists and Great Britain. But there is yet one more piece of evidence relevant here.

The *Gemeinnützige Unterhaltungsblätter*, the *Nordische Miszellen* edited by Alexander Bran, *Minerva* founded by Archenholz and the *Priviligierte Liste der Börsenhalle* were the mainstay of Kleist's sources for his newspaper; they all included political and scientific contributions sympathetic to England. Moreover, the *Berliner Abendblätter* was not the only newspaper circulating "police reports" designed to attract an audience and then to keep the pro-British spirit of insurrection alive. A tabloid similar to Kleist's and supported in much the same way by the local police chief was established during roughly the same period at Breslau. The weekly *New Breslau Tattler* (*Neuer Breslauer Erzähler*) edited by Carl Menzel and Carl

---

[107] *Report of the Manuscripts of J. B. Fortesque preserved at Dropmore*. Historical Manuscripts Commission (London: Herford Times, 1915) 9:292f.

[108] On 9 June 1809, Canning reported to King George about his meeting with Baron Heerdt and Herr Fagel, who brought him a letter from Stein's close associate, the Prince of Orange. Canning writes "the Hanoverian officer sent back with Mr. Kleist to ascertain the real state of the insurrection in the north of Germany" had returned with "highly favourable reports"; see *The Later Correspondence of King George III*, ed. Arthur Aspinall (Cambridge: Cambridge University Press, 1970): 295.

Schall contained the most reprints of articles from the *Berliner Abendblätter*,[109] and included "police reports," very much like those of Gruner, supplied by the chief of police in Breslau, Streit. There is a link here: according to the membership lists supplied by August Lehmann, Streit was the twenty-ninth member of the *Tugendbund* at Breslau.[110] This self-styled "League of Virtue" or "Moral Scientific Union," as it was also known, was deeply involved in Stein's insurrectionist strategy and secretly disseminated the works of the patriots throughout Germany and eventually beyond her borders. This suggests that both Streit and Gruner, working for Stein, sought to manipulate public opinion in favor of the activists' reform and anti-Napoleon policy through local newspapers. For Gruner, Kleist was simply the editor of the faction's publication in Berlin. Hitzig and Kuhn were chosen as the publishers in an effort to direct suspicion away from Georg Reimer, who, by the time, was already printing the work of most of Stein's literary allies. Moreover, Reimer may have been the proposed publisher for another journal which would sway public opinion in favor of re-organization: an "official" *Prussian Chronicle*. Thus Hardenberg would have an organ sympathetic to his reform policy, although Kleist's mass circulation newspaper would carry on the work of Stein. The original plan was proposed by Adam Müller.

Both Steig and Sembdner identified Müller's copious contributions to the *Berliner Abendblätter*.[111] Sembdner pointed out that Müller had authored articles with both retarding and progressive tendencies in order to discuss the *pros* and *cons* of government re-apportionments. Invariably, however, Müller's arguments conclude in favor of the reform under discussion.[112] But in three letters to the activists' financial expert, Friedrich Stägemann, Müller revealed that he had considerably more in mind. As early as August 29, 1809, Müller, insisting that the reorganizers of the Prussian state must speak out and articulate in a more popular way the reasons for such extraordinary measures, offered to produce: "1) publicly and with the authority of the governing body, an official government newspaper, 2) anonymously and with the consent and cooperation of the government a newspaper for all the people; in other words, I will write an

---

[109] See Sembdner, *Die Berliner Abendblätter* [Note 78], 332–341.

[110] August Lehmann, *Der Tugendbund* (Berlin: Haude & Spener, 1867): 214.

[111] Steig, *Kleists Berliner Kämpfe*, 9, 41–50 *et passim*; Sembdner, *Die Berliner Abendblätter*, 9, 31, 39ff.

[112] Sembdner, *Die Berliner Abendblätter*, 39f.

official and an opposition newspaper at the same time."[113] The opposition paper was to direct the debate over proposed changes, preempt the arguments of those opposed to a particular reform and win over large segments of the populace to the reorganization. To these ends, he would need authorization and instruction from the government as well as easy access to government agencies.

When Stägemann responded favorably, Müller sent him a detailed outline of his scheme. Among the more unusual items was: "#4 publication of official reports regarding the course of criminal trials and those of interest to the public."[114] In this way, the newspaper was to appeal to the people and, once an audience was established, manipulate public opinion in the interest of reform. The "official" newspaper was to be called the *Prussian Chronicle*, or the *Prussian Court and National Newspaper*. Although no name was suggested for the opposition journal, Müller refers to it as "semi-official," "a newspaper for the people," (*Volksblatt*) a journal which would present the arguments of the opposition even better than the conservatives could have, only to refute such contentions completely. Above all, Müller writes, "the individual patriots can be brought together in this way."[115] By early October 1809, Müller had gained the support of Beyme, who, as we have seen, had been one of Fichte's contacts, Stägemann and Sack — all of whom worked for the Prussian reform party.

It is likely that Müller persuaded Kleist, his co-editor for *Phoebus*, to join him in this new political venture. Although the "official" newspaper did not appear at this time; the *Berliner Abendblätter* bears the markings of Müller's outline. By October of the following year, the *Volksblatt* was ready for the press without an "official" *Prussian Chronicle*. Therefore, Müller began writing *pro*- and *contra*-reorganization in the same newspaper. Gruner was to supply the criminal reports and whatever other scandalous items he could find which would increase circulation. Whenever Kleist describes the *Berliner Abendblätter*, he uses the same vocabulary found in Müller's outline. The newspaper is "semi-official," dealing with "the business of the Fatherland,"depends upon an exchange of information with "the heads of interested government agencies," and has a co-editor, Müller, whose name must be kept secret.[116] Moreover, Stägemann, to whom Müller had sent his plan, contributed at least three articles to the

---

[113] *Briefe und Aktenstücke zur Geschichte Preußens unter Friedrich Wilhelm III.*, ed. Franz Rühl (Leipzig: Duncker and Humblot, 1899) 1:118.

[114] *Ibid.*, 1:125.

[115] *Ibid.*, 1:125–130.

[116] See Kleist's letter to Hardenberg, Sembdner 2:844; also 2:848f.

journal.[117] The parallels suggest that Kleist, encouraged by Gruner, co-operated with Müller in an unsuccessful attempt to manipulate public opinion in favor of the activists. He had, after all, worked for the reformers before.

Apparently, however, Kleist was not satisfied with his role as a mere editor of this politically oriented newspaper. He also sought to heighten artistic appreciation in his audience. This, according to Müller, precipitated the demise of the venture. In October 1810, after the first issues were out, Adam Müller wrote to Rühle von Lilienstern: "Kleist is editing with incredible success the *Berliner Abendblätter* and has made a lot of money. Unfortunately, he's started once more to re-educate his public to an appreciation of the bizarre and the shocking, which will simply not work. The PS, whenever you read it, is my sign."[118] Thus Kleist went beyond the precepts of the party, as he had done in *Prinz Friedrich von Homburg*, thereby losing the support of his political backers.

Was this not Kleist's problem from the outset? Perhaps the goals of the propagandist and those of the artist were incompatible from the first. Despite his apparent eagerness to serve the activist cause by working from a recommended blueprint and using the suggested components in the production of propaganda, he was unwilling, perhaps unable, to abandon artistic goals. On the one hand, he dealt with socio-political reality in accordance with party wishes. On the other hand, his rich artistic imagination, his multi-talented disposition, sought new modes of expression which would enable his audience to appreciate skillful representations of such aspects of poetic phantasy as the unusual, the bizarre and the shocking. Loath to respond, the inflexible public turned away from the more demanding Kleist to the more comfortable Iffland and Kotzebue whose trivializations of contemporary life dominated the German stage.

When Kleist looked to be paid for his efforts, he was greeted with blank stares. As we have seen, Gruner, castigated several times for failing to maintain strict censorship, had just been promoted to a position of authority over the political censors. It was inconceivable to Kleist that Gruner would have approached him without Hardenberg's knowledge. The minister of state reinforced this error himself when he answered one of Kleist's questions by saying that the state might support meritorious writers, when and if the resources became available.[119] But Gruner did not speak for Hardenberg; he was Stein's agent. In so precarious a position, he

---

[117] See Sembdner, *Die Berliner Abendblätter* [Note 78], 37f.

[118] As quoted by Steig, *Kleists Berliner Kämpfe* [Note 72], 528.

[119] Sembdner, *Die Berliner Abendblätter* 2:852f.

remained silent and allowed Kleist to believe that Hardenberg was responsible for the innuendos.

Furthermore, the project was not working according to plan. Censorship became too severe early in February 1811, when Schlechtendahl became the new police chief. Gruner could not risk exposing his operation to the minister of state because of Kleist. Hardenberg, as we have noted, did not enjoy the confidence of the Foreign Office, nor did he favor an anti-French propaganda campaign; he was unaware of Gruner's pledges which undoubtedly went far beyond anything he or the Chancellor's Office would have authorized. The hapless Kleist, plagued by debtors and a lack of success, sought relief from Gruner's superior, the man he felt had to be responsible. But Hardenberg knew nothing.

Bewildered and provoked, the sensitive Kleist became increasingly desperate: he challenged Friedrich von Raumer to a duel. Raumer contributed to his confusion by initially agreeing that the "government" might be prevailed upon to "offset monetarily the loss of popularity" likely to accompany increased contributions "suited to government purposes."[120] However, the political goals had been set by Stein through his agent Gruner. Hardenberg was kept in the dark, and the unfortunate Kleist fell victim, by his own hand, to an intrigue which had been revealed to him, as to so many others, only in bits and pieces.

---

[120] See Raumer to Kleist (12 December 1810): Sembdner 2:846f. Raumer recalls the incident in his memoirs (1:229–231); see also Steig [Note 72], 82ff.

4
Ernst Moritz Arndt and the "New Nation"

AS A MANIPULATOR OF PUBLIC OPINION, Kleist was ineffective. Although he gave to the Prussian myth of a German nation the highest degree of literary expression, Kleist was prevented by circumstances and individuals from reaching a broad segment of the reading public. The popularization of the myth was due less to Kleist's masterful efforts than to the essays and poems of Ernst Moritz Arndt. For this reason, we must distinguish those works Arndt produced for the activists from those written earlier which attracted their attention. As we shall see, volume one (1806) of *Spirit of the Times* gained Arndt notoriety as a political publicist, but volumes two (1808–09) and three (1813) were financed by Stein and circulated by Gruner as well as other activists.[1] We shall also analyze Arndt's style in the latter two volumes to ascertain how Arndt represented the nationalist myth and used the structures gleaned from the Vendée propaganda. Arndt's rhetoric, rhythm, imagery and pathos molded the myth of the German nation into a popular form which was then handed down, albeit with "adjustments," "re-interpretations," and "corrections," from father to son up to the end of the Second World War. Since, as we have seen, others who were less successful also articulated the message, Arndt's irrepressible representation of the myth is not just a matter of what he said, but how he said it. It can be shown that what he said differs markedly from the interpretations of his would-be disciples on the eve of German unification under Bismarck and thereafter.

Before the collapse at Jena, Arndt had expressed individualistic convictions in two works, *A Humane Word Concerning Freedom in the Old Republics* (1800) and *Attempt at a History of Serfdom in Pomerania and Rügen* (1803). In the earlier work he described the basic defect in the social structure of Sparta, Athens and Rome. Since no constitutional tradition existed

---

[1] The editor of Arndt's works, Wilhelm Steffens, discusses the connections to Gruner and Stein in his introduction, see *Arndts Werke* [Chapter III, Note 41], 6:13ff. Quotes from this edition, noted hereafter as Steffens.

in the ancient city-states to insure the rule of law, the aristocrats had ruthlessly exploited the masses.[2] The latter composition provided a blueprint for reforming the unjust institutions which placed an oppressive economic burden on the land-bound peasants in Pomerania and Rügen. As a motto for this book, Arndt chose the statement of Tiberius: "In a free country, tongue and spirit must be free." This and similar assertions earned Arndt the epithets "corrupter of the people" and "inciter to revolution" coined by the antagonized gentry and renters of large estates.[3]

In the first volume of *Spirit of the Times*, which made him an overnight celebrity in Germany, he persists in this criticism of autocratic privilege and north German particularism. His independent point of view allows the narrator, who uses scores of foreign words here, carefully avoided in later volumes,[4] to criticize friend and foe alike. Thus he heaps scorn upon German princes, who "are everything because of the people and nothing without them" (6:196). The ills which have befallen Germany as a result of Napoleon's superior foreign policy, he declares, were compounded by the self-interest of the princes:

> You cry out in your anxiety to the German nation; you act as if you believe in such a nation. To her you are criminals, you never believed in her, never loved or even knew her. It is all of your own making that no one is there, that the last public feeling for a common heritage and a single language have grown stale and that the illusion of a long tradition, a people's sacred life, has perished (6:171).

Such comments generally found a responsive audience among the latter-day founders of the activist party. Some fifty years later, when Arndt reminisced about his relationship to Baron vom Stein, he put similar words in the Prussian Minister's mouth in a response to the czarina (the former Princess Dorothea Auguste of Württemberg), who had declared that she would be ashamed to be a German if one French soldier escaped from Russia across the German border.[5] This suggests that Arndt and Stein agreed in their criticism of the German ruling class. On the other hand, Arndt, when he accuses the princes of acquiring land by unfair means and predicts that they will lose all of it (6:172), goes beyond captious assertions about Germany's plenipotentiaries which became a

---

[2] A paraphrase of this work in English and generous translations from *Spirit of the Times* are available in Alfred J. Pundt, *Arndt and the National Awakening in Germany* (New York: Columbia University Press, 1935): 34f.

[3] Pundt, *Arndt*, 35f.

[4] Steffens, *AW*, 12:242.

[5] "Meine Wanderungen und Wandlungen mit dem Freiherr vom Stein," Steffens, *AW*, 5:58f.

part of the reform party's platform. He also refuses to believe that the French are invincible; rather, he declares their German opponents are simply stupid and awkward.

The ten parts of this first volume also incorporate many arguments advanced earlier in the attempt to explain the lack of German unity. For example, when Arndt traces the political disunity to the absence of a cultural capital as the French have in Paris (6:106), he echoes Herder's commentary of 1792.[6] He also voices the German criticisms of the seizure and execution of the Duke d'Enghien in violation of German sovereignty (6:185). Volume one is a conglomeration of old and new political arguments and represents Arndt's most independent critical thinking on those national issues which were shaking the very foundation of the German social order. With the Peace of Tilsit, however, Prussia's *ancien regime* was, at least for a time, laid to rest. Napoleon sought to mold Germany's destiny, and Arndt was determined to resist the foreigner's intervention.

As the French troops advanced, Arndt quit Germany for Sweden in 1808. At Stockholm (from March 1808 to February 1809), he edited a short lived anti-Napoleon German language newspaper, *Der Nordische Kontrolleur*, written mostly by himself. More important is his collection of four independent essays, composed from January 1807 to the Fall of 1808, printed in book form. According to Gustav Erdmann, Arndt asked for and received permission from the Swedish Foreign Ministry to publish the book anonymously in Sweden. Johannes Paul, on the other hand, insists that King Gustav IV Adolphus commissioned Arndt to write this volume and paid him 500 *Reichstaler* for his services.[7] In any event, the first edition was published by Peter Sohm in Stockholm 1808–1809 in an edition of two-hundred and fifty copies.[8] In January 1809 a shipment arrived in Germany where a large portion was promptly seized by German censors and French agents. However, some of the books escaped confiscation to enjoy private circulation in northern Germany: in 1811, for example, Baron vom Stein recommended to Varnhagen von Ense that he imitate the style of

---

[6] See *Herders Sämtliche Werke*, ed. Bernhard Suphan (Berlin: Weidmann, 1877 1899) 17:25.

[7] Gustav Erdmann, *Ernst Moritz Arndt. Freiheitsträger und Patriot* (Vaterstetten: Arndt Verlag, 1970): 31. Johannes Paul, *Ernst Moritz Arndt* (Göttingen: Musterschmidt, 1971): 45. The confusion can be traced to the statement of the king's librarian Wallmark (1811–43), who recorded that the anti-French king paid for the book and thereupon sent it to Germany. Arndt disputes this in his correspondences with Stein, when he claims he paid the printing costs for volume two out of his own pocket and asks for compensation. See Steffen's notes 12:269. It is likely that Arndt, therefore, was paid twice for the same work.

[8] In his biography of Arndt for the *Allgemeine deutsche Biographie*, Gustav Freytag asserts that the book was printed in England. Later research has revealed, however, that the imprint: "Th. Boosey" London, is a cover for Georg Reimer's *Realschulbuchhandlung* in Berlin, which printed a second edition in 1813.

Arndt's second volume. "Since Burke," said Stein of volume two, "nothing has appeared with such genuine political eloquence, with such penetrating truths."[9] It is also likely that the activists smuggled in additional copies. Furthermore, when Arndt met with Schleiermacher, Kleist and the other members of the "Reading and Shooting Society" at Georg Reimer's house in Berlin 1809, the work was already well-known.[10]

The parallel between Arndt's procedure and Fichte's myth-making is striking. In the sixty-two pages of his "Last Word to the Germans," allegedly spoken in the Fall of 1808 (which constitute part four of volume II), Arndt calls for a return to genuine religious conviction and to "reason," which is "a sacred perception merged with the most heartfelt belief in the highest things" (7:138). The process whereby Arndt arrives at this definition is far from the precise mathematical statements Fichte juxtaposes when deducing postulates in his *Science of Knowledge;* yet it closely resembles the myth-making technique found in the *Addresses to the German Nation*. Arndt states categorically that a "belief in the highest things" rests not on philosophical proofs, but upon the feelings deep in the hearts of his readers. It relies, Arndt explains, on those things which good and wise men have sensed in previous ages, "the smiling dream of mankind under the first palm trees," that which appears to noble, educated men to be the sacred truth of fate and history (*Ibid.*). We recognize here Cicero's argument "optimus in rempublicam consensus," rejected as fallacious by Fichte in the *Science of Knowledge*, only to be resurrected in the *Addresses*.

With these words, Arndt simply broadens the base of Fichte's argumentation. The philosopher had postulated his statements on the "heart of the German"; the political publicist expands the foundation to include what he regards as the dream of all mankind. But this difference is soon obliterated as Arndt proceeds to interpret these dreams, sacred truths, fate and history in the same manner as did Fichte. Both writers simply tell their audience what is in the heart of the German, that is, of all mankind. Arndt's explanations are allegedly "proven" by the "one great feeling" in the name "German" (7:83), which will overcome the "devil in hell" (7:85) because it was instilled in the true German heart by the sacred will of providence (7:127).

How does Arndt interpret what is in the hearts of his countrymen? He uses the same three structural units underlying Fichte's social vision. First, the German heart calls for national education, which will instruct the upcoming generation in a bolder spirit. Hating tyranny and saving the na-

---

[9] As quoted in Varnhagen von Ense, *Denkwürdigkeiten und vermischte Schriften*, 3:198f.

[10] See Jerry F. Dawson, *Friedrich Schleiermacher, The Evolution of a Nationalist* (Austin: University of Texas Press, 1966): 115; also Pundt [Note 2], 87.

tion, "this [coming] generation must live proudly and learn to die in glory. The following generations should be instructed and educated in the same way, so that a courageous public spirit, a noble pride in the Fatherland and freedom will grow. May this direction and its fruits be youth's school and discipline!" (7:33f.). Any other school, he declares, should be shut down.

Second, the danger of French domination of the German conceptual capability must be eliminated (7:70). Germans must become worthy of their language (7:98). The French can never understand German thoughts because they refuse to recognize "our language and our disposition" (99). If the gallicizing tendency is not combated, Germany will be reduced to a country of despicable slaves without morals, language, science and art (166). Germans are all children of one language (104). In a phrase later adapted by Theodor Körner, Arndt curses those who taught Napoleon's German propagandists "to stammer their first German word" ["... das erste deutsche Wort lallen lehrte"] (153). After all, today's Germans live upon the soil of the ancient Germanic tribes and speak the language of their ancestors (93).

Third, the present generation should remember its vital link with a common cultural past and the duties implied in its rich heritage: "Men and friends, we are standing on the ashes of great men; we join hands over immortal memories and eternal obligations — swear here to do what is right, to live and die for freedom and manhood, and *their* mettle will pass to their offspring, while understanding and bravery will sustain the grandchildren" (122). In many passages, Arndt reiterates the common ties and the sacred obligations these bonds engender: Germans are Luther's people; they must gain strength and sustenance from Germany's unique heroic spirit.[11] A literary context of legendary heroes and immortal deeds emphasizes this mythic component. "We are all Germans," he tells his readers, "we live in a land of lofty memories and everlasting accomplishments" (88). In keeping with the myth, the most important of these ancient men of daring is Hermann, the leader of the Cherusci.

"Men of Germany," commands Arndt, "never forget Hermann! Pray to the Almighty for such a man and liberator ... and he will come and you will be *one* people, a free and strong people" (94). Throughout the narrative he refers to modern Germans as the sons (84) and to the "holy land of the Germanic tribes" (29). In a parallel to Kleist's drama, he refers not only to Hermann's battle with Varus in the Teutoburg Forest but also to Marbod, the Suevians and the Cattes (94). Finally, Arndt describes Bonaparte in much the same way Kleist had portrayed Roman politicians

---

[11] See Steffens, *AW*, 12:274.

in *Die Hermannsschlacht*. Since Napoleon had been unable to mar the stature of Germany's princes sufficiently, "he is still moderate to the petty princes. He sows old and new discord, flatters with old and new prejudices, keeps in power German princes who foster the helplessness and small-mindedness of their own people; with hopes and promises he points to the coming peace, baiting with secret institutions and good deeds those who will come to power when his plans become reality" (7:165). These are precisely the circumstances Hermann describes to Luitgar as he unfolds his strategy in *Die Hermannsschlacht*.[12] Moreover, as Arndt continues, the resemblance between his assertions and Hermann's words in Kleist's plays becomes greater:

> *Arndt*: Once he's finished, he'll have nothing more to fear or to worry about; then he'll knock one German prince after another from his seat and replace him with a French regent.... (7:165)
>
> *Hermann*: The fate of Germany has taught me all too well that Augustus' final goal is to destroy us both, him and me. And once he, Marbod, the Suevian prince, is destroyed, then I feel it vividly, Arminius's turn will come (lines 762–767).

This congruity suggest that *Die Hermannsschlacht* and volume II of *Spirit of the Times* derive from a common source. Another indication is found at the beginning of part four which Arndt wrote in the Fall of 1808. The section is introduced by a fragment from an unpublished tragedy entitled *Hermann* (7:113–116). Since this excerpt was included in the first printing and is not a later addition, we observe that both Kleist and Arndt worked on the same theme for a stage production at the same time. It is unlikely that Arndt knew Kleist's play firsthand — surely, he would have recognized the advantages of the rhythmically more natural pentameter over his own clumsy unrhymed hexameters! Both he and Kleist illustrated the same theme dramatically only weeks after Fichte had held up the Cheruscan prince to German youth as a model worthy of imitation. References in this connection to Klopstock's Hermann-trilogy, which was written forty years earlier and is void of all dramatic action, blur the more fundamental implication that the activists were encouraging a stage representation of the Hermann theme.

In the fall of 1809 two writers used the same theme for a drama; they had the same political contacts, made identical transitions from "individualism" to "nationalism," incorporated the activists' nationalistic myth in their respective works and indoctrinated their audience with a uniform socio-political philosophy. Moreover, the similarities between Arndt's writings and the works of other collaborators do not begin and

---

[12] Act II, Scene X.

end with Kleist's *Hermannsschlacht*. Besides basing the individual narratives in volume two upon the tripartite framework found in Kleist's play, Arndt incorporated ideas and rhetorical devices gleaned from Fichte, Stein and the Vendée propagandists. Volume two of *Spirit of the Times* promulgates the reform party's platform virtually *in toto*.

Arndt appeals to German writers to counteract Napoleon's propaganda. In "A Look Forward and Backward," he complains, as had Stein and Fichte, about the absence of German nationalist voices in the press (7:13); in the second part, "A Look Forward," he laments that the German people have no volunteer spokesman to interpret communal feelings (7:82); in the third part, "Peace Address of a German," he mocks the proclamation of a universal monarchy by pro-Napoleon factions in Germany. Although he denies their validity, he admits to their impact on public opinion (109). In part four, he calls upon German writers to become the leaders and interpreters of the times ("Wegeweiser und Dolmetscher der Zeit"). "The salvation of the people was in the hands of the writers" (148f.), but their lack of public spirit gave the French a great advantage. Arndt then begins to reflect the activists' strategy for manipulating public opinion: since the French tyrant has forbidden the citizenry "to think and speak like Germans," they have to resort to secret propaganda, to "a quiet accord and cooperation of the best German hearts and minds that will banish domestic discord, set aside despair and awaken German enthusiasm for the destruction of foreign power" (173). These appeals echo closely Stein's proposal to Frederick William III and his cabinet in the ensuing months.

Fichte's description of national life under foreign domination is rephrased in the section entitled "A Look Forward." Branding foreign control over Germany "intolerable" (*unerträglich*), he portrays the French march into Germany in terms similar to the narrative of the Roman incursion into the Teutoburg Forest in Kleist's *Hermannsschlacht*. Like Fichte, he argues that Germany must preserve its "self-rule," for without it the uniquely German national sovereignty and "the whole world" (*die ganze Erde*) would perish. Again in a close parallel to Fichte, Arndt states: "All the nourishing zeal, all the majestic desire, all the divine confidence of individuals and of peoples die out whenever only one [nation] rules the world." As he reminds his readers of their highest duty (*die höchste Pflicht*), he bids Germany's young men to sacrifice themselves gloriously for the nation, so that their children and grandchildren will have a Fatherland in which to enjoy their own sacred rights (81–83).

Pleas to tear down the old order and bring in the new permeate the four parts. In the second, for example, he points out that a return to particularist control, to the old constitution, to obsolete formulas and superfluous ornaments would not be feasible. "If that's what Germany wants, then I wish that the sword had never been drawn, not a drop of blood had been spilled and the beautiful country had been turned over to the foreigners" (78). France has uncovered Germany's most glaring weakness: disunity. Therefore, a new balance of power must be created, and the German princes must now dedicate their loyalty to the Fatherland for the mutual advantage of all Germans, just as they are now committed to Napoleon with the resulting national dissolution. In the future, they must owe their allegiance either to the Prussian crown or the Austrian emperor. Prussia must expand her dominion to the Rhine and the Danube; Austria must rule over the Alpine regions south of the Danube and west of the Rhine (79).

When Arndt wrote this particular passage in January 1807, he was content to let "wiser and mightier men" work out the details of German unification because he did not feel sufficiently familiar with the basic facts. By autumn 1808, he was privy to plans of the reformers and became more specific. After the war with France, he writes, "Austria will acquire Swabia, Franconia, Bavaria, Switzerland as well as all of her former territories; Prussia will take possession of Saxony, Brunswick, Holstein, Westphalia, Hesse and Mecklenburg" (171). He also offers a plan for organizing the ruling houses. To be sure, not all Prussian officials nor for that matter King Frederick William III agreed with this partitioning. This section received the brunt of criticism leveled against the second volume. Nevertheless, Varnhagen's description of Stein's boundless praise of the work, later efforts to have it reprinted and secretly distributed throughout Germany and, as will be shown later, the sum of money Arndt received for it, suggest that these recommendations correspond in essence to the reform party's program.

A conspicuous omission in this plan is the fate of Hanover. Corresponding to Stein's directives, England's interests on the continent are not to be tampered with. The Prussian minister of state had consistently demanded that Hanover be left in peace and that Prussia refuse to accept the rich province from Bonaparte's hand.[13] Arndt had been generally pro-British in the first volume, having defended the island kingdom from those German detractors who asserted that the political chaos in Europe was the result of machinations from across the channel (6:152ff.). Later, in the second volume, he shields England from the insidious French propaganda (7:19) by insisting that the French criticism of Britain is based on intrigues, not facts. He maintains also that Prussia, had the king only declared war earlier, could have counted on British support (60). Later, in

---

[13] See *Stein*, 2/1, (Stein an Vincke, 18. Dec. 1805) 153, (30. Jan. 1806) 165, (Immediatbericht, 25. March 1806) 187. He also pleaded against a commercial blockade of British ships and military conflict with England; see (Immediatbericht, 4. April 1806) 198f.; also 200f, 202, 204, 214, 219–223, 225, 226f, 234, 246f.

the third volume of *Spirit of the Times*, his praise of England in her effort against Napoleon will become rhapsodic (8:13) as he entreats Prussian policy makers to join in England's military stratagem (8:117). At the conclusion, he implores "free and proud England" to examine the fate of Europe's smaller states and not to be blinded by the wretchedness of their plight. Instead, he asks the British crown to help a just and happy world emerge from the present chaos (8:149). Cooperation with England, as we have noted, was central to the party's platform.

We have already uncovered several significant parallels in the second volume of *Spirit of the Times* to the works of Fichte and Kleist. The similarities are not limited to representations of Hermann, Marbod and the Suevians; they permeate motives as well. In part IV, for example, Arndt asks for a sword with which to end his life if the Germans choose to remain French slaves (7:170). Varus had vainly sought the same death as the Germanic tribes close in on him.[14] Arndt's exhortation to the German princes to submit to the rule of Emperor Francis I (7:165) is reminiscent of Kleist's "Proklamation" in his *Aphorisms, On the Liberation of Austria*.[15] His praise of the Spanish insurrection (7:164) goes hand in hand with Kleist's *Catechism*. Arndt also asks Napoleon's German and Austrian opponents to weave Hermann's wreath of oak leaves into their hair (7:77). In the opening scene of *Prinz Friedrich von Homburg*, written two years after the Swedish publication of Arndt's second volume, the prince seated under an oak tree similarly weaves a wreath. The correspondence shows that the prince's wreath, symbolizing a long and rich German heritage, marks those in agreement with the party.

Arndt also refers to the heroic General Count Zrinyi (7:122), who later becomes the subject of a play by another collaborator, Theodor Körner. Arndt's juxtaposition of Zrinyi with Jean de Lavalette, the victorious defender of Malta against the Turks in 1556, is repeated by Soliman during a key monologue in the first act of Körner's *Zriny*. Moreover, Arndt and Körner employ the same images: Napoleon is represented in volume two of *Spirit of the Times* as a Saracen, an Oriental; Körner's counterpart is Soliman, the Turk. For Arndt, Napoleon is a meteor which will burn up quickly; Körner uses the same metaphor.

After 1806 Frederick William III adopted as Prussia's emblem the eagle flying into the sun. Both Fichte and Arndt use this symbol to represent Prussia's eventual triumph over the French oppression and the old or-

---

[14] Sembdner, *Kleists sämtliche Werke*, 1:622 (lines 2476–2480).

[15] Sembdner, *Kleists sämtliche Werke*, 2:382. In his memoirs, "Erinnerungen aus dem äußeren Leben," Arndt confirms his association with Kleist in the winter of 1809 (Steffens, *AW*, 2:175).

der.[16] Volume two also contains the metaphor of iron valued higher than gold (7:102). This image, which is found in Arndt's poem "Praise of Iron," was popularized by Arndt's biographer, Ernst Müsebeck who, on the eve of World War I, entitled a patriotic anthology: *Gold I Gave For Iron* [*Gold gab ich für Eisen* (Berlin: Bong, 1913)].

The third volume of *Spirit of the Times* is also constructed upon the tripartite framework of the Prussian myth. Aside from the addition of an account of the French retreat from Russia based on a commentary by Arndt's and Kleist's good friend, Ernst Pfuel,[17] this volume is linked by allusion, imagery and phraseology with the work of the other collaborators. In his introduction Arndt admits that his book may be construed as an attempt to incite a national insurrection, but, he points out, only "un-Germans and weaklings will label it as such" (8:9). With this volume, the publicist reaches the zenith of his propagandist activities: he becomes a "priest ... in the public church,"[18] a leading contributor to the manipulation of public opinion in Germany.

He sees the weakness of the old system in the failure to integrate the various German court-schools, which led to a reliance on the "injurious foreign influences" to such an extent that the better German men and princes had been "de-germanized" (*entdeutscht*, 8:139). Focusing on the instructional process for future leaders, he calls for the founding of a major educational facility whose guardians shall be the select men of Germany. In this school the best pupils of noble birth, who are to be educated from their tenth to eighteenth year, must learn "German history, German virtue and the German language; they must prepare for their lofty calling in all physical and mental exercises" (8:144). The founding of an institution of this kind was a major proposal in the reform party's program.

Early in the first section entitled "To what did Bonaparte aspire and what did he accomplish," he describes the threat which the French language, "an old evil in Germany," poses for his countrymen. After a detailed account of the French retreat from Moscow, he comments at length on the "power of language and customs" (8:114) which bind people together. Whenever he thinks about the German people and the depth of the German language and disposition, he is overcome with tears and

---

[16] This emblem held in such high esteem by Fichte and Arndt with its motto "huic soli cedit" was mocked in the next generation by the Young German writer Karl Gutzkow in his description of Potsdam. See his *Skizzenbuch* (Kassel, 1839): 228.

[17] Ernst Pfuel, *Der Rückzug der Franzosen bis zum Niemen* (Berlin: Dümmier, 1813). The book was completed in Wilna on December 10, 1812, but not published until the next year.

[18] Ruth Flad, *Der Begriff der öffentlichen Meinung bei Stein, Arndt und Humboldt* (Berlin and Leipzig: de Gruyter, 1929): 77.

homesickness (151). He admonishes his compatriots to stop "stammering" in the tones of their foreign oppressors and to love fervently "your own language and your freedom" (170). Thus the language bond is emphasized once again in volume three.

Instances of Fichte's influence are evident not only in the reference to the linguistic consanguinity of all Germans but also in Arndt's catalogue of German characteristics. At one point, he insists that such outstanding features of the German personality as versatility, loyalty, frankness, a loving, understanding disposition for all times, peoples and nations, humility and piety will not be endangered by reforming existing institutions and the educational process (136). Fichte had described the German superpersonality in similar terms. Kleist had recommended that the Germans modify these positive traits in their own interests. In his *Addresses* Fichte had argued that once alien thought patterns are forced upon people, their power to think creatively and morally is seriously impaired. Arndt recasts this argument in more concrete terms: ". . . our every act of boldness shall cease, every bit of pride tremble, every virtue crawl; we shall be made to forget that we spoke and thought in German and learn instead to flatter our goaders in strange sounding tones and praise our wretchedness and shame as a new state of grandeur" (164).

The third volume also provides more insight into the policies of the reform party. Political leaders in favor of re-organization were inspired by the example of the Spanish insurrectionists, who inflicted heavy losses upon the French occupation army, and prompted the stationing of a considerable French force in Spain. In Arndt's writing, as in Kleist's *Hermannsschlacht*, partisan activities become a war of all the people, a "holy war" (18), while his panegyric for the Spanish General, José de Palafax (1780–1847), who defended Saragossa against numerically superior French assault troops in 1808 and again in 1809, is redolent of Kleist's praise "To Palafax" written in April 1809.[19]

As for Germany, "only a few high-spirited men hoped" for a similar popular upheaval. Between 1808 and 1811, "they saw the bottomless depravity; they recognized the bustling spirit of new creativity in the era; they did not regard England and Spain's struggle against France as dubious; above all they trusted in God and the spirit of retribution ever present in history" (25). These "few" are, of course, the members of the activist faction. Later he laments that all the work and all the blood will have been wasted if those who make the final decisions fail to raise the strength of their own convictions (112). The party whose policies Arndt espoused did

---

[19] Cf. Steffens, *AW*, 8:17 and Sembdner 1:30. For the dating of Kleist's poem, see his letter to Collin, April 20, 1809, Sembdner, *Kleists sämtliche Werke*, 2:823f.; also Sembdner, *Kleists sämtliche Werke*, note 1:913.

not have the final word. The reform faction was for the most part an opposition party, which counselled, but could not always persuade the Prussian monarch nor the more influential members of his cabinet.

This volume attests to Arndt's collaboration with that faction whose leaders advocated an alliance with Austria in 1808–09 and more support for such clandestine military volunteer groups as Major Schill's squadron (8:17); they praised England (8:13) and Spain (8:16–18) for resisting Napoleon and urged the king to adopt British military strategy (8:17) and accept British pound Sterling to finance guerrilla activities. Stein, Gneisenau and Scharnhorst pressed for a north German insurrection (8:177) as well as German unification under a strong Prussia (8:173). Arndt sought to manipulate public opinion in their favor. For this reason, he brands Bavaria and Württemberg "German turncoats." By enlisting such propagandists as Arndt who appealed to the public with "tongue and pen" ("Rede und Schrift," 8:168), the activists created a "spirit of dedication and sacrifice among the people" (8:134). On the other hand, these writers also sowed the seeds for future discord by holding forth the hope of a new and more liberal constitution for Prussia (8:180). On that score the government failed to make good on its promises.

A complex system of imagery, rhetorical devices and thoughts expressed by other collaborators is superimposed upon the tripartite structure of the nationalistic myth in this volume. In compliance with the reform party's program, Arndt calls upon the German states to rally around the German eagle on the Prussian banner (8:22), which then becomes a symbol of the unification movement (8:1113). Men of the "German tongue" (8:123), who must be liberated, are distinguished from the French sympathizers (*Franzosenaffen*), who know nothing of the majesty and honor of their own people (8:44). Napoleon is compared to the meteors and comets which burn brightly only for a short times and then are suddenly reduced to ashes. When Arndt describes the historical process in terms of a life-giving spirit "which travels like an invisible current of goodness through the generations, drifting like a spring wind over the nations and people, spreading its seeds of virtue" (8, 108), he anticipates Hegel's imagery by nearly a decade.

In volume two Arndt had included his translation of classical poems from the Greek to illustrate his arguments (7:34–38, 85). In volume three he combines Biblical phrases with rhetorical figures and imperatives to saturate the nationalistic myth with a lofty pathos. With parallelism, anaphora and modulation within the rhythmic pattern, Arndt raises the pathos to a crescendo. A good illustration can be found after a two part condemnation of those who believe the French propaganda and those who desert the cause of freedom until the battle is won. Arndt writes:

Eines gilt und eines ist not, daß du rufest: *Zusammen! zusammen! für Recht und Freiheit! für Gott und das Volk! Zu den Waffen, zu den Waffen! gegen die Welschen, die Franzosen, die Tyrannen!* Diesen Klang laß in deinen Tälern und Bergen, laß von deinen Türmen und Festen ertönen und versammele deine tapfere Jugend unter den Fahnen der Einmütigkeit und Gottseligkeit. Laß in den Staub versinken, was versinken muß; laß modern, was durch die lange Zeit verfault ist; laß ab von der unseligen Dummheit und Stumpfheit, womit du so lange nicht hast begreifen wollen, daß dein Leben, deine Verfassung, dein ganzer Zustand nicht mehr sind, wie sie vor zwanzig Jahren waren, und daß sie nimmer wieder ganz so sein können...(8:172).

One thing matters and one thing is necessary — that you cry out: "Together! Together! for justice and freedom! for God and country! To Arms! To Arms! Against the Latins, the French, the Tyrants! Let this sound ring from your valleys and mountains, from your towers and festivals and assemble your brave young men under the banner of unanimity and piety. Let fall in the dust, what must; let moulder what has decayed over a long period; refrain from the accused stupidity and indifference which has kept you from seeing that your life, your constitution, your entire condition no longer are what they were twenty years ago, and that they never can be again. . . ."

This lofty tone continues over several lengthy paragraphs until the writer interjects a personal comment, "My words burn because my heart is burning" (8:176), whereupon he resumes the pathos with himself as the subject (8:176–181).

In the paragraph quoted above, which goes on for another nine lines, the commands appear in a complex of parallel sentence structure and repetition. The imperative *laß* begins five separate dictums; *ergreife* introduces four. The anaphora creates a rhythmic quality simulating the beating of a drum; the repetition of a single imperative resembles a drummer's return to the initial beat of a drum roll. By shortening the rhythmic period towards the end of the paragraph, the narrator accelerates specific cadences. The conclusion of short commands are cast in trochaic meter: "was versinken muß" (x́x x́x x́), "Zeit verfault ist" (x́x x́x), "Treue deiner Väter" (x́x x́x x́x), "Gott dir geben will" (x́x x́x x́). Longer commands incorporate the cursus planus: "Tälern und Bergen" (x́xx x́x), "ergreife die Wahrheit" ([x]x́xx x́x), "Zeitalter hinwandeln" (x́xx x́x[x]), skillfully varied with cursus velox and oxytonic cadences: "die Franzosen, die Tyrannen" ([x]x́xx x́x x́x), "Geist und den Gott" (x́xxx́). As the more frequent trochaic beats and cursus planus cadences cluster toward the conclusion, they approximate the speeding up of the recurring drum beat pattern. The narrator gradually truncates the parallel sentence structure, which precipitates the flow of images. Truth, honesty and loyalty are personified by the "fathers"; Francophilism is represented as sinful, wanton and traitorous. Even time is divided metaphorically into "French" and "German." Just as an army moves forward with the drummer's return to the initial beat of his drum roll, so the images of good and evil advance upon the reader through rhetorical techniques. As the drum roll quickens, the reader, caught up in a flood of imagery and imperatives, is induced to rise and move forward in the nationalist cause.

As we have noted, the king and his closest advisors did not agree with Stein that massive propaganda would be effective in strengthening Prussia. On the contrary, they feared that Stein's proposal, if carried out, would incriminate the government and arouse Napoleon's ire. Frederick William III, Wilhelm von Humboldt, Hardenberg, Ancillon and others objected to the unleashing of chauvinistic sentiments, which would permit nationalism to infiltrate the school system and encourage young people to put Germany's interests ahead of Prussia's. To them the promises made to the people by the reform party smacked of Jacobinism. The activists disseminated their propaganda all over northern Germany nonetheless; from their base in Breslau, their members found ways of distributing volumes two and three of *Spirit of the Times* in southern Germany and Austria.

Stein paid his public relations man handsomely from funds provided by England and Russia for re-working volume two and writing volume three; he also covered the costs of printing, binding and distributing the books as is illustrated in a memorandum written at Wilna (June 18, 1812). Lamenting that Arndt's second volume produced in Sweden had not received wide distribution in Germany, Stein recommends that a new edition be prepared which would be sent secretly to Gruner, now in Prague, for circulation in Germany.[20] Arndt was to become Stein's secretary and the chief propagandist for the "German Legion" organizing in Russia. At the end of August 1812, Arndt arrived in Moscow, republished volume two, produced volume three and wrote poems, pamphlets, broadsheets and essays.[21] Reminiscing about his role in the collaboration, Arndt notes the physical resemblance between Stein and Fichte and confirms that the latter had exerted considerable influence on his own thinking;[22] he also documents Stein's arcane correspondence with England,[23] Gneisenau's se-

---

[20] *Stein* 3:652–657.

[21] See "Meine Wanderungen und Wandlungen mit dem Reichsfreiherrn Heinrich Karl Friedrich vom Stein" (Steffens, *AW*, vol. 5).

[22] Steffens 5:15.

[23] Steffens, *AW*, 5:27–29, 30.

cret missions,[24] also earlier meetings with Count Chasot,[25] leader of the paramilitary Berlin Committee (or Charlottenburg Club).

A letter from Stein at Breslau to Arndt dated March 12, 1813 reveals at least one way the literary agents were paid. With regard to volume three of *Spirit of the Times*, Stein writes: "If our capital suffices, have your little book printed and take an extra 400–500 *Taler* for yourself ... then bring the booklet, which is full of truth and common-sense, with you and pick up all our funds at [the Königsberg merchant] Ph[illips]."[26] Arndt received his money through that inconspicuous network of merchants, bankers, publishers, and military contacts which handled party funds and secretly remunerated activist collaborators.

From 1806 to his death in 1860 Arndt wrote scores of patriotic poems, including two large collections for the war effort against Napoleon: *Songs for Germans* [*Lieder für Deutsche* (1811)] and the series which concludes his *Catechism for the German Soldier and Militiaman* [*Katechismus für den deutschen Kriegs- und Wehrmann* (1814)]. Two among his many poems stand out on account of their popularity throughout the nineteenth and early twentieth centuries. *The Song of the Fatherland* [*Vaterlandslied* (1812)] and *The German's Fatherland* [*Des Deutschen Vaterland* (1813)] were set to music many times and reprinted in such anthologies as *Ergießungen deutschen Gefühles* (which we shall discuss in more detail in a later chapter) financed by the Prussian General Staff and circulated in German-speaking territories which remained loyal to the Confederation of the Rhine even after the Battle of Nations at Leipzig.

In Albert Methfessel's setting (1818), the *Song of the Fatherland* inspired generations of students and army recruits:

> Der Gott, der Eisen wachsen ließ,
> Der wollte keine Knechte,
> Drum gab er Säbel, Schwert und Spieß
> Dem Mann in seine Rechte,
> Drum gab er ihm den kühnen Mut,
> Den Zorn der freien Rede,
> Daß er bestände bis aufs Blut,
> Bis in den Tod die Fehde (1:100).
>
> The God who bids the iron grow,
> Wanted no slaves,
> So he put sabre, sword and spear
> In man's right hand,

---

[24] *Ibid.*, 19.

[25] *Ibid.*, 17 and 19.

[26] *Stein* 4:52.

> He gave him bravery and courage,
> The wrath of free speech,
> So that he would fight to the quick,
> Persisting in war until death.

The poem's six strophes of alternating four and three beat lines emphasize the idea of a single German nation ("Ihr Deutschen alle Mann für Mann / Fürs Vaterland zusammen"), incorporating such elements of the activists' myth as the language bond ("Der Zorn der freien Rede"), the desire for a spontaneous uprising and even a reference to the *Hermannsschlacht* in the Teutoburg Forest. Unfortunately, however, the last two verses contain ill-conceived imperatives which were subsequently, even in times of peace, impressed upon the minds of Germany's young people, who were often compelled by misguided, patriotic schoolmasters to learn the poem by heart. Verse five calls for Germans to "redden [their] swords with the blood of Frenchmen," and verse six demands "Victory or Death." These dictates were soon to be reinforced and expanded with disastrous consequences in the ensuing decades by writers, politicians and social institutions.

The first six stanzas of *The German's Fatherland* begin with the question: "What is the German's Fatherland?" After insisting in the first five verses that this Fatherland is more than just Prussia, more than Swabia or merely the Palatinate, etc., Arndt answers, "as far as the German tongue resounds," in a familiar rhyme at the middle of verse six:

> So weit die deutsche Zunge klingt
> Und Gott im Himmel Lieder singt,
> Das soll es sein! (1:127).

The poem concludes in typical activist fashion with the line: "It shall be all Germany!" No other poem by Arndt was so often recited or sung, more aggressively challenged, nor more often misunderstood.

The first to complain were the princes who took offense at the "demagogy" in a strophe which states that the princes had plundered the emperor and *Reich*. Arndt altered the line to read the "Latins' plunder," but that satisfied no one. Therefore, Arndt deleted the verse.[27] Next, in 1846, the poem, which was by now acclaimed as a folksong, became the object of a scathing criticism written by the Bonn academician, Ferdinand Delbrück. Observing that the song's popularity could be explained only by the "excessive naïveté" of Germans, who "take a lenient view of all that's

---

[27] See the discussion in Steffens, *AW*, 12:185.

wrong with the form because of the author's good intention,"[28] Delbrück rejected Arndt's "unthinkably wrongheaded" formulation of the question and took exception to the line in verse eight where Germany is represented as a country in which every Frenchman is regarded as an enemy, every German a friend. According to Delbrück, the answer the poem offers to its own question shows that the German's Fatherland is "a phantom, a chimera, an absurdity." He concludes with a plea urging Arndt to have the poem removed from the various anthologies of patriotic lyrics circulating at the time. Arndt refused. Describing Delbrück as "a strange, scholarly Don Quixote,"[29] he retorted that he could abandon the form, but not the content. Instead, he hoped the poem would last in the memory of the German people until a better one was written which expressed the same conviction in perfect form.[30]

A decade and a half later, Richard Wagner satirized the Germans in verse which parodied Arndt's poem:

Was ist des Deutschen Vaterland?
Ist's Nibelheim, Krähwinkelland,
Ist's wo der Jud' sich mausig macht,
Der Lump sich kühn ins Fäustchen lacht?
[...]
Wo dem, den sie zu Tod gehetzt,
Man Reden hält und Standbild setzt?
    etc. etc. etc.
O ja! O ja! Ja! Ja!
Sein Vaterland, da ist es, da! —[31]

What is the German's Fatherland?
Is it Nibel home or the land of the narrow-minded
Is it where the Jew gives himself airs,
The scoundrel laughs up his sleeve?
[...]
Where they give speeches and set monuments
To those they drove to their death?
    etc. etc. etc.
O yes! O yes! Yes! Yes!
His Fatherland, there it is, there! —

The lamentable expression of anti-Semitism found in Wagner's parody, not in Arndt's poem, is symptomatic of what lay ahead for Germany and

---

[28] *Das Volkslied: Was ist das Deutschen Vaterland. Würdigung desselben von Ferdinand Delbrück. Nebst Zuschrift an E. M. Arndt und Erwiderung von ihm* (Bonn: Marcus, 1846).

[29] *Ibid.*, see the conclusion.

[30] See also Steffens, *AW*, 12:184.

[31] Richard Wagner, *Gedichte* (Berlin: Grote, 1905): 34 and also footnote, 166.

her patriots. "Nationalism" was later to arouse latent German anti-Semitism, fostered over the decades by such stereotypes as the one found here. What separates the nationalist myth in the age of Napoleon from its ideological reworking in Wilhelminian Germany, not to mention the irrationality of Hitler's Third Reich, is, among other things, the emergence of anthropo-racial, selectionist and hereditaristic social theories which attempt to distinguish and then account for various racial characteristics. There is nothing inherently evil or morally indefensible about the observation and comparative study of different peoples; however, in Germany such investigations were seized upon to justify prejudice against certain minorities by passing value judgments on allegedly distinguishing traits. Nationalist ideology turned to barbarism in Germany when value judgments affixed to real and imagined racial differences became the basis for socio-political action and governmental policy. Anti-Semitism became part and parcel not of the myth of the German nation, but of nationalistic ideology as it evolved between two World Wars. Wagner's parody reflects the stereotypical thinking of his age and signals an ominous trend. It is also a reflection of his bitterness in 1863 over the regressive social policies of those petty princes who held mediocrity in high esteem and allowed musical genius to go begging.

Twenty-five years later, Friedrich Nietzsche quoted the lines:

So weit die deutsche Zunge klingt
Und Gott im Himmel Lieder singt

in the thirty-third of his "Sprüche und Pfeile" in *Twilight of the Idols* (*Götzendämmerung* [1888]) to illustrate the "simple mindedness" of the German who "imagines to himself even God singing songs." However, Nietzsche's misreading is possible only when a comma separates the first from the second line, which is not a part of Arndt's original. Hence the meaning of the line is "as far as the German tongue resounds and sings songs to God in heaven."

The criticism of Delbrück, Wagner and the misinterpretation by Nietzsche attest to Arndt's popularity, to his shortcomings and to the ways in which he was abused and misread. Praised and parodied, sung and satirized, Arndt's patriotic poetry attracted the interest and attention of Germans, great and small, throughout the nineteenth century. As the new century drew near, Arndt, along with his compatriots Fichte, Kleist and Körner, was about to be "re-examined" and "appreciated" in a more ideological context designed, as we shall see, to convert the myth of the nation into the national doctrine of Bismarck's Germany.

5
Reflections of the Myth: Presence and Absence (Schleiermacher, Süvern, Stägemann vs. Palm, Kotzebue and Iffland)

IN 1966 JERRY F. DAWSON OBSERVED A CORRELATION between Schleiermacher's sermon "A Nation's Duty in Time of War" (1813) and volumes two and three of Arndt's *Spirit of the Times*. Focusing on the remarkable resemblance between "one of the greatest national sermons ever preached" and Arndt's rhetoric, Dawson maintained that both Arndt and Schleiermacher jumped "to the same superficial conclusions about the possibility of a national state." He also called attention to Arndt's efforts at enlisting the theologian as an undercover agent for military headquarters at Königsberg in 1813.[1] However, the affinities between Arndt's propaganda and Schleiermacher's preaching extend beyond individual sermons and specific rhetorical patterns. Friedrich Schleiermacher made the same progression in his social thinking from an "individualistic" position to the activists' brand of nationalism. After moving to Berlin in 1807, he preached the gospel according to the reform party, as his efforts in support of national education endeared him to Stein. Moreover, as Schleiermacher politicized the pulpit in Berlin, his colleague on the National Education Reform committee at Königsberg, Johann Süvern, published poems exalting their party's leader. Another literary ally, Friedrich Stägemann, worked the Prussian myth as advocated by Fichte, Schleiermacher, Arndt and Kleist into a series of popular *War Songs* composed between 1807 and 1813. There were also anti-Napoleon writers who did not use the activists' literary blueprint. The anonymous author of the pamphlet *Germany in Her Low Abasement*, printed by the book dealer Johann Philipp Palm, did not work for the activists, nor did the popular

---

[1] Jerry F. Dawson [Chapter IV, Note 10], 99–116.

playwrights August Kotzebue and A. W. Iffland. Accordingly, as we shall see, their literary productions exhibit little structural congruity with the compositions of the party's myth-makers.

Initially Friedrich Schleiermacher voiced an "individualistic" political attitude similar to that of Fichte, Kleist and Arndt in their early works. In his *Speeches on Religion* (*Über die Religion*) of 1799, for example, he chastised his listeners for making "household gods" (*Hausgötter*) of "humanity and Fatherland," leaving no room for an individual concept of eternity.[2] He demanded that the church be relieved of its secular educational activities, which had resulted in state supervision of various ecclesiastical affairs, because, he argued, once the government assumed those responsibilities, the church would be free from state controls.[3] In the third of his *Soliloquies* (*Monologen*) in 1800, he stated categorically that love of Fatherland was not just demeaning, but an exercise in egotism. Representing the state as a necessary evil, an unavoidable restriction, like a huge machine designed to hide individual infirmities and render them harmless, he insists that freedom is the original condition, the initial and innermost sentiment. Everywhere, however, Germans find a limiting mechanism instead of a liberating process of education. Concerning the state, he remarks: "What there is of a spiritual community is degraded in the service of worldly interests." He asks Prussian political leaders bitterly, "Where is that power, which helps man attain the highest unfolding of existence, that consciousness of being a part of the nation's spirit, which each individual should have?" His answer is to look away from the social complex and group solutions toward one's own mental powers and inner strength.[4] Less than a decade later, Schleiermacher was to completely reverse this position as he became an ardent supporter of the political goals advocated by Stein and his faction.

Because of his desire for ecclesiastical reform, Schleiermacher attracted the attention of the reformers before the defeat at Jena. For this reason, the king refused to release him from Prussian service when he was called to Würzburg; instead Frederick William III appointed him university lecturer (*außerordentlicher Professor*) at Halle (May 6, 1804). Three years later, however, when the university city was lost to the Prussian crown after the Tilsit treaty, Schleiermacher was suspended from office. He continued

---

[2] *Friedrich Schleiermachers Sämtliche Werke*, ed. Georg Reimer (Berlin: Reimer, 1834–1864), *Zur Theologie I*: "Über die Religion, Reden an die Gebildeten unter ihren Verächtern," see the first speech entitled "Apologie."

[3] *Ibid.*, 374f.; see also 199f.

[4] See Friedrich Schleiermacher, *Monologen*, ed. Carl Schwarz (Leipzig: Brockhaus, 1869), 11f., 15, 47.

to preach at Halle until the end of the year, moving to Berlin in December 1807, where his homilies soon became more nationalistic. A comparison of his earlier sermons with those presented after he settled in Berlin points out the major differences.

On the last Sunday in 1806, Schleiermacher preached on the theme: "That recent times are no worse than former days."[5] Despite references to political institutions, the discourse remains intimate and "individualistic." He emphasizes the advantages of living in Prussia before the catastrophe at Jena, describing at length the inner tranquility attainable in the Prussian state. According to Schleiermacher, the aggregate fostered self-realization in one's chosen profession through wise laws, custom and tradition. His talk focuses on internal fortitude in the midst of chaos and calamity. All that has befallen Prussia, he maintains, should motivate each citizen to develop within himself a richer spiritual life. There is little in this sermon which reflects the Prussian myth of German nationalism.

His most famous exhortation of the period, "What we should and should not fear," is marked by the same intimacy and introspection.[6] Presented on New Year's Day, 1807, this sermon brought strength and encouragement to Baron vom Stein, who remembered it two years later as he hurried to safety across the Prussian border.[7] Schleiermacher argues that fear is worse than any loss, even worse than death. "Whoever fails to follow the voice of his heart out of fear, and instead suppresses his inner vital actions, will gradually lose even the ability to act; he will lose the most beautiful part of his life to an impassivity which grows with that fear, until he takes part in nothing other than his own, completely impoverished and shameful existence." The fearless Will, on the other hand, elevates the individual above and beyond fate; it makes him courageous and happy, diligent and undaunted, leading to inner satisfaction. Here again we detect a decidedly inward direction in Schleiermacher's counsel.

After the move to Berlin, however, his sermons begin to resemble Fichte's *Addresses*. As we have seen, the philosopher had requested help from the clergy in dispelling the false notions spread by the "old" religion, which had brought calamity upon Germany. As if in response, Schleiermacher echoes the activists' myth proclaimed in the "Addresses." In his opening remarks, Fichte had announced the dissolution of "the old order," and had declared Frederick the Great's political system destroyed and gone forever. Schleiermacher rephrased these thoughts in a sermon

---

[5] *Sämtliche Werke*, Section II: *Literarischer Nachlaß. Predigten* (1843) 1:268.

[6] *Ibid.*, 277f.

[7] See Wilhelm Dilthey, *Leben Schleiermachers*, ed. Hermann Mulert (Berlin: de Gruyter, 1922) 1:839f.

delivered on January 24, 1808, entitled "On the proper reverence of native greatness from an earlier time." His starting point is the esteem in which Frederick is held by contemporaries. "As we can readily see," the theologian asserts, "the greatness we enjoyed has disappeared from our midst once again."[8] Schleiermacher tells his congregation not to regard Frederick as the king who could have saved them: his time was fulfilled; it is now past and must be forgotten. Instead of looking to any single hero for deliverance, the people must turn to each other, to "the national group."[9] Prussia cannot go back to past institutions and to the old ways; everything gradually emerging from Prussian ruins is taking on a new form. The preacher then begins his argument in favor of proposals made by the reform party at virtually the same time to cabinet ministers at Königsberg.

"Our former condition," observes Schleiermacher, "was characterized by gross inequities among the state's components and members."[10] Pointing out that national harmony is a natural consequence of a united understanding and of united powers, he pleads for sacrifices from all the citizenry. The unfolding of the individual's existence is dependent upon the development of a "true sense of public spirit (*wahrer Gemeinsinn*)." "The business of our civic rebirth" is the order of the day. Schleiermacher predicates the worth of the individual on "the measure of his obedience and loyalty and by his activity for the whole." He no longer seeks to reinforce the positive traits of the individual's disposition, but directs the listener instead to the superpersonal strength in the national group. In his conclusion, he states that the German people, united by language, custom and heritage, will build a new national edifice "worthy of our ancestors."[11] With these words, Schleiermacher forsakes the theological path of rugged individualism and inner resourcefulness and turns down the road to Prussian myth-making.[12]

Later in 1808 he reworked an earlier text entitled "How much it increases the dignity of man, when he relies with his whole heart on those civic institutions to which he belongs." From the outset, he, like Fichte, criticizes the lack of public spirit in his listeners. "It is an evil," he main-

---

[8] Schleiermacher, *Predigten*, 355.

[9] *Ibid.*, 356.

[10] *Ibid.*, 361.

[11] *Ibid.*, 357, 365, 370.

[12] Schleiermacher's views on language are revealed most succinctly in his review of Johann Friedrich Zöllner's *Ideas on National Education* (1804); see Jerry F. Dawson [Chapter IV, Note 10], 77f.

tains, "that even in the best circles a mode of thinking prevails within which no real anxiety for public affairs and no ardent participation in the fate of the community can come into being."[13] In contrast to his earlier statements, he takes a decidedly negative view of cosmopolitanism, recommending instead strict devotion and zealous service to the Fatherland. Thus with each passing Sunday, the sermons of the pastor at Berlin's Trinity Church relied more and more on the mythic structure built by the philosopher from Lausitz.

The individual components of the socio-political myth fostered by Fichte, adopted for the stage by Kleist and popularized by Arndt reappear everywhere in Schleiermacher's sermons between late 1808 and the outbreak of the War of Liberation in 1813. His chief contribution to the myth is the inclusion of New Testament symbolism and Biblical allusions. During these five years, Schleiermacher superimposed a theological configuration upon the previously secular metaphysical context of the myth. Fichte's social vision of a liberated, united and "nationally" educated Germany emerges in these sermons as a sacred Messianic crusade. By 1812, for example, the theologian represents the myth in a hallowed Christian metaphor: addressing the question, "How we should use the time between major events," Schleiermacher likens the national evolution of the German people to the transfiguration of Christ. In this sermon the German people are equated with the apostles; the state is placed on a par with Jesus. As the disciples observed the transfiguration, so can the German people behold their own transformation into a nation-state.[14] Those who will have the opportunity to contribute to the establishment of "his" kingdom — Christ's in heaven and the German state on earth — are lauded in advance, and the congregation is instructed to pray, love and make use of each member's talents for the nation's fortification. In delineating national character ("unsere Sinnesart"), he outlines the individual's obligations to the state and refers to the language bond. He concludes by asking his parishioners to busy themselves in perfecting German potentials (*Deutschtum*) "before we lose those traits in which we readily perceive the image of God and our own nation."[15]

---

[13] According to Reimer's introductory note, this sermon represents the revised text of a sermon planned in 1806 for Halle, but never preached. However, Schleiermacher seldom wrote down any of his sermons and reconstructed them from memory for publication. In theme, tone, purpose and (aggressive) rhetoric, this sermon deviates so markedly from any extant homily preached before Tilsit that Reimer's dating becomes suspect. It is much more likely that this sermon was prepared from very succinct notes (jotted down in 1806 perhaps) and thoroughly revised in 1808 to conform with activists' goals.

[14] Schleiermacher, *Predigten*, 464.

[15] *Ibid.*, 476–470.

Schleiermacher's association with Fichte was marred by polemics. In the second and third "meditation" in his *Soliloquies*, for example, he had attacked Kant and Fichte because an absolute religious background to morality was lacking in their philosophy. Especially the Fichtean *Ich* with its supreme individualism appeared to have dispensed with a religious environment altogether. Yet because Schleiermacher's political thinking was shaped to a marked degree by the activists, he focused on the same problems Fichte had dealt with. Despite his break with Fichte and the Romantic poets, the theologian could not deny the widening of his horizons owing to their influences.[16] Fichte taught him to abandon casual and mechanistic socio-philosophical systems and to think "organically and dialectically."[17] The social postulates of both men derive from a bio-organismic theory of society. However, Fichte attacked France out of a desire to preserve the German nation; Schleiermacher proceeded from what he perceived as the spirit of Protestantism, arguing against a union of pope and emperor.

Although their relationship suffered from personal disagreements, both Fichte and Schleiermacher labored to create and disseminate an incisive nationalistic myth. This is particularly evident in the evolution of Schleiermacher's views on national education. Before 1806, he had little to say about public instruction[18] and had argued against church schools only because they led to state interference in ecclesiastical affairs. After moving to Berlin, however, his sermons abound in references to a process of national education devised to sustain the learner's intrinsic German potentials (*Deutschtum*). This concern for a program of national tutelage gained him the favor of the Prussian minister of state.

Schleiermacher's efforts to promote the myth coincide with his political activities in 1807/1808. Soon after settling in Berlin, he was approached by Lieutenant Baersch, the editor of the *People's Friend* (*Der Volksfreund*), who asked him to join the "Moral and Scientific Union" (*Tugendbund*). Almost ten years later, he would claim, in his response to the denunciation of this organization by Privy Councilor Theodor Schmalz, that he had refused to join such a group because he regarded affiliation with politically active associations "undignified."[19] Nonetheless, he soon became active in two clubs closely aligned with the "Moral and

---

[16] Wilhelm Dilthey, [Note 7], 36.

[17] *Ibid.*, 265, 285–288.

[18] Jerry F. Dawson [Chapter IV, Note 10], 77f.

[19] "An den Geheimrat," *Schleiermachers Sämtliche Werke* 9:655–665; see also John R. Seely [Chapter II, Note 27], 2:79–89 and Jerry F. Dawson, 69.

Scientific Union": he served as a courier for the "Charlottenburg Club" and was energetic in the service of the "Reading and Shooting Society."

The membership of the Charlottenburg Club presided over by Count Adolf von Chasot, who maintained close ties with the Königsberg triumvirate, included Johann Albrecht Eichhorn, an assistant supreme court justice and latter-day (1840) Prussian Minister of State!; Johann Reil, a Professor of Medicine at Halle and Berlin; General Hermann von Boyen, the Minister of War, and an officer named Hirschfeld. Because of the risks involved in meeting secretly, the club did not keep records. Schleiermacher did not know the names of all the members, nor how many belonged to the group in total.[20] This para-military organization was the Berlin branch of the activist faction constituted as a committee for planning a north German insurrection in 1808 or 1809 in concert with both the projected landing of British troops and an Austrian campaign in the south. Gneisenau, Scharnhorst and Stein controlled its movements; it maintained direct ties with Canning and was funded not only by the Foreign Office directly but also with British money delivered by Prussian officers dispatched from Königsberg.[21]

The Reading Society whose constituents included the more literary-oriented members of the Charlottenburg Club met irregularly in the house of the publisher, Georg Reimer, where the literary manipulation of public opinion was planned. It was at a meeting here in 1809 that Schleiermacher met Ernst Moritz Arndt, who had fled from Rügen and taken refuge in Reimer's home. In his Reimer-necrology, Arndt describes the target practice, paramilitary preparations and some of the members: Schleiermacher, Eichhorn, Cornelius and Niebuhr.[22]

Schleiermacher makes only veiled references to the operations of these groups in the correspondence with his fiancée, Henriette von Willich. He assures her on August 18, 1808, for example, that she need not worry about his covert political activities because "there is no lack of moderation and caution on my part, nor on the part of those who regulate my specific

---

[20] A membership list can be reconstructed from the following sources: E. Müsebeck, *Ernst Moritz Arndt. Ein Lebensbild* (Gotha: Perthes, 1914), 266–269, Heinrich Steffens, *Was ich erlebte* 6:153–234; *Schleiermachers Sämtliche Werke* 9:645–666; *Diltheys Gesammelte Schriften* 12:23ff.; John R. Seely [Chapter II, Note 27], 2:89f.

[21] Cf. Wilhelm Dilthey, "Schleiermachers politische Gesinnung und Wirksamkeit," *Gesammelte Schriften* 12:26.

[22] Steffens, *AW* 12:91; see also Alfred G. Pundt, *Arndt and the Nationalist Awakening in Germany* [Chapter IV, Note 2], 87; Jerry F. Dawson [Chapter IV, Note 10], 115. Varnhagen speaks of "Reimer's circle" (*Reimer Kreis*); see *Denkwürdigkeiten* [Chapter III, Note 95], 3:11.

tasks."[23] This statement reveals that Schleiermacher's activity was directed not solely by his own conscience, but rather by the needs of the faction he served.

During this period Schleiermacher served as a courier: from August 25 to September 22 (or 23), 1808 he embarked upon a secret mission to Königsberg, where he gathered information regarding Frederick William's meeting in August with Czar Alexander. He was to ascertain what preparations were being made for war against France and to consult with Stein, Gneisenau and Scharnhorst, who were convinced that another major campaign against Bonaparte was unavoidable. They, in turn, urged the king to mobilize the Prussian army, and assured Schleiermacher that the Charlottenburg Club was to play a significant role in a popular uprising. The letters of the theologian, turned espionage agent, to members of the Charlottenburg Club leave no doubt that England ("Freunde über See") was supporting with pound Sterling the north German insurrectionist movement, including the secretive paramilitary groups.[24]

After his meeting with the Czar, however, Frederick William decided not to wage war. The Charlottenburg Club, greatly distressed at the monarch's rejection of the triumvirate's plans for an offensive, sent Schleiermacher to Dessau in October 1808. Here he met with Steffens and Blanc in a plot to incite students at Halle to riot once the insurrection, planned at Königsberg, got underway in Hesse, Kassel and Magdeburg.[25] At Dessau, Schleiermacher also conferred both with Georg Reimer and the latter day founder of the "Black Raiders" guerrilla squadron, Major Leo von Lützow, as Bonaparte and the Czar made plans at nearby Erfurt. Steffens suggests that they also went to Dessau in order to thwart an attempt to assassinate Napoleon. Concocted by two Prussian officers and reported to the club, the scheme was to slay the emperor when he rode across the field at Auerstedt on the first anniversary of the battle. Schleiermacher and his friends feared that Prince Wilhelm, the king's brother, might be killed instead, thereby dealing the insurrectionists a setback. According to Steffens's account, Schleiermacher and his friends

---

[23] *Aus Schleiermachers Leben. In Briefen*, ed. Georg Reimer (Berlin: Perthes, 1858–1863) 2:125f.; Reimer edited volumes 1 and 2, Ludwig Jonas, vol. 3 and Jonas and Wilhelm Dilthey, vol. 4.

[24] These letters were decoded and published by Wilhelm Dilthey in his articles for the *Preußische Jahrbücher* 10 (September 1862):261–267, reprinted with notes in *Aus Schleiermachers Leben. In Briefen* [Note 23], 4:158–168, 171f.

[25] Steffens, *Was ich erlebte* [Chapter 3, Note 96], 6:173ff.

were unable to intercede; the officers' plan was frustrated nonetheless when Czar Alexander crossed into the projected line of fire.[26]

With the arrival of Schill's forces in Berlin, the club curtailed its activities because, according to Schleiermacher, "one cannot and must not encroach upon the government's prerogatives."[27] However, the watchful eyes of French agents had not failed to detect Schleiermacher's duplicity. It is also possible that he was denounced to French officials by German opponents of the reform party. On November 27, 1808, together with Provost Hanstein, he was brought to Marshall Davout's headquarters where he received a stern warning. French authorities listed him thenceforth as a "hothead" and "troublemaker."[28] With this, his undercover work abated.

From the pulpit of Trinity Church, however, he continued to preach the myth. He also corresponded with Baron Stein. An undated letter [summer?] of 1811 confirms that he had been asked not to communicate with Stein directly; but at this point he felt compelled to inform the departed minister that Hardenberg and other top cabinet members were abusing Stein's good name, ignoring his insights and wrecking his plans. In the conclusion, he offers the former minister of state his services once again as a secret agent.[29] This letter attests not only to the theologian's continued activism despite the admonition of Marshall Davout but also to the mounting opposition to Stein's initiatives coming from Hardenberg and other statesmen. We will recall that at this very time, Kleist had approached Hardenberg with regard to payments for the political propaganda he had produced. The circumstances described by Schleiermacher made it imperative for Gruner to avoid interceding on Kleist's behalf. In his answer, Stein called upon Schleiermacher to help counteract dissension by helping to mold public opinion along more positive lines.[30] Having been detected, however, Schleiermacher was of little use to the activists as an undercover agent. As early as 1808 he had confided to his fi-

---

[26] *Was ich erlebte* 6:173.

[27] As quoted by Dilthey, "Schleiermachers politische Gesinnung und Wirksamkeit," *GS* 12:34.

[28] See Dilthey, *GS* 12:32. The mild punishment meted out to Schleiermacher and Hanstein contradicts the image of the "cruel and tyrannical" Davout found in the third volume of Arndt's *Geist der Zeit*; see *Arndts Werke* 7:24. Later Arndt admitted that his portrait of Davout was exaggerated.

[29] *Stein* 3:536f.

[30] *Stein* 3:594f.

ancée that his usefulness was rapidly ending.[31] Nevertheless, his covert intelligence gathering activities and his Sunday sermons combined to make him the most renowned political preacher in German history.

When Stein decided to reorganize the Prussian school system, he appointed Schleiermacher to a committee studying reorganization. Fichte, Nicolovius and Wilhelm von Humboldt were also members of this task force. Here Schleiermacher worked together with Johann Wilhelm Süvern. It is generally believed that Humboldt was the key figure in Stein's educational reforms.[32] This is, however, incorrect. Humboldt's immediate superior was the minister of the interior, Count Karl Friedrich zu Dohna; but he was in reality responsible directly to the king. This is confirmed in Humboldt's report of December 1, 1809 to Frederick William III, which also points up some of the differences between Stein's and his own ideas on national education.[33] To be sure, Stein was favorably disposed to Humboldt when it came to the key position on the Education Committee; however, at that time, Humboldt was not interested.[34]

Contrary to Stein's thinking, Humboldt agreed with Frederick William that nationalism should not be taught in the public schools. Society could be improved only by self-education. The government should not hinder citizens from developing their personalities through cultural enlightenment; neither should it seek to indoctrinate them. According to Humboldt, the government should interfere in the lives of private citizens as little as possible. The idea of German unification left him cold, for he feared that the unique characteristics of each state would be lost if Germany were united.[35] Moreover, in a letter to Stein from Vienna (October 18, 1810), Humboldt laments never having worked with Stein and expresses his hope of fruitful cooperation in the future.[36] Stein's right-hand man on the Education Reform Committee was not Humboldt, but Johann Wilhelm Süvern. Humboldt, with whom Süvern had an excellent working relation-

---

[31] *Aus Schleiermachers Leben. In Briefen* [Note 23], 2:175f.

[32] See, for example, Jerry F. Dawson [Chapter IV, Note 10], 78f. For a more detailed perspective, see Paul N. Sweet, *Wilhelm von Humboldt. A Biography* (Columbus: Ohio State University Press, [Vol. 1] 1978, [Vol. 2] 1980).

[33] See *Denkschrift Wilhelm von Humboldts*. December 1, 1809 in *Wilhelm von Humboldts Gesammelte Schriften*, ed. Albert Leitzmann and Bruno Gebhardt (Berlin: Preußische Akademie 1903–1936) 1:199–234.

[34] See Sack's letter to Stein (January 28, 1809) in *Stein* 3:36 (also note 8).

[35] *The Spheres and Duties of Government*, 67; see also Reinhold Aris [Chapter II, Note 28], 137f., 145, 162.

[36] *Stein* 3:414.

ship, supervised both his and Schleiermacher's activities on the committee.

Little has been written about Süvern. In 1860 W. A. Passow drafted a brief commemorative.[37] Wilhelm Dilthey dedicated one of the lengthier articles in the *Allgemeine Deutsche Biographie* to Süvern. In 1914 Richard Wagner (from Rostock) traced the relationship between Fichte and Süvern in a dissertation.[38] From these sources, we can piece together the following portrait: before the Battle at Jena, Süvern was the director of the Gymnasium at Elbing. In 1806 he was appointed Professor of Classical Literature at Königsberg, where his colloquium on the "History of Europe since Charlemagne" held in the winter semester 1807 won him the acclaim of Stein's faction. Thereupon Süvern's lectures were printed and circulated at the court; Stein warmly recommended them to the royal family.[39] In December 1808, Stein arranged for Süvern's appointment to the Education Reform Committee in the education department (ministry of the interior) together with Fichte, Süvern's former teacher at Jena, who had introduced him to the theories of Pestalozzi. Süvern's task was to reform the elementary school system according to those theories, which had made a very favorable impression on Stein.

As they worked together in Königsberg and Berlin, Fichte wrote to his wife that Süvern's appointment was the only one about which he was completely happy.[40] During Süvern's colloquium in Königsberg, Fichte delivered his *Addresses* in Berlin. As counselor to the education department, Süvern did his utmost to realize the program of national instruction which Fichte had outlined. When Stein entrusted him with drafting a "Proclamation for the Citizens of Prussia" in October 1808, Süvern tried to transform Fichte's proposals into reality in the name of the king by writing that the process of national instruction was designed to educated "youth to a mighty race in which the noble purpose of the state will endure and develop."[41] Throughout this proclamation, Süvern's description of the reforms reflects the tenets of Fichte's (and Stein's) social vision.

---

[37] W. A. Passow, *Zur Erinnerung an J. W. Süvern* (Thorn, 1860).

[38] Richard Wagner, *Die Beziehungen Fichtes zu Süvern und die Entsendung der preußischen Eleven nach Yverdon* (Diss. Erlangen, 1914).

[39] See the Princess Wilhelm of Prussia's letter to Stein of December 14, 1810 in *Stein* 3:438.

[40] *Fichte Briefwechsel* [Chapter 2, Note 25], 1:176.

[41] See "Entwurf einer 'Proklamation an sämtliche Bewohner des preußischen Staates' " (October 21, 1808) in *Stein* 2/2:902–905.

Süvern's efforts at poetic creativity are as important as his attempt at legislating the Fichtean myth into political reality. However, in this regard he enjoys a dubious distinction among the collaborators: he published two poems which greatly endangered the literary endeavor and might have led to its complete public disclosure. A journalist in Berlin who read these lyrics in the "Königsberg Newspaper" (*Königsberger Zeitung*) came dangerously close to unmasking the covert operation.

News about the interception of a letter from Stein to Prince Wittgenstein by French agents arrived in Königsberg in September 1808. Stein's impending dismissal hurled the activists into turmoil. On October 14, Süvern drafted a petition signed by Scharnhorst, Gneisenau, Nicolovius, Grolmann, Röckner and himself in defense of the minister of state and against the ratification of the Paris convention, which would have enlarged Napoleon's power in Prussia.[42] Meanwhile Count Dohna circulated a petition among the people in East Prussia requesting Stein's retention. The Court Party (*Hofpartei*) and other anti-reform factions, recognizing an excellent opportunity to rid themselves of the statesmen responsible for the loss of their rights and privileges, protested such "encroachment on the king's prerogatives." With a reference to parallel developments during the French Revolution, they asked the monarch to prohibit the activists from "manipulating the spirit of the people any way they care to."[43]

As the petition circulated, Süvern published the following poem[44] in the Königsberg newspaper:

> Fest, Edler steh! ein Fels, an dem in grausen Wettern
> Des Sturmes Grimm vertobt, der Wogen Drang sich bricht.
> Empörtes Element umschlag' ihn rings — zerschmettern,
> Verrücken mag es ihn, den Ur-Granit-Stein, nicht!
> Bleib unser Hort! Geführt von Dir, mit Dir verbündet,
> Hofft noch der Biedermann, hegt unverzagten Mut!
> Und unerschüttert steht, unwandelbar gegründet
> Der Bau, der fest auf Dir, dem starken Grundstein ruht!
> Wer Dich besitzt ist reich, ist sicher in Gefahren
> Ein Schatz von Geist und Kraft, vereint in Dir, ist sein.
> O mög er sorgsam Dich, dem Volk zum Heil, bewahren,
> Dich, seines Diadems kostbarsten Edelstein.
>
> Stand fast, o noble one, a rock on which the raging
> Storms subside, the force of waves in turbulence break up.

---

[42] *Stein* 2/2:891–895.

[43] *Stein* 2/2:913–915.

[44] Reprinted in *Stein* 2/2:908.

Agitated elements surround him — they will not
Overwhelm or unsettle him, the arch-granite-Stone.
Remain our shield! led by you, allied with you,
The man of honor harbors dauntless courage!
And unshakable the immovably established building
Stands when it rests on you, the strong cornerstone;
Whoever has you, is rich, is safe in danger
A treasure of intellect and power united in you is his.
O may he carefully preserve you for the people's sake
You, his diadem's most precious noble stone.

Süvern's verse addresses itself to Baron Stein by means of the play on words involving "Stein." With this poem, the incautious Süvern sought to rally popular support not for the cause but for its chief exponent. Nor did Süvern stop here. On November 3, 1808 he published in the *Königsberg Newspaper* a "Folksong Addressed to the King" in which the minister is portrayed as a friend whom the throne urgently needs. Addressing God, the rhapsodist places "the friend" (Stein) on a par with the king — it is he who is removing the heavy burden from the people, thereby enabling the princes to sleep more peacefully.[45] Such ill advised digressions from the cause in defense of their embattled leader had grave consequences for the reform party.

On November 8, 1808 the *Vossische Zeitung* in Berlin reprinted the first poem and followed it with a stinging commentary. Mocking the contrived word play on the name Stein, the critic blasted this aggrandizement which elevated the minister of state to an idol (*Abgott*). "It (the poem) is the wretched clumsy work of an insane, inflated head," writes the commentator, "not unlike those, who have brought so much calamity upon our regent and our country."[46] The poem is then dismissed as the creation of a dreamer (*Schwärmer*) who must have an idol, to whom he can burn incense; eventually, however, the idol will destroy him. But the most devastating comment is reserved for the conclusion.

Claiming to have the best interests of the country at heart, the anonymous commentator admonishes his reader to respect those who dedicate their talent to fellow citizens, but to despise those who incite petty passions with their pens. To this latter group, he implies, belongs this idolizer of Stein, "whom we loathe as much as Gentz, Kotzebue and other men of their calibre, whose every line is paid with British pound Sterling."[47] This accusation reaches to the core of the collaboration between Prussian politi-

---

[45] *Stein* 2/2:918f.

[46] *Vossische Zeitung*, No. 134, 1808; see *Stein* 2/2:927.

[47] *Ibid.*

cians and men-of-letters. To be sure, Friedrich Gentz, who had formerly worked for Prussia, had taken service in Austria where he continued to receive British remuneration, and the journalist is wrong about Kotzebue, who was paid by the czar; yet the anonymous critic did touch upon one reason for the zeal of many collaborators: England was supplying Stein with money. With his verse, Süvern, the overzealous advocate, very nearly exposed the covert operation.

On November 15, 1808 the *Vossische Zeitung* published a second satirical article directed against Süvern's poetry. This time the *Folksong* came under attack. For the most part, the critic complains about the demagogy and the "system of leveling" (the writer's definition of "anarchy") expressed in the poem. Strong criticism is directed against the reform party's platform, which pits "the people against the nobility and the army."[48] Absent from the commentary is any reference to England as the financial source of the party's literature, which suggests that the journalist had suspected British complicity, but had no proof. Had he checked farther, he might have uncovered the intricate network of financial expediters in the British-Prussian operation, which Austrian intelligence agents in Prague uncovered three years later. The publication of the poems hurt the activists nonetheless. On November 22, 1808 Wittgenstein, who now refused to correspond with Stein, complained that the circulation of Süvern's poems in Königsberg and the ensuing castigation in the *Vossische Zeitung* were having serious repercussions abroad: the derision between political factions adversely affected Prussia's credibility in other countries.[49]

Another of the lesser known literary collaborators was the undersecretary of the Prussian treasury, Friedrich Stägemann (1763–1840), who joined the activists no later than 1808 and was named councilor of state (*Staatsrat*) in 1809. From 1806 to 1813, Stägemann produced approximately fifty poems, many of which appeared in Berlin and Königsberg newspapers; in April 1813 they were collected and published by Reimer under the title *Kriegsgesänge* (*War Songs*). For the most part, these "songs" were constructed along the lines of the Vendée propaganda as emended by Stein. Stägemann combined the three components characteristic of the myth-makers work with a complex system of references to Greek and Roman mythology. In a cumbersome apparatus of annotations, he explains these advertences, the meaning of his symbols and his poetic intentions.

---

[48] *Stein* 2/2:945.

[49] *Stein* 2/2:984.

The poems from 1806 to early 1807 bear little resemblance to the productivity of Stein's literary agents, indicating that the blueprint had not yet been circulated. However, in the ode, "After the Peace of Tilsit," dated Memel, 1807, the three structural units appear together with apostrophes to "Hermann's offspring," admonitions to neutrals and the faint-hearted, and a curse upon Bonaparte. Having called upon the muse to banish "unmanly melancholy," and to "fire up the fury" in his song, the poet envisions nymphs covered with hoarfrost drinking the "last breath of Germanic speech" and then shouting for joy at the impending feat-of-arms against Napoleon. The power of the Romans lies now in dead letters, but Germans, with spiritual aid from Chlodowich and his Germanic warriors, will band together to defeat the French. The lyrical persona then appears as a national educator, informing the people that Stein and Hardenberg, united, will show them the way to "eternal fame."[50] The three components marking the activists' literature are reassembled here in the midst of copious references to mythological gods, heroes and victories. Appropriately, the poet's intention, he claims, is to pay homage to Stein and his co-workers for Prussian reform.

The collected poems resound with variations on the three themes. Castigating the princes who have joined the Confederation of the Rhine, the poet emerges again as a national educator who warns the fatherland's renegades to heed the "wailing in unsettled times" and teaches them to "see the warning reflection of willful fire-raising." He undertakes the task because "the blessed shores of the Ilm no longer reverberate the German swan's melodic songs." This strained image stretches the language-bond argument to the breaking point, as the strophe ends with the personified *Teutona* struck dumb by "bloody steel."[51]

More important are the eight poems dedicated to Major von Schill and his squadron, in which the lyricist, in sharp contrast to Frederick William's denunciation, praises Schill as a hero and urges Germany to take up arms, join the valiant Britains and drive the invaders out. Far less complicated and with fewer allusions to the mythology of classical antiquity, these songs are addressed to all "German brothers," and reflect the reform party's position on Schill and the desirability of a north German insurrection. They concur with *Prinz Friedrich von Homburg* inasmuch as Kleist sought to vindicate the Major in his play and to Theodor Körner's poetry which, as we shall see, was intended to rally public opinion in favor of a guerrilla campaign similar to the war effort initiated by Schill.

---

[50] Friedrich Stägemann, *Kriegsgesänge aus den Jahren 1806–1813* (Berlin: Reimer, 1813), 24–27.

[51] *Ibid.*, 46.

As might be expected, Fichte had the highest praise for Stägemann's *War Songs*. When the collection appeared, the philosopher thanked the poet for absolving (*entsündigen*) those who had risen above the era's decadence. "Whoever belongs to that group," writes Fichte, "must thank you for having expressed his convictions in your poetic language . . . I include myself . . . Therefore, I thank you."[52] In contrast to his odes modeled after the lyric poet, Alchaeus of Mytilene (600 B.C.), which were directed to the educated upper class, his songs about Schill spoke to Germans in various walks of life. Coupled to his contributions in Kleist's *Berliner Abendblätter*, these songs of inspiration mark Stägemann as a literary agent for the reform party. His far-reaching correspondence with Nagler, Niebuhr, Theodor Schön, Kiesewetter, Adam Müller and especially Justus Gruner bears witness to his deep involvement with the clandestine activities of Stein and the activists.

Authors involved in the literary collaboration with Baron von Stein's faction can be distinguished from other anti-Napoleon writers of the period by the specific tripartite structure common to their works. In each major genre, the activists' myth of one German nation provided the foundation for the work of the collaborators. This structure is not found in the anti-French diatribes of those not in the service of the reform faction. In order to shows the structural differences, we shall examine the work of three anti-Napoleon German writers who, as we know from other sources, did not work for the reform party. The first is a pamphlet by an anonymous author written before the literary collaboration got underway; the second and third objects of scrutiny are plays by Kotzebue and Iffland.

In 1806 the Stein publishing house in Nuremberg, owned by Johann Philipp Palm, printed a 144-page pamphlet entitled: "Germany in its Low Abasement."[53] Neither the author's name, the publisher nor place of printing appeared on the title page. Palm forwarded a copy to the Stäge publishing house in Augsburg, which in turn sent it to a priest. This pamphlet fell into the hands of German-speaking French officers quartered in the clergyman's house, who, insisting that their honor had been offended, turned over the brochure to the French government. The ensuing investigation lead ultimately back to Palm. On August 25, 1806, the book dealer,

---

[52] *Briefe und Aktenstücke zur Geschichte Preußens unter Friedrich Wilhelm III* [Chapter III, Note 113], 1:302.

[53] *Deutschland in seiner tiefen Erniedrigung*, translation is that of Holtman, who does not discuss the pamphlet. Perhaps "Germany in her Deep Humiliation" might be closer to the original. See Robert B. Holtman, *Napoleonic Propaganda* (Baton Rouge: Louisiana State University Press, 1950).

who refused to name the author, was condemned to death for disseminating slander against Napoleon. Palm's execution by firing squad at Braunau was vividly described by Chaplain Thomas Pöschell, in two letters to Palm's widow, which were widely distributed in Germany, provoking an uproar against French brutality.

It was apparent to Germans that the courageous book-dealer had been a scapegoat whose fate was intended to set an example. The verdict against Palm states emphatically that authors, printers, and book distributors had engaged in leading south German citizens astray by calling for mutiny and revolution against France and for the assassination of French soldiers. Moreover, such book dealers incited the people to disobedience and neglect of duty towards Napoleon's puppet governments.[54] Henceforth the death penalty was ordered for all German writers and book dealers who spread libel against France.[55] Although it has been argued that this pamphlet was no worse than others written at this time,[56] we must examine its contents judiciously. The emperor's wrath was undoubtedly aroused by three invectives: the insults directed against the soldiers of the Grand Army, the repeated derision of Bonaparte's lineage and family, and the exultation because of England's forthcoming victory in her struggle with France. From this perspective, *Germany in her Low Abasement* represents the strongest expression of anti-Napoleon sentiment produced in Germany to fall into French hands before the battle of Jena.

The day of the French soldier, maintains the anonymous author, is spent in "gluttonous eating, animal-like drinking and raping women." Demanding the most elegantly prepared meals, he "hurries to his [German]

---

[54] For the text of the verdict against Palm, see *Deutschland in seiner tiefen Erniedrigung*, ed. Heinrich Meckens (Würzburg: Stubens, 1877): p. XVf.

[55] On August 5, 1806, Napoleon issued a demand for the exemplary punishment of German authors and distributors guilty of libel against France or himself. Specially named are the publishing houses of Kupfer in Vienna, Enrich in Linz and Stein in Nuremberg. In a letter to Talleyrand (same date), he points out that Nuremberg is responsible for the slander of Frenchmen in Germany. If the senate of this city, he maintains, does not have the responsible publishers arrested and punished for their libel, he will, before leaving Germany, punish the municipality in an exemplary manner. He also writes to Marshal Berthier, demanding the arrest of the responsible book dealers in Augsburg and their execution in twenty-four hours. He emphasized that these libels are not ordinary crimes, but incite the inhabitants against the French army and thus represent high treason; the authors and spreaders of such libels are guilty of murder and must be sentenced to death. See *Correspondence de Napoléon Ier*, ed. H. Plon and J. DuMaine (Paris: Henri Plon, 1869) 13:36–38. Noted hereafter as *Corr*. For a contemporary account of the impact of Palm's execution on public opinion in Germany, see Heinrich Steffens, *Was ich erlebte* [Chapter III, Note 96] 6:158ff.

[56] See, for example, Johannes Braun's argument in his article on Palm in the *Allgemeine Deutsche Biographie*.

quarters like a starved wolf." He is a wolf in human form, who shamefully abuses German women and particularly young girls. "Public opinion claims," he continues, "that the French soldier has degenerated from a civilized European to a ferocious cannibal."[57] Throughout the discourse the writer stresses the physical maltreatment to which German maidens must submit and the financial ruin brought to German households by "the burdens and unpleasantness caused by the most oppressing billeting of unpaid Frenchmen" (47). The pamphleteer heaps scorn and ridicule on all the Bonapartes: the marriage of Eugène de Beauharnais to the oldest daughter of the Bavarian king was necessary, "in order to transfuse the first noble blood into Bonaparte's dark family" (45f). Criticizing Germans for their lack of unity and determination to resist the "upstart," he argues that no one can witness in silence the moral, social, economic and cultural decline concomitant with the political humiliation of Germany.

The pamphlet also refers to the competition in the textile market between France and England, and emphasizes the benefits Germany would derive from trading with Britain rather than with France (41). The author defends the emperor of Austria and encourages his compatriots to support a pro-British, Austrian policy and to reject French domination. Napoleon's anonymous antagonist argues that Bonaparte's plans concerning Egypt and Malta have been frustrated by British naval superiority. Despite the author's pro-British bias and open hostility toward Bonaparte, his work bears virtually no structural affinity to the literature of the activist myth-makers which begins after the Treaty of Tilsit. Nevertheless, this pamphlet, which has been attributed at various times to Julius von Soden, Johann Konrad von Yelin and Johann Leuchs, rubbed salt in Napoleon's wounds and openly provoked retaliation.

Another detractor who worked outside the collaboration was the popular and prolific playwright, August Kotzebue, whose journal, *The Bee*, had been an early irritant to French policy-makers in Germany. However, in his stage productions of 1809 and 1810, Kotzebue carefully avoided serious political commentary. Instead he wrote such historical plays as *The Little Gypsy* (1809), set in sixteenth century Spain. Kotzebue's reluctance to deal with contemporary socio-political issues derives to some extent from the strict censorship to which his plays were subjected. He complained that each word of his *Needless Tribulations* (*Sorgen ohne Not*), banned from many German theaters in 1810, had been critically revised in order to pass a severe censorship.[58] In the same year, he re-worked a play by Holberg, *The Arabian Powder*, in which he aims a few barbs at contemporary "coffee

---

[57] *Deutschland in seiner tiefen Erniedrigung* [Note 54], 33–44.

[58] *Theater von August Kotzebue* (Leipzig & Vienna: Kummer & Klang, 1841) 26:134.

house politicians." When the swindler Taps remarks, for example, that he will always be able to make a living because there will always be playing cards and fools in the world who like to play, his co-conspirator Pack quickly adds: "with cards and maps."[59] But none of Kotzebue's stage productions contain the familiar structure of the nationalist myth.

The differences between Kotzebue's representations of patriotic sentiment and those of the Prussian myth-makers have gone largely undetected because critical inquiry over the past decades has focused less on his political activities than on the reasons for his contemporaneous popularity. Quoting from Adelbert von Chamisso's diary, which notes that by 1819 Kotzebue's renown had spread to such far away places as Hawaii, Gerhard Schulz has suggested that such widespread acceptance of Kotzebue's entertaining plays may have paved the way for a better understanding of the dramas in iambic verse by Lessing, Schiller and Goethe.[60] Harley U. Taylor chronicled the huge success Kotzebue's plays enjoyed in New York and Philadelphia from 1798 to 1805; A. Denis traced the rise and fall of Kotzebue's "literary fortune" in France.[61] The causes for such prominence have been discovered both in the social conditions of the time and in genre manipulation. According to Leif Albertsen, the playwright's reputation resulted from his uncanny ability to portray in a de-sensitized context those socio-economic ambitions of the emerging bourgeoisie hampered by the middle class moral code.[62] Doris Maurer, on the other hand, argued that Kotzebue's widespread acclaim was attributable to his clever manipulation of key elements common to playwriting aimed at amusing and entertaining rather than edifying the audience.[63] One result of this focus on Kotzebue's world-wide fame and the reasons for it is the current scholarly quest for instances of his influence on equal and greater talents. The persistence of Kotzebue's influence was proven

---

[59] *Ibid.*, 247.

[60] Gerhard Schulz, *Die deutsche Literatur zwischen Französischer Revolution und Restauration*. Erster Teil. 1789–1806. (Geschichte der deutschen Literatur, ed. Helmut de Boor und Richard Newald [Munich: Beck, 1983] vol. 7/1:478.) See the discussion of Kotzebue, 472–478 and Iffland, 469–472.

[61] Harley U. Taylor, "The Dramas of August von Kotzebue on the New York and Philadelphia Stages from 1798 to 1805," *West Virginia University Philological Papers* 23 (1977): 47–58; A. Denis, "La fortune littéraire et théâtrale de Kotzebue en France," see *Dissertation Abstracts International* 38 (1978): 3125C.

[62] Leif Ludwig Albertsen, "Internationaler Zeitfaktor Kotzebue: Trivialisierung oder sinnvolle Entliterarisierung und Entmoralisierung des strebenden Bürgers im Frühliberalismus?" *Sprachkunst* 9 (1978): 220–240.

[63] Doris Maurer, *August von Kotzebue. Ursachen seines Erfolges: Konstante Elemente der unterhaltenden Dramatik* (Bonn: Bouvier, 1979).

recently when situations and dialogues from *The Stranger* (*Menschenhaß und Reue* [1789]) were detected in Dickens's *David Copperfield* written more than six decades later (1849/50).[64] Such influence may have come about in a more roundabout way since it has also been shown recently that Kotzebue and Richard Brinsley Sheridan (1751–1816), a precursor of George Bernard Shaw, used similar techniques to entertain and amuse their respective audiences.[65] Parallels have also been drawn between Kotzebue and Nestroy[66] as well as between Kotzebue and Iffland, to whom we shall turn momentarily.

For the most part, any discussion of the political ramifications of Kotzebue's work has been limited to brief biographical sketches in familiar handbooks[67] without proceeding much beyond those generalities formulated by the literary historians of *fin de siècle* Germany. Nevertheless, Kotzebue's fame and fortune as a playwright in Germany rest on his talent not only for de-sensitizing current issues plaguing middle class conscience but also for satirizing those forces and personalities tending to destabilize the socio-political status quo in the smaller German states. His dominance of the German stage, even in Weimar under Goethe's direction, indicates that bourgeois class-consciousness had not yet reached the point of open rebellion against aristocratic rulers nor of widespread insistence on German unification. The favorable reception afforded Kotzebue suggests instead that he, in the minds of his viewers, perceived accurately the more ludicrous aspects of grandiose plans for Germany's future, whether dictated by Napoleon or heralded by Prussian myth-makers, and cleverly mocked them by articulating through his characters the same suspicions, doubts and, sometimes, outright hostility to certain proposals, which troubled his non-Prdussian, middle class audiences. Determining whose interests his plays served and thereby fixing Kotzebue's place on the ideological spectrum is but one path of inquiry; another leads to those reflections of thought patterns, attitudes and social aspirations already established as part of the viewer's mindset. Kotzebue's popularity stems, at least in part, from his knack for presenting characters on the German stage

---

[64] Stanley Friedman, "Kotzebue's *The Stranger* in *David Copperfield*," *Dickens Studies Newsletter* 9 (1978): 49–50.

[65] Martin Brinkhorst, "Kotzebue und Sheridan: Erfolgsstrategien von 1799" *Orbis Litteraum* 34 (1979): 17–32.

[66] Peter Pütz, "Zwei Krähwinkeliaden 1802/1848. Kotzebue: *Die deutschen Kleinstädter*. Nestroy: *Freiheit in Krähwinkel*," *Die deutsche Komödie: Vom Mittelalter bis zur Gegenwart*, ed. Walter Hinck (Düsseldorf: Bagel, 1977): 175–194.

[67] Fritjof Stock, "August von Kotzebue," *Deutsche Dichter des 18. Jahrhunderts*, ed. Benno von Wiese (Berlin: Schmitt, 1977): 958–971.

who express the political views, doubts and critical opinions of the contemporary political scene held by audiences outside of Prussia. When those convictions changed, when later in the century the reservations about social and political reforms articulated by the characters were no longer shared by the public in the smaller German states, when optimism replaced trepidation, Kotzebue's popularity declined. From this perspective, he represents a primary source for helping to determine which beliefs were widely held after 1813/14 and which were rejected during the *Restauration*.

It has gone undetected that Kotzebue's work took a new direction once Stein left Prague for the more friendly environs of St. Petersburg. On August 21, 1812 Kotzebue offers the statesman living in exile the service of his pen and, without waiting for an answer, begins writing political satire.[68] In 1813 he produced "The Revenge of Hate and Love" in five acts — a play set against the background of the Spanish insurrection. The theme had been recommended to poets by Stein on several occasions. Kotzebue also wrote "The Return of the Volunteer or the Patriotic Oath" in which three wealthy and beautiful women take an oath to marry only a soldier crippled in battle. Kotzebue satirizes such foolish and meaningless outbursts of momentary patriotism by having the ladies rationalize in typical bourgeois fashion their decision to break their oath. Despite their well-intentioned, but shallow pledge, each marries her suitor as he returns unscathed from battle. The ironic twist comes when Luise, who refused to take such an oath and was ridiculed for her refusal, falls in love with Fritz Webb, the only wounded veteran among the characters. In this little play, Kotzebue draws attention to the superficial attitudes regarding the war effort; he mocks the hypocrisy of those who declare an initial willingness to sacrifice for the good of the nation. He also shows that things tend to return to "normal," that is, to the way they were before the war, after the enemy is driven out. His play reflects in this way the hypocritical and ambiguous position of the bourgeoisie regarding the struggle against Napoleon.

Kotzebue's *Hermann and Thusnelda* was also staged in 1813. Certain motives are reminiscent of Kleist's play of 1808/1809: the Romans completely misunderstand German traditions and conceptualizations; they kill children and manhandle German women. Hermann and Varus speak monologues similar to those of Kleist's counterparts. When Varus realizes, for example, that he is outnumbered and surrounded in the forest, he says:

Schon waren sie gewöhnt an unser Joch,

---

[68] *Stein* 3:725.

> Und prangten gern mit röm'schen Ehrenzeichen,
> Und manche wähnten uns von höherer Abkunft,
> Des röm'schen Adler Macht unüberwindlich!
> Woher dies kühn erwachte Selbstgefühl?
> Warum von unsern Fahnen wich der Schrecken?
> Sie wagen es, mich drohend zu umringen,
> Sie sperren mir des Waldes Felsenpfade —
> Ha, Jupiter! sind deine Donnerkeile
> Nicht uns're Waffen mehr? ist sie gefallen,
> Die Zauberbinde, die so fest wir knüpften?
> Muß ich, der Römer, vor Barbaren zittern?[69]

> They were already used to our yoke
> And liked to show off their Roman medals,
> And many thought we were higher beings,
> Rome's eagle insurmountable,
> From whence this bold awakened confidence?
> Why does our flag no more spread terror?
> They dare to surround me menacingly
> They block the rocky path through the woods —
> Ha, Jupiter, are your thunderbolts no longer
> Our weapons? Has the magic blindfold fallen
> Which we had so tightly fastened?
> Must I, a Roman, tremble before barbarians?

These lines bear resemblance to Varus's monologue in the third act of Kleist's play. Likewise the motif of the blond German hair sent back as souvenirs to ladies in Rome occurs in both plays, also the symbol of the iron ring worn on the arm denoting German enslavement. Kotzebue and Kleist both employ impressed Germanic tribesmen as guides to lead the Romans to their death, and the mythic figure of the "Norn" plays a prophetic role in both plays.

In contrast to Kleist's Hermann, however, Kotzebue's figure lacks subtlety or persuasive arguments and is less cautious in his methods. Outraged by Varus's injustice and the harsh sentences meted out to his tribesmen, Hermann openly challenges Varus and is backed up by all the other German princes except Segest, another Cheruscan prince and Thusnelda's father. Kotzebue's Arminius is particularly appalled by Varus's unrelenting conscription of Germans into his mercenary army and states that the Cheruscan goal is only to be free. In Kotzebue's play "Weeping Germania" appears on the stage, Thusnelda is killed by Varus and the "Norn" allows Hermann, Marbod and their kinsmen a view of Thusnelda sitting among the fallen heroes in Walhalla.[70] The play was apparently in-

---

[69] *Theater von August Kotzebue* 39:138.

[70] Ibid., 149.

tended to win the favor of Baron Stein. Nevertheless, apart from certain common motives, images and, of course, characters, the structure of Kotzebue's three act "heroic opera," as it is subtitled, shows little structural congruity with Kleist's drama.

One of Kotzebue's later efforts includes a likeness of Napoleon in the figure of "Somebody Else." His *The Rivergod Niemen and Somebody Else* was presented at the theater in Reval as the Russians chased the last French soldiers across the Niemen River. But neither this "joyous play" (*Freudenspiel*), nor its "Seitenstück," *Somebody Else's Travel Adventures* shows any parallels to the writings of the Prussian collaborators. In the latter "heroic tragi-comedy" dedicated with irony to the "friend of truth, Mr. Moniteur in Paris," Napoleon (Somebody Else) and his Mamluke bodyguard scheme to save themselves and the Grand Army. Despite his last minute strategy and the many orders issued to "General Dumaret" — a veiled reference to the French General Charles Dumouriez (1739–1823) who had defected to the Austrian side in 1799 — which can no longer be carried out, Somebody Else is unable to save his army and takes flight to Paris. He also encounters the mythic Rübezahl, Libussa (the legendary queen of Bohemia), Gustavus Adolphus, the book dealer Johann Philipp Palm, Major von Schill and the Tyrolean patriot Andreas Hofer. The structure of the play is like that of the Barock station-drama: at each point, one of these characters reveals to "Somebody Else" the hopelessness of his life. This, as the play's popularity suggests, is what audiences wished to see in 1813/14. The conspicuous absence of pleas for a united Germany suggests that German nationalism was not yet dominant in the minds of the middle class everywhere in Germany. It was the historians of Bismarck's era, searching fervidly for earlier examples of nationalistic yearnings, who perceived a "spontaneous outpouring" of a "German spirit." Kotzebue's plays and the success they enjoyed imply that such was an exaggeration. The opposition to Napoleon did not necessarily go hand in hand with a desire for a single German nation once the wars of liberation ended.

Kotzebue's plays may share certain figures and symbols with the activists' literary supporters, but exhibit little structural affinity with their work. Before Stein moved to St. Petersburg his interests corresponded to those of England; therefore, Kotzebue, who worked for the czar could not write for him. Once such collaborators as Arndt, Count Chasot, Kleist's friend Ernst Pfuel and others set up shop in St. Petersburg under Stein's leadership and Czar Alexander's protection, Kotzebue was free to offer his services — as long as Stein and the czar saw eye to eye. But Stein espoused Russian foreign policy only when it corresponded to British interests and, for this reason, had little use for Kotzebue and declined his offer.[71] As a result, the playwright was not privy to the activists' literary design and did not employ their myth of the German nation in his dramas. One who came closer to imitating the myth-makers was August Wilhelm Iffland (1759-1814), whose plays contained an occasional motif of central importance to the activists' strategy. As we shall see, at least one of his plays after 1811 took up the theme of insubordination a half-decade before Kleist's more masterful *Prinz Friedrich von Homburg*. Nevertheless, it can also be shown that Iffland was not concerned, as was Kleist, with dramatizing the consequences of living and acting in agreement with the myth of a new and morally superior German nation.

Over the past decades remarkably few critical studies of Iffland's work have appeared. Scholarship has dealt instead with his life and his fame as an outstanding actor.[72] He is generally named in the same breath with Kotzebue[73] — a juxtaposition to which he strenuously objected.[74] His most famous plays, *The Hunters* (1785) and *The Old Bachelors* (*Die Hagestolzen* [1796]), were written long before the Peace of Tilsit and need not concern us here.[75] His anti-Napoleon attitude and his loyalty to the Prussian king and queen have been documented by Rudolf Genée and Erwin Kliewer.[76] During the occupation, he wrote *The Cockades* which, according to Kliewer, represents an attack on party affiliation of any kind; it reveals that Iffland himself avoided identification with any political faction.[77]

The occupation also threatened to establish a French theater as a competitor if Iffland failed to produce the latest plays from Paris on the Berlin stage. Under such pressure, he avoided antagonizing French sympathizers and in his productions contented himself with occasional references to the

---

[71] Kotzebue's play, *Somebody Else's Travel Adventures*, ends with the line, "Long live Alexander!" For Stein's and his own reaction to Kotzebue, see Arndt's description in "Wanderungen und Wandlungen mit dem Reichsfreiherrn Heinrich Karl Friedrich vom Stein" Steffens, *AW* 5:88f.

[72] Alois Wierlacher, "August Wilhelm Iffland," *Deutsche Dichter des 18. Jahrhunderts* [Note 67], 911–930.

[73] Karl-Heinz Klingenberg, *Iffland und Kotzebue als Dramatiker* (Weimar: Böhlau, 1962).

[74] See Gerhard Schulz [Note 60], 473.

[75] For a discussion of these pieces, see the introduction to Iffland's *Hunters* by Adolf Hauffen, "Das Drama der klassischen Periode," *Deutsche National-Literatur* (Stuttgart: Union, n.d.), vol. 139.

[76] Rudolf Genée, *Ifflands Berliner Theaterleitung 1796–1814* (Berlin: National-Zeitung, 1896); Erwin Kliewer, *A. W. Iffland*, Germanische Studien, vol. 195 (Berlin: Ebering, 1937).

[77] Kliewer, *Iffland*, 140.

king and queen.[78] His play *Wohin?*, begun in the summer of 1806,[79] was staged with considerable success in 1808. The hero, Thomas Germanicus, and his son Hermann, deeply disturbed by the French menace, attempt to rally public opinion for the Fatherland and are promptly threatened with banishment. Hermann, who pens an uncensored call-to-arms addressed to all Prussian citizens, encounters increasing hostility from his timid superiors in the Ministry of State. His plea to the nation to remember Arminius and Germany's honor falls on deaf ears, whereupon he emigrates to Lapland with his father so that their families will never have to endure servitude. Despite the call for the upper class to sacrifice or the references to Hermann and the Cherusci, the play bears little structural similarity to the work of the reform party's myth-makers.

His most ambitious stage production after 1806, *Albert von Thurneisen*, which he had written in 1781, contains the motif of a military leader caught between love and duty, who disobeys orders, as did Kleist's *Prinz Friedrich*. Concerning the Prince's infraction, however, Kleist dramatizes a man's fear of death, a woman's love and a patriot's vision of a new nation. Iffland, on the other hand, is unable to rise above social conventions with his illustration of Thurneisen's insubordination. Such basic human experiences as war, fear, resistance, forgiveness, love and dreams motivate Kleist's characters, whereas rigid canons as well as an uncritical acceptance of military codes and social *mores* move Iffland's figures. Succumbing to Sophie's pleas for a meeting, Captain von Thurneisen disobeys General von Dalzig's orders and leaves his post on the eve of a siege. The General resolves to safeguard his daughter Sophie by giving her in marriage to Count Hohenthal, whom she does not love. As Thurneisen tells Sophie that his honor prevents him from deserting his troops to flee with her, the enemy overruns his abandoned position, and he is discovered in Sophie's chamber. His execution before the firing squad during the General's offensive restores his lost dignity and stained honor.

Although this tragedy shares scarcely more than a central motif with Kleist's masterpiece, the similarity was sufficient for Iffland to regard Kleist as a competitor. His rejection of *Prinz Friedrich von Homburg* assured that Kleist's play would not be staged in Berlin. Nor was this the only time Iffland stood between Kleist and a theater audience. His preference for Karl Wohlfahrt's mediocre *Hermann* (1808) shut out Kleist's *Hermannsschlacht* from the repertoire in Berlin and contributed to Kleist's decision to send the play to Vienna.

---

[78] Gustav Höcker, *Die Vorbilder der deutschen Schauspielkunst* (Glogau: Flemming, n.d.), 220.

[79] Otto Tschirch, *Geschichte der öffentlichen Meinung in Preußen vom Basler Frieden bis zum Zusammenbruch des Staates 1795–1806* (Weimar: Böhlau, 1933) 1:415–417.

The pamphlet published by Palm and the plays of both Kotzebue and Iffland may serve as examples of the anti-Napoleon literature not commissioned by the reform party. Structurally, this literature has little in common with the work of party myth-makers, who re-cast an ever present basic tripartite framework in new combinations within different genres. The literary collaborators may be identified by their advocacy of national education, their reference to the language bond, their representation of the individual as a link between past and future along with specific images, rhetorical patterns and heroic personalities from Germany's past. When these characteristics are not present in his work, an anti-Napoleon writer might have promoted the idea of a single German nation, but he was not working for the party. On the contrary, as we have seen, his own productivity could stand in the way of party goals and he might unwittingly block the dissemination of the patriot's myth.

6
The Extremist: Friedrich Ludwig Jahn

FRIEDRICH LUDWIG JAHN'S POPULARISTIC NATIONALISM added a fanatical dimension to the myth of the German nation. More than any other patriot, Jahn represented a one-sided view of national essence which revered the primitive as the motivating aspect of human behavior, the source of everything physical and spiritual. With Jahn, bombast, racism, anti-Semitism, also boorishness in speech and bearing became part and parcel of the mythic thought model. His rejection of all non-Germans led to a spiritual constriction in the German national consciousness which was easily exploited and intensified during the Third Reich. However, it can also be shown that Jahn's patriotism developed into fanaticism as he saw the goal to which he and many of his friends aspired, that is the formation of a single German nation, frustrated by the maneuvering of the nobility. Jahn's early work, *Deutsches Volkstum* (1810), which to be sure already contained the ideological seed of perverted patriotism, is in its own right less extreme. An examination will show that it reflected many of the tenets advocated by Stein and the activist party to which Jahn belonged.[1]

When Peter Viereck examined the foundation upon which Hitler built his *Reich*, he uncovered the potential lurking in Jahn's Folk-State.[2] Louis L. Snyder traced the "tragic" aspects of German nationalism to *Turnvater* Jahn, who "believed that the Germans, infected with Gallic cosmopolitanism, had become soft and effeminate, and that they needed rugged training to bring them into the great German outdoors. He called for a self-assertive, self-confident nation, which, far from taking orders from a foreign conqueror, would be ready to throw its might around in

---

[1] Unfortunately, Jahn's letters from 1807 to 1813, which might have shed more light on his political activities were destroyed by fire in August 1838. Cf. Carl Euler, *Friedrich Ludwig Jahn. Sein Leben und Wirken* (Stuttgart: Krabbe, 1881).

[2] Peter Viereck, *Metapolitics: From the Romantics to Hitler* (New York: Scribner, 1941): 88f.

world society."[3] Hans Kohn counted Jahn among those Germans who had rejected the humanitarian traditions of the West and precipitated "the moral catastrophe, into which the malady of self-centered nationalism and the accompanying *trahison des clercs* can lead."[4] In an attempt to discover the *Roots of German Nationalism*, Snyder pointedly labeled Jahn "an eccentric demagogue."[5]

Jahn's peculiar behavior had already prompted criticism from contemporaries. Heine and the Young Germans of the next generation were especially harsh in their castigation. In *Die Romantische Schule*, for example, Heine accused Jahn of systematizing "idealistic rudeness" and opposing "in the meanest, coarsest manner those convictions, the most majestic and holy Germany ever produced, namely humanity, the brotherhood of man and cosmopolitanism."[6] Heine distinguished sharply between Jahn's popularist notions and the patriotism of Lessing, Herder, Schiller, Goethe, Jean Paul and "all educated people."[7]

A similarly negative attitude was expressed by Karl Immermann, who noted thankfully that the generation of eccentrics ("Geschlecht der Sonderlinge") was rapidly dying out. Germany's foremost representative had been Jahn, the "crackpot par excellence," who was "obsessed with education and language, and wanted to fashion the world so it would correspond with the thinking of a clever, old-Prussian peasant."[8] For the most part, however, these appraisals are kneejerk reactions to Jahn's later activities and behavior and do not reflect upon *Deutsches Volkstum*. Another contemporary, Adolf von Beurmann, for example, denounced the Jahn of 1815–19 as typical of "those characters who never achieve anything because they dressed the new in the garb of the old and forgot the goal because they worry too much about the form"; yet he also contends he would have respected Jahn greatly, had he simply refrained from writing after *Deutsches Volkstum*, which is "far more noble than his bizarre

---

[3] Louis L. Snyder, *German Nationalism: The Tragedy of a People* (Harrisburg: Stackpole, 1952): 22. Reprint Port Washington, N. Y.: Kennikat Press, 1969; see also the extensive bibliographical notes on Jahn, 38–43.

[4] Hans Kohn, *The Mind of Germany: The Education of a Nation* (New York: Scribner, 1960): 20.

[5] *Roots of German Nationalism* (Bloomington: Indiana University Press, 1978): 61. Selected bibliography on nationalism, 295–300.

[6] *Heinrich Heines Sämtliche Werke*, ed. Ernst Elster (Leipzig: Bibliographisches Institut, 1887–1890), "Die Romantische Schule" 5:237; noted hereafter as Elster.

[7] *Ibid.*

[8] *Karl Immermanns Werke in fünf Bänden*, ed. Benno von Wiese (Frankfurt: Athenäum, 1973) 4:523.

meanderings through French prisoner camps."⁹ Based on this testimony, we may separate the latter day eccentric from the thirty-two year old author committed to ridding his homeland of the oppressive French occupation. Because Jahn's popularist nationalism became more constrictive, more bigoted, in the course of time, we may differentiate between the activist under Napoleon's yoke and the "father of German gymnastics," the physical fitness exponent of the *Restauration*.

This is not to deny a continuity in Jahn's thinking and writing. On the contrary, *Deutsches Volkstum* foreshadows the zealous, spiteful and "tragic" side of the later, more contracted notions of German nationalism. However, the responsibility for the later depreciation of the myth lies squarely with Jahn, his disciples and interpreters, not with any political faction for which he may have produced *Deutsches Volkstum*. The popularist tendency of the work isolates Jahn from those Stein supporters we have examined, who wrote for an upper class reading public. Yet, as we have observed, Fichte, Kleist, Arndt, Schleiermacher and others refashioned the literary components of the activist's myth in different genres for different audiences. Therefore, it is not inconceivable that the activists entrusted Jahn with addressing the growing Prussian lower middle class. As we shall see, considerable evidence points in that direction.

Unlike Fichte, who appeared to derive social imperatives for the citizen of 1808 from his own system of critical idealism (as embodied in the *Science of Knowledge*), Jahn sought to develop his brand of nationalism from the writings of popular philosophers. He cites works by Thomas Abbt, Joseph von Sonnenfels and K. G. Kapf.[10] These middle class moralists had generated widespread popular acclaim in the preceding decades with essays on love and death for the Fatherland, the principles of patriotism and "education" for patriotic citizens. By pointing to these "predecessors" in an effort to justify his claims, Jahn sought to endow his own teachings with a sense of historical continuity, permanence and durability within a middle class context. He claims to derive his concept of *Staatsgeist* from these popular writings which he, in turn, projects into an alleged tradition reaching back to Polybius and such works as the *Ernesti de private Romanorum disciplina*. However, Jahn's procedure produced contradictions which he, not unlike Fichte, simply swept under the rug.

Thomas Abbt (1738–1766), for example, wrote his *Death in the Service of the Fatherland* (1761) not as a German nationalist, but as a Prussian particularist. On the first anniversary of Frederick the Great's military set-

---

[9] Adolf von Beurmann, *Vertraute Briefe über Preußens Hauptstadt* (Stuttgart: Cotta, 1837).

[10] *Friedrich Ludwig Jahns Werke*, ed. Carl Euler (Hof: Grau, 1884) 1:282. Quotes in text from this edition; noted hereafter as Euler.

back at Kunersdorf, Abbt tried to console Prussian subjects concerning the heavy casualties. Born outside Prussia in Ulm, Abbt was under consideration at that time for a position at the university of Frankfurt an der Oder. His popular essay was intended to prove regional loyalty to his newly adopted monarch. In view of his deepening anti-Semitism, it is surprising that Jahn recommended the work of Joseph von Sonnenfels (1733-1817) who had converted to Catholicism in Vienna around 1741. Nevertheless, Sonnenfels's *On Love of the Fatherland* (1771, reworked between 1783 and 1787) comprises anecdotes illustrating devotion to the Austrian crown. Written under Abbt's influence, Sonnenfels's treatise provided an Austrian counterbalance to Prussian patriotism. Hence neither work reflected a genuine concern for all Germany, because the two authors championed opposing particularist interests.

On the other hand, Herder had praised both writers. In Abbt's essay he embraced the concept of a nation governed by law and by a ruler who regarded himself as the "father or the mother of happy people."[11] Yet this image had been created by Frederick the Great for the Prussian monarchy, not for all the German states. In Sonnenfels's anecdotes, Herder saw a masterful portrayal of social circumstances.[12] Unlike Jahn, Sonnenfels had delighted in social satire and criticism directed at all segments of society. As editor of the journal *A Man Without Prejudice* (*Mann ohne Vorurteil*, 1765–1767), he had gained notoriety by unmasking the hypocrisy and infirmities of "civilized" society. Like Rousseau, he had proclaimed the life of the savage superior to that of either the courtier or the cleric. Unfortunately, however, both he and Jahn suffered from a lack of organizational skills: their work suffers from superficiality and illogical meanderings. Nowhere are such characteristics more in evidence than in *Deutsches Volkstum*.

Despite ten discernible chapters surrounding a ten point program, the structure of Jahn's book is chaotic. Excerpts appear in these pages from dozens of other writings, ranging from contemporaneous popular philosophy to the more remote works of classical antiquity, with little by way of introduction and even less explication. Although the innumerable references to a potpourri of literary sources exonerates Jahn from the charge of being "thoroughly uncultivated,"[13] the lack of organization and logical sequence confounds his message and, upon close scrutiny, blunts his arguments. With Jahn begins that intemperance and obfuscation characteristic

---

[11] *Herders Sämtliche Werke* [Chapter 4, Note 6], 1:23.

[12] *Ibid.*, 4:320; see also 1:453; 4:123, 189, 429; 32:234.

[13] Treitschke refers to Jahn as "einen lärmenden Barbaren"; see *Treitschke's History of Germany in the Nineteenth Century*, trans. Eden and Cedar Paul [Chapter III, Note 16], 1:307.

of later myth-makers. Aggressive assertion replaces more dispassionate discourse: the claims for German superiority are neither clarified nor substantiated.

A twisted interpretation of a biblical verse[14] forms the basis for Jahn's insistence that any German who marries a foreigner forfeits all civil liberties. A blinding desire to prove an archetypal affinity (*Urverwandtschaft*) between Germans and the Aryans of Persia and India[15] induces him to accept historical improbability. Neither his assertions regarding the "purer" Christianity found in Germany[16] nor the negative similes of "gypsies and Jews"[17] prove that the proper education of Germans is "something different, something higher."[18] However, such negative metaphors, ahistorical yearnings and contorted Biblical exegesis intensify the image of racial supremacy which Jahn integrated into the myth.

Does *Deutsches Volkstum* contain the tell-tale structure of the activist's myth? Despite the disorganized ramblings, Jahn's book reproduces the framework prepared at Königsberg and Memel in virtually every detail. Although none of the other works we have scrutinized have the same anthropo-racial implications, Jahn's *Deutsches Volkstum* belongs to the attempts at literary collaboration promoted by Stein's literary supporters. In brief, Jahn's work may be described as an activist's *vademecum* for the Prussian middle class. Chapter five entitled "National Education" includes all the ingredients we have uncovered. The purpose of national education, Jahn proclaims, is to "realize in each individual an archetypal model of a perfect human being, citizen and link in the chain of his people" (1:234). Before citizens can be molded, each must master the mother tongue — a process to which Jahn dedicates several paragraphs (1:234–245). Once men and women become social beings, they become, "something special . . . a link in a never ending chain" (1:283). We observe here not only a reassembling of familiar components but also a structuring reminiscent of Fichte, Arndt and, as we shall see in the next chapter, Theodor Körner. *Deutsches Volkstum* resounds with reform party rhetoric and strategy. At the center, however, are near quotes from party documents. Jahn's thoughts on national education were gleaned from Wilhelm von Humboldt's "Report to the King" (December 1, 1809), which contained a plan for the reorganization of the Prussian school system endorsed by

---

[14] Nehemiah 13: 23–36; Euler, *Jahns Werke* 1: 287.

[15] Euler, *Jahns Werke* 1: 225.

[16] Euler, *Jahns Werke* 1: 225f.

[17] Euler, *Jahns Werke* 1: 234.

[18] Euler, *Jahn*, 234f.

Stein.[19] With simplified vocabulary and other names for the schools described by Humboldt, Jahn presents the same plan. Whereas Humboldt sought to establish elementary, district and "scholarly schools"(*Elementar-, Kreis* und *Gelehrtenschulen*), Jahn calls for community (*Gemeinschafts-*) district (*Kreis-*) and "schools of the margraviate" (*Markschulen*). The similarities between the two descriptions suggest a common effort:[20]

> [Humboldt] In den Elementar-Schulen soll nur gelehrt werden, was jeder als Mensch und Bürger notwendig wissen muß; in den gelehrten sollen stufenweise diejenigen Kenntnisse beigebracht werden, die zu jedem, auch dem höchsten Berufe notwendig sind und der Grad der Ausbildung, den jeder verlangt, muß nur von der Zeit abhängen, die er in der Schule zubringt, und der Klasse, die er darin erreicht [*Stein* 3:231f.].

> [Jahn] Was der Mensch als Mensch und Staatsbürger wissen muß — lernen alle Schüler gemeinsam. Die besonderen Vor- und Hülfskenntnisse des Berufes und Erwerbes — lernt jede Schülerart besonders (1:185).

Despite differences in detail and syntax, both Humboldt and Jahn advocate earlier instruction in civics for everyone; specific knowledge required in the various professions would follow. In addition, both place mathematics, mechanics and natural sciences on a par with the "scholarly languages" (*Gelehrtensprachen*) of antiquity. Better training for teachers, more rigorous standards for admission to the university and earlier aptitude testing are but a few of the congruous aspects found in both works.

A revealing difference between Humboldt's and Jahn's description can be detected in their respective points of departure. "Education should be firmly grounded in religious feeling," writes Humboldt, "its base is the fear and love of an omnipresent higher being" (3:233); for Jahn that "higher being" is the state itself: "Uniform public institutions represent the means for developing a popular sense of civic duty and a patriotic way of thinking. Uniform institutionalization can produce conformity as well as originality in the individual. A noble nationalism will be expressed in the consensus of all educated people" (1:193). This distinction points out the gap between Humboldt and the activists, and identifies Jahn with the latter. In his *Brünn Memorandum*, Stein came closer on this point to Jahn than

---

[19] See *Stein* 3:231–235.

[20] (Humboldt:) In the elementary schools only those subjects should be taught which each person and citizen must know; in the secondary schools knowledge of those things should be gradually imparted which are needed in even the most lofty profession. The degree of learning achieved by each pupil should depend only on the amount of time spent in school and the class-level attained.
(Jahn:) Whatever an individual needs to know as a person and a citizen, all pupils learn together. The specialized knowledge and auxiliary skills needed in professional or commercial life should be taught separately to different groups of pupils.

to Humboldt: "Educational institutions must not work simply toward perfecting mechanical abilities and imparting a body of knowledge, but toward awakening a civic as well as militaristic spirit in the nation and toward the general dissemination of a knowledge of martial arts via instruction in gymnastic exercises" (*Stein* 3:297). Stein and Jahn saw eye to eye on the question of national education.

With a humorous illustration reminiscent of Kleist's *Hermannsschlacht*, Jahn chides his compatriots for failing to perfect proficiency in standard German. The confusion and resulting demise of the Romans in Kleist's play was brought about by the similarity of two camp names. In a similarly humorous anecdote, Jahn illustrates the linguistic problems facing citizens in different parts of Germany who have not developed proficiency in the standardized language. A Prussian general requested twelve chaff-cutters (*zwölf Futterschneider*) from the mayor of a Saxon city. He was astonished to receive several horse-drawn wagons full of tailors (*zwölf Fuder Schneider*) with a promise that the others would be sent as soon as possible (1:197f.). The similarity between "chaff-cutter" and "wagon-loads" produced the humorous befuddlement. Nevertheless, Kleist's and Jahn's amusing treatment of the language argument may have been called for in the blueprint drafted by the politicians. As Euler points out, Jahn did not know Kleist's play (1:344). The fact that two writers, working in different genres postulated similar arguments in the same humorous way suggests a common source for both. There are several other parallels.

Jahn's hero is Hermann, "the incomparable" (1:297), who "waged war and risked battle against the destroyers of our people" (1:206). He chides Marbod for not joining forces with Hermann from the outset (1:207). Like Kleist, he calls for total war against the enemy regardless of cost and human sacrifice (1:299), and describes education as "basic military training" (1:270f). Moreover, the focal point for the movement toward unified resistance is Prussia (1:147f.), where activists agitate "... in print and speech from the stage, from the pulpit and from the teacher's lectern" (1:157). In addition to parallels with Kleist's play and subtle references to the collaboration itself, Jahn's work includes a partitioning of Germany to favor Prussia (1:205) reminiscent of Arndt's projections in volume two of *Spirit of the Times*. Arndt himself receives considerable praise,[21] whereas political neutrals are decried and denounced. Jahn also cites the heroic defense of Saragossa (1809) by Spanish insurrectionists, which inspired Stein and Kleist; he anticipates Theodor Körner's dramatic portrayal of the heroic Count Zriny (1:297) and formulates activists' proposals in unadorned language. The presence of the tell-tale structure, the correspondence to the

---

[21] For details, see Euler, *Friedrich Ludwig Jahn* [Note 1], 49, 386, 508ff.

work of other collaborators, the heroic images and the familiar reform proposals mark Jahn as a literary agent for Stein and his faction in 1810.

In the introduction, Jahn explains that he had no intention initially of having his "weak effort" printed. However, "a few statesmen and patriots showed some interest in the manuscript and declared it to be worthy of publication" (1:150). It is not difficult to recognize these political leaders as members of the reform faction. More important, the presence of the telltale components of the myth shed some light on an episode Jahn related in his memoirs published in 1835: he served as a guide for a British agent in northern Germany shortly before the British landing on the banks of the Scheldt (1:435). In short, Jahn's service to the activists began before he wrote *Deutsches Volkstum* and had included direct contact with secret British emissaries en route to Stein, Gruner or members of their group.[22]

With this discovery, it is easy to understand why Jahn joined Major Lützow's "Black Raiders." In a letter to Lützow (June 16, 1814), he implies that he had been "cooperating" with political leaders since at least 1810.[23] His correspondence also reveals a close association at this time with Justus Gruner, Adolf von Chasot, Friedrich Stägemann and Wilhelm Süvern.[24] Beyond the structural indicators in *Deutsches Volkstum* the most revealing evidence is a reminiscence written down three decades later. On December 17, 1837 Jahn describes, in a letter to Mützell, dining one evening with Stein, Wallmoden and Fouqué during which they discussed plans for liberating the fatherland.[25] We see, then, the few extant letters from 1807 to 1813, the memoirs and the later correspondence support the contention that *Deutsches Volkstum* was written in the service of Stein and his faction.

Jahn's efforts to relate his popularist notions to an alleged tradition cannot conceal that he took many of these ideas from supporters of the French Revolution.[26] His concept of transferring power from the aristocracy to the people, his distrust of the nobility, even popularist nationalism itself constitute the legacy of 1789. These French elements became so thoroughly integrated with activist reform strategy in his thinking that he embraced them as originally German,[27] although they are of

---

[22] "Denknisse eines Deutschen oder Fahrten des Alten im Bart," Euler, *Jahns Werke* 1: 435–497; Jahn mentions his ties to Gruner at this time: see Euler 1:433f.

[23] *Die Briefe F. L. Jahns*, ed. Wolfgang Meyer (Dresden: Limpert, n.d.): 74.

[24] *Briefe*, 71, 79, 120.

[25] *Briefe*, 146.

[26] Heinrich Pröhle, *Friedrich Ludwig Jahns Leben*. 2nd. ed. (Berlin: Reimer, 1872): 31ff.

[27] Michael Antonowytsch, *Friedrich Ludwig Jahn. Ein Beitrag zur Geschichte der Anfänge des deutschen Nationalismus* (Berlin: Ebering, 1933): 17.

much more recent origin. Also, Jahn departs from the cosmopolitan, humanistic heritage of such patriots as Herder, Lessing and Klopstock by constricting this complex to favor immediate ends. Along with Fichte, Kleist, Arndt and Schleiermacher, Jahn conducted his literary activity according to a political mandate.

Some of his recommendations were carried out within a few years. With regard to literature, for instance, he called for a collection of German sagas and fairy tales to help in the creation of a national identity (1:345). The brothers Grimm obliged with such a collection two years later. Yet other proposals, including the complete Germanization of all family names (1:338) and the destruction of "un-German, un-patriotic" books (1:345) went far beyond planned reforms. Such tragic aspects as the insistence on German superiority in thinking ability (*Volksfaßlichkeit*, 1:342), or the aggressive militarism promoted by the gymnastic devotees would propel the defenders of a unified Germany into the trenches of the First and Second World Wars.

Because Jahn's idea of total war, his perception of Hermann and Marbod, his humorous treatment of the language-bond argument so closely parallel Kleist's, we suspect a common source. So many correlations can be found between Fichte's speeches and *Deutsches Volkstum* that Jahn either had direct access to Fichte's manuscripts or both worked from the same blueprint.[28] Quotes from Arndt's work and praises to his name occur with such frequency that an interrelationship is easily established. As we have seen, however, Jahn did not know Kleist's plays. Moreover, Fichte's speeches were first published in a very limited edition. Although volume one (1806) of Arndt's *Spirit of the Times* is cited by footnote in Jahn's work, similarities in the arguments about the mother tongue point to influence from volume two (1808/9), which, as we have noted, circulated in limited quantities among the activists.

The most significant distinction remains the explicit callousness toward others and the narrow-mindedness regarding national essence. Moreover, Jahn addressed a different segment of the populace. Kleist, Fichte and Arndt appealed to an upper class reader by setting in place a moral, theoretical cornerstone for the nationalist myth. Jahn, by contrast, was concerned with the practical implementation of the patriots' strategy and the potential contributions of the lower middle class to a future insurrection. Fichte addressed the intelligentsia when he argued that devotion to Germany was a step in becoming a world citizen; once the German na-

---

[28] Paul Piechowski, *Friedrich Ludwig Jahn: Von Turnvater zum Volkserzieher* (Gotha: Klotz, 1928): 110: "The correlations between *Deutsches Volkstum* and the *Reden* seem so great that it can be concluded that Jahn was both influenced in general by Fichte and knew the *Reden* even before publication of his great book."

tion was established, the German blueprint for patriotism would spread throughout the human race. Jahn, on the other hand, abandoned even the pretense of the cosmopolitanism inherited from Classical Weimar. "Civic mindedness" was meant to benefit the German state, the Fatherland, not all mankind. By the time Rudolf Virchow got around to linking Jahn's nationalism to the more cosmopolitan views of German idealism, the gymnastic movement had become a front for aggressive military training.[29]

Deutsches Volkstum solicits the support of the middle class for Stein's reforms and attempts to recruit able-bodied men for military and paramilitary service. Jahn's proposals for the development of a national militia, for the abolition of serfdom and for more humane forms of army discipline echoes Gneisenau's memorandum of 1808, which, with the support of Stein and Scharnhorst, had petitioned the king to authorize an insurrection in northern Germany.[30] There can be little doubt, therefore, that gymnastics on the Hasenheide were intended as paramilitary training for a popular uprising. Combining physical fitness with zealous devotion to Germany, the gymnasts were the future soldiers who would free the Fatherland in wars of liberation.

A physical education center was nothing new in Germany. As early as 1774 J. B. Basedow had proclaimed the benefits of physical fitness. In 1784 Christian Salzmann (1744–1811) had founded a gymnastic facility at Schnepfenthal in Thuringia. By 1793 Johann Guts-Muths (1759–1839) could describe the principles of athletic training in *Gymnastics for Young People*. And in 1794–95 Gerhard Ulrich Vieth published his three volume *Attempt at an Encyclopedia of Physical Exercise*. Efforts at combining physical prowess with intellectual development mark German educational theory in the second half of the eighteenth century. Jahn added the socio-political dimension when he recognized the potential in such pedagogical theories for circumventing the restriction of the Prussian army to 42,000 men imposed by the Peace of Tilsit. Once trained on the field in Berlin, the gymnasts were ready to take their places whenever the insurrection ignited. In order to ensure discipline without official military authority, character training had to be integrated into the athletic program.

The paramilitary enterprise got underway in the Spring of 1810 when Jahn led a few students "into the woods and onto a field" (2:4) where he initiated "youth games." As more young people joined in, he founded the field on the Hasenheide, south of Berlin. On June 19, 1811 a small group

---

[29] Horst Ueberhorst, "Der Barrenstreit und sein politisch-historischer Hintergrund," *Leibesübungen* 9 (1967): 5; see also *Friedrich Ludwig Jahn 1778/1978* ed. Horst Ueberhorst (Bonn-Bad Godesberg: Inter Nationes, 1978).

[30] Euler, *Friedrich Ludwig Jahn* [Note 1], 110.

celebrated the first general "Gymnastic Day." Two years later, when Frederick William III issued the long awaited call for volunteers, Jahn enlisted, taking most of the gymnasts (*Turner*) with him. While Jahn served in Lützow's squadron, Ernst Eiselin (1793–1846) kept the movement alive. In 1814 Jahn returned after seeing little action. Yet by 1816 he could boast over a thousand followers.[31] Moreover, the Finns and Slavic peoples, who were also awakening to national consciousness, were adopting his ideas. On August 24, 1816 Jahn assured Th. Müller, "Those who exercise with us on the fields will be loyal to the Fatherland."[32]

But to whose Fatherland? For Jahn, Germany was to be molded in Stein's image. He and Arndt had already mapped out the geographical boundaries favoring Prussia. Fichte had systematized the process by which a unified national identity would be achieved; Kleist had dramatized the moral implications and Schleiermacher had appended the religious pageantry and Christian symbolism. Gymnastics would then ensure middle class support and train future defenders of the newly united and administratively reformed Germany. But Stein's vision on the road from Tilsit to Leipzig was not to be. Germany's unification à la Jahn was still a half century away. As the *Restauration* began in earnest, Jahn discovered that he like Arndt, Schleiermacher and Reimer was a thorn in the reactionary side.

In the meantime, gymnastic fields had opened in other towns. Preserving the unification tendencies by helping to mitigate class differences, the *Turner* soon found themselves confronted by Metternich and his sympathizers who intended to restore the *ancien regime*. In short order, the fields became political arenas where, on the one side, such nationalistic gymnasts as Franz Passow championed the "new centers" for the cultivation of patriotism and, on the other, more cautious athletes, including Heinrich Steffens, condemned the uncontrollable chauvinism displayed by some members. After a bitter dispute among the gymnasts, suspicious government officials closed the field at Breslau in 1818. By March 1819, all activities on the Hasenheide had been barred, and on January 20, 1820 the Prussian government ordered more than a hundred gymnastic centers to shut down. With the *Restauration*, Jahn's training schools became "undesirable."

He responded with outlandish behavior and extravagant claims. Dressed in a toga-like costume of coarse material, with long, flowing, un-

---

[31] *Briefe* [Note 23], 91.

[32] *Briefe*, 93.

kempt hair and often carrying a spear or club,[33] he publicly castigated his particularist opponents and all friends of Metternich's policies. His political posture became increasingly more constricted: in order to guard against "intellectual submission," a German should never deal with foreigners in their language;[34] to protect the new nation, hungry bears, wolves and other wild animals should be stocked in artificially created woodlands at Germany's borders;[35] as a preparation for defense Germans should live in the wilds and confront life and death struggles daily.[36] Such incredible statements alienated many would-be supporters and played right into Metternich's hands.

Together with Friedrich Friesen and P. Luden, Jahn drafted a national program for German schools of higher learning in which physical exercise was placed on a par with academic subjects. His disciples, C. E. L. Dürre and H. F. Massmann, spread the gospel of "German essence" at various German universities, linking the fraternities (*Burschenschaften*) to gymnastics and patriotism. When August von Kotzebue ridiculed such excesses and satirized gymnastics in general, he was assassinated in March 1819 by Karl Sand, both a *Turner* and a *Burschenschafter*. This act gained Metternich the support he needed to eliminate resistance to his restoration policies by striking hard at the advocates of a reformed and united national state under Prussian leadership. In the night of the 13th to the 14th of July 1819, Jahn was arrested "on suspicion of secret treasonable affiliations" in connection with a second murder, that of a police inspector, and taken to Küstrin, the fortress at Spandau.[37] What followed is, as we shall see, similar to the way other literary supporters of Prussia's reform party were treated.

For the next half dozen years, Jahn was embroiled in time-consuming legal maneuvers just to stay out of jail. This went on for the next two decades until Frederick William IV pardoned him and other "demagogues" in 1842. During these twenty years Jahn was effectively separated from the gymnastic movement. His departure from the field was so complete that Johann Guts-Muths, not Jahn, was honored in Germany in the 1850s

---

[33] See the contemporary description of Jahn by Adolf Streckfuss, *500 Jahre Berliner Geschichte*, ed. Leo Fernbach (Berlin: Haude and Spene, 1900).

[34] Willi Schröder, *Burschenturner im Kampf um Einheit und Freiheit* (Berlin: Sportverlag, 1964): 190.

[35] Euler, *Friedrich Ludwig Jahn* [Note 1], 488.

[36] *Ibid.*, 489.

[37] See Jahn's account in Euler 2:161ff.

and 1860s as the founder of modern physical fitness.[38] Not until the establishment of Bismarck's Germany did Guts-Muths take a backseat to Jahn when nationalistic historians heralded him as an early promoter of national unification.[39]

We see, then, that the radical consequences of nationalism emerged gradually from Jahn's collaboration with the activists in 1810 and gained momentum later in his desperate attempts to ward off a particularist victory after the Congress of Vienna. These negative components were subsequently resurrected in the service of national unification in 1871. Severe nationalistic contractions set in with the German Gymnasts Association's Kaiser-cult, its summons to accelerated military training and its aggressive affirmation of Bismarck's Reich.

Our investigation has shown that *Deutsches Volkstum* contains the structure common to activist myth-making. Like Fichte, Kleist, Arndt and Schleiermacher, Jahn worked from a reform party outline; yet unlike his fellow collaborators, he sought to carry out Stein's, Gneisenau's and Scharnhorst's strategy in a practical way which would appeal to the middle class and attract able-bodied defenders of a new nation. With his lectures on *Deutsches Volkstum* in 1817 and his crudeness in manner and speech, Jahn, in defense of his aspirations for a united Germany, superseded his party's mandate. His hyperbolic assertions, eccentric behavior and ceaseless agitation provoked reprisals from Metternich's camp, bent in 1819 on crushing the drive toward unification the better to secure particularist interests.

Later, in the 1860s and 1870s, the German Gymnastic Association persistently advocated military training and physical exercise as preparation for armed service in time of war. Such untempered militarism prepared the way for E. Neuendorff[40] with his "Back to Jahn" and the anti-Semitic regulations of 1933. In 1810 however, Jahn embraced the activist myth and exaggerated the benefits of "undefiled German potentials" to impress the middle class.[41] The persecution he endured when the unification movement became unfashionable remains to be shown. As a test case, however,

---

[38] *Deutsche Turnzeitung* 5 (1860): 22.

[39] Willi Schröder, *Das Jahnbild in der deutschen Turn- und Sportbewegung* (Diss. Leipzig, 1958).

[40] Cf. E. Neuendorff, "Turnverein oder Wehrverband," *Deutsche Turnzeitung* 47 (1932): 847ff.; see also *Die deutsche Turnerschaft von 1860–1936* (Berlin: Limpert, 1936): 226–230.

[41] For details of the significance and function of gymnastic clubs and singing societies in the development of German nationalism, see Dieter Düding, *Organisierter gesellschaftlicher Nationalismus in Deutschland (1808–1847)* (Munich: Oldenbourg, 1984). We shall examine this study later in another context.

Deutsches Volkstum provided us with an example of how structural and stylistic evidence can link an author, writing during the French occupation, to Stein and his reform faction.

7
Theodor Körner: The Myth Personified

SEVERAL PARALLELS MAY BE DRAWN between the works of Heinrich von Kleist and those of Theodor Körner. Although he never achieved the artistic mastery and aesthetic harmony[1] found in Kleist's compositions, Körner picked up where Kleist had left off and carried on, especially in his lyrics, the socio-political myth-making which characterizes *Die Hermannsschlacht*. This is not surprising in view of their close personal friendship. In 1808 Kleist was a frequent guest at the Körner home where he called upon Julie Kunze.[2] Theodor's father, the justice Christian Gottfried, famous for his friendship and exchange of letters with Schiller, was her legal guardian. The relationship between Kleist and Julie was severed when she refused to correspond secretly with the enamored dramatist. The episode was a painful experience for Kleist and may have formed the nucleus for his *Käthchen von Heilbronn* (1808).[3]

During this period, Kleist made an impact on the seventeen year old Körner and probably initiated him into the association of writers and politicians with whom he worked. Initial examples of Kleist's influence are found in Körner's *Toni: A Drama in Three Acts* (1812) and in his poem, *Saint Cecilia (Die heilige Cäcilie)*.[4] Written for the Viennese stage, the drama *Toni* is a dramatization of Kleist's short story, *The Engagement in St. Domingo*

---

[1] Cf. Heinrich August Erhard, *Theodor Körner. Sein Leben nebst einer ausführlichen Beurteilung seiner Schriften* (Armstadt: Hildebrand, 1821).

[2] See Karl Berger, *Theodor Körner* (Bielefeld and Leipzig: Velhagen und Klasing, 1912).

[3] This connection was first proposed by Eduard von Bülow in 1848; see Sembdner, *Kleists Werke* 1:938; also Hans R. von Jaden, *Theodor Körner* (Vienna: Frick, 1913).

[4] *Körners Werke*, ed. Augusta Weldler-Steinberg (Berlin and Leipzig: Bong, n.d.) 1:146. For the relationship Kleist-Körner, see the editor's introduction, p. xvi.

(1811),[5] and the poem was inspired by Kleist's *St. Cäcilie or the Power of Music* (*Die heilige Cäcilie oder die Gewalt der Musik*, 1810). Similarities also link Körner's five act tragedy, *Zriny*, which enjoyed considerable success in the Vienna of 1812, to Kleist's political writings, particularly to *Die Hermannsschlacht*.

Kleist and Körner share an idealistic framework and promulgate the same socio-political message. Both writers perceived the poet's role as that of an agitator for armed resistance and military action. The Hungarian hero, Count Zrinyi, fights and dies for "Freedom, Honor, Faith and Fatherland" (2:140). These are the same ideals set forth in Kleist's *Catechism*, his aphorisms *On the Liberation of Austria* and *Die Hermannsschlacht*. When Juranitsch questions Zrinyi's plan to burn down the city before Turkish troops can occupy it (2:113ff.), he echoes contentions found in Kleist's ironic *Letter of a Mayor in a Fortress to a Petty Official*.[6] The arguments presented by the Count's prospective son-in-law in an effort to save the city correspond to the prescript of the mayor who attempts to save his own property. They derive from the same short-sighted convictions expressed by the German princes in the third scene of act one of *Die Hermannsschlacht*. Zrinyi's determination to die with honor surrounded by his family rather than accept slavery and humiliation parallels Hermann's decision to risk women and children in the liberation of Germany.[7] The heroes of both plays welcome death for the Fatherland; the heroines of both plays imitate their male counterparts by assuming an active part in the enemy's demise. The secondary characters of both dramas unite loyally behind their leaders determined to triumph over superior forces or die in the effort.

The personalities of Soliman the Great and Quintilius Varus share several features. Both resemble Napoleon in their despotism, impatience and insistence on victory regardless of cost. The mandrake (*Alraune*) tells Varus that he has come from nothing, will return to nothing and that he stands only two steps from the grave.[8] Varus is depicted as a constellation mighty for the moment but destined to pass into oblivion as rapidly as he ascended to prominence. Soliman is also represented as a powerful man on the brink of physical ruin. Whereas Varus is unable to interpret the omen, Soliman is painfully aware of his impending doom and, before

---

[5] The heroines in both works are named Toni, which was also the name of Körner's fiancée, Toni Adamberger, the Viennese actress. See Georg Feierfeil, '*Die Verlobung in St. Domingo*' *von Heinrich von Kleist und Theodor Körners 'Toni'* (Brenau: Prgar, 1892).

[6] Sembdner, *Kleists Werke* 2:371f.

[7] Sembdner, *Kleists Werke* 2:592.

[8] Sembdner, *Kleists Werke* 2:603.

passing into the next world, seeks to make a mighty impact on this one. In his monologue of scene two in act one, he compares himself to the phoenix diving into the flame.⁹ The dominant imagery of falling stars and all-consuming fire underscores the transiency of the destructive man. Soliman's premonitions not only parallel the prophecy of Kleist's mandrake regarding Varus but also reverberate contemporary predictions of Bonaparte's fate. German critics equated Napoleon with a volcanic phenomenon, a meteor appearing suddenly on the horizon, destined to burn out quickly and disappear.¹⁰

Körner adds a significant aspect to this general framework: Soliman is not the only strongman in his day and must acknowledge that great men have opposed him. When comparing himself to Alexander the Great and the Roman conquerors, Soliman accentuates the heroic aspects of his adversary, the Austrian emperor: "No emperor Charles stood in their way; no La Valette hindered their victory. Charles, Charles, you should not have lived in this day and age and your Europe would lie at my feet" (2:73). With these words, Körner expresses his confidence in Francis II and his brother, Archduke Charles: only they can stop Napoleon. Therefore, the Austrian emperor should wage war against the French despite the cost. The historical settings for both Kleist's *Die Hermannsschlacht* and Körner's *Zriny* shielded the authors against possible reprisals. Neither the dramatist in Prussian service, nor the playwright in Vienna dared be more explicit. Nevertheless, *Die Hermannsschlacht* could not be performed on the German stage after the Austrian disaster at Wagram in July, 1809 and was first presented on 29 August 1839. The success of *Zriny* in the Vienna of 1812, on the other hand, led to Körner's appointment as playwright for the Royal Court Theater (*Hofburgtheater*).

Despite Kleist's influence, the socio-political myth discernible in *Die Hermannsschlacht* is not a significant structural component in Körner's *Zriny*. One reason for this is Count Zrinyi's Hungarian extraction. Körner was unable to use language as a common bond because Zrinyi, although loyal to the Holy Roman Emperor, led an Hungarian army. Nevertheless, Körner found in the historical Zrinyi a good example of the leadership and unwavering loyalty to the Habsburg dynasty so desperately needed in the Austrian campaign against Napoleon. His dramatization of Zrinyi's heroism incorporates some of the political arguments found in *Die Hermannsschlacht*: Zrinyi, like Hermann, educates the audience regarding

---

⁹ *Körners Werke* 2:73.

¹⁰ Arndt writes in volume three of *Geist der Zeit*, "But every so often extraordinary events and individuals cut across these [established] circles like comets; nevertheless, they only glow and threaten like comets and meteors, shine brightly for a short time and then burn out and disappear" (Steffens, *AW* 8:106).

the national struggle; the characters illustrate an ideal relationship to their leader (and to the Austrian crown). In this way, Körner made use of principles set forth by Fichte and Kleist; however, he adapted them for maximum appeal to his Austrian audience.

Körner's purpose led him to portray his characters as static personalities. Neither Zrinyi, Juranitsch, the women, nor for that matter the antagonist Soliman undergo any significant transition in thinking, behavior or disposition. In Kleist's *Die Hermannsschlacht*, by contrast, Thusnelda and Marbod, the Cherusci and the other tribal princes reconsider their political and social attitudes during the play; they gain a better understanding of the enemy and their duties to the national group. Hermann, though he undergoes little personality development, reveals his strategy gradually. For this reason, the audience is able to participate in an edifying process. *Zriny*, on the other hand, stands closer to the exemplum of the Baroque theater. By his conduct, the Count illustrates what should and must be done in the face of adversity. The audience observes a personification of specific ideals (loyalty, bravery, wisdom, etc.) and is encouraged to imitate the protagonist's behavior. Körner did not seek to persuade, but rather to fortify his Austrian audience for the forthcoming military tribulations. When Kleist sent *Die Hermannsschlacht* to Vienna in 1809, he had hoped his play would promote cooperation between Austria and Prussia, resulting in a unified front against Napoleon. Körner's intention was to move his audience to defiance by a dramatized example.

His last play, *Josef Heyderich*, is another exemplum. Once again, Körner glorifies loyalty, bravery and discipline; his purpose is again to fire the passions of his audience. More recent events rather than past history provide the setting for this play, which calls for united action against the French. The Battle of Montebello (1800) sets the scene for Corporal Heyderich's act of heroism. The subtitle: "German loyalty" indicates the specific national characteristic Körner intended to exemplify. Instead of seeking medical help for himself, the loyal Heyderich stays with his injured lieutenant until the officer is provided with medical attention. The steadfast corporal thereupon succumbs to his own, much more serious wounds. The dialogue reflects the solidarity and suffering of the Austrian combatants. The townspeople display a lack of patriotism when they callously refuse to aid the wounded soldiers of their own army. By dramatizing acts of heroism from Austria's past and recent history, Körner sought to promote ideals as well as armed resistance to France. Because the Habsburg domain comprised many nationalities, he was unable to use all the structural components of the socio-political myth propagated in Prussia. Nevertheless, he presented similar arguments and assumed a comparable political posture in these plays.

In March, 1813, Körner suddenly abandoned his promising career as playwright in Vienna to follow the Prussian eagle. With his father's blessing, he joined Lützow's "Black Raiders," a semi-official guerrilla organization which harassed French patrols and attacked French supply convoys. Lützow's raiders were made up of men from outside Prussia; the troops expressed intent was to incorporate the idea of German unity.[11] Körner inspired and glorified his comrades in a series of poems entitled *Lyre and Sword* (published in 1814). The myth disseminated by other Prussian men-of-letters serves as the cornerstone of this collection; certain poems are structured entirely upon the mythic framework.

Körner named one of the poems in the collection "The Rifleman's Song":

Frisch auf, ihr Jäger, frei und flink!
 Die Büchse von der Wand!
Der Mutige bekämpft die Welt
Frisch auf den Feind, frisch in das Feld
 Fürs deutsche Vaterland!
Aus Westen, Norden, Süd und Ost
 Treibt uns der Rache Strahl,
Vom Oderflusse, Weser, Main,
Vom Elbstrom und vom Vater Rhein
 Und aus dem Donautal.
Doch Brüder sind wir allzusamm';
 Und das schwellt unsern Mut.
Uns knüpft der Sprache heilig Band,
Uns knüpft ein Gott, ein Vaterland,
 Ein treues deutsches Blut.
Nicht zum Erobern zogen wir
 Vom väterlichen Herd;
Die schändlichste Tyrannenmacht
Bekämpfen wir in freud'ger Schlacht
 Das ist des Blutes wert!
Ihr aber, die uns treu geliebt,
 Der Herr sei euer Schild,
Bezahlen wir's mit unserm Blut!
Denn Freiheit ist das höchste Gut,
 Ob's tausend Leben gilt.
Drum, wackre Jäger, frei und flink,
 Wie auch das Liebchen weint! —
Gott hilft uns im gerechten Krieg!
Frisch in den Kampf! — Tod oder Sieg!

---

[11] *Treitschke's History of Germany in the Nineteenth Century*, trans. Eden and Cedar Paul [Chapter III, Note 16], 1:511; also Adolf Kofahl, "Theodor Körners Leben," *Theodor Körners Sämtliche Werke* (Leipzig: Folk, n.d.), p. V.

> Frisch, Brüder, auf den Feind. [12]
>
> Step lively, soldiers, free and bold!
> Take rifles from the walls!
> Courageous men will fight with zeal
> On to the foe, on to the field
>   The Fatherland now calls!
> From West and North, from South and East
>   We move on vengeance' beam,
> From river Oder, Weser, Main
> From Elbe and from father Rhine
>   And from the Danube stream.
> We're brothers all together here;
>   That prods our dauntless pace.
> Bound by our language holy band,
> Bound by one God, one Fatherland,
>   A truly German race.
> For not to conquer we went forth
>   From family home and life;
> Against the vilest tyrant's might,
> We gladly wage our joyous fight
>   That's worth the bloody strife!
> But you, who always loved us true,
>   The Lord, be he your shield;
> We're paying for it with our lives!
> For freedom is the highest prize,
>   Though thousand men we yield.
> So, gallant soldiers, free and bold,
>   Though sweethearts weep with woe! —
> To our just cause, the Lord does call!
> On to the fight! — succeed or fall!
>   On brothers! At the foe!

The poem has a tripartite circular structure with the concluding verse repeating the call to action expressed in the opening lines. The initial command does not lead to an immediate response; instead time is suspended in the next four strophes as the poet presents an argument. The "Drum" of the last stanza denotes a summation of the principles set forth in the main body and returns the poem to that point in time arrested in the first verse. The individual's duty to the national group is emphasized in the initial strophe: when the fatherland summons, the individual rushes to the defense. In verses two through five the poet draws from his idealistic axioms the logical conclusion for concrete reality — military action. However, the axioms from which this is deduced are not reflected upon within the poem's structure, but are accepted as posited. These unscrutinized postu-

---

[12] *Körners Werke* 1:27f.

lates constitute the socio-political myth proclaimed by the other Prussian literary collaborators.

The poem is constructed upon the myth inasmuch as it revolves around the nationalistic (rather than particularistic) point of view expressed in verse two and also accentuates the language bond in verse three. The structure pivots in four and five on the educational process embarked upon by the poet who teaches his comrades the nature of this struggle: we fight not to conquer, but to defend the Fatherland and national identity. In a line attesting to Schiller's influence,[13] the speaker declares freedom the highest prize and proceeds from this ideal to his summation. Thus the first and last stanzas, dealing with the individual's obligations to the national group, constitute one structural unit, the second and third (nationalistic perspective and language as a social bond) stand at the center, and the structure's pivot is the instructional process begun in strophes four and five. With this the socio-political myth disseminated in Prussia is reproduced in lyrical form.

Meter and rhythm complement the structural affinity to the myth. The dominant iambic four beat line corresponds to common-time march tempo; the alternation with three beat lines suggest a pattern of drum beats. Consistent masculine endings not only stress the underlying drum sequence but also connote a marching army. These cadences act in concert with the metrical conformity of the stanzas, producing a distinct drum beat configuration. This is then sustained by alliteration: the reiteration of *f* sounds: *Frisch auf!, frei, flink, Vaterland*, together with a consistent metrical variance (four beat / three beat lines) within each verse and a constant masculine cadence corresponds to a drummer's beat and propels the poem forward. This rhythmic quality is augmented in the central verse by anaphora: in the second stanza, lines three and four begin with "Von" and the name of a river; lines three and four of the third strophe start with "Uns knüpft. . . ." The repetition accentuates the drum roll in these lines. Just as a drummer repeats the initial beat as he advances, the poet reiterates key words in the stanzas, thereby increasing the forward mo-

---

[13] The choir concludes Schiller's *Braut von Messina* with the lines:

Das Leben ist der Güter höchstes nicht.
Der Übel größtes aber ist die Schuld.
(*Säkularausgabe* 7:120)

Körner interjects the notion of freedom as the highest possession and plays on the double-meaning of *Gut* both as possession and the abstract good. Later in the era, Heine parodied the thought when he wrote in *Ideen Das Buch Le Grand*. "Das Leben ist der Güter höchstes, und das schlimmste Übel ist der Tod." See *Heinrich Heines Sämtliche Werke*, ed. Ernst Elster (Leipzig: Bibliographisches Institut, n.d.) 3:136. Schiller exerted a profound influence on the plays and the poems of Körner; see Gustav Reinhard, *Schillers Einfluß auf Theodor Körner* (Strasbourg: Trübner, 1899).

mentum called for thematically. The anaphora in these two strophes provides the basis for a rhythmic pattern which underscores the nationalistic point of view and the language bond.

The rhyme scheme places additional stress on the rhythmic quality. After the blank rhyme (a) of the first line, the arrangement (bccb) couples the four beat lines at the center and connects the three beat lines before and after. In this way, the drum beats are reinforced and the stylistic analogy to the drummer's cadences is completed. The blank rhyme at the beginning of each stanza signifies a step forward; the central four beat couplets and the rhymed three beat lines imply a union of like things. With this the rhyme scheme presents a stylistic parallel to the theme of national homogeneity.

This is not to deny that metrical necessities taxed Körner's skill. The apocope in the first line of the third stanza (*zusamm'* for *zusammen*) is a dubious choice. In the third line of verse four the accent falls unnaturally on the superlative ending (*-ste*). The elision in *freudig* [*er*] on the next line, "[in] freud'ger Schlacht" contributes negligibly to the total rhythmic harmony, tending instead to set off a ponderously strained oxymoron. The futile attempt to unite Eros and Mars results in an anacoluthon since the sweetheart has little to do with the summation implied in "Drum" of the previous line and with either the call-to-arms or the invocation of God in the next. In the last verse the key word "death" (*Tod*) is unstressed whereas the less significant "oder" takes the accent. Although one may argue that the poet intended here to stress victory (*Sieg*) over death, the phrase is cumbersomely set off by a dash, indicating a balanced alternative. Therefore, in this metrical context the unaccented "Tod" undermines the thematic symmetry. Despite these and other stylistic imperfections, the poem is significant for our study because Körner effectively incorporated the structural components of the Prussian-nationalist myth into these lines.

The imagery is especially suggestive of the social vision contained in Fichte's *Addresses*. Visual images dominate: the parental hearth symbolizes the connection between family and homeland; Germany's rivers denote the geographical expanse of the nation, thus underpinning the nationalist argument; vengeance is rendered metaphorically as an abstruse ray which penetrates simultaneously the heart of each soldier. The tactile imagery focuses on the bonds of language, God and country that join men in a single brotherhood. When juxtaposed to images of blood and lineage these tactile bonds assume an organic quality. The kinesthetic images of joyous battle, a thousand falling soldiers and victory or death not only increase the poem's forward thrust but also urge the reader to resolve national ideals in concerted military action against a tyrannical enemy. As the kinesthetic imagery builds up toward the conclusion, the theme of frontal assault reinforced by meter, rhythm and rhyme receives additional impetus.

The "Rifleman's Song" occupies a central position in Körner's *Lyre and Sword*. It is the eighteenth poem in a collection of thirty-six,[14] and assumes numerically a special meaning. "The Rifleman's Song" is a composite of those structural components found in other poems in the collection, uniting in one structure the essential principles outlined in poems before and after it. The language is colloquial and readily comprehended by the soldiers to whom it spoke encouragement. As we have seen, its nucleus is the socio-political myth which underlies Fichte's popular philosophy, at least one of Kleist's dramas, Schleiermacher's sermons and Arndt's *Spirit of the Times*.

Having examined the structure of Körner's "Rifleman's Song" in detail, we can readily perceive similarities to other poems in the collection. The basic three structural units constituting the myth reappear in several texts. The "Dedication" (*Zueignung*) composed on April 24, 1813, urges all German poets to heed the call-to-arms in "our ancestors holy language" (9), and contains instructions for honoring the poet should he fall. The one hundred twenty lines of "On the Battlefield at Aspern" (1812) repeat in lyrical form many facets of Fichte's *Addresses*. The battle is equated with Hermann's struggle ("Römerschlacht," 12); the poet instructs posterity about its eternal debt to those who have fallen (13) and the German people in its collective duties to the nation (14). The language bond is underscored in the third stanza when the poet, imitating Arndt, claims that the names Aspern and Duke Charles will resound "where'er a lip can stammer in German" ("Wo nur Deutsch die Lippe lallen kann"). The poem, "My Fatherland" (*Mein Vaterland*), written in 1813, resembles Arndt's "The German's Fatherland" (*Des Deutschen Vaterland*) published in spring of the same year. In both poems the reader receives instructions pertaining to duties to the national group, as German poets are called upon to support a specific socio-political platform. In the "Confederate's Song Before the Battle," written shortly before the engagement at Dannenberg on May 12, 1813, Körner uses a motif from the fifth scene of act three in Kleist's *Die Hermannsschlacht* when he claims that foreign aggressors have cut down the sacred oak trees; he also accuses them of defaming the German language. Therefore, he instructs the reader to avenge these crimes against the German lineage. The third and fourth stanzas delineate a social vision similar to that outlined in Fichte's *Addresses*. Such other poems as "To the King," "Prayer" and "Courage" reflect in varying degrees the structures which produce the Prussian myth of a German nation.

---

[14] Körner subsequently added a three poem appendix (*Anhang*).

The most famous poem in *Lyre and Sword* is undoubtedly "Lützow's Wild Chase" (*Lützows Wilde Jagd*) written on the Schneckenberg mountain near Leipzig on April 24, 1813, and set to music by Carl Maria von Weber. This composition, which has attained the status of a folk song in Germany, became the patriotic legacy of generations of German students, who served in two World Wars. Aesthetically, however, it has little to recommend it. The meter tends toward irregularity and incongruity: each of the opening lines in the first three stanzas must be scanned differently. The rhymes are redundant and often hastily chosen (*meinte/Feinde, Schlacht/Schlacht, Angesicht/nicht*, etc.).[15] The imagery is at times so strained that it tends to confuse or even baffle the reader. In the first verse we encounter a glitter in the sunshine which we are asked to hear (rather than see) — over the shrill-sounding trumpets. Although lying in ambush, the raiders shout a cheer — which would have assured their rapid demise no doubt! In the ensuing stanzas, grape vines glow, thunderstorms brighten rather than darken and the "black raiders" bed down amidst whimpering, moaning enemies. Stylistically, the poem is not harmonious. Nevertheless, it prompted praise from such Prussian historians as Heinrich Beitzke and Heinrich von Treitschke, who quote copiously from Körner's lyrics in their descriptions of "the origin and character of the great movement."[16]

Körner's poetic veneration of Lützow and his raiders assured them a special place in German history. Treitschke, for instance, points to the clandestine operation as an heroic example of German strength and determination.[17] His perception was pre-conditioned by the political and military advisors of Körner's day who applauded Lützow and his volunteers. Gneisenau, in his *Memorandum to Friedrich Wilhelm III* and Blücher, in a letter to Scharnhorst of January 5, 1813, lauded Lützow's military success and prowess. Both men urged the king to provide for more such covert insurrectionist organizations.[18] Not all contemporaries, however, expressed so positive an opinion of Major Lützow and his guerrilla band. A more sober picture is offered, for example, by Varnhagen von Ense:

---

[15] *Körners Werke* 1:37f.

[16] Quote from *Treitschke's History of Germany in the Nineteenth Century*, trans. Eden and Cedar Paul, [Chapter III, Note 16] I:510f. See also, Heinrich Beitzke, *Geschichte der deutschen Freiheitskriege* (Berlin: Duncker and Humblot, 1864) 1:156.

[17] *Treitschke's History of Germany in the Nineteenth Century*, 1:509–513; see also Fritz von Jagwitz, *Geschichte des Lützowschen Freikorps* (Berlin: Mittler, 1892).

[18] See Neithardt von Gneisenau, *Denkschriften zum Volksaufstand von 1803 und 1811* (reprinted, Berlin: Kriegsgesch. Bücherei, 1936) and *Blüchers Briefe*, ed. Wilhelm Capelle (Leipzig: Insel, 1915).

Theodor Körner: The Myth Personified 153

Viewed strictly as a military unit, Lützow's squadron soon displayed incompatible elements: splendid youths and men from the city, many taken away from their studies and government posts and still with the innocence and enthusiasm of higher education, were thrown together with both the coarsest companions, for whom savagery was more important than freedom, and crafty hypocrites who concealed their rapacity under the guise of fervent patriotism. Hence the innumerable complaints regarding all sorts of cruelty, which the people claimed to have suffered at the hands of the so-called Black Raiders.[19]

Varnhagen's analysis points out the importance of higher education in persuading German upper-class youths to join such military volunteer groups (*Freikorps*). Their teachers had been Fichte, Schleiermacher and Jahn whose social vision was often decisive. The Prussian myth of a new Germany provided the ideals which motivated these young men.

Another disapproving opinion was voiced by Gustav Parthey in his *Memoirs*:

When it came to courage and skill Lützow was certainly any officer's equal; yet his military career consisted almost entirely of serious injuries and imprisonment. The volunteers (*Freikorps*) were first deployed in Mecklenburg and in the area around Hamburg against the Danes. However, nowhere did all go well for them because their leader was either wounded or captured. Several copies of Körner's *Lützow's Wild Chase* sung to various melodies were circulated; but the last line was a travesty of the Black Raiders: 'That was Lützow's quiet, embarrassed chase!' Neither in those battles decisive for Germany after the truce of 1813 nor in the glorious campaigns in France at the beginning of 1814 were Lützow's raiders able to participate.[20]

According to the Prussian *Junker*, Major Ludwig von der Marwitz, Frederick William III had summoned volunteers for these *Freikorps*, but had no intention of using them against France.[21]

The later veneration of Lützow and his men illustrates the potency of the mythopoeic process which engendered counterfigures to Napoleon

---

[19] K. A. Varnhagen von Ense, *Denkwürdigkeiten und vermischte Schriften* [Chapter III, Note 95], 3:234.

[20] Gustav Parthey, *Jugenderinnerungen*, ed. Ernst Friedel (Berlin, 1907) 1:116. The last line of Körner's poem reads:

Das war Lützow's wilde verwegene Jagd (1:38)
(That was Lützow's wild daring chase)

The parody quoted by Parthey reads in German:

Das war Lützows stille, verlegene Jagd

[21] F. A. Ludwig von der Marwitz, *Ein märkischer Edelmann im Zeitalter der Befreiungskriege*, ed. F. Meusel (Berlin: Mittler, 1908–1913) 2:206.

and the heroic soldiers of the Grand Army. Distortions and fabrications became part of the German patriot's biography as the next generation of historians hastened to sustain Napoleon's anti-myth in Germany. Perhaps the greatest impetus given to this direction came from the death of Körner himself. At least seven witnesses presented testimony on how Körner was killed. They contradict each other on several points. Only one account, however, found its way into the authoritative German annals — the one most flattering to the central figure.[22]

According to Fritz Helfritz, an officer's son, Körner disobeyed orders to retreat, urged the troops onward and was killed twenty paces in front of the charging line. Ferdinand Zenker claims that Körner was trying to persuade Helfritz that he should disobey orders to retreat when the fatal shot came from behind a bush. On the other hand, Anton Probsthan recalled that the poet was hit while the attack was being planned. Another account related by Schönborn suggests that Körner was not killed by a Frenchman at all, but rather by a German musketeer named Franz! A month after the shooting, Emma Körner complained that she still had no accurate description of her brother's death; she was dissatisfied with a report stating that a French prisoner had grabbed a rifle from the wagon in front of him and had shot the poet from his horse.[23]

None of these versions found a way into the patriotic literature of the next decades. It was rather the more romanticized narrative of Peter Stiefelhagen which attracted such Prussian historians as Heinrich Beitzke, Julius von Pflugk-Harttung and Friedrich Kerst.[24] According to this report, Körner was killed after the raiders had seized a supply convoy. When Lieutenant Körner remarked that the French escort had disgraced itself in the skirmish, one of the French officers understood the insult and shot Körner down with a concealed weapon. Stiefelhagen records the spontaneous outrage of Lützow's men at the murder of their lieutenant and the reprisals taken against all the prisoners. The appeal of this rendition lies in the vindication of the *Freikorps*. It emphasizes a victory over the disgraced French soldier, who in turn is represented as vile and treacherous. The culpability of the indignant French officer becomes collective guilt since the other prisoners must bear the consequences. Stiefelhagen makes no mention of disobeyed orders nor of a possible German assassin:

---

[22] The testimony was gathered and published by Emil Peschel and Eugen Wildenow, *Theodor Körner und die Seinen* (Leipzig: Seemann, 1898) vol. 2.

[23] *Ibid.*, 2:235.

[24] See Heinrich Beitzke, *Geschichte der deutschen Freiheitskriege* [Note 16], 1:155–160; Julius von Pflugk-Harttung, *1813–1815. Illustrierte Geschichte der Befreiungskriege* (Stuttgart: Union, 1912); Friedrich Kerst in *Daheim*, 48 (1912), Nr. 47.

Körner is a conquering hero, murdered at a triumphant moment by a vanquished and insidious enemy.

The preference for this version illustrates the interaction between historical fact and myth-making. Writing for a socio-political crusade, the myth-maker seizes upon the historical deposition most favorable to his cause in order to influence his audience by means of a specific heroic image. His purpose is not to disseminate knowledge impartially, but to exemplify a behavioral pattern pre-conceived as a worthy course of action in keeping with the state of consciousness engendered by the myth. The description of a traitorous act will not benefit the cause. Therefore, a report like that of Schönborn is ignored. Eyewitness accounts which fail to do homage to the "heroic death" of the central figure are discarded. The rendition which, from the vantage point of the myth, places the hero in the best light possible is constantly reiterated until it becomes "authoritative."

Stiefelhagen's affidavit is quoted and referred to again and again in studies of this period in German history despite his own admission that he was elsewhere when the fatal shot was fired. He, as well as W. Krimer and the Chaplain Jüngst who corroborated this account, claim to have heard only that Lieutenant Körner had fallen; they ascertained the details later. Both Zenker and Probsthan claim they were present when Körner was hit: both testified to seeing Körner fall. Nevertheless, their testimony was rejected by "authoritative" historians in favor of a more emotionally charged version which substantiates the socio-political image of Körner produced by the myth-maker. Körner glorified Lützow's raiders — a rather impotent instrument in Napoleon's demise — and his own death was envisioned not in terms of military achievement, but rather against the background of the myth he labored to create.[25] Life and death, fact and objective were fused together by latter-day myth-maker historians, striving to create a desired state of consciousness within the national group.

But what induced Körner to forsake a promising career in Vienna for the guerrilla campfires in the woods of north central Germany? In sharp contrast to Kleist, Fichte, Schleiermacher and Arndt, he did not need the compensation. His father, a wealthy man, was a patron of the arts. Körner did not need to write propaganda for money. Why was he asked to compose lyrics, glorifying Lützow and his raiders? We have already examined the first reason — his link in Dresden with Kleist and Adam Müller. Körner was a trusted native of that city which served as a focal point outside of the Hohenzollern monarchy for the activities of the Prussian, Aus-

---

[25] For a recent discussion, see Erhard Jöst, "Der Heldentod des Dichters Theodor Körner: Der Einfluß eines Mythos auf die Rezeption einer Lyrik und ihre literarische Kritik," *OL* 32 (1977): 310–340; also Helen A. Szépe, "Opfertod und Poesie: Zur Geschichte der Theodor Körner Legende," *CG* 9 (1975): 291–304.

trian, Russian and British war parties. Since Körner was privy to their plans and had already demonstrated considerable literary talent, he was called upon to write songs for Lützow's volunteer army comprised of Germans outside Frederick William's domain ready for military action against France. The corps itself was affiliated, for the most part, with the regiment under Stein's father-in-law, Count von Wallmoden.

A propagandist was also considered important to the success of Lützow's operation. The failures of such earlier guerrilla leaders as the "Black Duke" of Braunschweig-Oels and Major Ferdinand von Schill were blamed, at least in part, on the vain and half-hearted attempt to rally the populace to their cause. No such mistake was to be made with Lützow. Körner's job was to manipulate public opinion in favor of the Black Raiders. Stein's Brünn Memorandum of 1810 had made the need for prior myth-making clear. Stein, moreover, renewed his personal ties with the Körner household when he visited Christian Gottfried in April 1813; at the time, Arndt was a guest in the Körner home.[26] Ernst Pfuel, a close friend of both Kleist and Arndt brought Stein, himself deeply involved in directing Lützow's maneuvers, the news of Körner's fatal wound (*Stein* 4:249). Theodor apparently perceived his "duty" clearly. Heeding the call from family friends among the patriots in Dresden and Vienna, he joined Lützow and began to poeticize his comrades according to the blue print laid down years earlier in Königsberg and Berlin. His death, in turn, was eulogized by his fellow collaborator Stägemann, who ended the first cycle of his *Kriegsgesänge* with a testimonial to the "heroic" Körner.

Beginning with Fichte and ending with Körner we have followed an intellectual movement which within half a decade proceeded from speculative myth-making in the name of critical idealism to armed resistance on a national scale. Körner carried the philosopher's postulates to extremes and helped to create by word, deed and in death a counterpart to French propaganda — an anti-myth which could replace the established image of the heroic Napoleon. Before insurrection and "German liberation" could be achieved a new state of consciousness had to take form in the minds of the citizenry. When the intellectuals were won over to the cause of political engagement and armed resistance, the Prussian populace followed.

On May 16, 1803, the Prussian government had sent out a call-to-arms, which was met by a total lack of enthusiasm and commitment and, in some regions, by open disobedience. Parents sent their children of military age out of the country, causing recruiting agents, who were assigned huge conscription quotas, to press teenagers and old men into the king's service. The result was public unrest: government officials were trounced

[26] Steffens, *AW* 5:121–123.

and those drafted were often freed by force. By 1813–14 the political outlook had changed significantly: first, the myth-makers had persuaded the intelligentsia to support the Prussian insurrectionists; second, Napoleon had suffered a disastrous setback in Russia. At this historical juncture, the myth could be converted effectively into military action. During the previous six years, public opinion had been manipulated to the advantage of the ruling class. As we have seen in our discussion of Kotzebue's plays, the middle class was not of one opinion. Nevertheless, the myth for which Körner lived, wrote and died, had proven to be a most potent instrument delivered into the hands of Prussian politicians by their literary collaborators.

8
Victory and Aftermath

ACCORDING TO THE STATISTICS OF Count von der Osten-Sacken, a general in the Russian forces and later corps commander in Blücher's army, 612,000 men invaded Russia in 1812; only 50,000 lived through the ordeal.[1] The devastation of the Grand Army fired the hopes of the patriots for the repulsion of all French troops from German soil. Pamphlets circulated with titles that appeared to praise the emperor, but with contents designed to stir up anti-Napoleon sentiment. One anonymous author ironically entitled his collection of poems: *Hymns to Napoleon. The Campaign in Russia of Napoleon the Great in the Year 1812*. The subtitle pays lip service to the hero, claiming that the rhymes were constructed by "one of his most zealous supporters and admirers;" yet the poems themselves contain scathing criticism:

> Es hatte der Kaiser
> Sich trefflich basirt,
> Ich glaube, daß weiser
> Ein Fähnrich agirt,
> Ohn' alles Replie,
> Wo blieb das Genie?[2]
>
> There was the emperor
> Excellently based,
> Wiser, I think, an
> Ensign would act,
> But for a reply
> Where was his genius?

The author questions whether Napoleon had ever shown real genius. The invasion of Russia had proven that he had set his sights too high. In one section he asks Bonaparte to stop the bloodshed:

---

[1] *Kampf um Freiheit. Dokumente zur Zeit der nationalen Erhebung 1789–1815*, ed. Friedrich Donath and Walter Markov (Berlin: Verlag der Nation, 1954): 208.

[2] *Lobgesänge auf Napoleon. Napoleons des Großen Feldzug nach Russland in Jahre 1812. In saubre Reime gebracht von einem seiner eifrigsten Anhänger und Verehrer* (1814): 5.

Laß vom Blutvergießen, Menschenmorden
Endlich ab, O Tiger wildester Art,
Welches Scheusal ist aus dir geworden
Stolzer Weltverwüster, Bonaparte? (p. 17)

Stop the bloodshed, the murder
At last, O Tiger of the wildest kind,
What sort of monster have you become
Proud devastater of the world, Bonaparte?

Similar themes were worked for pamphlets in the ensuing months. The writer of *Napoleon the Charlatan or Bliss Through Destruction* points out that Napoleon had the opportunity to show true greatness in the midst of adversity, but had utterly failed.[3] Ferdinand August (1795–1870), one of Jahn's students, authored a poem destined to remind generations of German school children about Napoleon's defeat in Russia:

Mit Mann und Roß und Wagen:
Mit Mann und Roß und Wagen
So hat sie Gott geschlagen!
Es irrt durch Schnee und Wald umher
Das große mächtige Franzenheer;
Der Kaiser auf der Flucht,
Soldaten ohne Zucht.

With man and horse and wagon
Did God defeat them!
Lost in the snow and woods
Wanders the mighty French army;
The emperor in flight,
Soldiers out of control.

In 1813 Arndt wrote his *Catechism for the German Soldier and Militiaman*, which contains a distillate of his political thinking along party lines at that historical juncture. Attempting to rally public opinion to the cause of German liberation, Arndt offers the following description of the French emperor:

> This terrible and cruel man justified all means for increasing his power; through treason and force and treachery he deceived all countries and people, divided them and subjected them to his rule; he dishonored and disgraced all thrones and majesty and banished as much as he could of this world's happiness, freedom and joy. To our dear fatherland, the holy German empire, he did the same![4]

---

[3] See *Napoleon der Gaukler oder Glückseligkeit durch Zerstörung* (Deutschland, 1814).

[4] Steffens 10:134.

Arndt intensifies the negative representation with an unembellished rhetorical formula: linking treachery, violence, deceitfulness and fraud on the one hand, he forms the antithesis to the sequence uniting legitimate thrones, grandeur, fortune, freedom and human happiness on the other. Bonaparte is portrayed as the personification of the maleficence which divides countries and people, a symbol of oppression and the embodiment of negation. For Arndt, the sinister image of Napoleon provided a vehicle through which the reader might be induced to hatred and defiant action.

The J. C. Hendel publishing house at Berlin and Halle was commissioned to produce a steady supply of literature similar to Arndt's catechism. Such brochures calling men to arms reduced the Prussian myth to a simple formula: "... if you don't want to become a degenerate, despicable race completely unworthy of your ancestors, if your children and their children are not to curse you: then act in unison."[5] Many pamphlets listed non-existent printing firms in mythical cities. One author calling himself simply Friedrich published *The Angel of Death or Sermon for a Crusade against the Devil*, in which he entreats all contemporary heroes to free the world from Bonaparte, the Monster: "— young heroes and knights of our day — behold! The time is at hand to free the earth of this abomination, who has united in himself what history has told us of those abortions from the world of fables" (p. 11). As the troops aligned on the fields outside Leipzig, the popular literature was taking the Prussian myth to extremes. The Prussian intelligentsia had been stirred into political and military action; now appeals to the masses followed.

When Prussia emerged victorious from the Battle of Nations, cries of jubilation resounded throughout the German literary world. Some writers like Carl Martini hurried to thank Bonaparte for taking his leave of contemporary history.*Dankadresse für Napoleon Bonaparte im Namen der geretteten Nationen. Ein Gedicht — aber keine Dichtung! Von Carl Martini* (Germanien, 1814).> Others like Kotzebue hastened to point out that they had predicted Napoleon's rapid demise.[6] One skillful composer put together a "New Opera with Old Songs" from various librettos popular at the time; all tended to glorify the Prussian role in the French defeat. Thus with great fanfare Napoleon was routed, at least for a time, from German heroic literature, as the myth of German superiority appeared vindicated by the judgment of history.

---

[5] *Aufruf an die Deutschen zum gemeinschaftlichen Kampfe gegen die Franzosen* (Berlin and Halle: J. C. Hendel in Commission, 1813): 7.

[6] *Endliches Schicksal Napoleons vorhergesagt im Jahre 1806 von A. v. Kotzebue* (Berlin and Halle: J. C. Hendel, 1813).

With the victory at Leipzig several authors in other parts of Germany voiced nationalistic sentiments nurtured in the shadow of the Confederation of the Rhine. Friedrich Jacobs (1743–1819), for example, who had moved to Jena in 1810 after a bitter feud with entrenched academicians at Munich, authored two nationalistic pamphlets: *Dangers and Hopes for Germany* [*Deutschlands Gefahren und Hoffnungen* (Gotha: Becker, 1813)] and *Germany's Honor*, [*Deutschlands Ehre* (Gotha: Becker, 1814)]. In the first, "F. J." summons Germans to forget all that divides them and to gather around the old German oak tree, where he draws parallels between contemporaneous circumstances and events in the history of ancient Greece and Rome. At the conclusion, he pleads for the establishment of a new nation in which Austria and Prussia work in unison for the common good of all Germans. In *Germany's Honor*, he criticizes the arrogance of Frenchmen, rejects the notion that their language is superior and portrays France as the victim of its own servitude. Jacobs calls for the unification not just of Germany, but of Europe, which would permit "the principles of the British merchants" to become "the principles of all people engaged in commerce" (p. 9). Thus Jacobs aligns the economic goals of the bourgeoisie with the unification movement. Characteristically, however, neither of his pamphlets bear any structural affinity to the work of the Prussian mythmakers.

In Bavaria, the criminal lawyer Paul Johann Anselm von Feuerbach (1775–1833) was among the first to speak in favor of national unification. He was also among the first to express doubts that the German princes would permit it. In his pamphlet, *On the Subjugation and Re-Liberation of Europe* (Munich: Finsterlin, 1813), Feuerbach warned his readers against those who would break their promises of unification and freedom; instead Germans must, "Be united! Oppose the world's enemy with a single will and collective strength." He observes nonetheless that the common people whose power could revitalize the nation were "despised and feared" (p. 23). Feuerbach echoed the sentiment, though not the structures of the north German poets, when he called for the dawn of a new era, the establishment of a new nation and under no circumstances "a return to the old days" (p. 31).

On November 14, 1813, Johann Andreas Schmeller wrote the following lines, which he later presented to Crown Prince Ludwig of Bavaria as part of a collection:

Gekommen sind sie, Deutschlands schönste Tage
o seid der Tage werth, seid Deutsche wieder,
Und wo noch Deutsche seufzen, da seid Brüder,

Da helfet! Jubel werd auch ihre Klage!⁷

Germany's most beautiful days have come
O be worthy of these days, be Germans again
And where e're Germans still sigh, be brothers,
Help there. May rejoicing too be their lament.

Schmeller published several other nationalistic poems which, he claims, were written much earlier and recorded in his diary.

In 1814 the publisher Engelmann in Heidelberg printed a small volume of poetry entitled simply *German Poems* [*Deutsche Gedichte*], containing a dozen "war songs of scorn and honor," two dozen "fiery sonnets" (literally: "armored"), "another four war songs" and twenty more "patriotic sonnets" written by "Freimund Raimar." Behind the pseudonym stood the Franconian poet Friedrich Rückert who combined in 79 pages individual features of the north German presentation with nationalistic sentiment in the south. This partial synthesis helps to explain the popularity of the "Fiery Sonnets" [*Geharnischte Sonette*] in later years, particularly in Wilhelminian Germany.

In these poems, Germans are called upon to rise in unity from all the different provinces:

Auf, Deutsche, auf, aus allen euren Gauen!⁸
(Rise, Germans, rise, from all your tribal lands!)

He summons Prussia (Borussia) to take the lead in resisting the French; he dedicates sonnets to Frederick the Great and to the women of Prussia. However, in contrast to the Prussian myth-makers, Rückert depicts the Wars of Liberation as a necessary evil, not as a glorious moment of history; these wars can be justified only by the need for liberation and unification:

Der blutdurchwirkte Vorhang ist gehoben,
Das Schicksal geht an seine Trauerspiele.⁹

(The blood-drenched curtain is lifted,
Fate sets to work on its tragic plays)

---

⁷ Johann Andreas Schmeller, *Tagebücher 1801–1862*, ed. Paul Ruf (Munich: Beck, 1956) 1:219.

⁸ *Friedrich Rückerts Gesammelte Poetische Werke in zwölf Bänden*, (Frankfurt: Sauerland, 1882) 1:15.

⁹ *Ibid.*, 12.

Whereas Arndt strives for a lofty tone and Körner for unbridled enthusiasm, Rückert imparts his reflections and formulates convictions which serve to rationalize the bloody and costly war just concluded. As the years went by, Rückert added to his collection of *Fiery Sonnets* until by 1868, when Sauerland prepared a special edition of the poems, their number had grown to seventy-four. Structurally, none of them reflect the pattern common to north German representations. Instead of "national education,""the bond of language" or links in the great chain binding ancestors with posterity, Rückert constructs his poems around indictment, apostrophe and expressions of hope, culminating in a prophetic-religious vision. For him, the poet's duty is to begin the deliberations, regarding the necessities of a war, leading to "freedom" and "unity." He guides his readers, that is the "German *Volk*," in the process of reflection. As Vierengel aptly put it, Rückert was "no bard who leads everyone to war with a song, but rather an uncomfortable critic."[10]

There were other reasons for the favorable reception of Rückert's poetry in northern Germany. Although Rückert does not propose a program of national education, his prophetic and religious perspectives yield similar results; his many apostrophes serve the same purpose inasmuch as they seek to rally southern Germany to the Prussian cause, which, it is argued, has become a European crusade:

Borussia! in diesem Augenblicke
Ist Deutschlands ganzes Aug' auf dich gerichtet.[11]

(Prussia! in this moment
All Germany's eyes are focused on you)

As had the north German myth-makers, Rückert exhorts all classes to join in the battle against the French and appeals to each German's sense of political responsibility. More important, however, he blames the war on those German princes who had joined the Confederation of the Rhine, for they had turned France's ("die mit fremden Degen") war of expansion into a "war between brothers."[12] The French are enemies who know why they murder Germans:

Denn Feinde sind's, geschaffen uns zum Leide,

---

[10] Heinz Vierengel, "Die *Geharnischten Sonette* von Friedrich Rückert," *Rückert-Studien* 1 (1964): 25; see also Helmut Prang, *Friedrich Rückert. Geist und Form der Sprache* (Wiesbaden: Harrassowitz, 1963): 49.

[11] Rückerts *Poetische Werke*, 1:24.

[12] *Ibid.*, 13f.

Wenn sie uns tödten, wissen sie weswegen.[13]

(For they are enemies, made to cause us suffering,
When they kill us, they know why)

More wretched, therefore, are those Germans who constitute Bonaparte's "entourage of thieves" and have thereby disgraced themselves in the eyes of future generations. Rückert shares with the north German myth-makers a poetic yearning for a new nation; however, he does not wish to see this new Germany established by sheer force or blind patriotism, but rather after careful consideration of the intellectual and emotional foundation necessary for success. For this reason, he subjects the expression of his political convictions to the rigid rules of the sonnet, an intricate form which lends itself to a reflective, critical stance, yet is so demanding that contemporaries had already initiated debate on the future of the sonnet in German literature.

In a review entitled: "On the Poet Freimund Raimar and the German Sonnet" for *Die Musen* (No. 3, 1814), Friedrich de la Motte-Fouqué heralded Raimar as the one German poet who had secured the sonnet a place in German literary history. With this volume, Fouqué argued, Raimar had proven that the form of the sonnet could be reproduced successfully in German as long as its content was patriotic. Raimar had shown that the German sonnet need be neither limp nor un-German, but to be effective in German the sonnet must "wear the suit of mail and armor" — it must be patriotically inspired.

Few contemporary critics shared Fouqué's views on Rückert's sonnets. An anonymous reviewer for the *Heidelberger Jahrbücher*, maintaining that the form itself led to poems in stilted German, found in the volume by Raimar, "not one such sing-song which [. . .] could save its own honor." For this reviewer the more "naive chansons" were decidedly superior poems. He was more impressed with the *Cossack Song* and the *Devil's and Drummer's Song* than by any of the "Fiery Sonnets"; he praised the "natural" poems "in folktones" such as *Marschall Ney* and *Marschall Vorwärts*[14] and dismissed the sonnets as "unnatural." Likewise, I. O., the reviewer for the *Jenaischer Allgemeine Literatur-Zeitung*, favored the "War and Victory Songs in a modern folktone" because they were "vivid and powerfully naive" and rejected the "unpoetic rhymes" of the "Fiery Sonnets." I. O. [probably Count Otto Heinrich Loeben (1786–1825) who wrote under the pseudonym Isidorus Orientalis] pointed out lines in the sonnets, "where

---

[13] *Ibid.*, 14.

[14] *Heidelberger Jahrbücher der Literatur*. No. 49 (1814): 775–778.

the language is not given freedom, but rather appears to have had force applied to it."[15] Contemporaries were drawn to the other poems in the collection, not to the *Fiery Sonnets*. It remained for the ideologues of Bismarck's Germany to resurrect Fouqué's assessment on their search for earlier signs of nationalistic sentiments. Conrad Beyer, for example, promulgated a Rückert cult by publishing popular editions of the sonnets and an exuberant biography in 1895. In 1814 Rückert's sonnets did not necessarily reflect a deeply felt or even widespread sentiment in favor of a unified nation in other parts of Germany. An anonymous pamphleteer in Munich asked in November 1813, *What do We Want* [*Was Wollen Wir?*] only a few weeks after King Maximilian Joseph declared independence from the Confederation of the Rhine, and answered unequivocally: "We want to stay Bavarians!" (p. 4). Despite Rückert's call for German unity, Bavaria could still boast its share of particularists.

At Dresden, the efforts of Kleist, Müller, Cavalry Captain (later General) von Carlowitz in whose home they met, and Dietrich von Miltitz whose castle *Siebeneichen* hosted many a secret meeting of Napoleon's enemies in Saxony had not rallied the Saxon king to the nationalist cause. On the contrary, when pressed by Baron von Gagern to explain why he supported Bonaparte to the end, Frederick August responded: "Twice this almighty man had it in his power to destroy me, but he did not. I shall always remember that."[16] Even when it became apparent that continued allegiance to France would prove detrimental to Saxony, Frederick August did not embrace nationalism, but nurtured instead a gradual return to regional loyalty. In 1816 he commissioned K. H. L. Pölitz to collect examples from Saxon history to illustrate "the purest form of patriotism," which, according to Pölitz, is found in Saxony: "Our state's history shows that the people of Saxony have enjoyed a most fortunate relationship between the royal governing house and those governed."[17] The crucial importance of Dresden notwithstanding, the literary activists had not succeeded in firing nationalistic emotions in Frederick August's kingdom.

The state of Baden proved even less susceptible to nationalistic fervor. After Napoleon's defeat at Leipzig, Baden's rulers refused to break with Imperial France. For this reason, the Prussian general staff financed the publication and distribution in Baden of an anthology comprised of patriotic lyrics. The purpose of *Outpourings of German Emotion in Songs and Mel-*

---

[15] *Jenaischer Allgemeine Literatur-Zeitung.* No. 171 (Sept. 1814), 421–424.

[16] Heinrich Christian Freiherr von Gagern, *Mein Antheil an der Politik* (Stuttgart: Cotta, 1823) 1:161.

[17] K. L. H. Pölitz, *Über das Verhältnis des Studiums der sächsischen Geschichte zur Belebung und Erhöhung eines reinen Patriotismus* (Leipzig: Hinrichs, 1816): 17f.

odies which appeared in Heidelberg in the Spring of 1814 was to persuade the citizens of Baden that they were, as Germans, part of a larger German nation. The anthology, forty percent of which consisted of E. M. Arndt's poems, was intended to manipulate public opinion away from France by creating a German nationalistic attitude in the citizenry. The attempt failed.[18] The people remained loyal to the ruling house, as the anthology found no resonance even after the fall of Paris (March 31, 1814) and Napoleon's unconditional abdication (April 12, 1814). The public's interest shifted away from such lyrics and toward the panegyric, oration and other more intricate verse forms better suited to commemorate the victories.[19] With the exception of Theodor Körner's *Lyre and Sword*, which his father published in a handsome edition in 1814, nationalist literature did not attract the following anticipated. Hence the movement toward unification was held in check by both the unsympathetic governments in the individual states and by the reading public which adopted a wait-and-see attitude. Outside of Prussia, at any rate, it did not clamor for nationalistic literature nor for the creation of a new nation.

Even in Prussia the unification movement was in trouble from the moment the cannons ceased firing. By the time Rückert published his "Fiery Sonnets" the exultation of the nationalists in northern Germany was dying down. No sooner had the "Wars of Liberation", *Befreiungskriege*, which Frederick William III refused to call "Wars of Freedom" (*Freiheitskriege*), ended, than the forces of the *Restauration* ushered in a new era of repression and territorial particularism. In 1813 Scharnhorst died. Shortly thereafter, Stein turned his back on politics, rejecting offers of prominent positions in the post-war government because he neither agreed with the emerging structure of the German alliance (*Deutscher Bund*) nor trusted *Restauration* reactionaries.[20] At the head of his "German Legion," organized and equipped at St. Petersburg and Moscow, Stein had chased the French out of Königsberg, where he had instructed local officials not simply to restore the old feudal relationships, but to carry out reform. His plan was to unite the German states between Prussia and Austria in five districts, depose those rulers who had aligned with France and to permit the bourgeoisie some voice in government. However, the entrenched bureaucracy at Königsberg refused to proceed with reform without written

---

[18] *Ergießungen deutschen Gefühles in Gesängen und Liedern bey den Ereignissen dieser Zeit* (n.p. [Heidelberg: Engelmann], 1814). Neudruck: Hildesheim: Gerstenberg, 1983. See Ernst Weber's "Nachwort," 1*-19*.

[19] *Ibid.*, 15*.

[20] Cf. *Stein* 6:138. In this letter to his eldest daughter, Stein expresses his dismay at the turn of events, describing the proposed constitution ("die ständische Verfassung"), which was never passed, a farce ("ein Possenspiel").

instructions from the king and his cabinet. When, after this setback, Prince William failed to press forcefully for the national assembly requested by the Westphalian representatives, Stein sensed that Frederick William III and his key advisors had no intention of keeping promises the activists had made to the people. Bourgeois notions of freedom and unity were to be suppressed.

The political fate of Stein's design for German unification under a more representative government was sealed at the Congress of Vienna. As the British delegation headed by Castlereagh reported back to London, [21] bankers and financiers on the continent had flatly refused to extend credit for any new bourgeois-republican social scheme. The enormous capital needed to rebuild Europe would be lent only to sovereigns who, as personifications of their individual states, signed obligations in the name of the country, which thereupon assumed the indebtedness. Only "legitimate" rulers — those whose lineage had traditionally accepted the responsibility for repayment — were considered credit-worthy. Republican governments like the one established in France after the Revolution had created the financial crisis now facing all the European powers. Therefore, financing new forms of government, whether republican, democratic or centrally administered and controlled, was deemed too risky and, it was feared, would lead to bankruptcy all around.

Even those blueprints for partial unification discussed at the Congress were totally unacceptable to Prussia: one included expanding the Prussian state to the Rhine by consolidating large, but segmented, territories on the left bank under Hohenzollern control; another would have returned large Slavic populations to the Prussian state. Both were rejected by Hardenberg, who insisted that Prussia be permitted to annex the state of Saxony outright. This proposal met with staunch opposition from England and Austria. The representative from Hanover, Count Münster, sought to thwart Prussian territorial ambitions because he recognized an opportunity to enlarge Hanover through acquisitions in the north of Germany. As a result, Stein saw his dream of a unified Germany vanish. He also contributed to a rift with England over the question of Hanoverian expansion. Hardenberg had succeeded at the Congress of Vienna only in isolating Prussia completely and sabotaging any plan for unification which might alter Prussia's traditional identity.

---

[21] Cf. Castlereagh to Liverpool (Jan. 1, 1815) in: *British Diplomacy 1813–1815*. Selected Documents dealing with the reconstruction of Europe, ed. Charles Kingsley Webster (London: G. Bell, 1921) Nr. 42:277 et passim. See also the Memoirs of Count Münster in: FO. Hanover, 6 (March 30, 1813); also Karl Goldmann, *Die preußisch-britischen Beziehungen in den Jahren 1812–1815* (Würzburg: Triltsch, 1934): 69ff.

Within a few months of the Congress, Theodor Schmalz, a privy councilor in the Prussian Justice Department, published an innocuous-looking "correction" to an article which had appeared four years earlier. Devoted to the year 1808, the fifth volume of the *Chronik des neunzehnten Jahrhunderts* had identified Schmalz as a member of "a revolutionary party which Baron Stein had established at court."[22] In 1811, working with material gathered three years earlier by Carl Venturini, the editor of volume five, G. G. Bredow, noted that Schmalz, in collaboration with this party, had written an "Address to the Prussians" intended to "awaken the spirit of the populace, while outlining a general plan for developing as successfully as possible the power of the people."[23] As a result, Bredow continued, Schmalz had been arrested in Berlin by French occupational authorities, who found among his papers many letters "proving that he had been commissioned by influential people in Königsberg to write political commentary."[24] Nevertheless, after a brief period of detainment, Schmalz was released by Marshal Davout who "had found nothing incriminating in any of the documents."[25]

With the conclusion of the Wars of Liberation and the Congress of Vienna, Schmalz felt compelled, so he stated, to set the record straight. He admitted that he had been paid to write his "Address"; but then many writers had received compensation for agitating against the French oppressors. He had been arrested, however, not because of the "Address," but because the French had discovered that he had been offered the post of director in a secret society. Davout pressured Schmalz to reveal all he knew about the society. But, as Schmalz went on, he had turned down this position in the "League of Virtue" (*Tugendbund*) and had been made to suffer for it, as the members continued to harass him. The "League" had not been, in a strict sense, a covert organization since the members had applied for and received a charter from the king in 1808; yet, in the following year, Frederick William III ordered the group to disband. At that point, "other such societies were founded behind the scenes, to some extent on the ruins of the 'League'. Their efforts were laudable as long as their purpose had been to free the Fatherland from foreign invaders, damnable, however, if they continued to pursue aims inside the country which ran

---

[22] *Chronik des neunzehnten Jahrhunderts*. Vol. 5 (1808), ausgearbeitet von Dr. Carl Venturini, ed. G. G. Bredow (Altona: Hammerich, 1811): 410.

[23] *Ibid.*, 411.

[24] *Ibid.*, 412.

[25] *Ibid.*

contrary to the king's wishes."[26] According to Schmalz, the League's members, now active in veiled, oath-bound brotherhoods, were attempting, "to unify Germany by instigating a war, pitting German against German [...], with hatred [they are trying] to establish a single government."[27] Moreover, the propaganda these groups had commissioned and disseminated throughout the German states both during and after the French occupation had been and still was completely ineffective. After all, "it was not their literature which had inspired Prussians; in the final analysis, the oppression itself and the king's own signal had set the liberating process in motion."[28] The people had not freed Germany, Schmalz remarked, but rather the princes and the king had done so.

Schmalz's sixteen pages provoked a furor. Propagandists paid with secret funds? Secret societies plotting against king and country? The League conspiring against Frederick William III? The rebuttals and new allegations by Kamptz and Tschoppe kept the presses rolling for months. The reference to the Chronicle was damaging to Stein and his faction since the public was reminded that the Berlin newspapers in 1808, official documents and the letter from Stein to Wittgenstein, intercepted by French agents and published on Napoleon's orders in the Parisian tabloids, had discredited the Minister of State, showing him to be at the center of covert activities directed at undermining France and conducted without the Prussian king's knowledge or consent. Moreover, the French warrant for Stein's arrest had branded him not only an enemy of the French empire but also of the German states. In a letter from Madrid to Champagny (December 16, 1809), Napoleon had instructed French authorities and the police of the Confederation of the Rhine to regard Stein as a traitor in the employ of the British ("comme traitre et employé par les Anglais").[29]

A few weeks after the appearance of Schmalz's correction, Friedrich Rühs published a refutation that likely did more harm than good. In *Fairytales about Conspiracies*, Rühs did not simply rebuke Schmalz, but rather called for the establishment of a representative form of government for all Germany. The German people had fought for freedom from all despots, Rühs argued; if they were not represented in a new German gov-

---

[26] [Ritter] Theodor A. Schmalz, *Berichtigung einer Stelle in der Bredow-Venturinischen Chronik für das Jahr 1808. Über politische Vereine, und ein Wort über Scharnhorsts und meine Verhältnisse zu ihnen* (Berlin: Maurer, 1815): 11.

[27] *Ibid.*, 12.

[28] *Ibid.*, 11f.

[29] Gerhard Ritter, "Die Ächtung Steins," *Nassauische Annalen* 52 (1931): 1ff.; Alfred Stern, ed., *Abhandlungen und Aktenstücke zur Geschichte der preußischen Reformzeit 1807–1815*. (Leipzig: Duncker and Humblot, 1885): 3, 266ff.

ernment, then as subjects they will have created "hell on earth."[30] Sensing that such pamphlets served only to align nationalists with republicans bent on overthrowing the monarchy, the son of Christoph Martin Wieland, Ludwig, urged caution: it would be best to ignore Schmalz, who "doesn't know what he's talking about. He's speculating or day-dreaming."[31] B. G. Niebuhr concluded that Schmalz's would-be "correction" contained not a shred of evidence about the existence of secret societies in Prussia or Germany. "What privy councilor Schmalz is decrying, is a fairy tale"[32]; if he does know anything about a plot against the king, he is obliged to report it to the proper authorities. Niebuhr called for a thorough investigation.

He should have known better. As we have seen, Niebuhr, a close associate of Stein, Gneisenau and Scharnhorst, was well informed of reform party connections to various covert paramilitary organizations throughout Prussia and beyond her borders. It was he who had recommended to Stein that incentives be provided for writers to promote the cause of reform and liberation. Within a few weeks, Schmalz responded. Claiming that Niebuhr had defamed his good name, Schmalz detailed the founding and evolution of secret societies in Prussia. More importantly, he identified Ernst Moritz Arndt's essay *Über Preußens Rheinische Mark* as typical of the work done by the initiated; he thereupon aligned all nationalist thinkers with revolutionaries and traitors[33] and called for an investigation of his own. Schmalz accusations were the first sign that what had comprised a united front against Napoleon in Prussia had begun to crumble as the ink dried on the treaties.

As Schmalz knew, the investigation Niebuhr and he were requesting was already in the making. As early as 1812 Hardenberg had begun to suspect the existence of anti-government conspiracies. For this reason, he instructed the spy E. J. Th. Janke to infiltrate an organization built on the

---

[30] Friedrich Rühs, *Das Märchen von den Verschwörungen* (Berlin, 1815). Contradicting Rühs' statements, an anonymous author in Leipzig confirmed Schmaltz's account, and named Arndt and Görres among those nationalist conspirators bent on "enriching themselves at the expense of the state." See *Die deutschen Roth- und Schwarz-Mäntler. Eine Seiten-Patrouille zu den Französischen schwarzen und weißen Jakobinern*, (Neubrandenburg: Graff [Leipzig], n.d. [1815]).

[31] Ludwig Wieland, *Bemerkungen gegen die Schrift des Geh. Rats Schmalz zu Berlin über politische Vereine. Nebst einem Anhang über des Gouvernementsraths Koppe, 'Stimme eines preußischen Staatsbürgers'* (Erfurt: Keyser, 1816): 16.

[32] Barthold Georg Niebuhr, *Über geheime Verbindungen im preußischen Staat und deren Denunciation* (Berlin: Realschulbuchhandlung, [Oktober] 1815.)

[33] *Über des Herrn B. G. Niebuhrs Schrift wider die meinige, politische Vereine betreffend* (Berlin: Maurer, 1815): 10.

ruins of the League, that is the *Deutscher Bund* founded in Berlin by Friedrich Ludwig Jahn and Friedrich Friesen. Janke reported that the League, since its dissolution, continued to function as an umbrella organization. Besides the *Deutscher Bund* which had formed a year after the League's dislodgement, such other organizations as the *Gesellschaft der Vaterlandsfreunde in Pommern*, the *Königsberger Deutsche Gesellschaft* and the *Gelehrten Gesellschaft von Prenzlau* were controlled by former members of the League, who continued to pursue its aims. Janke went on to describe an earlier plot to assassinate Napoleon concocted in Berlin and thwarted by Schleiermacher.[34] Janke's reports so alarmed Frederick William III that he wrote to Hardenberg on January 22, 1813, "I am certainly not mistaken in the belief that the League of Virtue has been resurrected and that a popular government (*Volksregierung*) will soon appear here."[35] Upon Schmalz's denunciation of secret societies followed an investigation by the Berlin police chief von Bülow who concluded that at least some of the members were allied with the reform faction and were preparing to establish a republic or at the least a constitutional monarchy which would include the German princes and be modeled after England or Sweden.[36] In the ensuing years, the Prussian Ministry of the Interior conducted several lengthy investigations which brought to light the British financial backing Ludwig Kleist had received, Bishop Eylert's role in a possible *coup*, and the hiring of literary agents to produce propaganda for the "good cause."[37] Friedrich von Müller testified that Napoleon was well aware of the machinations of secret societies and the "wild political speeches" of the academicians at Jena aimed at German youth.[38] He confirmed that the object of these organizations had been to "get to know those with opinions similar to ours, and together with them to disseminate our conviction that

---

[34] Akten des ehemaligen preuss. Geh. Staatsarchiv. Deutsches Zentralarchiv II (Merseburg), Rep. 77, Tit. XVII, Nr. 21, Vol. II, fol. 16; see also Percy Stulz, *Fremdherrschaft und Befreiungskampf* (Berlin: Rütten and Loening, 1960): 143. See our account in Chapter V, 110f; also Heinz Kamnitzer, *Wider die Fremdherrschaft* (Berlin: Rütten and Loening, 1956).

[35] As quoted by Willi Erler, *Die schlesische Volksstimme in den Jahren der inneren Wiedergeburt Preußens 1807 bis 1813*. Diss. phil. Leipzig 1900, 207.

[36] "Report of Police Minister Bülow." in: *Deutsches Zentralarchiv* II (Merseburg), Rep. 77. HX, Nr. 58, fol. 38.

[37] *Deutsches Zentralarchiv* II (Merseburg), Rep. 77. Tit. XVII, Nr. 21. Vol. I. The Bishop of Potsdam, Rulemann Eylert, testified that he had been approached by Stein regarding a possible *coup*. Stein wanted Eylert to crown Prince William, "King of Prussia in the name of God." Gneisenau vehemently denied that any *coup* had been planned.

[38] Friedrich von Müller, *Erinnerungen aus den Kriegszeiten von 1806 bis 1813* (Brunswick: Vieweg, 1851): 288.

the French must be defeated."[39] One of the more thorough investigations was conducted at Mainz where a specially appointed commission concluded that Fichte's *Reden*, Schill's insurrection, Jahn's German *Bund*, the fraternities, the athletic clubs and Lützow's "black raiders" had all been closely aligned and were seeking to start a revolution in Germany.[40] Since virtually all the writers we have examined are named in these investigative reports, we can confirm the existence of a literary collaboration which we have already identified through structural and stylistic scrutiny. Moreover, the denunciators of the *Restauration* were not merely jousting with windmills; they were correct on two major points: first, at least some of the Prussian activists who advocated the creation of one German nation were willing, if necessary, to overthrow the king; second, covert, paramilitary organizations, supporting this nationalist cause in an all-out effort to rid Germany of Napoleon, were accepting British financial support. With these discoveries, the concept of a new German nation as opposed to a confederation of sovereign states fell into disrepute. From the perspective of Schmalz and others, nationalism was a treasonable, revolutionary force identified with plots to overthrow the king.

Once Frederick William III widened the investigation, the leaders of the reform party became the targets of reprisals and censorship. Blücher offered his resignation at once. Gneisenau, whose list of "Useful Men in the Monarchy to Prepare and Influence Public Opinion" drawn up as part of a master plan in 1811 included the names Schleiermacher and Süvern, was summoned to testify about ties to England. He maintained that he never received any of the British money obtained by Major Ludwig von Kleist for the Charlottenburg Club. These funds were intended for the purchase of military hardware.[41] He had never been a member of the *Tugendbund*, and was guilty only of trying to get England involved more deeply in the Prussian war effort. However, such disclaimers made under duress must be understood in terms of the pending investigations. Their credibility was questioned by Pertz when he proved, for example, that despite such denials Gneisenau's political opinions in 1808 were those of the *Tugendbund* (1:332) and that Gneisenau was a co-ordinator for just about all of the secret organizations directed by Stein (1:425).

Without their high-ranking political and military contacts to protect them, the literary collaborators were virtually defenseless. To be sure,

---

[39] *Deutsches Zentralarchiv* II (Merseburg), Rep. 77, XXV, fol. 91.

[40] Cf. Erwin Rundnagel, *Friedrich Friesen. Ein politisches Lebensbild* (Berlin/Munich: Oldenbourg, 1936): 175ff.

[41] Georg Heinrich Pertz, *Das Leben des Feldmarschalls Grafen Neithardt von Gneisenau* [Chapter III, Note 51], 1:615.; see also 2:404, 436.

Kleist had committed suicide in 1811; Körner had fallen in August of 1813; Fichte had succumbed to typhoid in 1814. Only Jahn, Arndt, Schleiermacher and the publisher Georg Reimer remained of the reform party's primary myth-makers. Each was to feel the sting of *Restauration* censorship and repression because of their part in the conspiracies of days past, or whenever they reminded the Prussian government of those earlier promises made to the people regarding a constitution and German unification.

In his *Memoirs*, Arndt recalled the years after Karl Sand murdered August Kotzebue. In 1819 Arndt's papers were confiscated and sealed; in 1820 he was relieved of his professorial duties and forbidden to speak or write about the ensuing investigation. The charges leveled against him included "participating in secret societies and alliances, leading young people astray, spreading delusions about a Republican political order, advocating the restoration of the Fatherland."[42] Arndt was branded a "demagogue" and forced into early retirement. Twenty years later, the seventy year old historian and political commentator received a royal pardon and was reinstated in his position at the University of Bonn. Nevertheless, as Arndt conceded, the ordeal cost him the potentially most productive years of his life.[43] When he reminded the princes of their pledge to the people, the super-patriot, who had been initially rewarded with money and an honored academic position, was declared *persona non grata*. Like Schleiermacher and Reimer, he had fostered a myth only to discover that those whose interests it once served were concerned with power, not unity.

In his Reimer-Necrology (1842), Arndt also described the tribulations of the book publisher accused of "plotting against king and country" (12:91ff). His home was searched, his papers seized, his friends questioned because, as Arndt points out, Reimer continued to call for German unification and to decry German territorial fragmentation. Denouncing the "demagogue hunters of the last twenty-five years," Arndt insists that Reimer, also Schleiermacher, Eichhorn and Niebuhr (12:91) were "demagogues in a good sense," who worked between 1809 and 1813 for German liberation and unity.

Because Schleiermacher continued preaching the virtues of nationalism and castigating the evils of particularism after the Napoleonic wars, he was soon embroiled in bitter conflicts with Prussian authorities. In 1814 the circulation of a sermon he had delivered in 1812 provoked a furor. Intended to fire the emotions of the young men of military age two years

---

[42] Steffens, *AW* 2:244.

[43] *Ibid.*

earlier, this appeal was now construed as an attack upon post-Napoleonic Prussia.[44] Moreover, on March 24, 1814, he presented a paper to the Royal Academy in which he compared the political systems of democracy, aristocracy and monarchy. Insisting upon the right of the people to take part in the decision-making process, he asserted not only that Germans desired a constitutional government but also that the Hohenzollern monarchy was an unnatural social order out of harmony with the contemporary *Volksgeist*.[45] By 1815 he was invoking the wrath of God upon those unwilling to keep earlier pledges of German unification.

For the next fifteen years he suffered persecution at the hands of the monarchy he had so fervently protected. Because of Schleiermacher's constant Sunday reminders of the government's unpaid debt to the citizenry, Altenstein engineered his departure from the section on instruction in the Ministry of the Interior. More harassment was precipitated by his involvement in three major controversies: union between the Reformed and Lutheran confessions, the text of the liturgy and his role in the *Tugendbund*. His stance on each issue strengthened his image as a vigorous nationalist and provoked reprisals from those determined to return to the *ancien regime*. On October 18, 1818 he preached on the theme, "Rejoicing before God." This commemoration of the Battle of Nations contained a warning to the king that God had given Germany a victory in the holy cause of national unification, which Frederick William dare not ignore. Statements of this kind brought him ever closer to dismissal from his post at the University of Berlin. As Jerry Dawson points out, Schleiermacher found after 1815 that, "he was now almost an enemy of the state which he had served as a loyal teacher and preacher before the reaction."[46]

Jahn fared no better. As with Arndt, Reimer and Schleiermacher, Jahn was charged and acquitted, harassed and exonerated. He lost valuable years in legal maneuvers, house arrest and self-defense. At first, he was imprisoned for "treasonable affiliations"; later the complaint was reduced to "repeated disrespectful comments about the present constitution and state institutions" (1:161). The truth of the latter is indisputable; but what about the former? If the latter is a lesser charge for which the perpetrator could be pardoned, what provoked the accusation of treason?

---

[44] See *Schleiermachers Sämtliche Werke. Predigten.* 1:449–461. The complaint filed against Schleiermacher by Police Minister Schuckmann and the king's order to exile him in: *F. D. Schleiermacher. Ausgewählte Vorlesungen und Pädagogische Schriften*, ed. Heinz Schuffenhauer (Berlin: Volk und Wissen, 1965): 267ff.

[45] *Schleiermachers Sämtliche Werke. Zur Philosophie*, 2:249.

[46] Jerry Dawson [Chapter IV, Note 10], 123.

The myth-makers invited retaliation by clamoring for a united Germany under Prussian leadership after the Congress of Vienna had decided otherwise. However, their outspoken opposition, though culpable, was hardly treasonable. Since they were arrested on the same charge and subjected to the same police procedures, the initial reasons for their condemnation must lie deeper. The pattern suggests that they were excoriated not because of their criticism but for disloyal activities reaching back to the conspiracy with Great Britain in 1809 and earlier. Treitschke points out that Jahn played a key role in the planned ouster of Frederick William III in favor of his brother Prince William (1:354). These machinations exposed by Schmalz and Kamptz and attested to by Bishop Eylert prompted the harassment of those who continued to press for the nationalist scheme. Conservative government officials in high places linked the myth-makers to the treasonable pursuits aimed at deposing the king.[47] The intrigues of those earlier years were ultimately responsible for the fierce denunciation and may well have influenced Stein's decision to retire from political life.

[47] Cf. R[ichard]. C[harles]. Raack, *The Fall of Stein*. (Cambridge: Harvard University Press, 1965). Raack disputes any notion of a conspiracy to oust Frederick William III, arguing that all the plans of the activists were, at least between 1807 and the fall of 1808, known to the king. More recent evidence tends to undermine Raack's conclusions. See Rudolf Ibbeken [Chapter I, Note 38] and my article, "British Espionage and Prussian Politics in the Age of Napoleon," *Intelligence and National Security: An Interdisciplinary Journal*, 2 (1987): 26–40.

9
Transformations: The Little Corporal and Little Germany

AS EARLY AS SPRING 1814, SCHLEIERMACHER wrote of his disillusionment with the emerging Prussian policy towards unification. Germany, he writes to Charlotte von Kathen, would have been better off if Prussia had been defeated.[1] With these words, the political preacher closed ranks with those who expressed misgivings over the victory. After the Congress of Vienna, he was joined by many intellectuals who had begun to wonder if Napoleon had been the enemy portrayed in the propaganda. In retrospect, the age of Napoleon appeared to have enjoyed moments of glory and adventure, all the more appealing when compared with the mediocrity of the *Restauration* era. In the ensuing years, a new image of the French emperor emerged in European literature: the little corporal, the man in the three-cornered hat, the friend of the common people.

One of the first re-evaluations of the French leader to appear in Germany after the Battle of Nations was Ernst Wahrlieb's (a pseudonym for the political publicist Johann Adam Bergk) *Napoleon the Great and Bonaparte the Small. A Summary of his Heroism and his Wretchedness* (1814), which described two sides of the emperor. "Napoleon" is depicted as the great general, the military genius, the expert strategist; "Bonaparte" signifies the despot, the tyrant who sacrificed thousands on the altar of the Russian invasion. This dichotomy was to reappear several times as the *Restauration* disappointed nationalistic aspirations. Wahrlieb's characterization is a forerunner of the ambivalent representations of such Napoleon-sympathizers as Heine (who claimed he had written his *The Grenadiers* as early as 1816), Börne and Grabbe, who used the image of the "great Napoleon" to underscore the lackluster leadership displayed by rulers in their own day, yet could not forgive "vile Bonaparte" for taking on the trappings of the aristocracy and practicing absolutist tyranny.

---

[1] *Aus Schleiermachers Leben in Briefen* [Chapter V, Note 23], 2:309f.

By the late 1820s critics like Wilhelm Hauff could satirize the German reaction to the emperor by contrasting the anti-Bonaparte hatred of the myth-makers with the pro-Napoleon sentiment of proto-socialists in Prussia and other parts of Germany. In his short story, *The Picture of the Emperor* (published posthumously in 1828), Hauff illustrates the anti-French attitude in the persons of Baron Albert von Rantow and his uncle. The pro-Napoleon point of view is represented by General Willi, the uncle's best friend despite his years of service in the Grand Army. In a series of discussions, the divergent attitudes are expressed on several issues. At one point the General comments on the view of Napoleon in parts of Germany outside Prussia:

> "All the people? — rebelled?" replied the General laughing bitterly. "Then Germany must have revolted before the Germans took up arms. For some it was beautiful, but foolish ardour; many were motivated by arrogance; for others it was simply the fashionable thing to do; and you forget that Austria, Bavaria, Württemberg, that Swabia and Franconia did not, as you claim, rise up — and they too belonged to Germany."[2]

Although Albert's uncle and his friend, the General, express with equal eloquence completely opposite positions regarding Napoleon, and thereby articulate the opposing opinions in the Germany of Hauff's day, the author reveals his sympathies at the conclusion of the story. It turns out that the rabid Napoleon-hating uncle had unknowingly met the French leader and had been rescued by him from marauding soldiers. A copy of the famous painting by Jacques Louis David of Napoleon crossing the Great St. Bernard Pass reveals to the aged man that the French captain who saved his life, and whom he had revered for many years, was none other than Napoleon Bonaparte. With this discovery a reconciliation of all parties is brought about as the story ends with fifty voices shouting, "Vive l'Empereur!"

Impetus for the exploitation of Wahrlieb's two-sided image in later German texts came from the European context which supplied basic themes, motives and images for the unfolding of the Napoleonic cult in Germany. A contributing aspect was the commercial success of the pro-Bonaparte literature aided by the rise of large commercial publishing houses and the international promotion of "best sellers." Nowhere is the lack of historical authenticity and the influence of the general European trend more evident than in Heine's prose. An often quoted passage from the *Ideen. Das Buch Le Grand* ends with the following statement:

---

[2] *W. Hauffs Werke*, ed. Max Mendheim (Leipzig and Vienna: Bibliographisches Institut, n.d.), 3:499f.

... and St. Helena is the hollowed grave to which the peoples of East and West pilgrimage in ships with many-colored flags, there to strengthen their hearts through the great memory and deeds of the secular savior, who suffered under Hudson Lowe, as is written in the gospels Las Cases, O'Meara and Antommarchi.[3]

In a series of tightly linked images, the narrative persona prophesies Napoleon's future renown and Britain's eternal infamy. With a reference to Napoleon's secretary, Count Emanuel Las Cases, his personal physician, Dr. Barry O'Meara and his last medical consultant, Francesco Antommarchi, whose memoirs recorded the emperor's last days in exile on St. Helena, Heine acknowledged that the international best sellers of these writers had a profound influence on his own point of view. Assuring the European reading public that Napoleon had never been the oppressor the aristocrats say he was, these memoirs revered the French leader as an immortal whose deeds will be remembered as long as mankind survives. In his own presentations, Heine portrayed the emperor as a quasi-religious entity suggested by the three disciples of St. Helena, and in so doing brought the Napoleonic cult to Germany. He differs markedly from such reform party collaborators as Arndt and Kleist because he views Napoleon from the vantage point of the emerging European literary legend, and skillfully articulates a position contrary to that of the Prussian myth-makers. Heine is not concerned with the French occupation of Germany nor the despotic aspects of the French emperor, but rather with the legendary man of action, the literary hero.

From this point on, the legendary Napoleon and the anti-French perspective of Prussia's nationalist myth-makers exist side by side in German literature. One of the most humorous and ironic treatments of this duality is found in the eleventh chapter of the second book in Karl Immermann's *Münchhausen* (1838–39), where a schizophrenic captain appears. At certain times he is an ardent Bonapartist and at others a chauvinistic German nationalist: "For a time he's a Frenchman completely engrossed in the glory of the Napoleonic era; then he becomes once again just as ardent a Prussian, praising the impetus of that great national movement." Later in the passage, Immermann explains the meaning behind his character's strange behavior: "Many a German, who for a time didn't know what he

---

[3] Elster 3:160. For the European context, see my article, "The Emergence of the Napoleonic Cult in German Literature," *Revue belge de Philologie et d'historie*, 52 (1974): 613–625. See also Jacob Presser, *Napoleon. Die Entschlüsselung einer Legende* (Hamburg: Rowohlt, 1979).

was, Frenchman or German, would have maintained a simple, more genuine dignity by acting as he did."[4]

The "Young Germans" Theodor Mundt, Gustav Kühne and Karl Gutzkow studied under Hegel who influenced their literary development. Seated at the philosopher's feet at the newly established Humboldt University in Berlin, they had heard Hegel's mandate to step out of individual, self-absorbed flights of subjectivity and into the real world. Hegel prodded this generation of writers with bold directives:

> For man, this total focal point of the ideal, is alive; he is here and now, presence, individual infinity. To life belongs the antithesis of a surrounding external nature in general, hence a connection to her and an activity in her. As such activity is to be perceived through art, not only as such but also in specific manifestations, artistic production ought to move into the realm of actual existence, making itself felt, reacting to and inspiring the living through and in its very material.[5]

Yet when they examined that "reality" on the quest for new themes, neither Heine nor Immermann, nor any of their acquaintances among the "Young Germans," found the Absolute Spirit's divine plan for the universe as the master had promised; instead they discovered the economic misery which had accompanied industrialization and the social restrictions inherent in the political institutions of the *Restauration*. Therefore, the Young Germans sought an end to the literature of seclusion engendered, for example, by Goethe, and to the widespread ignorance of socio-political reality in Germany promoted by the "Old German" Romantics; they wanted to strengthen belletristic ties with the great historical movements and the social aspirations of the day. They had little use for those writers who refused to help resolve the significant issues of the period and had opted instead for the eremite aspects of life and thought which ended inevitably in arbitrary and despotic self-glorification. Art and life, so argued Heinrich Heine, Karl Gutzkow, Theodor Mundt, Heinrich Laube and Ludolf Wienbarg, should interact in a dialectic of reciprocal action. In their writing, Napoleon is both the man of history as well as the hero of legend; therefore, cross-overs from one aspect to the other abound in their literary presentations.

---

[4] *Karl Immermanns Werke in fünf Bänden*, ed. Benno von Wiese (Frankfurt: Athenäum, 1973) 3:223.

[5] *Hegels Sämtliche Werke*, ed. Hermann Glockner (Stuttgart: Fromm, 1949–1953) 12:331. Mundt's description of the experience is found in the *Leipziger Blätter für Unterhaltung*, Jg. 1833, p. 234 and Jg. 1835, p. 348f. Heine also heard Hegel's lectures, but not those on aesthetics, which were delivered one semester (Winter 1820/21) before Heine arrived in Berlin. By the time Hegel presented them again (in revised form in 1823), Heine had returned to Göttingen.

Heine's family, moreover, belonged to the Jewish minority in Düsseldorf whose hopes were fired by the Code Napoléon only to be dashed by the return of Prussian troops. In the midst of "imperial splendor," Heine's mother even dared to dream of a career for her son in the emperor's civil service — an impossibility under the *ancien regime*. But the dream vanished with Napoleon's exile and, as the Jews were thrust back into the old Pariah conditions, Heine's mother encouraged her son to switch from engineering to banking and economics (7:463f.).[6] Such reversals of fortune help to explain Heine's negative reaction to any appeal for German unity since, in his portrayal, such a movement was dictated to the people from above; it did not emerge "spontaneously" or "impulsively" in the hearts and minds of the German people: "They commanded us to be patriotic and we became patriots, because we do everything our princes command us to do." This quote from the first book of the *Romantische Schule* published initially for a French audience in *L'Europe littéraire* (March, April and May 1833) introduces Heine's delineation of the major differences between French and German patriotism:

Der Patriotismus der Franzosen besteht darin, daß sein Herz erwärmt wird, durch diese Wärme sich ausdehnt, sich erweitert, daß es nicht mehr bloß die nächsten Angehörigen, sondern ganz Frankreich, das ganze Land der Zivilisation, mit seiner Liebe umfaßt; der Patriotismus des Deutschen hingegen besteht darin, daß sein Herz enger wird, daß es sich zusammenzieht wie Leder in der Kälte, daß er das Fremdländische haßt, daß er nicht mehr Weltbürger, nicht mehr Europäer, sondern nur ein enger Deutscher sein will (5:237).

The patriotism of Frenchmen consists in a warming of the heart, which, because of this warmth, expands, broadens and encompasses not only his next of kin but also all of France, the whole civilized world, with his love; the patriotism of the German, by contrast, consists in a narrowing of the heart, which contracts like leather in the cold, in hating all that is foreign, in not wanting to be a citizen of the world any longer, not a European anymore, but only a narrow German.

In Heine's account, the evolution of the Romantic school in German literature went hand in hand with political developments. During this period, literature became the handmaiden of the government and those "se-

---

[6] This more traditional view of Heine's relationship to the Jewish minority in the Rhineland has been questioned both by Jeffrey Sammons, *Heinrich Heine. A Modern Biography* (Princeton University Press, 1979): 33–35 and Franz Futterknecht, *Heinrich Heine. Ein Versuch* (Tübingen: Narr, 1985): 55, 69–71, 93–98. Futterknecht argues that the Continental Blockade hurt Samson Heine's textile business more than anything instituted by Prussia. However, in this passage from the "Memoiren," Heine depicts his mother's concern for the difference in career opportunities available under Napoleon and later under the Prussians. These changed considerably, especially for Jews.

cret societies" whose members worked to further government plans. As far as Heine was concerned, August Wilhelm Schlegel had "conspired" against Racine in his critical writings for the same reason and to the same ends that Stein intrigued against Napoleon. For Heine there was no doubt that the causes for the Romantic interest in "Volk" and "Volkstümlichkeit," in Germanic "origins" and Christian religiosity, in fairy tales and "nationality" were ultimately political. German "patriotism" and German "nationalism" were no more than literary art's misguided attempts to join in the struggle against France. This prompts Heine to imagine Napoleon, "the great classic, as classical as Alexander and Caesar," crashing down, while August Wilhelm and Friedrich Schlegel, "the little Romantics," who were "just as Romantic as Tom Thumb and Puss and Boots," emerging as victors (5:238). As he had explained in the "Journey from Munich to Genoa" in the third volume of his *Travelogues* (1829), German nationalism "with its vanity and hatred" was simply "the main lever which ambitious and greedy princes set in motion for their own purposes" (3:272). For Heine, therefore, the most significant issue of the day was not Germany's political unification, but rather her social emancipation.

Standing apart from the nationalistic undercurrents is also the figure of Goethe, who remained aloof from the political developments of such consequence for other writers and expressed a consistently favorable opinion of Napoleon. When Arndt approached him with the request that he add his voice to those who opposed the French emperor, Goethe answered: "Go ahead and rattle on your chains; the man is too great for you; you'll not break them" (Steffens, *AW* 2:151). Between 1810 and 1812 he wrote a series of poems to Bonaparte and his family entitled: *In the Name of the Citizenry of Karlsbad*. In later years, he was fascinated by the "daemonic" figure of Napoleon whom he had met in Erfurt. In his conversations with Eckermann he repeatedly expressed a desire to understand fully this "Compendium of the world."[7] He translated Alessandro Manzoni's ode, *Il cinque maggio*, in the night of January 14, 1822, publishing his translation in the following year in *Über Kunst und Altertum*. The ode itself constitutes one of the more influential poems in the emergence of a European cult of Napoleon.

---

[7] *Eckermanns Gespräche mit Goethe*, ed. Fritz Bergemann (Baden-Baden: Insel, 1981): 16 February 1826 (1:162). See also Ilse Peters, "Das Napoleonbild Goethes in seiner Spätzeit," *Viermonatsschrift der Goethe Gesellschaft* 9 (1944): 140–171. Andreas Fischer, *Goethe und Napoleon* (Frauenfeld and Leipzig: Huber, 1900); Peter Berglar, *Goethe und Napoleon. Die Faszination des Geistes durch die Macht* (Darmstadt: Roether, 1968); also Dirk von Eck, *Napoleon im Spiegel der Goetheschen und Heineschen Dichtung* (Diss. Amsterdam, 1933); August Raabe, *Das Erlebnis des Dämonischen in Goethes Denken und Schaffen* (Berlin: Junker and Dünnhaupt, 1942): 267ff.

Upon Napoleon's death in 1821 Franz Grillparzer composed an ode which raised the question of the emperor's moral and psychological motivation. In the fifth verse, Grillparzer states that he cannot love Bonaparte because he brought war and not peace to the continent. By the seventh verse, however, he has turned the emperor into a hero, although he concludes with the epitaph:

Und sühnend steh' auf deinem Leichenstein:
Er war zu groß, weil seine Zeit zu klein![8]

And may the atoning words stand on your tombstone:
He was too great, for his time was too small!

The more polemic writer, Ludwig Börne, emphasized the dualism in the name Napoleon Bonaparte. His *Aphorisms* contain the comment, "*Napoleon* was great, high-minded and magnanimous; he fought for freedom and justice. But *Bonaparte* was tyrannical, autocratic, evil and deceitful."[9] This love-hate relationship is indicative of the political activists in the 1820s and 1830s who could admire Napoleon for his heroic qualities, but could not forgive Bonaparte for his despotic tendencies. In his "Lectures on Contemporary German Literature," Robert Prutz contrasted the figure of Napoleon to the unheroic German university professor and "the sly-nosed, cunning German diplomats."[10] Despite their outspokenness against the tyranny of Metternich's regime, these writers represented nationalistic views of their own: Georg Herwegh, for example, called for Germany to turn to the pages of its own history for such heroes as the French had in Napoleon.[11]

Foremost among the playwrights influenced by the political evolution of Germany after the Wars of Liberation is Christian Dietrich Grabbe. Molding the historical personality into a dramatic protagonist, Grabbe

---

[8] *Franz Grillparzers Sämtliche Werke*, ed. August Sauer (Vienna: Schroll, 1909–1948), part I, 10:61. See also Grillparzer's diary in part II, 8:101, 109–111; also his poems *Krakau* (1838) and *Rußland* (1839) in part I, 12:96 and 11:150ff. respectively. For studies, see P. Busse, "Grillparzer und Napoleon," *Jahrbuch der Grillparzer Gesellschaft* 19 (1910): 39–60; M. M. Cizek, *Grillparzers Napoleonbild* (Diss. Vienna, 1944); Joseph Nadler, *Grillparzer* (Vaduz: Liechtenstein, 1948): 56, 154, 167 et passim.

[9] *Börnes Sämtliche Werke*, ed. Inge and Peter Rippmann (Düsseldorf: Melser, 1964) 2:255.

[10] *Vorlesungen über die Deutsche Literatur der Gegenwart* (Leipzig: Mayer, 1847): 37f.

[11] *Herweghs Werke*, ed, Hermann Tardel (Berlin: Bong, n.d.) 1:56–59: See the poem "Ufnau und Sankt Helena":

Wie lang mit Lorbeern überschütten
Wollt ihr die korsische Standarte?
Wann hängt einmal in deutschen Hütten
Der Hutten statt des Bonaparte?

perceived the French emperor as a tragic Titan motivated by lofty ideals but doomed by his time. Perhaps no other nineteenth century play in German so completely captures the contemporary milieu and intense atmosphere as *Napoleon or the Hundred Days* (1831). One of the more significant points the author makes is found in Napoleon's prophecy in the seventh scene of act five. The opening lines underscore the unfulfilled promises, the disillusionment and the bitterness of the period under Metternich's iron rule: "Rather than one great tyrant, as they like to call me, they'll soon have a thousand petty ones."[12] Thus Grabbe elevates Napoleon to a symbol of lost liberty.

As early as 1832, Heine, reporting from Paris, observed the political ramifications of the increasingly popular Bonaparte-literature in France. One of the more commonly acclaimed poets in Paris was Pierre Jean de Béranger (1780–1851), who penned songs and poems in which Napoleon appeared, not as the emperor, but as the Little Corporal, the friend of the powerless, who roamed the streets of Paris in his shabby uniform and three cornered hat, listening to the common people. In Béranger's poems, veterans, children and grandmothers keep the Napoleonic legend alive:

> On parlera de la gloire
> Sous le chaume bien longtemps,
> L'humble toit, dans cinquante ans,
> Ne connaîtra plus d'autre histoire,
> Le viendront les villageois
> Dire alors à quelque vieille:
> Par des récits d'autrefois
> Mère, abréges notre veille,
> Bien, dit-on, qu'il nous ait nui,
> Le peuple encore le révîre
> Oui, le révîre.
> Parlez-nous de lui, grand'mère,
> Parlez-nous de lui.[13]

> They will speak of his glory
> Under the thatched roofs for a long time
> The humble roof, in fifty years,
> Will know no other story.
> Then the villagers will come to say
> To old woman of him.
> Mother, shorten our long night,

---

[12] *Christian Dietrich Grabbe. Werke und Briefe*, ed. Alfred Bergmann (Emsdetten: Lechte, 1960–1973.) 2:457f. Cf. Wolfgang Hegele, *Grabbes Dramenform* (Munich: Fink, 1970): 89ff.; also Alan Walter Hornsey, *Idea and Reality in the Dramas of Christian Dietrich Grabbe* (Oxford: Pergamon Press, 1966): 100; Friedrich Sieburg, *Grabbe, Napoleon, Dichtung und Wahrheit* (Frankfurt: Ullstein, 1963).

[13] *Oeuvres de Béranger* (Paris: Perrotin, 1847) 2:186.

By telling of other times.
Although they say he may have harmed us,
The people again revere him,
Yes, revere him.
Tell about him, grandmother,
Tell about him.

Reporting on the widespread popularity of such poetry with all its political implications, Heine, in an article for the *Augsburger Allgemeine Zeitung*, wrote:

> In the meantime the Bonapartistic poetry is more significant and more dangerous for the [French] government. There isn't a working class woman in Paris who doesn't sing and feel Béranger's songs. The people understand this Bonapartistic poetry best of all — and that's what the poets are counting on and on the poets other people are counting (March 25, 1832).[14]

Eight years later, he commented on the politicization of the Napoleonic legend over the course of the decade. In an article for the *Augsburger Allgemeine Zeitung* on May 14, 1840, Heine, observing the enthusiasm with which Parisians greeted the return of Napoleon's remains from St. Helena, points out that Bonaparte's legend had now become France's "point d'honneur."[15] Crafty politicians are using it more than ever to further their own goals.

In the meantime, however, the "Little Corporal" had been imported by German poets. Those who could not articulate the Napoleonic legend as well as Heine sought to outdo him in exuberance. In the last stanzas of "The Nightly Review" by Joseph Christian von Zedlitz (1790–1862), for example, Napoleon, a modern Caesar, continues to review the troops:

> Das Wort geht in die Runde
> Klingt wieder fern und nah':
> "Frankreich" ist die Parole,
> Die Losung: "Sankt Helena!"
> Dies ist die große Parade
> Im elyseischen Feld,
> Die um die zwölfte Stunde
> Der tote Cäsar hält.[16]

> The word makes the rounds
> Resounding far and near:
> "France" is the password,
> The countersign: "St. Helena!"

---

[14] "Französische Zustände,"Elster 5:86.

[15] "Lutezia," Elster 6:169.

[16] Joseph Christian Freiherr von Zedlitz, *Gedichte* (Stuttgart: Cotta, 1832): 23f.

> This is the big parade
> On the Elysian fields,
> Which, at the twelfth hour,
> The departed Caesar observes.

The most fervent and sentimental German poet to venerate Napoleon was Franz von Gaudy, whose "Songs of the Emperor" [*Kaiserlieder* (1835)] exploit Béranger's images and sentimentalizing stylistic devices:[17]

> Schlummern denn in deiner Laute solche, mächtig-große Klänge,
> Die den Namen voll beziffern, Und du fürchtest nicht, es sprenge
> Deines Saitenspieles Wölbung dröhnend jener Riesenton,
> Der der Erde Ball erschüttert, der Accord: Napoleon?

> Does there slumber in your lute such great and mighty tones,
> Which can fully decipher the name, And you do not fear, that giant tone
> May break the strings on which you play with such resounding
> That shakes the globe, the chord: Napoleon?

Despite the lack of originality, one thing about Gaudy's creation is remarkable: No other German poet so consistently exalted Napoleon in such elated terms. Moreover, Gaudy, a Prussian officer, was born and died in the same cities as Heinrich von Kleist.

It was not simply disillusionment with Metternich's system which prompted the rebirth of enthusiasm for Napoleon. The commercial success of the memoirs written by those who had accompanied the emperor to St. Helena prompted German novelists to look at the Napoleonic era as material for the German historical novel. One writer indebted to the Young Germans, Ludwig Rellstab (1799–1860), fashioned themes and situations from incidents involving the emperor for short stories and novels. The four volumes of his novel *1812* (1834) exhibit many antiquated stylistic practices and a bewildering entanglement; he creates, for example, a most unrealistic picture of Russia at the beginning of the nineteenth century. Nevertheless, in abridged versions the novel enjoyed a modest popularity in Germany for more than a century.[18]

---

[17] Franz Freiherr von Gaudy, *Kaiserlieder* (Leipzig: Brockhaus, 1835), "Vorspiel," 4.

[18] Concerning the popularity of the work, see Ernst Alker, *Die deutsche Literatur im 19. Jahrhundert (1832–1914)* (Stuttgart: Kröner, 1961): 309f. See also Werner Hegemann, *Napoleon oder Kniefall vor dem Heros* (Hellerau: Hegner, 1927); Milian Schömann, *Napoleon in der deutschen Literatur* (Berlin: de Gruyter, 1930); Friedrich Stählin, *Napoleon Glanz und Fall im deutschen Urteil* (Brunswick: Westermann, 1952); Fritz L. Cohn, "The Worship of Napoleon in German Poetry," *Modern Language Quarterly*, 1 (1940): 539–549; T. Ziolkowski, "Napoleon's Impact on Germany. A Rapid Survey," *The Myth of Napoleon*, Yale French Studies, 26 (1960/61): 94f.; J. Tranié, *Napoleon et L'Allemagne* (Paris: Lavuzelle, 1984).

Taking full advantage of the popularity of the emerging Napoleonic cult in Germany, Ferdinand Stolle (1806–1872) made a handsome income from his six Napoleon novels, in which he glorified the emperor and toned down Prussia's role in his demise. His works include: *1813* (1838), *Elba und Waterloo* (1838), *Der neue Cäsar* (1841), *Napoleon in Ägypten* (1844), *Boulogne and Austerlitz* (3 vols. 1848) and *Die Granitenkolonne von Marengo* (1855). The most successful was *1813* which reflects the plight of Dresden as it falls into French hands and is then besieged and retaken by the Prussian army aided by Cossacks. With penetrating psychological insight, Stolle depicts the shifting political and moral attitudes of the citizenry: the *Bürger* adapts his system of values to the tide of economic and social expediency. Stolle also attempts to show the influence of secret societies, particularly the *Tugendbund* on political developments.

Commercial opportunity motivated many German writers of the 1830s and 1840s. The Napoleonic cult became big business as the European reading public displayed more and more interest in news about the Titan of the century. The complete *Oeuvres de Napoleón Bonaparte* published in Paris in 1821, for example, underwent six separate editions by 1852. Collections of his writings, culminating in an *Encyclopedie Napoléonienne*, edited by E. Judenne and G. Franceschi (Paris 1870) went through eleven editions. Between 1833 and 1881 four separate editions were made of the German translations of this collection. By 1857 sixteen editions were made of the manuscripts left after Napoleon's death at St. Helena, also thirteen editions of his memoirs. In Carl Arledter's translation (Göppingen, 1822), they were reprinted often. The *Mémorial de Sainte Hélène* by Las Cases was edited sixteen times between 1822 and 1895. More than a dozen editions of O'Meara's *A Voice from St. Helena* were in circulation. Between 1846 and 1864, six reprints were made of selections edited by Achille Moreau from the memoirs of Las Cases, O'Meara, Montholon, Santini and some lesser intimates of the hero. In view of this commercial success, it is not surprising that in Germany, quite apart from the novels, poems and plays, several anthologies of songs in praise of the emperor appeared, especially in those areas in which sympathies had been strong: *Mainzer Liederbuch für die Veteranen der großen Napoleonsarmee von 1803 bis 1814* (Mainz, 1837); *Napoleon'sche Gedichte. Zum Besten der Unglücklichen in Lyon* (Leipzig, 1840); *Napoleon Bonaparte, der große Kaiser der Franzosen. Sein Leben, seine Heldentaten und sein Ende* (Nuremberg, 1842); *Napoleonslieder von Victor Hugo, Rückert, Byron, Zedlitz, Barthelmy, usw. zusammengestellt von Ernst Ortlepp* (Ulm, 1843); *Napoleons-Album* (1843).

One counterbalance to this pro-Napoleon attitude in Germany came initially from an unexpected quarter and was intended merely to entertain and amuse the reader. As most of Germany read Napoleon novels, plays and anthologies, Frederick William Hackländer (1816–1877), secretary to the crown prince of Württemberg, introduced a different genre with a peculiar realism: the "soldier story." His *Pictures of a Soldier's Life in Peace* (*Bilder aus dem Soldatenleben in Frieden* 1840) and the three volumes of his *Adventures in the Guardroom* (*Wachstubenabenteuer* 1845) quieted the enthusiasm for Napoleon literature inasmuch as they sentimentalized military life, engrossing the reader (who had more than likely already served in the army) by poking fun at superior officers and their more ludicrous orders. He followed these stories with two more sober volumes of *Bilder aus dem Soldatenleben im Krieg* (1849–1850) based on the reports he wrote during the campaign against Piedmonte.

Whereas Hackländer sought to show the funny side of life in the military, Prussian writers seized the opportunity the genre presented both to entertain and to rally the reading public around the flag. In 1853 Julius von Wickede (1819–1896) published three volumes of his *Stories of Prussian Hussars* (*Preußische Husarengeschichten*) which, to be sure, satirized life in the cavalry and played upon those resentments felt by many former members of other branches of military service toward the hussars; nevertheless, this work and to an even greater extent the three volumes of his *Stories of an Austrian Veteran* (1855) tended to counteract sympathies for the French by pointing to them as the enemy who made military service necessary in the first place. A more pronounced anti-French, pro-military bias was expressed by the Prussian officer Adolf von Winterfeld (1824–1889) who published fourteen volumes of *Humorous Stories about Soldiers* (*Humoristische Soldatennovellen*) from 1860 to 1877. These stories, though often amusing, reinforce attitudes of blind obedience in the military chain of command and civilian subservience to the army.

For the most part, however, literary interest during the *Restauration* had focused away from the Prussian myth of German nationalism and upon diametrically opposed artistic adaptations of Bonaparte's image, as particularism rather than nationalism played the decisive role. After the failure of the March Revolution of 1848, German readers were attracted to the more intimate details of the emperor's rule. In 1861, for example, Luise Mühlbach could still contribute to pro-Napoleon sentiment by detailing Napoleon's private life. Her novel, *Empress Josephine*, evokes sympathy for Bonaparte and the woman who loved him. Yet in the same year, Julius von Wickede edited the posthumous papers of a German "freedom fighter" under the popular title, *Against Napoleon. The Life of a German Cavalryman 1806–1815* (*Wider Napoleon. Ein deutsches Reiterleben* [in three parts] 1861). Once again both aspects of Napoleon's personality were placed simultaneously before the German reading public. Whereas Mühlbach stressed those elements which aroused sympathy and understanding, Wickede's popular volume, which was re-edited in the twentieth century by the German biographer of Napoleon, Friedrich von

Kircheisen, tended to emphasize the hardship and misery the emperor had brought to the German states.

By this time, national hatred was being rekindled on the other side of the Rhine as well. Louis Napoleon had begun to establish his "Liberal Empire" which Germans regarded with mistrust and alarm. During his detention at the fortress of Ham for his part in the insurrection at Boulogne-sur-mer in 1840, Louis had written letters, pamphlets and books, among them the mildly socialistic *Extinction du pauperisme*, which served to revive nostalgic memories of the glorious Napoleonic era for his own political profit. In the same year, Adolph Thiers who headed the French cabinet made an unfortunate remark which quickly rallied German public opinion against France and later became identified with the regime of Louis Napoleon: echoing the war party's sentiment, Thiers observed that since geographical boundaries provide the most secure national defense, France's interest might best be served by extending her borders to the Rhine. The German response was an immediate revival of francophobia. Nikolaus Becker penned his *Song of the Rhine (Rheinlied)*:

Sie sollen ihn nicht haben,
Den freien deutschen Rhein[19]

They shall not have him,
The free German Rhine.

which became so popular that, for a time, it could vie for the honor of becoming the German national anthem. As Friedrich Engels pointed out, only the Germans could be united so quickly in "national animosity"; only Germans would desire a national anthem predicated on negation.[20] Alfred du Musset countered with a poem which opens "Nous l'avons eu votre Rhin allemand." Heinrich Heine, who satirizes both Becker's *Song of the Rhine* and Musset's "shamefully mocking tongue" ("schändliche Spötterzunge") in Caput V of *Germany. A Winter's Tale* (1844), had noted even earlier that the revival of Bonapartism and the rekindling of national resentment went hand in hand.

Ironically, Germans repulsed by Thiers's observations failed to recognize that similar statements on their part would produce the same resentment in other ethnic groups. No other poet, for example, used river imagery to greater advantage for Germans nor greater disadvantage to other nationalities than Heinrich Hoffmann von Fallersleben (1798–1874),

---

[19] Nikolaus Becker, *Gedichte* (1841) in: *Der deutsche Vormärz*, ed. Jost Hermand (Stuttgart: Reclam, 1967): 128. For a discussion of subsequent developments, see E. Ann Pottinger, *Napoleon III and the German Crisis 1865–66* (Cambridge: Harvard University Press, 1966).

[20] Friedrich Engels, "Der 'welsche' Erbfeind" in *Der deutsche Vormärz*, 140.

when he wrote his *Song of the Germans* [*Lied der Deutschen*] on 28 August 1841 during a visit to Heligoland. Later set to a melody from Joseph Haydn's *Emperor's Quartet*, this *Song*, rather than Becker's *Song of the Rhine*, became the German national anthem on 11 August 1922. Nevertheless, when Hoffmann von Fallersleben published his poem, anti-German sentiment was growing among non-Germans in the Prussian and Austrian domains. The poem was, therefore, not received as the poet had intended. Just as Thiers's remark was regarded by Germans as a military threat to their borders, Hoffmann von Fallersleben's *Song of the Germans* was perceived by others as a poetic expression of the belligerent, expansionist attitude held by many Germans. The poet had intended merely to induce Germans to put loyalty to that new nation in the offing ahead of regional patriotism; however, his description of the new nation's geographical expanse provoked resentment among those national groups whose rivers symbolized Germany's borders in the first verse of the poem:

> Von der Maas bis an die Memel,
> Von der Etsch bis an den Belt. . . .

Little of the territory through which these waters flow had ever belonged to "Germany" and corresponded only loosely to the expanses of the then defunct Holy Roman Empire. The *Maas* or Meuse, for example, rises at Pouilly on the Plateau du Langres and heads generally northward for 590 miles through Belgium and the Netherlands to the North Sea. Few of the inhabitants of these regions considered themselves "Germans." The "Memel" cuts through territory seized in 1252 by Teutonic knights who built a fortress called *Memelburg*. The city which sprang up around the fortress was settled by Germans who were considerably outnumbered by Slavs particularly Lithuanians, who called the river *Neman*, the town *Klaipéda*, and hated their German landlords.

The *Etsch* or Adige river is hardly a natural boundary since it flows south, away from Germany. Although it rises from two Alpine lakes below the Passo di Resia and passes south through the Val Venosta and east past Merano and Bolzano, the "heartland" of Tirol, the inhabitants of the region, except for a brief interlude between 1805 and 1814 when they belonged to Bavaria, had been Hapsburg subjects for centuries. As the river continues on its 255 mile journey to the Adriatic Sea just north of the Po delta, it passes through the southern part of Tyrol with its large Italian-speaking population. These *Welschtiroler*, as they were called, were not at all unhappy about Napoleon's proposal in 1808–09 to unite the entire so-called Etsch-district with the kingdom of Italy ruled by Bonaparte's stepson. These Tyroleans were Austrians who spoke Italian. They never considered themselves to be Germans. They supported the guerrilla war fought by Andreas Hofer and the German-speaking Tyroleans from April to November 1809 (resulting in Hofer's execution in Mantua on 20 Feb. 1810) in defense of the Tyrol, not for the liberation nor for the unification of Germany.

Even Hofer and his German-speaking compatriots didn't consider themselves "Germans." Although they were heralded by such Prussian-oriented poets as Max von Schenkendorf, Friedrich de la Motte-Fouqué, Theodor Körner, and others as the embodiment of popular resistance to Napoleon throughout German-speaking territories, Andreas Hofer and his sharpshooters shared little of the Prussian enthusiasm for a new Germany and even less for a rejuvenated Prussia. The insurrection Hofer led was neither a war of liberation (*Befreiungskrieg*) nor a war for freedom (*Freiheitskrieg*), as the resistance movement was regarded in Prussia, but a war for independence (*Unabhängigkeitskrieg*) from the French Emperor and his Bavarian allies. Hofer sought to free the Tyrol from Bavaria's rule in order to rejoin the Austrian empire and return to the old constitution. The founding of a "new" Germany was not even remotely his goal.

There are three bodies of water to which "der Belt" can refer: the large Belt or *Store Bælt*, the small Belt (*Lille Baelt*) or the *Beltsee*, all of which belong to Denmark. The large *Belt* separates Seeland and Lollard on the eastern end and Fünen and Langeland on the western side. The little *Belt* flows between Fünen and Jutland, while the *Beltsee* designates the northern part of what Germans call the *Kieler Bucht*. These waters are behind Danish borders and can hardly be claimed by Germany in any other way but by right of military conquest. This is precisely what Germany's neighbors feared whenever Germans talked about establishing "their" nation.

Like the statement by Thiers, Hoffmann von Fallersleben's poetic description of that new Germany's borders is historically questionable; it went beyond what representations of German ethnicity or references to the bond of language could justify. The poet's freewheeling geography lesson was never meant as a declaration of imperialistic intent, but rather as a call for unity in the face of particularistic allegiances. Unfortunately, little in the poem itself prevented others in the next decades from holding up the *Song of the Germans* as the true poetic representation of the geographical expanse of the new German nation to be established, if need be, at the expense of others.

There was yet another problem with the poem. Originally, it was not sung to the famous melody by Haydn, but to "God save Francis, the Emperor." The melody implied that the Hapsburgs should lead the unification movement of the 1840s. But the German princes had deserted Francis by joining the Confederation of the Rhine under Napoleon's protectorate. This forced Francis II to lay down the imperial crown and dissolve the Holy Roman Empire in 1806 lest Napoleon crown himself Emperor of the Germans! With this, Austria turned her attention more toward the growing Slavic and Italian populations within her imperial borders. By the middle of the nineteenth century, ethnic German comprised less than 25% of Austria's population. The crown could ill afford to lead a "Germans only" movement as many German nationalists demanded. Even if Austria had been willing to give up her claims to non-German subjects, the unified German nation she was supposed to lead would be threatened from the outset by the very minorities she had abandoned. It was feared that Russia would then exert an undesirable influence on these Slavic groups, which would then threaten any newly established "German" nation. For these reasons among others, the Hapsburg rulers refused to resurrect the Holy Roman Empire or accept the crown of a new German nation even after the revolution of 1848 when Frederick William IV of Prussia encouraged Austria to do one or the other.

By 1847 when the Perrotin publishing house in Paris printed a popular edition of Béranger's poems, Germany and France were steering a collision course. Initially, Louis Napoleon could use the old antagonism to his advantage; ultimately, however, it led to war with Germany and disaster for his Second Empire. The renewal of national hatred, which Heine witnessed in the making some thirty years earlier, not only contributed to the Franco-Prussian War of 1870–71 but also played right into the hands of those ideologues of Bismarck's *Reich* who banished the heroic Napoleon from German literature by recasting and reshaping the anti-Napoleon sentiments and war chants of Prussian myth-makers. At this historical juncture, the cultural identity which, for example, the brothers Grimm had promoted with their collection of German fairy tales was reshaped into the ideology rising upon the economic base of Friedrich List's German customs union. Political unification became less and less a matter of fulfilling older dreams and aspirations and more a question of economic expansion. The battle between German and American pork from 1879 to 1891 provides a concrete example of economic rivalry which nurtures national prestige.[21] Colonial expansion, particularly the German penetration into South West Africa from 1880 to 1885, intensified the desire for national unity and determined to a remarkable degree Germany's foreign policy.[22] As the authoritarianism of Bismarck's belated nation began to mold a "German national character" after 1871, nationalism evolved into a complex social, political and economic phenomenon.

---

[21] Louis P. Snyder, *Roots of German Nationalism* [Chapter VI, Note 51], 92–111. For a more recent discussion which includes cultural factors, see Arlie J. Hoover, *The Gospel of Nationalism* (Stuttgart: F. Steiner, 1986).

[22] Louis P. Snyder, 75–91.

The dichotic image of Napoleon rather than the myth of the nation dominated German literature up to unification in 1871. As late as 1873 Luise von Françoise could exploit this literary ambivalence in her popular novel, *Frau Erdmuthens Zwillingssöhne*, in which Pastor Gottfried Bleibtreu narrates the story of Liska, the girl he secretly loves. On the one hand, she is the bride of the Prussian chauvinist and German nationalist, Hermann Roc von Fels; on the other, she is the paramour of Hermann's twin, Raoul, who venerates Napoleon. The rivalry, conflict and impassioned jealousy between the different brothers produces a tragedy, resulting in Raoul's death. Luise von Françoise's characters reflect that strange blend of reactionary-liberal politics which marked the thinking of her German contemporaries. Yet this example from the pages of trivial literature in the early 1870s may also be seen as foreshadowing literary prophecies of the next decade: when Hermann does battle with Raoul, the German nationalist myth will triumph over sympathies for the French. However, before writers of the next generation could seize upon the more irrational aspects of the myth, thereby promoting that historical process which would lead Germany to wrack and ruin, German nationalism had undergone additional transformations. As we shall see, the myth had become ideology.

This transformation was, as Dieter Düding (last footnote, Chapter VI) cogently argued, the work of "socially organized nationalists," who, from 1808 to the March Revolution and beyond, filled the ranks of student fraternities, singing societies, athletic leagues and civic clubs. Censorship and the resulting limitations on the commercial success for pan-German literary points of view turned German nationalism into an "underground" movement subsequently resurrected and reshaped by forces sympathetic to Bismarck's political goals. Nevertheless, as the Iron Chancellor laid the foundation for the new German empire, academics assumed an increasingly significant role as "advocates of the nation" (Scherer). As the Hohenzollern influence on the other German states increased, political and literary historians marched dutifully, though often unwittingly, into the ideological swamp. As early as 1854, for example, Ludwig Häußer, fed up with the stultifying effects of the *Restauration* and a failed bourgeois revolution, published an influential *History of Germany from the Death of Frederick the Great to the Founding of the Old Alliance*. As a member of the legislature in the state of Baden, he had witnessed firsthand the retarding influence of the old order buttressed by dynastic treaties which hindered trade, "family friendships" of questionable value in times of crisis and, generally, a lack of public pride and faith in the country. Therefore, in three mighty volumes, Häußer contrasted these "infirmities in the life of our state" with what he considered to be the "inherent power of the nation." This compelling force had surfaced briefly during the French occupation and had enabled the Germans to drive out Napoleon's armies.

Häußer sought to revive this "spirit of the nation" whose nucleus at that time had been Prussia but, now, as far as he was concerned, could be any German state.

In his description of the resistance movement, Häußer envisioned "the seeds of fermentation in the masses." In times of emergency, only the inborn strength of the people could achieve victory. During the occupation, a premonition overwhelmed the "German heart," as deep and lasting transformations took place in the disposition (*Gemüt*) of the populace: "As in the external order of life, a change came about in the intellectual mood of the nation."[23] In the midst of virtual dissolution, a consciousness of collective strength and an urgent need for self-denial and exertion became paramount in the thinking of all citizens.

Grammatically, Häußer's account abounds in reflexive and passive verb forms, intended to illustrate the unfolding of a process which held out the hope that the German states would become a nation. But grammar and syntax of this kind tend to omit the agent by whom historical events are brought into being. By omitting names and personal pronouns responsible for specific actions at key historical junctures, Häußer imbued the era with a metaphysical quality: a transcendent historical force produced a sense of collective consciousness in the German psyche simultaneously experienced by thousands of people, each of whom was thereby motivated to act according to a preconceived plan for the founding of a German nation. After the Wars of Liberation, the ruling families had conspired to impede the progress of this "national spirit." Häußer's narration is among the first to depict the establishment of a unified *Deutschland* as the expression of a "higher" force.

Once Bismarck had succeeded in uniting most of the German princes, Heinrich von Treitschke used similar grammatical structures to vindicate and justify the formation of this specific union of states behind the Hohenzollern throne, rather than a more inclusive national unification. Twenty-five years after Häußer penned his account, Treitschke turned the public's attention to those transformations in Germany's intellectual life which, according to him, were brought about by developments internal to Prussia. In his chronicle of the nineteenth century, the disaster at Jena in 1806 had started a psychic process in the German mind which led to active resistance to Napoleon:

> All things that could animate a strong people to despairing resolve, pride and hatred, pain and repentance, were fermented in a thousand valiant spirits, and every new misdeed of the foreign oppression increased the bitterness

---

[23] Ludwig Häußer, *Deutsche Geschichte vom Tode Friedrich des Großen bis zur Gründung des alten Bundes* (Meersburg: Hendel, 1933 [First Edition 1854]) 3:159f. For a statement of his purpose, see Häußer's introduction to volume three.

until at length all that was Prussian was united in the passionate desire for reprisal.[24]

Like Häußer, but with a different goal, Treitschke portrayed the "spontaneous" and "contagious" aspects of a German rebirth, emphasizing the "mass reaction" of German citizens, especially the resolve of Prussians, after the humiliation suffered at Tilsit. In an effort to vindicate Prussian hegemony in the newly established German Empire, Treitschke stressed the two-hundred year old rivalry between Austria and the new "Germany." Eight years after the founding of Bismarck's *Deutschland* he sought to strengthen that central authority which had, allegedly, harnessed this psyche and, in so doing, accelerated the national spirit's progress. The expression of this spirit was the Germany as constituted in Treitschke's own day.

This *History of Germany in the Nineteenth Century* prompted a flood of imitations, interpretations and supplements. Heinrich von Sybel argued that the history of this newly created "nation" represented the progress of an ethical ideal.[25] August von Rochau seized upon Hegel's claim that the Absolute is accessible in manifestations unique to each age as a justification and apology for those political and religious institutions recently established on a national level. Julius von Pflugk-Harttung wrote stirring, imaginative narrative accompanied by monumental illustrations of the battles, personalities and acts of heroism in the era of liberation.[26] What unites these historians is the aura of spontaneity and urgency ascribed to the German response to French occupation. Despite differing attitudes within German historiographical tradition, their phraseology implies that the historical process from 1807 to 1813/14 had been guided by a transcendent force and had served a "higher" purpose. They may have disagreed about the exact nature of this goal; yet they traced the growth of a "faith in the power" of the German character as it evolved from Tilsit to Leipzig with remarkable congruity.

In such authoritative accounts of Germany under Napoleon, an "intellectual mood" takes possession of the individual, as "national passion" begins to rage in each soul. A newly acquired consciousness seeks expression after the Peace of Tilsit in the taking-up of arms against the French invaders. Historians subscribing to such notions acknowledged that many

---

[24] *Treitschke's History of Germany in the Nineteenth Century*, trans. Eden and Cedar Paul [Chapter III, Note 16], 1:312. For details of the German attitude toward von Treitschke, see Ludwig Lorenz, *Heinrich von Treitschke in unserer Zeit* (Leipzig: Hirzel, 1916).

[25] For details, see Hellmut Seier, "Sybels Vorlesungen über Politik und die Kontinuität des 'staatsbildenden' Liberalismus," *Historische Zeitschrift* 187 (1959): 105.

[26] See Julius von Pflugk-Harttung, *1813–1815. Illustrierte Geschichte der Befreiungsgeschichte* (Stuttgart: Union, 1912).

people were instrumental in organizing and channeling these unharnessed sentiments; yet they perceived Germany's liberation as a necessary expression of national consciousness engendered by a historical force which had permeated the era and inspired national action.

This is not to suggest that such fanciful metaphysical explanations of Germany's evolution went unchallenged. As early as 1868, Johann Gustav Droysen urged caution when writing history from subjective viewpoints founded on metaphysical speculation.[27] More recently, George Iggers discerned a shift in emphasis in German historiography before 1871 and thereafter.[28] He also outlined the differing attitudes among north and south German historians. After World War I, these conceptualizations of Germany's national resurgence were analyzed with a critical eye as historians sought to discover their own contributions to the causes of the catastrophic war. Friedrich Meinecke, for example, denounced the cornerstone of radical Machiavellianism which Hegel had set in place and Treitschke had affirmed.[29] Otto Hintze insisted that there was nothing holy about the state which warranted such devotion from German historians since Hegel.[30] These and other critics promoted the decline of the German "idea."

Earlier, however, in the wake of unification, German historians, inspired by the idea of an unfolding historical process and captivated by the possible application of a dialectical method, involving especially Prussia and Austria, fused pseudo-metaphysical explanations with cultural aspects to describe the "German metamorphosis" between 1807 and 1813. Yet they tended to omit the agents responsible for the events they described, thereby focusing attention on a presupposed benevolent historical force at work in the era. Because they exaggerated the effusion of general sentiment and the spontaneity of the popular response to Napoleon's domination, it is not the individual who stands at the center of their accounts, but rather the relationship of individual actions to the unidentified force which had somehow commandeered the superpersonal German psyche.

---

[27] Johann Gustav Droysen, *Grundriß der Historik* (Leipzig: Veit, 1868).

[28] George Iggers, *The German Conception of History* (Middletown: Wesleyan University Press, 1968): 130ff.

[29] Friedrich Meinecke, *Weltbürgertum und Nationalstaat* (Munich: Oldenbourg, 1928); see also "Die Idee der Staatsräson" (1924) in *Friedrich Meineckes Werke*, ed. H. Herzfeld and Carl Hinrichs (Munich: Oldenbourg, 1957) 1:411–427.

[30] Otto Hintze, "Wesen und Wandlung des modernen Staates," *Sitzungsberichte. Preußische Akademie der Wissenschaften* (1931): 790–810.

Literary scholars in the newly created nation followed their lead by producing monumental "assessments" (*Würdigungen*) of those authors briefly described by the historians as having contributed to the national effort. Employing the same terminology, corresponding grammatical structures and equally imaginative narrative techniques, literary historians described the patriotic literature of the Napoleonic era in Germany as the vehicle through which "national destiny" had been fulfilled. Inquiries into the "historical consciousness" of the individual writer took precedence over examinations of his or her artistic talent. The a priori political persuasions of individual literary historians at the turn of the century account for variances in their presentations.

Wilhelm Scherer, for example, perceived a link between Fichte and Arndt, yet he does not analyze the bond in terms of his own approach to literature; instead he neglects the "experienced, inherited and learned" (*das Erlebte, Ererbte, Erlernte*) in the life and works of these authors and analyzes them as instruments of that "higher" force which called into being the new German state: "But the transfigured picture of the nation, which they [Arndt and Fichte] carried in their hearts and communicated to the masses, was a tremendous ethical force, upon which rested courage and hope and the power to resist during the time of crisis. Everywhere the cosmopolitan attitude was in retreat as the national standpoint asserted itself."[31] No one was more convinced of the validity of this national standpoint than Scherer himself. According to him, literary scholars were "advocates of the nation"[32] who examined literary history in this period with a view toward national destiny and showed their "appreciation" of those who had helped Germany attain a unified political identity.

Friedrich Vogt and Max Koch, also avid nationalists, saw a connection between Fichte's *Addresses* and Arndt's essays and poems. In their *History of German Literature*, Fichte and Arndt are related not because of style, parallel organizational structures or linguistic patterns, but rather because "Out of the *Address* [and out of Arndt's compositions] there speaks a [. . .] spirit."[33] The same spirit, moreover, speaks out of Heinrich von Kleist's *Die Hermannsschlacht*: "Since Jena the feeling for the Fatherland had burst

---

[31] Wilhelm Scherer, *Geschichte der deutschen Literatur*. 5th ed. (Berlin: Weidmann, 1889): 632.

[32] For a discussion, see Jost Hermand, *Synthetisches Interpretieren*. 3rd ed. (Munich: Nymphenburg, 1971): 165. Additional information in *Germanistik — eine deutsche Wissenschaft*, ed. E. Lämmert et al. (Frankfurt: Suhrkamp, 1967). See also Wolfgang Emmerich, *Germanistische Volkstumsideologie: Genese und Kritik der Volksforschung im dritten Reich* (Tübingen, 1968).

[33] Friedrich Vogt and Max Koch, *Geschichte der deutschen Literatur*. 5th ed. (Leipzig: Bibliographisches Institut, 1934) 2:266.

into flame ["war ... hell aufgelodert"] in the descendant of a family of soldiers."[34] In *Prinz Friedrich von Homburg* it was Kleist's "love of his homeland and faith in the Fatherland's future"[35] which received concrete expression.

Waldemar Oehlke binds Fichte, Arndt, and Kleist together also, but points to Schleiermacher as the source for their spiritual inspiration. Regarding these four patriots, Oehlke comments: "It is the spirit which brings together the diversity of the Romantics and molds it into one powerful force."[36] There are similarities also in the presentation of Rudolf Gottschall, who ties "the activity-creating power of the spirit" found in Fichte's *Addresses* to Kleist's *Hermannsschlacht* in which "the fanaticism of national hatred and bitter anger boil over."[37] Gottschall describes *Prinz Friedrich von Homburg*, with the vocabulary of mystics when he talks about "that repressed patriotism animated with power and consecration."[38]

The hero of the authoritative, nationalistic "founders" of modern German literary scholarship was Theodor Körner. Oehlke put it perhaps most concisely: "It was the national concept which awoke during the suffering of the Napoleonic period and now [in the poems of Körner] towered up in radiant flames."[39] Even so observant a literary critic as Hermann A. Korff could not escape the thought patterns or the vocabulary of the earlier school. Comparing Uhland's lyrics to the poems in Körner's collection, *Lyre and Sword*, for example, he speaks of the "historical necessity we carry within ourselves, not only out of the depths of the spirit but also out of the depths of our blood."[40]

Each of these spokesmen for earlier German literary historiography perceived certain connections among these five patriotic writers. Fichte's *Addresses to the German Nation* influenced Arndt's *Geist der Zeit*; both were affected in turn by Schleiermacher's *Sermons*, which, in these accounts, are also somehow tied to Kleist's dramas *Die Hermannsschlacht* and *Prinz*

---

[34] *Ibid.*, 279.

[35] *Ibid.*, 280.

[36] Waldemar Oehlke, *Die deutsche Literatur seit Goethes Tod* (Halle: Niemeyer, 1921): 54.

[37] Rudolf Gottschall, *Die deutsche Literatur des 19. Jahrhunderts*. 4th ed. (Breslau: Trewendt, 1875): 485–490. See also his description of Fichte's *Addresses* as the results of "the action-creating power of the spirit" (p. 291).

[38] *Ibid.*, 485.

[39] See Oehlke [Note 36], 57.

[40] Hermann A. Korff, *Geist der Goethezeit*. 5th ed. (Leipzig: Koehler & Amelang, 1959–62) 6:226. First edition 1923–53.

Friedrich von Homburg. The tendencies older literary historians found here culminate mysteriously in Körner's collection of poems and war songs known as *Lyre and Sword*. But the parallels allegedly discovered in such diverse genres as popular philosophy, sermons, the drama or lyric poetry are traced to the psyche of the individual author, which had been mysteriously commandeered. The authoritative literary scholar, moreover, depends on the political annalist for his vocabulary and phraseology. With statal passive verb forms, reflexives and separable prefixes, which tend conveniently to omit the agents, these literary scholars described events between 1807 and 1813 as simply "coming into being" rather than produced by men and women and subject to their personal initiatives.

Presupposing that a benevolent omnipotence was at work at this juncture in German history, specialists in the period, whose works became authoritative in the evolution of German literary scholarship, concentrated on the complex of events, rather than on the congruence of deeds. In so doing, they overlooked the unprecedented cooperation between Prussian political leaders and men-of-letters. Political historians and, in their wake, literary scholars sought to ascertain the "higher purpose" of the events leading to the Wars of Liberation, thereby endowing the era with an ulterior significance: in their accounts, German resurgence proceeds from a state of consciousness predicated upon personal sacrifice, heroism and a concerted, unified effort which they considered to be worthy of emulation by future generations. They attribute to this period a wealth of symbolic relationships, thus producing an emotive portraiture in agreement with preconceived notions. This is not objective historiography; it is production of ideology based on a myth.

The events of these years were portrayed not with regard to concrete causes and effects, but as an undefined spiritual power affecting the Prussian state as a "superindividual" personality. Such abstractions incorporate symbolic associations, underscore human dignity and courage by illustrating what these historians regarded as exemplary conduct, which promoted the myth of German strength, homogeneity and superiority. Above all, however, the convictions of these scholars, their own political belief in German nationalism over territorial particularism, manifest themselves in their accounts. The a priori interests of the researcher determined what was found. Buttressing their political commentary on contemporary events with illustrations from the Napoleonic era, the annalists fashioned the earlier Prussian myth-makers into the heroes of Wilhelminian Germany. Literary scholars followed with detailed accounts of those writers who had pleaded for that political unification which was then another half century away. In so doing, the political and literary historians contributed to an ideological superstructure designed to give the newly formed German Empire the semblance of historical inevitability and permanence. They simply argued that Bismarck had achieved what the German writers of the Napoleonic era had longed for six decades earlier.

As authoritative historians and literary scholars at the turn of the century recast and circulated the myth in ideological garb, the flourishing interest in Napoleon was branded "undeutsch,"[41] the product of by-gone provincialism, to be understood as a regional oddity.[42] Once Bismarck's ideologues began to think less in terms of the "new nation" envisioned by Fichte, Kleist, Arndt and Schleiermacher and more in terms of defending that very different configuration constituted after 1871, the fascination with Napoleon waned. As apologists constructed thought models in support of the "new" Germany, only recently threatened by the Second French Empire, Napoleon's image, once a symbol of revolutionary ideals now very much out of vogue, was retired from Germany's "serious" literature. Banished to the pages of an occasional trivial novel, to be resurrected only by such literary titans as Friedrich Nietzsche, Napoleon, the revolutionary hero, gave way to a new configuration of the German nationalist myth laced with ideology, a half-baked biological determinism and irrational sentiments.

Although it is beyond the scope of this study to examine the many ways in which the German nationalist myth was recast and pressed into ideological servitude, it is nevertheless a noteworthy irony that academicians were ascribing German unification tendencies to the power of a rational, quasi-metaphysical, historical force, but writers delved into the irrational undercurrents. The ancient God, for example, who reveals himself to the narrator in Arthur Bonus's *German Faith. Dreams From Solitude* (1897), castigates the German people whom, he says, he will rescue, in words reminiscent of Arndt's poem.[43] Willibald Hentschel's would-be

---

[41] Cf. Carl Voretzsch, "Gaudys *Kaiserlieder* und die Napoleondichtung," *Preußische Jahrbücher* 95 (1889): 412–496. Georg Schneider, "Napoleon und die Napoleoniden auf der Bühne," *Velhagen und Klasigs Monatshefte* 16 (1901/02): 653–657; Paul Friedrich, "Napoleondichtungen," *Literarisches Echo*. 12 (1909/10), Column 690–696.

[42] V. G. Lutta, *Die deutschen Volkslieder auf Napoleon* (Diss. Berlin, 1931); Walter Klein, *Der Napoleonkult in der Pfalz* (Berlin and Munich: Beck, 1934); Paul Holzhausen, "Napoleon im deutschen Drama," *Bühne und Welt* 2 (1901): 725–734; also by Holzhausen, *Heinrich Heine und Napoleon I* (Frankfurt a.M., Diesterweg, 1903); *Napoleons Tod im Spiegel der zeitgenössischen Presse und Dichtung* (Frankfurt a.M., 1902); "Napoleon in der deutschen lyrischen Dichtung," *Zeit und Völker* 8 (1911): 20–26; "Napoleon im Deutschen Epos und Drama," *Zeit und Völker* 8 (1911): 142–146; See also Eduard Niemeyer, "Die Schwärmerei für Napoleon in der deutschen Dichtung," *Archiv für Literaturgeschichte* 4 (1875): 507–517.

[43] Arthur Bonus, *Deutscher Glaube. Träumereien aus der Einsamkeit* (Heilbronn: Salzer, 1897): 87: "Eine stinkende Verwesung ist eure Anbetung geworden, ohne Freiheit, ohne frische Luft, ohne Zorn freier Rede." For a discussion of "nationalism" in the works of

utopian *Mittgart* (1904) incorporates some aspects of Fichte's educational program, Jahn's dress code, Körner's confidence in sabre and song, and Arndt's vision of contemporaries linked in an eternal chain uniting ancestors with descendants. Yet Hentschel's stereopsis is decidedly more absonant to the myth, as he searches for that "super human being whose countenance reflects divine thoughts from pre-historic millennia — that true representative of the Germanic race."[44] The attitude of Kleist's Hermann is reflected in Joachim G. Boeckh's *Königsbühl* (1925), when the campers sing:

> Ich habe Lust im weiten Feld,
> Zu streiten mit dem Feind.

> My desire is to fight with the enemy
> Upon an outstretched field.

and the chauvinist Christoph Markwart observes:

> Auf allen euren Wimpeln seht ihr das schwarze Balkenkreuz und das Zeichen der Sendung. Ich will sie euch deuten: Es heißt, daß ihr deswegen Wölflinge seid, daß ihr deswegen in euren Sippen lebt, weil ihr einst als wackere Kämpfer dienen sollet in der großen Heerschau, die gesandt ist, nicht vom Menschenhand, sondern vom ewigen Schicksal, ein neues Deutschland zu schaffen.[45]

> On all your pennants you see the black crossbars and the sign of your mission. I shall interpret them for you: it means that you are wolf cubs, that you live in your packs because you will serve one day in the great legion sent not by human hands, but by eternal fate, in order to create a new Germany.

Such contrived ties between the new Germany and the dream of writers in the age of Napoleon, based on irrational sentiments, yearnings and premonitions, were underscored by Julius Petersen in his *Yearnings for the Third Reich* (1934), when he drew a parallel between the crisis facing Germany in 1813 and the results of events after 1914:

> As did the War of Liberation in 1813, the year 1914 fired up the smelting oven in which a new communal feeling was fused together. At that time, the French occupation had gone before, this time it came after. There had been

---

other writers, see Ernst Keller, *Nationalismus und Literatur* (Berne and Munich: Francke, 1970).

[44] Willibald Hentschel, *Mittgart. Ein Weg zur Erneuerung der germanischen Rasse* (Leipzig: Hammer, 1904): 13.

[45] Joachim G. Boeckh, *Königsbühl* (Potsdam: Voggenreiter, 1925): 145f.

no lack of voices calling for a purifying, hardening fate engendered in national suffering.[46]

On the eve of World War I, one character in particular personified the German nationalist myth turned ideology — blond Wiltfeber, the eternal German, who taught his audience to "love out of the depths of your blood."[47] Martin Wiltfeber was a "true seeker of the *Heimat*," one who searched for "that messiah who must come, if we are not to remain indifferent forever, or to live a lie in order to survive."[48] As the German reading public was "edified" by Lanz von Liebenfels who dreamed of blond-haired, blue-eyed Aryans ruling Germany and subjugating the rest of Europe, Germans by the score were soon to line up for a place in such *Thingspiele* as Euringer's *German Passion* (1933), Heydicke's *The Way into the Reich* (1935) and Möller's *Frankenburger Würfelspiel*, performed in conjunction with the Olympic Games in 1936. But it was Burte's *Wiltfeber* of 1912, sold in forty thousand copies by 1928, who served as the model for Egger's *Job der Deutsche* of 1933, thus heralding the movement away from the cultural evolution envisioned by Lessing, Klopstock and Herder, away from the "new nation" to which Fichte, Kleist, Arndt, Schleiermacher and Körner aspired and toward organized barbarism in the name of German supremacy.

For German literature, it was but one contorted leap from the ideologues' cultural nationalism to Hitler's Germany. Other historical developments intensified and complicated the process. Claiming to reinforce that distinct "national art," which Caspar David Friedrich allegedly initiated, Adolf Stoecker promoted a Christian Social Nationalism. As more "patriotic societies" were established, Friedrich von Bernhardi began to glorify war.[49] Behind Turnvater Jahn and his tirades against foreigners

---

[46] Julius Petersen, *Die Sehnsucht nach dem Dritten Reich in deutscher Sage und Dichtung.* Erw. Abdruck aus der Zeitschrift 'Dichtung und Volkstum' (Stuttgart: Metzler, 1934): 60.

[47] Hermann Burte, *Wiltfeber der ewige Deutsche. Die Geschichte eines Heimatsuchers* (Leipzig: Haessel, 1912). The novel was written in the summer of 1911 and published in January 1912. By 1928 forty-thousand copies had been printed. Numerous editions and reprints were circulated between 1933 and 1945. Quote here from the 1928 edition, p. 62.

[48] *Ibid.*, 225. According to Wiltfeber, a Messiah is needed for protection from "half-breeds": "Ein Strom ist die Zeit, eine Bewegung der Dinge untereinander und nach einem Ziele; wenn aber Jauche hineinkommt und kotige Losung, so sterben an ihrer Zeit zuerst die Edlen und werden vom Strome geschwemmt. Denn sie können einfach nicht leben im verjauchten Elemente; die Mischlinge aber sind immer der Zeit gemäß und angemessen und fragen verwundert: warum siechen die Edeln und serbeln und sterben aus? Wir leben doch fröhlich und sind gesund!" (p. 223).

[49] See Louis L. Snyder, *From Bismarck to Hitler* (Williamsport: Bayard, 1935): also Hermann Glaser, *Spießer-Ideologie. Von der Zerstörung des deutschen Geistes im 19. und 20. Jahr-*

lurked that peculiar form of German anti-Semitism which stood ever ready to serve the political advantage of Hitler and his henchmen. By 1934 the message had been distorted and the distortions repeated so often that Goebbels, Hess, not to mention Hitler himself, had only to press on the mythic lever of nationalism to produce the behavioral response the Nazis sought in the populace. It is no surprise, therefore, that a storm trooper band in Leni Riefenstahl's *The Triumph of the Will* serenades the *Führer* specifically to the strains of Carl Maria von Weber's setting for Körner's *Lützow's Wild Chase*, and Albert Methfessel's setting (1818) for Arndt's *God, Who Bids the Iron Grow*. By that time, the myth had gone awry. A structured argument in defense of a fragmented nation dominated by a foreign power had degenerated into a conglomerate of uncritically accepted beliefs justifying *Lebensraum, Heim ins Reich* and the supremacy of an imagined "Aryan race," which had somehow miraculously survived in Germany. As the brown-shirted musicians under Hitler's window conjured visions of Arndt's pathos and Körner's legendary heroism, the German nationalist myth as it developed in Prussia had exploded into fanaticism.

hundert (Freiburg: Rombach, 1964) [Trans. by Ernest Menze: *The Cultural Roots of National Socialism* (London: Croom Helm, 1978).].

Selected Bibliography

I. Documents. Memoranda. Letters

A. Unpublished Archival Material located at:

    1. Akten des ehemaligen Preußischen Geheimstaatsarchivs. Deutsches Zentralarchiv. Merseburg. Deutsche Demokratische Republik. Historische Abteilung II.

    2. Geheimstaatsarchiv. Preußischer Kulturbesitz. Berlin.

    3. Bayerisches Haupt-Staatsarchiv. Munich.

        I. Allgemeines Staatsarchiv.

        II. Geheimstaatsarchiv.

        III. Geheimes Hausarchiv.

        IV. Kriegsarchiv.

    4. Staatsarchiv Bamberg.

    5. Bundesarchiv. Militärarchiv (Militärisches Forschungsamt). Freiburg im Breisgau.

    6. Foreign Office. London. Correspondence: Prussia, Hanover, Austria.

    7. Österreichisches Staatsarchiv. Vienna. Abteilung I: Haus-, Hof-, und Staatsarchiv.

B. Published Records. Posthumous Papers.

Aspinall, Arthur, ed. *The Later Correspondence of George III.* London: Cambridge University Press, 1970.

Bailleu, Paul, ed. *Preußen und Frankreich von 1795 bis 1807. Diplomatische Correspondenzen.* 2 Parts, Leipzig: Hirzel, 1881–1887.

Botzenhart, Erich and Hubatsch, Walter, eds. *Freiherr vom Stein. Briefe und amtliche Schriften.* 10 vols. Stuttgart: Kohlhammer, 1954–1963.

Copies of the Original Letters and Despatches of the Generals, Ministers, Grand Officers of State, and Company at Paris to the Emperor Napoleon at Dresden. (No editor) London: Printed for John Murray, 1814.

Defénse des Officiers de la troupe de Schill. Lüttich, 1814.

Donath, Friedrich und Markov, Walter, eds. *Kampf um Freiheit. Dokumente zur Zeit der nationalen Erhebung 1789–1815*. Berlin: Verlag der Nation, 1954.

Doris, Charles de Bourges. [*Mémoires Secretes sur Napoléon Bonaparte*] *Geheime Nachrichten über Napoleon Bonaparte*. Leipzig: G. Fleischer, 1815.

Dyroff, Heinrich D. *Der Wiener Kongreß 1814/15*. Munich: Deutscher Taschenbuch Verlag, 1966.

Fortesque, J. B. *Reports of the Manuscripts of J. B. Fortesque preserved at Dropmore. Historical Manuscripts Commission*. 10 vols. London: Herford Times, 1882–1927.

Griewank, Karl, ed. *Luise, Königin von Preußen, Briefe und Aufzeichnungen*. Bielefeld: Velhagen und Klasing, 1928.

Klein, Tim, ed. *Die Befreiung 1813/15. Urkunden, Berichte, Briefe mit geschichtlichen Verbindungen*. Ebenhausen: Langewisch and Brandt, 1913.

Kleßmann, Eckart, ed. *Die Befreiungskriege in Augenzeugenberichten*. Düsseldorf: Rauch, 1966.

L[enz]., M[ax]., ed. "Vier Denkschriften Scharnhorsts aus dem Jahr 1810". *Historische Zeitschrift* 58 (1887): 55–105.

Ompteda, Ludwig, *Politischer Nachlaß des Hannoverischen Staats- und Cabinet-Ministers Ludwig von Ompteda aus den Jahren 1804 bis 1813*. Jena: Frommann, 1869.

Pflugk-Harttung, Julius von, ed. *Das Befreiungsjahr 1813 aus den Akten des Geheimen Staatsarchivs*. Berlin: Union, 1913.

Plon, Henri und DuMaine, Jean, eds. *Correspondance de Napoléon Ier*. Paris: Henri Plon, 1869.

Preußen, Geheimes Staatsarchiv. *Berichte aus der Berliner Franzosenzeit 1807–1809*. Neudruck der Ausg. [ed. Hermann Granier] 1913. Osnabrück: Zeller, 1969.

Rühl, Franz, ed. *Briefe und Aktenstücke zur Geschichte Preußens unter Friedrich Wilhelm III. vorzugsweise aus dem Nachlaß von F. A. Stägemann*. 4 vols. Leipzig: Duncker und Humblot, 1889–1904.

Schoeps, Hans J., ed. *Aus den Jahren preußischer Not und Erneuerung*. Berlin: Haude und Spene, 1963.

Stern, Alfred, ed. *Abhandlungen und Aktenstücke zur Geschichte der preußischen Reformzeit 1807–1815*. Leipzig: Duncker und Humblot, 1885.

Webster, Charles Kingsley, ed. *British Diplomacy 1813–1815. Selected Documents Dealing with the Reconstruction of Europe*. London: G. Bell, 1921.

Wertheimer, Eduard, ed. "Berichte des Grafen Friedrich Lothar Stadion über die Beziehungen zwischen Österreich und Baiern 1807–1809" *Archiv für österreichische Geschichte* 63 (1882): 149–238.

Winter, Georg, ed. *Die Reorganisation des preußischen Staates unter Stein und Hardenberg*. 2 vols. Leipzig: Hirzel, 1931.

C. Letters.

Bailleu, Paul, ed. *Friedrich Wilhelm III. und der Königin Luise Briefwechsel mit Kaiser Alexander*. Leipzig: Hirzel, 1900.

Capelle, Wilhelm, ed. *Blüchers Briefe*. Leipzig: Insel, 1915.

Dühr, Albrecht, ed. *Ernst Moritz Arndt Briefe*. Darmstadt: Wissenschaftliche Buchgesellschaft, 1972.

Briefwechsel zwischen Friedrich Gentz und Adam Müller 1800–1829, no ed., Stuttgart: Cotta, 1857.

Granier, Hermann, ed. *Hohenzollernbriefe aus den Freiheitskriegen, 1813–1815*. Leipzig: Hirzel, 1913.

Höltei, Karl von, ed. *Briefe an Ludwig Tieck*. Breslau: Trewendt, 1864.

Meyer, Wolfgang, ed. *Die Briefe Friedrich Ludwig Jahns*. Dresden: Limpert, n. d.

Norvin, William and Gerhard, Dietrich, eds. *Die Briefe B[arthold]. G[eorg]. Niebuhrs*. 2 vols. Berlin: de Gruyter, 1926–1929.

Raich, J. M. ed. *Dorothea von Schlegel geb. Mendelssohn und deren Söhne Johann und Philipp Veit, Briefwechsel*. 2 vols. Mainz: Kirchheim, 1881.

Reimer, Georg, ed. *Aus Schleiermachers Leben. In Briefen*. Berlin: Perthes, 1858–1863.

Schmidt, Erich, ed. *Caroline. Briefe aus der Frühromantik*. Leipzig: Insel, 1913.

Schulz, Hans, ed. *J[ohann]. G[ottlieb]. Fichte Briefwechsel*. Kritische Gesamtausgabe. Leipzig: Haessel, 1930.

Sydow, Anna von, ed. *Wilhelm und Caroline von Humboldt in ihren Briefen*. Berlin: Mittler, 1909.

Walzel, Oskar, ed. *Friedrich von Schlegels Briefe an seinen Bruder August Wilhelm*. Berlin: Speyer und Peters, 1890.

II. Contemporaneous Publications. First editions. Journals and Newspapers.

Adlerjung, Johann L. *Unterhaltungen eines Lehrers mit seinen Schülern*. Leipzig and Prague: Wildtmann, 1792.

Albrecht, Heinrich Eph. *Versuch über den Patriotismus*. Hamburg: Gundermann, 1793.

Allgemeine Literatur-Zeitung, ed. C. F. Schütz, vols. 1–39, Jena and Halle, 1785-1823.

[Anon.]. *Aufruf an die Deutschen zum gemeinsamen Kampfe gegen die Franzosen*. Berlin und Halle: J. C. Hendel, 1813.

_____. *Die deutschen Roth- und Schwarz-Mäntler. Eine Seiten-Patrouille zu den französischen schwarzen und weißen Jakobiner*. Neubrandenburg: Graff. Leipzig, n. d.

_____. *Ergießungen deutschen Gefühles in Gesängen und Liedern bey den Ereignissen dieser Zeit*. Heidelberg: Engelmann, n. d. [Neudruck, ed., Ernst Weber. Hildesheim: Gerstenberg Verlag, 1983].

_____. *Lobgesänge auf Napoleon. Napoleon des Großen Feldzug nach Rußland im Jahre 1812. In saubre Reime gebracht von einem seiner eifrigsten Anhänger und Verehrer*. n. p. 1814.

_____. *Napoleon der Gaukler oder Glückseligkeit durch Zerstörung*. Deutschland, 1814.

_____. *Norddeutschlands Gränzen und Vertheidigung zur Beherzigung beim künftigen Frieden*. n. p. 1814.

_____. *Versuch von der Erziehung und Unterweisung der Kinder*. 2nd ed. Zürich: Orell, 1748.

_____. *Was war Deutschland? Was ist es jetzt? Was darf es von der Zukunft hoffen?* Germanien, 1813.

_____. *Was wollen wir?* Munich: Fleischmann, 1813.

Aretin, Johann Christoph Freiherr von. *Die Pläne Napoleons und seiner Gegner besonders in Teutschland und Österreich.* Munich: Fleischmann, 1809.

Bahrdt, Karl Friedrich. *Philanthropinischer Erziehungsplan.* Frankfurt a. M.: Eichenberg, 1776.

Beauchamp, Alphonse. *Histoire de la guerre de la Vendée et Chouans.* Paris: Giguet et Michaud, 1806.

Beurmann, Adolf von. *Vertraute Briefe über Preußens Hauptstadt.* Stuttgart: Cotta, 1837.

Brumbey, K. W. *Kurzer theoretischer Plan zur Menschenerziehung nach den Bedürfnissen unserer Zeit.* Berlin: Sander, 1784.

Burke, Edmund. *Reflections on the Revolution in France.* London: J. Dodsley, 1790.

Chronik des neunzehnten Jahrhunderts, ausgearbeitet von Dr. Carl Venturini, Ed. Georg G. Bredow. Altona: Hammerich, 1811. vol. 5.

Europäische Annalen, Ed. Ernst L. Posselt. Stuttgart: Cotta, 1805–1812.

Feuerbach, Paul Anselm von. *Was sollen wir? Eine Rede an das bayerische Volk.* Munich: Fleischmann, 1813.

_____. *Über die Unterdrückung und Wiederbefreiung Europens.* Munich: Finsterlin, 1813. Gleichzeitig in Leipzig bei Rein.

Fichte, Johann Gottlieb. *Reden an die deutsche Nation.* Berlin: Realschulbuchhandlung [Reimer], 1808.

Geschichte und Politik. Eine Zeitschrift. Ed. Karl Ludwig Woltmann. vols. 1–6. Berlin: Reimer, 1800–05.

Gneisenau, Neithardt von. *Denkschriften zum Volksaufstand von 1803 und 1811.* Neudruck. Berlin: Kriegsgesch. Bücherei, 1936.

Heidelberger Jahrbücher der Literatur. Heidelberg: Mohr und Zimmer, 1808–1810, 1811–1816.

Jacobs, Friedrich. *Über Sinn und Absichten einiger Stellen der zu München erschienenen Flugschrift 'Die Pläne Napoleons und seiner Gegner'.* Munich: Franz, 1809.

_____. *Deutschlands Ehre.* Gotha: Becker, 1814.

_____. *Deutschlands Gefahren und Hoffnungen. An Germaniens Jugend.* Gotha: Becker, 1813.

Kern, Wilhelm H. L. *Napoleon und sein Zeitalter.* Koblenz: Pauli, 1808.

Koppe, Karl Wilhelm. *Die Stimme eines preußischen Staatsbürgers.* Cologne: Dümont-Schauberg, 1815.

Krause, K. H. *Mein Vaterland unter den hohenzollerischen Regenten.* Halle: Schwetschke, 1803.

Lachmann, Karl Ludulf Friedrich. *Allgemeine Ideen über die jeder Menschenklasse Deutschlands zu wünschende Ausbildung und Aufklärung.* Leipzig: Barth, 1790.

Leonhardi, Friedrich Gli. *Erdbeschreibung der preußischen Monarchie.* 5 vols. Halle: Schwetschke, 1791–1798.

Martini, Carl. *Dankadresse für Napoleon Bonaparte im Namen der geretteten Nationen. Ein Gedicht – aber keine Dichtung!* Germanien, 1814.

Materialien zur Geschichte des österreichischen Revolutionierungssystem. 3 Hefte [Nuremberg: Stein], n. p., 1809.

Minerva. Ed. J. W. Archenholz. Berlin and Hamburg: Hoffmann, 1792–1811.

Mirabeau, Honoré Riquetti, Comte de. *Travail sur l'éducation publique trouvé dans les papiers de Mirabeau l'ainé*, publié par P. J. G. Canabis. Paris 1791.

Morgenblatt für gebildete Stände. Tübingen: Cotta, 1807–1832.

Der Morgenbote. Eine Zeitschrift für die österreichischen Staaten. Ed. Franz Xavier Huber. Vienna: Feil, 1809.

Neuer literarischer Anzeiger. Ed. Johann Christian von Aretin. Munich: Fleischmann, 1806–1808.

Niebuhr, Barthold Georg. *Preußens Recht gegen den sächsischen Hof.* Berlin: Reimer, 1814.

Pfeil, Johann G. Benjamin. *Zuruf eines Patrioten an seine Mitbürger.* Leipzig: Baygang, 1794.

Pölitz, Karl L. H. *Über das Verhältnis des Studiums der sächsischen Geschichte zur Belebung und Erhöhung eines reinen Patriotismus.* Leipzig: Hinrichs, 1816.

Rühs, Friedrich. *Das Märchen von den Verschwörungen.* Berlin: Reimer, 1815.

Schmalz, Theodor A. [Ritter]. *Berichtigung einer Stelle in der Bredow-Venturinischen Chronik für das Jahr 1808. Über politische Vereine, und ein Wort über Scharnhorsts und meine Verhältnisse zu ihnen.* Berlin: Maurer, 1815.

_____. *Über des Herrn B. G. Niebuhrs Schrift wider die meinige, politische Vereine betreffend.* Berlin: Maurer, 1815.

Schöttgen, Christian and Kreysig, Georg. *Diplomatische und curieuse Nachlese der Historie von Obersachsen und angrentzenden Ländern.* 3rd Part. Dresden 1731.

Stägemann, Friedrich. *Kriegsgesänge aus den Jahren 1806 1813.* Berlin: Reimer, 1813.

Thiersch, Friedrich. *Betrachtungen über die angeblichen Unterschiede zwischen Süd- und Norddeutschland.* Leipzig: Fleischer, 1810.

Thuiskon. Über Deutschlands Einheit. Ed. Johann August Zeune. Berlin: Hitzig, 1810.

Villaume, Peter. *Abhandlungen das Interesse der Menschheit und der Staaten betreffend.* Altona: Hammerich, 1794.

Wieland, Christoph Martin. "Über teutschen Patriotismus," *Neuer teutscher Merkur*, 5 Stück, 1793: 12ff.

Wieland, Ludwig. *Bemerkungen gegen die Schrift des Geh. Raths Schmalz zu Berlin über politische Vereine. Nebst einem Anhang über des Gouvernementsraths Koppe 'Stimme eines preußischen Staatsbürgers'.* Erfurt: Keyser, 1816.

Zailonow, Anton [Ernst Anton Imman Truhart]. *Freimütige Bemerkungen über den Preußischen Staat in politischer, militärischer und bürgerlicher Hinsicht von einem Russen.* Ruthenien [Riga], 1806.

Zimmermann, Johann Georg. *Vom Nationalstolz.* Zurich: Orell, 1758.

Zöllner, Johann Friedrich. "Über deutsche Aussprache." *Beyträge zur deutschen Sprachkunde.* Zweite Sammlung. Berlin: Maurer, 1796.

_____. *Ideen über Nationalerziehung.* Berlin: Reimer, 1804.

III. Editions and Bibliographies.

Baumgartner, Hans M. and Jacobs, Wilhelm G. *J. G. Fichte Bibliographie.* Stuttgart-Bad Cannstatt: Frommann, 1968.

Baxa, Jacob, ed. *Adam Müller. Ausgewählte Abhandlungen.* Jena: Fischer, 1921.

_____. *Adam H. Müller: Elemente der Staatskunst.* Jena: Frommann, 1922.

Eckardt, Hans von, ed. *Friedrich Gentz. Staatsschriften und Briefe.* 2 vols. Munich: Drei Masken Verlag, 1921.

Elster, Ernst, ed. *Heinrich Heines Sämtliche Werke.* Leipzig: Bibliographisches Institut, n. d. [1887–1890].

Euler, Carl, ed. *Friedrich Ludwig Jahns Werke.* Hof: Grau, 1884.

Fichte, Immanuel H., ed. *Johann Gottlieb Fichtes Sämtliche Werke.* Berlin: Veit, 1845.

_____. *Johann Gottlieb Fichtes Nachgelassene Werke.* Bonn: Marcus, 1834.

Glockner, Hermann, ed. *Hegels Sämtliche Werke.* Stuttgart: Frommann, 1949.

Iffland, August Wilhelm. *Ifflands Theatralische Werke.* Leipzig: Göschen, 1859.

Jacobs, Friedrich. *Vermischte Schriften.* Leipzig: Dyk, 1840.

Kanzog, Klaus, ed. *Heinrich von Kleist. Prinz Friedrich von Homburg. Texte, Kontexte, Kommentar.* Munich: Hanser, 1977.

Kircheisen, Friedrich von. *Bibliographie des napoleonischen Zeitalters.* Berlin: Mittler, 1928.

Kotzebue, August von. *Theater von August Kotzebue.* Leipzig and Vienna: Kummer & Klang, 1841.

_____. *Endliches Schicksal Napoleons vorhergesagt im Jahre 1806 von A. v. Kotzebue.* Berlin and Halle: J. C. Hendel, 1813.

Lange, Fritz, ed. *Neithardt von Gneisenau. Schriften von und über Gneisenau.* Berlin: Rütten and Loening, 1954.

Lauth, Richard and Gliwitzky, H. eds. *J. G. Fichte. Gesamtausgabe der bayerischen Akademie der Wissenschaften.* Stuttgart: Frommann, 1981.

Leffson, August and Steffens, Wilhelm, eds. *Arndts Werke.* Berlin: Bong, n. d.

Leitzmann, Albert and Gebhardt, Brunno, eds. *Wilhelm von Humboldts Gesammelte Schriften.* Berlin: Preuß. Akademie der Wissenschaften, 1903–1936.

Menckens, Heinrich, ed. *Deutschland in seiner tiefen Erniedrigung.* Würzburg: Stubens, 1877.

Pareyson, Luigi. "Fichte. Bibliografia essenziale," *Grande Antologia Filosofica,* eds. M. F. Sciacca and M. Schiavons. Milan: Mursia, 1971.

Ranke, Leopold von. *Sämtliche Werke.* Leipzig: Duncker und Humblot, 1890.

Raumer, Kurt von, ed. *Die Autobiographie des Freiherrn vom Stein.* 2nd ed. Münster and Cologne: Böhlau, 1955.

Reimer, Georg, ed. *Friedrich Schleiermachers Sämtliche Werke.* Berlin: Reimer, 1834–1864.

Rückert, Friedrich. *Gesammelte poetische Werke in zwölf Bänden.* Neue Ausgabe. Frankfurt: Sauerländer, 1882.

Schäfer, Karl–Heinz and Schawe, J., eds. *Ernst Moritz Arndt. Ein bibliographisches Handbuch.* Bonn: Röhrscheid, 1971.

Schlesier, Gustav, ed. *Friedrich von Gentz. Memoires et lettres inédites.* Stuttgart: Hallberger, 1841.

_____. *Friedrich von Gentz Schriften. Ein Denkmal.* Mannheim: Hof, 1838–1840.

Schmidt, Günther, ed. *Freiherr vom und zum Stein. Schriften von und über Stein.* Berlin: Rütten und Loening, 1955.

Schuffenhauer, Heinz, ed. *F. D. Schleiermachers Ausgewählte Vorlesungen und pädagogische Schriften.* Berlin: Volk und Wissen, 1966.

Sembdner, Helmut, ed. *Heinrich von Kleists Sämtliche Werke.* 5th ed. Munich: Hanser, 1970.

―――. *Heinrich von Kleists Lebenspuren.* Vol. 8 of dtv Gesamtausgabe. Munich: dtv, 1969.

Suphan, Bernhard, ed. *Herders Sämtliche Werke.* 33 vols. Berlin: Weidmann, 1877–1913.

Steinberg, Augusta, ed. *Körners Werke.* Berlin: Bong, n. d.

Stenzel, Gerhard, ed. *Die deutschen Romantiker.* 2 vols. Salzburg: Bergland, 1954.

Walsh, Robert, ed. *Selected Speeches of George Canning.* Philadelphia: Key and Biddle, 1835.

Weniger, Erich, ed. *Wilhelm Diltheys Gesammelte Schriften.* Stuttgart: Teubner, 1960.

Wieck, Wilderich, ed. *Friedrich von Gentz Ausgewählte Schriften.* 5 vols. Stuttgart and Leipzig: Rieger, 1836–38.

Wiese, Benno von, ed. *Karl Immermanns Werke in fünf Bänden.* Frankfurt: Athenäum, 1973.

IV. Reminiscences. Diaries. Memoirs.

Ense, Varnhagen von. *Denkwürdigkeiten und vermischte Schriften.* Mannheim: Hof, 1837–59.

―――. *Ausgewählte Schriften.* 3 vols. Leipzig: Brockhaus, 1871.

Eylert, Rulemann Friedrich. *Charakter-Züge und historische Fragmente aus dem Leben des Königs von Preußen Friedrich Wilhelm III.* Magdeburg: Heinrichshofen, 1842–47.

Fürst, Julius, ed. *Henriette Herz. Ihr Leben und ihre Erinnerungen.* Berlin: H. Hertz, 1880.

Gagern, Heinrich Christian Freiherr von. *Mein Antheil an der Politik.* 4 vols. Stuttgart: Cotta, 1823–30.

Hardenberg, Karl August, Fürst von. *Denkwürdigkeiten.* 5 vols. Ed. Leopold Ranke. Leipzig: Duncker und Humblot, 1876–77.

Harnisch, Christian Wilhelm. *Mein Lebensmorgen. Nachgelassene Schriften von Wilhelm Harnisch zur Geschichte der Jahre 1787 bis 1822*, Ed. Hans Erich Schneider. Berlin: Hertz, 1865.

Hiller von Gärtringen, August. *Denkwürdigkeiten.* Berlin: Mittler, 1912.

Hüser [also Huesser], Johann Hans Gustav Heinrich. *Denkwürdigkeiten aus dem Leben des Generals der Infantrie von Hüser größtenteils nach dessen hinterlassenen Papieren. Zusammengestellt und herausgegeben von M[athilde]. Q[uedrow]..* Berlin: Reimer, 1877.

Keller, Ludwig. "Der preußische Staat und die Patrioten im Urteil eines französischen Staatsmannes." *Monatsschriften der Comenius Gesellschaft* 22 (1913): 4–25.

Kircheisen, Friedrich von. *Feldzugserinnerungen aus dem Jahre 1809.* Bibliothek wertvoller Memoiren. Hamburg: Gutenberg, 1909.

Müller, Friedrich von, *Erinnerungen aus den Kriegszeiten von 1806 bis 1813.* Brunswick: Vieweg, 1861.

Parthey, Gustav. *Jugenderinnerungen.* Ed. Ernst Friedel. Berlin: Frensdorf, 1907.

Philippart, John. *Campaign in Germany and France.* London: Barrington, 1814.

Ranke, Leopold von. "Zur eigenen Lebensgeschichte." *Sämtliche Werke.* Leipzig: Duncker und Humblot, 1890.

Ruf, Paul, ed. *Johann Andreas Schmeller. Tagebücher 1801–1852.* Munich: Beck, 1956.

Schubert, Gotthilf Heinrich. *Der Erwerb aus einem vergangenen und die Erwartungen von einem zukünftigen Leben. Eine Selbstbiographie.* Erlangen: Palm und Ancke, 1854–56.

———. *Ansichten von der Nachtseite der Naturwissenschaft.* Dresden: Arnold, 1808.

Steffens, Heinrich [also Henrik]. *Was ich erlebte.* Breslau: Max, 1842.

Streckfuss, Adolf von. *500 Jahre Berliner Geschichte,* Ed. Leo Fernbach. Berlin: Goldschmidt, 1900.

Von der Marwitz, F. A. Ludwig. *Ein märkischer Edelmann im Zeitalter der Befreiungskriege,* Ed. Friedrich Meusel. Berlin: Mittler, 1908–1913.

Walter, Jakob. *A German Conscript with Napoleon.* Lawrence, Kansas: Department of Journalism Press, 1938.

V. Secondary Sources.

A. The Era in Political Perspective.

Anderson, Eugene N. *Nationalism and the Cultural Crisis in Prussia 1805–1815.* New York: Farrar and Rhinehart, 1939.

Andreas, Willy. *Das Zeitalter Napoleons und die Erhebung der Völker.* Heidelberg: Quelle und Meyer, 1955.

Aris, Rheinhold. *A History of Political Thought in Germany from 1789 to 1815.* London: Allen and Unwin, 1936.

Backus, David P. "Stein and Russia's Prussian Policy from Tilsit to Vienna." Ph.D diss., Yale University, 1949.

Bassewitz, M. F. von. *Die Kurmark Brandenburg im Zusammenhang mit den Schicksalen des Gesamtstaates Preußen während der Zeit vom 22. Okt. 1806 bis 1808.* 2 vols. Leipzig: Brockhaus, 1851–52.

Beitzke, Heinrich. *Geschichte der deutschen Freiheitskriege.* Berlin: Duncker und Humblot, 1854–55.

Bornhak, Konrad. *Preußen unter der Fremdherrschaft 1807–1813.* Leipzig: Frankenstein and Wagner, 1925.

Cavaignac, Godefroy. *La formation de la Prusse contemporaine, 1806–1813.* 2 vols. Paris: Hachett, 1891–1898.

Coker, Francis William. *Organismic Theories of the State.* New York: Columbia University Press, 1910.

Doeberl, Michael. *Entwicklungsgeschichte Bayerns.* Munich: Oldenbourg, 1912.

Droysen, Johann Gustav. *Grundriß der Historik.* Leipzig: Veit, 1868.

Eisner, Kurt. *Das Ende des Reiches. Deutschland und Preußen im Zeitalter der großen Revolution.* Berlin: Buchhandlung Vorwärts, 1907.

Epstein, Klaus. *The Genesis of German Conservatism*. Princeton: Princeton University Press, 1966.

Erler, Willi. *Die schlesische Volksstimme in den Jahren der inneren Wiedergeburt Preußens*. Diss. Leipzig [Fock], 1910.

Ernstberger, Anton. *Eine deutsche Untergrundbewegung*. Munich: Beck, 1955.

_____. *Böhmens Freiwilliger Kriegseinsatz gegen Napoleon*. Munich: Lerche, 1963.

Flad, Ruth. *Der Begriff der öffentlichen Meinung bei Stein, Arndt und Humboldt*. Berlin and Leipzig: de Gruyter, 1929.

Ford, Guy Stanton. *Stein and the Era of Reform in Prussia*. Princeton: Princeton University Press, 1922.

Förster, Friedrich C. *Preußen und Deutschland unter der Fremdherrschaft*. Berlin: Hempel, 1842.

Freymark, Hermann. *Die Reform der preußischen Handels- und Zollpolitik von 1800–1821 und ihre Bedeutung*. Jena: G. Fischer, 1898.

Gebhardt, Brunno. *Handbuch der deutschen Geschichte*. 8 vols. Stuttgart: Union, 1960.

Goette, Rudolf. *Das Zeitalter der deutschen Erhebung 1807–1815*. Gothe: Parthers, 1891.

Goldmann, Karl. *Die preußisch-britischen Beziehungen in den Jahren 1812–1815*. Würzburg: Triltsch, 1934.

Gooch, George Peabody and Ward, A. W. *The Cambridge History of British Foreign Policy 1783–1919*. London and New York: Cambridge University Press, 1922.

Hahlweg, Werner. *Preußische Reformzeit und Revolutionärer Krieg*. Wehrwissenschaftliche Rundschau. Supplement 18. Berlin: Mittler, 1962.

Hartung, Fritz. *Deutschlands Zusammenbruch und Erhebung 1792–1815*. Bielefeld: Velhagen und Klassing, 1922.

Hassel, Paul, ed. *Geschichte der preußischen Politik 1807 bis 1815. Erster Teil 1807/08* [No more published]. Leipzig: Hirzel, 1881.

Hashagen, Justus. *Das Rheinland und die französische Herrschaft*. Bonn: Hanstein, 1908.

_____. *Das Rheinland und die preußische Herrschaft*. Essen: Baedeker, 1924.

Häußer, Ludwig. *Deutsche Geschichte vom Tode Friedrich des Großen bis zur Gründung des alten Bundes*. Meersburg: Hendel, 1933. [1st ed. 1854.]

Heitzer, Heinz. *Insurrektion zwischen Weser und Elbe*. Berlin: Rütten und Loening, 1959.

Helke, Fritz. *Preußische Rebellion*. Stuttgart: Union, 1942.

Helmert, Heinz. *Der Befreiungskrieg, 1813/14*. Berlin: Deutscher Militärverlag, 1963.

Hintze, Otto. "Wesen und Wandlung des modernen Staates." In *Sitzungsberichte. Preußische Akademie der Wissenschaften*. 1931: 790–810.

Holtman, Robert B. *Napoleonic Propaganda*. Baton Rouge, Louisiana: Louisiana State University Press, 1950.

Hoover, Arlie J. *The Gospel of Nationalism*. Stuttgart: Steiner, 1986.

Ibbeken, Rudolf. *Preußen 1807–1813. Staat und Volk als Idee und in Wirklichkeit*. Cologne and Berlin: Grote, 1970.

Iggers, Georg. *The German Conception of History*. Middletown: Wesleyan University Press, 1975.

_____. *New Directions in European Historiography.* Middletown: Wesleyan University Press, 1975.

Jaenicke, Hermann. *Von Tilsit bis Leipzig.* Berlin: Eisenschmidt, 1913.

Jeisman, Karl Ernst. *Staat und Erziehung in der preußischen Reform.* Göttingen: Vandenhoeck und Ruprecht, 969.

_____. *Das preußische Gymnasium in Staat und Gesellschaft.* Tübingen: Niemeyer, 1974.

Kamnitzer, Heinz. *Wider die Fremdherrschaft.* Berlin: Rütten und Loening, 1956.

Knemeyer, Franz Ludwig. *Regierungs- und Verwaltungsreformen in Deutschland zu Beginn des 19. Jahrhunderts.* Cologne: Grote, 1970.

Kosselleck, Reinhardt. *Preußen zwischen Reform und Revolution.* Stuttgart: Klett, 1967.

Krieken, Albert Theodor. *Über die sogenannte organische Staatstheorie.* Leipzig: Duncker und Humblot, 1873.

Krones, Franz von. *Zur Geschichte Österreichs im Zeitalter der französischen Kriege und der Restauration 1792–1816.* Gotha: Pethes, 1886.

Lehmann, August. *Der Tugendbund.* Berlin: Haude and Spene, 1867.

Lehmann, Konrad. *Die Rettung Berlins im Jahre 1813.* Berlin: Ebering, 1933.

Ludz, Peter Christian, ed. *Geheime Gesellschaften.* Heidelberg: Schneider, 1979.

Mehring, Franz. *1807 bis 1812.* 2nd. ed. Stuttgart: Dietz, 1913.

Meinecke, Friedrich. *Weltbürgertum und Nationalstaat.* Munich: Oldenbourg, 1928.

_____. *Das Zeitalter der deutschen Erhebung.* Bielefeld: Velhagen und Klassing, 1906.

Mitchell, Harvey. *The Underground War Against Revolutionary France.* Oxford: Clardon, 1965.

Neubauer, Friedrich. *Preußen Fall und Erhebung, 1805–1815.* Berlin: Mittler, 1908.

Oncken, Wilhelm. *Österreich und Preußen im Befreiungskriege.* 2 vols. Berlin: Grote, 1876.

Pflugk-Harttung, Julius. *1813-1815. Illustrierte Geschichte der Befreiungskriege.* Stuttgart: Union, 1913.

Pfuel, Ernst. *Der Rückzug der Franzosen bis zum Niemen.* Berlin: Dümmler, 1813.

Pirenne, Jacques Henri. *La Sainte Alliance. Organisation européenne de la paix mondiale.* 2 vols. Neu Chatel, 1946-1950.

Rambaud, Alfred. *L'allemagne sous Napoléon Ier. (1804–1811).* Paris: Perrin, 1897.

Raumer, Kurt von. *Deutschland um 1800.* Constance: Hatchfeld, 1958.

Roessler, Wilhelm. *Die Entstehung des modernen Erziehungswesen in Deutschland.* Stuttgart: Kohlhammer, 1961.

Scheibeck, Ludwig. *Die deutschnationale Bewegung in Bayern.* Diss. Munich, 1913.

Schnabel, Franz. *Deutsche Geschichte im neunzehnten Jahrhundert.* 5th ed. Freiburg: Herder, 1959. [1st ed., 1927].

Sherwig, John. *Guineas and Gunpowder: British Foreign Aid in the Wars with France 1793–1815.* Cambridge: Harvard University Press, 1969.

Simon, Walter Michael *The Failure of the Prussian Reform Movement 1807–1819.* Ithaca: Cornell University Press, 1955.

Snel, John M. *The Democratic Movement in Germany 1789–1914*. Chapel Hill: University of North Carolina Press, 1976.

Sorel, Albert. *L'europe et la révolution française*. 9 vols. Paris: Plon, 1885–1911.

Springer, Max. *Die Franzosenherrschaft in der Pfalz 1792–1814*. Stuttgart: Deutsche Verlagsanstalt, 1926.

Streisand, Johann. *Deutschland 1789–1815*. Berlin: Deutscher Verlag der Wissenschaften, 1973.

Stulz, Percy. *Fremdherrschaft und Befreiungskampf*. Berlin: Deutscher Verlag der Wissenschaften, 1960.

Towne, Ezra Thayler. *Die Auffassung der Gesellschaft als Organismus*. Halle: Kaemmerer, 1903.

Treitschke, Heinrich von. *Deutsche Geschichte im neunzehnten Jahrhundert*. 10th ed. Leipzig: Hirzel, 1918. [1st ed. 1879. Trans. Eden and Cedar Paul (New York: McBride and Nast, 1915)].

Tschirch, Otto. *Geschichte der Öffentlichen Meinung in Preußen vom Basler Frieden bis zum Zusammenbruch des Staates 1795–1806*. 2 vols. Weimar: Böhlau, 1933.

Ulmann, Heinrich. *Geschichte der Befreiungskriege 1813/14*. 2 vols. Munich: Oldenbourg, 1914.

Valjavec, Fritz. *Die Entstehung der politischen Strömungen in Deutschland 1770–1815*. Munich: Oldenbourg, 1951.

Voigt, Johannes. *Geschichte des sogenannten Tugendbundes oder des sittlich-wissenschaftlichen Vereins*. Berlin: Decker, 1850.

Wohlfeil, Rainer. *Spanien und die deutsche Erhebung*. Wiesbaden: Steiner, 1966.

Young, Peter. *Blücher's Army*. Reading, Pennsylvania: Osprey Publ., 1973.

B. Individual Statesman.

Abs, Hermann Josef. *Die finanzpolitischen Anschauungen des Freiherrn vom Stein in der Perspektive unserer Zeit*. Troisdorf, 1972.

Bach, Ernst. *Stein*. Stuttgart: Kohlhammer, 1957.

Baersch, Georg. *Ferdinand von Schills Zug und Tod im Jahre 1809*. Leipzig: Brockhaus, 1850.

Barth, Georg Karl. *Der Lützower und Pestalozzianer W. H. Ackermann*. Leipzig: Teubner, 1913.

Baur, Wilhelm. *Das Leben des Freiherrn vom Stein*. Karlsruhe and Berlin: Reuther, 1885.

Benicken, Friedrich Wilhelm. *König Friedrich Wilhelm III. Sein Leben und Wirken*. 3rd ed. Quedlinburg and Leipzig: Basse, 1840–43.

Bock, Helmut. *Schills Rebellenzug 1809*. Berlin: Deutscher Militärverlag, 1972.

Botzenhart, Erich. *Freiherr vom Stein*. Münster: Aschendorff, 1952.

Butz, Philipp. *Der Ritter auf der Bettenburg*. Heidelberg: Peters, 1906.

Delbrück, Hans. *Das Leben des Feldmarschalls Grafen Neithardt von Gneisenau*. 2 vols. 2nd ed. Berlin: Walter, 1894.

Dieckmann, Karl. *Der Staatsgedanke des Freiherrn vom Stein. Ein Weg zum deutschen Einheitsstaat*. Berlin: Jungdeutscher Verlag, 1931.

Droysen, Johann G. *Das Leben des Feldmarschalls Grafen Yorck von Wartenburg.* Leipzig: Insel, 1913.

Ergang, Robert Reinhold. *Herder and the Foundation of German Nationalism.* New York: Columbia University Press, 1931.

Faure, Elie. *Napoleon.* Dresden: Aretz, 1938.

Fahrner, Rudolf. *Gneisenau.* Munich: Delfinverlag, 1942.

Fiedler, Siegfried. *Scharnhorst. Geist und Tat.* Herford and Bonn: Maximilian Verlag, 1963.

Fournier, August. "Stein und Gruner in Österreich." *Deutsche Rundschau* 53 (1887): 120–142, 214–247, 348–362.

Funder, Walter. *Freiherr von Stein.* Leipzig and Jena: Urania, 1954.

Grimme, B. *Der Föderalismus des Reichsfreiherrn vom Stein.* Diss. Marburg, 1952.

Grunwald, Constantine. *Stein. L'ennemi de Napoléon.* Paris, 1936.

Hans, Ludwig. *Arndt und Stein. Erlebnis und Darstellung.* Phil. Diss. Bonn, 1948.

Hausherr, Hans. "Stein und Hardenberg." *Historische Zeitschrift* 190 (1960): 267–289.

_____. *Hardenberg. Eine politische Biographie. Aus dem Nachlaß.* Ed. E. Born. Cologne: Böhlau, 1963.

Heilmann, Joseph. *Feldmarschall Fürst Wrede.* Leipzig: Duncker und Humblot, 1881.

Henderson, Ernest. *Blücher and the Uprising of Prussia Against Napoleon. 1806–1815.* New York: AMS Press, 1978.

Henningsen, Nikolaus, ed. *Major von Schill und seine Tapferen.* Cologne: Schaffstein, 1913.

Herre, Franz. *Freiherr vom Stein. Sein Leben—Seine Zeit.* Cologne: Kiepenheuer and Witsch, 1973.

Holmsten, Georg. *Freiherr vom Stein.* Hamburg: Rowohlt, 1975.

Isenburg, Wilhelm. *Das Staatsdenken des Freiherrn vom Stein.* Bonn: Bouvier, 1968.

Jagwitz, Fritz von. *Geschichte des Lützowischen Freikorps.* Berlin: Mittler, 1892.

[Janke, J. E. Th.] *Erinnerungen an den preußischen Staatsminister Freiherrn vom Stein und seine Wünsche für Preußen.* Leipzig: Nauck, 1832.

Just, Leo. *Franz von Lassaulx.* Bonn: Marcus und Weber, 1926.

Kamnitzer, Heinz. "Stein und das deutsche Comité in Rußland 1812–13." *Zeitschrift für Geschichtswissenschaft.* 1 (1953): 50–69.

Kircheisen, Friedrich von. *Napoleon I. Sein Leben und seine Zeit.* 9 vols. Munich and Leipzig: Müller, 1911–1934.

Klatt, Tessa. *Das politische Wirken der Königin Luise von Preußen.* Berlin: Junker and Dünnhaupt, 1937.

Kleßmann, Eckhart. *Prinz Louis Ferdinand von Preußen 1772–1806.* Munich: List, 1972.

Klippel, Georg Heinrich. *Das Leben des Generals von Scharnhorst.* 3 vols. Leipzig: Brockhaus, 1869–1871.

Kraehe, Enno E. *Metternich's German Policy.* Princeton, NJ: Princeton University Press, 1963.

Krauel, R. "Stein während des preußisch-englischen Konflikts im Jahre 1806," *Preußisches Jahrbuch* 137 (1909): 429–457.

Lentner, Ferdinand. *Der Freiherr vom Stein in Österreich*. Vienna: Braumüller, 1873.

Manfred, Albert. *Napoleon Bonaparte*. 2nd ed. Berlin: Verlag der Wissenschaften, 1981.

Mann, Golo. *Friedrich von Gentz. Geschichte eines europäischen Staatsmannes*. Zurich and Vienna: Europa Verlag, 1947.

Möller, Horst. *Aufklärung in Preußen. Der Verleger, Publizist und Geschichtsschreiber Friedrich Nicolai*. Berlin: Colloquia Verlag, 1974.

Mommsen, Wilhelm. *Stein, Ranke, Bismarck. Ein Beitrag zur politischen und sozialen Bewegung des 18. Jahrhunderts*. Munich: Bruckmann, 1954.

Müsebeck, Ernst. *Ernst Moritz Arndt. Ein Lebensbild*. Gotha: Perthes, 1914.

_____, ed. *Gold gab ich für Eisen*. Berlin: Bong, 1913.

Neuendorff, Edmund. *Die deutsche Turnschaft von 1806–1936*. Berlin: Limpert, 1936.

Otto, Hans. *Gneisenau. Preußens unbequemer Patriot*. Bonn: Keil, 1979.

Ouvry, Heinrich Aimé. *Stein and his Reform in Prussia*. London, 1873.

Paret, Peter. *Yorck and the Era of Prussian Reform*. Princeton, NJ: Princeton University Press, 1966.

Paulig, Friedrich R. *Friedrich Wilhelm III. König von Preußen*. 2 vols. Frankfurt an der Oder: Paulig, 1905.

Pertz, Georg Heinrich. *Das Leben des Feldmarschalls Grafen Neithardt von Gneisenau*. Berlin: Reimer, 1869.

_____. *Das Leben des Ministers Freiherrn vom Stein*. 6 vols. Berlin: Reimer, 1849–1855.

Pottinger, E. Ann. *Napoleon III and the German Crisis 1865–66*. Cambridge: Harvard University Press, 1966.

Presser, Jacob. *Napoleon. Die Entschlüsselung einer Legende*. Hamburg: Rowohlt, 1979.

Raack, Richard Charles. *The Fall of Stein*. Cambridge: Harvard University Press, 1965.

Ranke, Leopold von. *Hardenberg und die Geschichte des preußischen Staates von 1793–1813*. 2 vols. Leipzig: Duncker und Humblot, 1879.

Ritter, Gerhard. *Stein. Eine politische Biographie*. 3 vols. Stuttgart: Kohlhammer, 1958.

_____. *Die Staatsanschauung des Freiherrn vom Stein*. Berlin: Deutsche Verlagsgesellschaft, 1927.

Rössler, Hellmuth. "Buol." *Schriften der Kleist Gesellschaft* 18 (1938): 98–109.

_____. *Österreichs Kampf um Deutschlands Befreiung*. 2 vols. Hamburg: Hanseat. Verlagsanstalt, 1940.

_____. *Reichsfreiherr vom Stein*. 2nd ed. Göttingen: Musterschmidt, 1964.

_____. *Graf Johann Philipp Stadion. Napoleons deutscher Gegenspieler*. 2 vols. Vienna and Munich: Herold, 1966–67.

Rothfels, Hans. *Stein und der deutsche Staatsgedanke*. Königsberg: Gräfe and Unzer, 1931.

Rundnagel, Erwin. *Friedrich Friesen. Ein politisches Lebensbild*. Munich and Berlin: Oldenbourg, 1936.

Schmidt, Otto Eduard. *Drei Brüder Carlowitz. Lebensbilder und Briefe*. Leipzig: Koehler und Amelang, 1933.

Schnabel, Franz. *Freiherr vom Stein*. Leipzig and Berlin: Teubner, 1931.

Schneidawind, Franz J. *Prinz Wilhelm von Preußen in den Kriegen seiner Zeit*. Berlin: Decker, 1856.

Schwab, Dieter. *Die 'Selbstverwaltungsidee' des Freiherrn vom Stein und ihre geistigen Grundlagen*. Frankfurt: Athenäum, 1971.

Seeley, John R. *The Life and Times of Stein*. 3 vols. London: Cambridge University Press, 1878. Reprinted New York, 1968.

Stern, Sigismund. *Stein und sein Zeitalter*. Leipzig: Brockhaus, 1855.

Sweet, Paul N. *Wilhelm von Humboldt: A Biography*. Columbus, Ohio: Ohio State University Press, [vol. 1] 1978, [vol. 2] 1980.

———. *Friedrich von Gentz: Defender of the Old Order*. 2nd. ed. Westport: Greenwood, 1970.

Thiede, Klaus. *Die Staats- und Wirtschaftsauffassung des Freiherrn vom Stein*. Jena: Fischer, 1927.

Thielen, Peter Gerrit. *Karl August von Hardenberg*. Cologne and Berlin: Grote, 1967.

Trainé, Jean. *Napoléon et l'Allemagne*. Paris: Lavauzelle, 1984.

Tümmler, Hans. *Der Freiherr vom Stein und Carl August von Weimar*. Cologne and Berlin: Grote, 1974.

Vobiahn, Bernhard. *Barthold Georg Niebuhr und der Freiherr vom Stein*. Diss. Leipzig, 1934.

Wagner, R. *Das Bild des Freiherrn vom Stein in der deutschen Geschichtsschreibung*. Diss. Munich, 1947.

Wentzchke, Paul. *Justus Gruner der Begründer der preußischen Herrschaft im Bergischen Lande*. Heidelberg: Winter, 1913.

Weise, Heinrich von. "Generalleutnant Friedrich Wilhelm Graf von Götzen." *Preußische Jahrbücher* 68 (1891): 804–835.

Wuppermann, Leonie. *Prinzessin Marianne von Preußen, geborene Prinzessin von Hessen-Homburg in den Jahren 1804–1808*. Diss. Bonn, 1942.

C. The Era in Cultural and Literary Perspective.

Blackall, Eric A. *The Emergence of German as a Literary Language*. London: Cambridge University Press, 1959.

Blumenberg, Hans. *Arbeit am Mythos*. Frankfurt: Suhrkamp, 1979.

Brunswig, Henri. *Societé et romantisme en Prusse au XVIIIe siècle*. Paris: Flammarion, 1973.

Buhr, Manfred. *Revolution und Philosophie*. Berlin: Deutscher Verlag der Wissenschaften, 1965.

Cassirer, Ernst. *Idee und Gestalt. Fünf Aufsätze*. Berlin: Bruno Cassirer, 1921.

Czygan, Paul. *Zur Geschichte der Tagesliteratur während der Freiheitskriege*. Leipzig: Duncker und Humblot, 1911.

Deutsch, Karl. *Der Nationalismus und seine Alternativen*. Munich: Piper, 1972.

Düding, Dieter. *Organisierter gesellschaftlicher Nationalismus*. Munich: Oldenbourg, 1984.

Emmerich, Wolfgang. *Germanistische Volkstumsideologie. Genese und Kritik der Volksforschung im Dritten Reich.* Tübinger Vereinigung für Volkskunde, 1968.

_____. *Zur Kritik der Volkstumsideologie.* Frankfurt: Suhrkamp, 1971.

Engelsing, Rolf. *Der Bürger als Leser. Lesergeschichte in Deutschland. 1500–1800.* Stuttgart: Metzler, 1974.

Frank, Horst Joachim. *Geschichte des deutschen Unterrichts von den Anfängen bis 1945.* Munich: Hanser, 1973.

Frank, Manfred. *Der kommende Gott: Vorlesungen über die neue Mythologie.* Frankfurt: Suhrkamp, 1982.

_____. *Der unendliche Mangel an Sein: Schellings Hegelkritik und die Anfänge der Marxschen Dialektik.* Frankfurt: Suhrkamp, 1975.

Glaser, Horst Albert, ed. *Deutsche Literatur. Eine Sozialgeschichte.* Hamburg: Rowohlt. Vol. 5 (1786–1815) [1980], vol. 6 (1815–1848) [1980].

Goldfriedrich, Johann Adolf. *Geschichte des Deutschen Buchhandels vom Beginn der Klassischen Literaturperiode bis zum Beginn der Fremdherrschaft (1740–1804).* Vol. 3 of *Geschichte des deutschen Buchhandels. Im Auftrag des Börsenvereins der deutschen Buchhändler,* hg. von der historischen Kommission desselben. Leipzig, 1909.

_____. *Geschichte des deutschen Buchhandels vom Beginn der Fremdherrschaft bis zur Reform des Börsenvereins im neuen deutschen Reiche.* Vol. 4. Leipzig, 1913.

Gottschall, Rudolf. *Die deutsche Nationalliteratur des 19. Jahrhunderts.* 4th ed. Breslau: Trewendt, 1875.

Günther, Karl Heinz. *Geschichte der Erziehung.* 10th ed. Berlin: Volk und Wissen, 1971.

Hammer, Helmut. *Österreichs Propaganda zum Feldzug 1809.* Munich: Zeitungswissenschaftliche Vereinigung, 1935.

Heinrich, Dieter and Wagner, H., eds. *Subjektivität und Metaphysik.* Frankfurt: Klostermann, 1966.

Höcker, Gustav. *Die Vorbilder der deutschen Schauspielkunst,* Glogau: Flemming, n. d. [1899].

Houben, Heinrich Hubert. *Verbotene Literatur von der klassischen Zeit bis zur Gegenwart.* Bremen: Schünemann, 1928.

Kaemmel, Otto. *Geschichte des Leipziger Schulwesens vom Anfang des 13. bis gegen Mitte des 19. Jahrhunderts (1214–1846).* Leipzig and Berlin: Teubner, 1909.

Kaiser, Konrad. *Bilder aus der Zeit der Volkserhebung 1813.* Leipzig: Seemann, 1955.

Keller, Erwin. *Nationalismus und Literatur.* Berne and Munich: Fink, 1970.

Kelly, George Armstrong. *Idealism, Politics and History. Sources of Hegelian Thought.* Cambridge: Harvard University Press, 1969.

Klein, Walter. *Der Napoleonkult in der Pfalz.* Münchner Historische Abhandlungen. Heft 5. Munich and Berlin: Beck, 1934.

Koenig, Helmut. *Zur Geschichte der Nationalerziehung in Deutschland im letzten Drittel des 18. Jahrhunderts.* Monumenta Paedagogica. vol. 12. Berlin: Akademie Verlag, 1960.

_____. *Zur Geschichte der bürgerlichen Nationalerziehung in Deutschland zwischen 1807 und 1815.* Monumenta Paedagogica. vol 13. Berlin: Akademie Verlag, 1972.

Kohn, Hans. *The Mind of Germany: The Education of a Nation.* New York: Scribner, 1960.

_____. *Nationalism. Its Meaning and History*. Princeton: Van Nostrand, 1960.

_____. *The Age of Nationalism. The First Era of Global History*. New York: Harper, 1962.

_____. *Prelude to Nation-States: The German and French Experience, 1789–1815*. Princeton: Van Nostrand, 1967.

Korff, Hermann August. *Geist der Goethezeit*. 4 vols. Leipzig: Koehler, 1923–1953.

Lämmert, et al., eds. *Germanistik. Eine deutsche Wissenschaft*. Frankfurt: Suhrkamp, 1967.

Lemberg, Eugen. *Geschichte des Nationalismus in Europa*. Stuttgart: Schwab, 1950.

Leyhausen, Wilhelm. *Das höhere Schulwesen in der Stadt Köln zur französischen Zeit (1794–1814)*. Studien zur rheinischen Geschichte. heft 6. Bonn: Marcus und Weber, 1913.

Lukács, Georg. *Deutsche Realisten des neunzehnten Jahrhunderts*. Berlin: de Gruyter, 1951.

_____. *Die Zerstörung der Vernunft*. Darmstadt und Neuwied: Luchterhand, 1973.

Mayer, Hans. "Zur historischen Dimension des Romantischen" *Colloquia Germanica* 2 (1960): 70–108.

Mehring, Franz. *Aufsätze zur Literaturgeschichte*. Frankfurt: Roderberg, 1972.

Mosse, George Lachman. *The Nationalization of the Masses*. New York: Fertig, 1976.

_____. *The Crisis of German Ideology*. New York: Grosset and Dunlap, 1966.

Oehlke, Waldemar. *Die deutsche Literatur seit Goethes Tod*. Halle: Niemeyer, 1921.

Politzer, Heinz. *Hatte Ödipus 'nen Ödipuskomplex? Versuche zum Thema Psychologie und Literatur*. Munich: Piper, 1974.

Platt, Washington. *National Character in Action*. New Brunswick: Rutgers University Press, 1961.

Poag, J. F. and Scholz-Williams, Gerhild, eds. *Das Weiterleben des Mittelalters in der deutschen Literatur*. Königstein: Athenäum, 1983.

Schalk, Adolf. *The Germans*. Englewood Cliffs: Prentice Hall, 1971.

Scherer, Wilhelm. *Geschichte der deutschen Literatur*. 5th ed. Berlin: Weidmann, 1889.

Schulz, Gerhard. *Die deutsche Literatur zwischen Französischer Revolution und Restauration. Erster Teil. 1789–1806*. Vol. 7 of *Geschichte der deutschen Literatur*. Eds. Helmut de Boor und Richard Newald. Munich: Beck, 1983.

See, Karl von. *Deutsche Germanenideologie vom Humanismus bis zur Gegenwart*. Frankfurt: Suhrkamp, 1970.

Shafer, Boyd Carlisle. *Nationalism. Myth and Reality*. New York: Harcourt and Brace, 1972.

_____. *Nationalism. Interpreters and Interpretations*. New York: Macmillan, 1963.

_____. *Faces of Nationalism*. New York: Harcourt and Brace, 1972.

Snyder, Louis L. *From Bismarck to Hitler: The Background of Modern German Nationalism*. Williamsport: Bayard, 1935.

_____. *Race. A History of Modern Ethnic Theories*. New York: Longmans and Green, 1939.

_____. *German Nationalism: The Tragedy of a People*. Harrisburg: Stackpole, 1952.

_____. *The Idea or Racialism*. Princeton: Van Nostrand, 1962.

_____. ed. *The Dynamics of Nationalism*. Princeton: Van Nostrand, 1964.

_____. *Varieties of Nationalism*. New York: Holt, Rinehart and Winston, 1976.

_____. *Roots of German Nationalism*. Bloomington: Indiana University Press, 1978.

Spranger, Eduard. *Der Anteil des Neuhumanismus an der Entstehung des deutschen Nationalbewußtseins*. Berlin: Norddeutsche Buchdruck- und Verlagsanstalt, 1923.

Tatar, Maria M. *Spellbound. Studies on Mesmerism and Literature*. Princeton: Princeton University Press, 1978.

Timm, Hermann. *Gott und Freiheit: Studien zur Religionsphilosophie der Goethezeit*. Frankfurt: Klostermann, 1974.

_____. *Die heilige Revolution: Das religiöse Totalitätskonzept der Frühromantik. Schleiermacher, Novalis, Friedrich Schlegel*. Frankfurt: Syndikat, 1978.

Viereck, Peter. *Metapolitics: From the Romantics to Hitler*. New York: Scribner, 1941.

Vogt, Friedrich und Koch, Max. *Geschichte der deutschen Literatur*. 5th ed. Leipzig: Bibliographisches Institut, 1934.

Ziolkowski, Theodore. "Der Hunger nach dem Mythos." In *Die sogenannten Zwanziger Jahre*, Eds. Reinhold Grimm und Jost Hermand. Bad Homburg: Athenäum, 1970.

D. Individual Writers and Literary Problems.

Albertsen, Leif Ludwig. "Internationaler Zeitfaktor Kotzebue: Trivialisierung oder sinnvolle Entliterarisierung des strebenden Bürgers im Frühliberalismus." *Sprachkunst* 9 (1978): 220–240.

Albrecht, Egon-Erich. *Heinrich von Kleist 'Prinz Friedrich von Homburg' auf der deutschen Bühne*. Diss. Kiel, 1921.

Allemann, Beda. "Der Nationalismus Heinrich von Kleists," *Nationalismus in Germanistik und Dichtung*. Eds. Benno von Wiese and R. Henß. Berlin: Schmitt, 1967: 305–311.

Angress, Ruth. "Kleist's Treatment of Imperialism: Die Hermannsschlacht and Die Verlobung in St. Domingo" *Monatshefte für deutschen Unterricht* 69 (1977): 17–33.

Antonowytsch, Michael. *Friedrich Ludwig Jahn*. Berlin: Ebering, 1933.

Baumanns, Peter. *Fichtes ursprüngliches System. Sein Standort zwischen Kant und Hegel*. Stuttgart: Frommann, 1972.

Berger, Karl. *Theodor Körner*. Bielefeld und Leipzig: Velhagen und Klasing, 1912.

Berglar, Peter. *Goethe und Napoleon. Die Faszination des Geistes durch die Macht*. Darmstadt: Roether, 1968.

Bergner, Dieter. *Neue Bemerkungen zu J. G. Fichte*. Berlin: Deutscher Verlag der Wissenschaften, 1957.

Bethke, Johann. *Heinrich von Kleist und Österreich*. Diss. Vienna, 1932.

Beyer, Conrad. *Friedrich Rückert. Leben und Dichtungen*. Koburg: Sandelbach, 1866.

_____. *Friedrich Rückert. Ein biographisches Denkmal*. Frankfurt: Sauerländer, 1868.

_____. *Neue Mitteilungen über Friedrich Rückert*. 2 vols. Leipzig: Frohberg, 1873.

Birkenhauer, Klaus. *Heinrich von Kleist. Rätselhaft und Frühvollendet*. Tübingen: Wunderlich, 1977.

Blöcker, Günther. *Heinrich von Kleist oder das absolute Ich*. Berlin: Argon, 1960.

Brinkhorst, Martin. "Kotzebue und Sheridan: Erfolgsstrategien von 1799" *OL* 34 (1979): 17–32.

Burkhardt, Sigurd. "Heinrich von Kleist: The Poet as Prussian." *Centennial Review of Arts and Sciences* 8 (1964): 435–462.

Busch, Ernst. "Die Stellung Gotthilf Heinrich Schuberts in der deutschen Naturmystik und in der Romantik:" *DVjS* 20 (1942): 305–339.

Dawson, Jerry F. *Friedrich Schleiermacher. The Evolution of a Nationalist.* Austin: University of Texas Press, 1966.

Decker, Gebrand. *Die Rückwendung zum Mythos. Schellings letzte Wandlung.* Munich and Berlin: Oldenbourg, 1930.

Denis, Arthur. "La fortune littéraire et théâtrale de Kotzebue en France." *DAI* 38 (1978): 3125c.

Dilthey, Wilhelm. *Das Leben Schleiermachers.* Berlin and Leipzig: de Gruyter, 1922.

Diwald, Hellmut. *Ernst Moritz Arndt—Das Entstehen des deutschen Nationalbewußtseins.* Munich: Bechtle, 1970.

Durst, Rolf. *Heinrich von Kleist. Dichter zwischen Ursprung und Endzeit.* 2nd ed. Berne: Francke, 1977.

Eck, Dirk von. *Napoleon im Spiegel der Goetheschen und Heineschen Dichtung.* Diss. Amsterdam, 1933.

Eimer, Gerhard. *Caspar David Friedrich und die Gotik.* Hamburg: von der Ropp, 1963.

Engelbrecht, Helmut Carol. *Johann Gottlieb Fichte. A Study of his Political Writings.* New York: Columbia University Press, 1933.

Ergang, Robert Reinhold. *Herder and the Foundation of German Nationalism.* New York: Columbia University Press, 1931.

Erhard, Heinrich A. *Theodor Körner. Sein Leben nebst einer ausführlichen Beurteilung seiner Schriften.* Arnstadt: Hildebrand, 1821.

Euler, Carl. *Friedrich Ludwig Jahn. Sein Leben und Wirken.* Stuttgart: Krabbe, 1881.

Feierfeil, Georg. *`Die Verlobung in St. Domingo´ von Heinrich von Kleist und Theodor Körners `Toni´.* Bernau: Prgar, 1892.

Fischer, Andreas. *Goethe und Napoleon.* Frauenfeld and Leipzig: Huber, 1900.

Fischer, Maximilian. *Heinrich von Kleist. Der Dichter des Preußentums.* Stuttgart: Cotta, 1916.

Fortlage, Carl. *Friedrich Rückert und seine Werke.* Frankfurt: Sauerländer, 1867.

Freund, Michael. *Napoleon und die Deutschen.* Munich: Callwey, 1969.

Fricke, Gerhard. *Gefühl und Schicksal bei Heinrich von Kleist.* Berlin: Junker und Dünnhaupt, 1929.

Friedman, Stanley. "Kotzebue's `The Stranger´ in `David Copperfield´." *Dickens Studies Newsletter* 9 (1978): 49–50.

Frühwald, Wolfgang. "Der Regierungsrat Joseph von Eichendorff," *Internationales Achiv für Sozialgeschichte der deutschen Literatur* 4 (1979): 36–67.

Futterknecht, Franz. *Heinrich Heine. Ein Versuch.* Tübingen: Narr, 1985.

Gajek, Benjamin. "Achim von Arnim: Romantischer Poet und Preußischer Patriot (1789–1831)." *Sammeln und Sichten. Festschrift für Oskar Fambach zum 80. Geburtstag.* Ed. Joachim Krause et al. Bonn: Bouvier, 1982. 264–282.

Genée, Rudolf. *Ifflands Theaterleitung 1796–1814*. Berlin: National-Zeitung, 1896.

Gerlach, Kurt. *Heinrich von Kleist. Sein Leben und Schaffen in neuer Sicht*. Dortmund: Ostdeutsche Forschungsstelle, [vol. I] 1971, [vol. II] 1972, [vol. III] 1977.

Grathoff, Dirk. "Die Zensurkonflikte der `Berliner Abendblätter´." In *Ideologiekritische Studien zur deutschen Literatur*, Ed. Volkmar Sander. Frankfurt: Athenäum, 1972.

Hans, Ludwig. *Arndt und Stein: Erlebnis und Darstellung*. Diss. Bonn, 1948.

Härtel, Heinz. "Unbekannte Äußerungen Arnims über Kleist." *WB* 23 (1977): 178–181.

Hausenstein, Wilhelm. "Heinrich von Kleist. Gestorben am 21. November 1811." *Mannheimer Volksstimme*, 22. November 1911.

Hegele, Wolfgang. *Grabbes Dramenform*. Munich: Fink, 1970.

Hellmann, Hanna. *Heinrich von Kleist. Darstellung des Problems*. Heidelberg: Winter, 1911.

Herling, Max und Schroeder, H. D. *1769–1969. Ernst Moritz Arndt*. Greifswald: Arndt Universität, 1969.

Herzog, Wilhelm. *Heinrich von Kleist*. Munich: Beck, 1914.

Holzhausen, Paul. *Heinrich Heine und Napoleon I*. Frankfurt: Diesterweg, 1903.

Hooverland, Lillian. "Heinrich von Kleists `Michael Kohlhaas´ jenseits der Gerechtigkeit." *Colloquia Germanica* 9 (1975): 269–290.

Hornsey, Alan Walter. *Idea and Reality in the Dramas of Christian Dietrich Grabbe*. Oxford: Pergamon Press, 1966.

Hunter, Charles K. *Der Interpersonalitätsbeweis in Fichtes früher angewandter praktischer Philosophie*. Meisenheim: Hain, 1973.

Jacoby, Daniel. "Fichte und sein Verhältnis zu Preußen." *Euphorion* 21 (1914): 237–251.

Jaden, Hans R. von. *Theodor Körner*. Vienna: Frick, 1913.

Janke, Wolfgang. *Fichte. Sein und Reflexion. Grundlage der kritischen Vernunft*. Berlin: de Gruyter, 1970.

Jöst, Erhard. "Der Heldentod des Dichters Theodor Körner: Der Einfluß eines Mythos auf die Rezeption einer Lyrik und ihre literarische Kritik." *Orbis Litterarum* 32 (1977): 310–340.

Kaufmann, F. W. "Kleist und Fichte." *Germanic Review* 9 (1934): 1–8.

Kliewer, Erwin. *August Wilhelm Iffland*. Germanische Studien, vol. 195. Berlin: Ebering, 1937.

Klingenberg, Karl-Heinz. *Iffland und Kotzebue als Dramatiker*. Weimar: Böhlau, 1962.

Knaack, Jürgen. *Achim von Arnim—Nicht nur Poet*. Darmstadt: Thesen, 1976.

Körner, Josef. *Recht und Pflicht*. Leipzig: Teubner, 1926.

Kühnemann, Eugen. "Kleist und Kant." *Schriften der Kleist Gesellschaft* 2 (1922): 1–30.

Kunisch, Hermann. "J. A. Schmellers geistesgeschichtliche Stellung," *Historische Jahrbücher* 62 (1949/1950): 69–81.

Lachs, John. "Fichte's Idealism." *American Philosophical Quarterly* 9 (1972): 311–318.

Lindsay, John M. "Figures of Authority in the Works of Heinrich von Kleist." *Forum of Modern Language Studies* 8 (1972): 107–119.

Loose, Hans-Dieter. *Kleists `Hermannsschlacht´. Kein Krieg für Hermann und seine Cherusker*. Karlsruhe: von Loeper, 1984.

Lorenz, Ludwig. *Heinrich von Treitschke in unserer Zeit.* Leipzig: Weicher, 1916.

Luther, Bernhard. "Kleists `Prinz Friedrich von Homburg´ und Müllers `Elemente der Staatskunst´." *Zeitschrift für deutschen Unterricht* 30 (1916): 171–183.

Maaß, Joachim. *Heinrich von Kleist.* Berlin und Munich: Scherz, 1977.

Maurer, Doris. *August von Kotzebue. Ursachen seines Erfolges: Konstante Elemente der unterhaltenden Dramatik.* Bonn: Bouvier, 1979.

Meyer-Benfey, Heinrich. "Die innere Geschichte des `Michael Kohlhaas´." *Euphorion* 16 (1908): 99–140.

_____. "Kleists politische Anschauungen." *Schriften der Kleist Gesellschaft.* Jahrbuch 1931. 13 (1932): 10–28.

Müller-Seidel, Walter, ed. *Heinrich von Kleist. Aufsätze und Essays.* Darmstadt: Wissenschaftliche Buchgesellschaft, 1967.

Müsebeck, Ernst. *Ernst Moritz Arndt. Ein Lebensbild.* Gotha: Perthes, 1914.

Muth, Ludwig. *Kleist und Kant.* Kantstudien. Suppl. No. 68. Cologne: Universität, 1954.

Nadler, Joseph. *Grillparzer.* Vaduz: Liechtenstein, 1948.

Paul, Johannes. *Ernst Moritz Arndt.* Göttingen: Musterschmidt, 1971.

Peschel, Emil und Widenow, Eugen. *Theodor Körner und die Seinen.* Leipzig: Seemann, 1898.

Petersen, Julius. *Die Sehnsucht nach dem dritten Reich in deutscher Sage und Dichtung. Erw. Abdruck aus der Zeitschrift `Dichtung und Volkstum´.* Stuttgart: Metzler, 1934.

Piechowski, Paul. *Friedrich Ludwig Jahn. Vom Turnvater zum Volkserzieher.* Gotha: Klotz, 1928.

Prang, Helmut. *Friedrich Rückert. Geist und Sprache.* Wiesbaden: Harrassowitz, 1963.

Pröhle, Heinrich. *Friedrich Ludwig Jahns Leben.* 2nd ed. Stuttgart: Krabbe, 1872.

Prutz, Robert. "Fichte in Königsberg." *Allgemeine Zeitung.* Beilage 181. Nr. 218. Munich: den 8. August 1893.

Pundt, Alfred J. *Arndt and the National Awakening in Germany.* New York: Columbia University Press, 1935.

Pütz, Peter. "Zwei Krähwinkliaden 1802/1848. Kotzebue: `Die deutschen Kleinstädter´. Nestroy: `Freiheit in Krähwinkel´." *Die deutsche Komödie. Vom Mittelalter bis zur Gegenwart.* Ed. Walter Hinck. Düsseldorf: Bagel, 1977, 175–194.

Raabe, August. *Das Erlebnis des Dämonischen in Goethes Denken und Schaffen.* Berlin: Junker and Dünnhaupt, 1942.

Reinhard, Gustav. *Schillers Einfluß auf Theodor Körner.* Strasbourg: Trübner, 1899.

Rogge, Helmut. "Heinrich von Kleist letzte Leiden. Nach unveröffentlichten Zeugnissen aus dem Nachlaß Julius Eduard Hitzigs." *Schriften der Kleist Gesellschaft* 2 (1922/23): 31–74.

Rudolf, Günther. "Adam Müller und Kleist." *WB* 24 (1978): 121–135.

Sammons, Jeffrey. *Heinrich Heine. A Modern Biography.* Princeton: Princeton University Press, 1979.

Samuel, Richard. "Kleists `Hermannsschlacht´ und der Freiherr vom Stein." *Jahrbuch der deutschen Schiller Gesellschaft* 5 (1961): 64–101.

_____. "Heinrich von Kleist und Neithardt von Gneisenau," *Jahrbuch der deutschen Schiller Gesellschaft* 7 (1963): 352–370.

Schneider, Hermann. *Studien zu Kleist*. Berlin: Weidmann, 1915.

Scott, D. F. S. "Kleist's Kant Crisis." *Modern Language Review* 42 (1947): 474–485.

Scurla, Herbert. *Ernst Moritz Arndt. Der Vorkämpfer für Einheit und Demokratie*. Berlin: Kongreß Verlag, 1952.

Seier, Helmut. "Sybels Vorlesungen über Politik und die Kontinuität des `staatsbildenden´ Liberalismus." *Historische Zeitschrift* 187 (1959): 90–112.

Sembdner, Helmut. *Die Berliner Abendblätter Heinrich von Kleist*. Berlin: Weidmann, 1939.

Scheibner, Eberhard. "Zu Kleist politischen Ansichten zur Zeit der Berliner Abendblätter." *WB* 23 (1977): 144–166.

Sieburg, Friedrich. *Grabbe, Napoleon. Dichtung und Wahrheit*. Frankfurt: Ullstein, 1963.

Stamm, Israel Soliman. "Note on Kleist and Kant." *Studies in Honor of Johann Albrecht Walz*. Lancaster, Pennsylvania: Prince and Lemon, 1941: 31–40.

Stefansky, Georg. "Ein neuer Weg zu Heinrich von Kleist." *Euphorion* 23 (1921): 639–696.

Steig, Reinhold. *Heinrich von Kleists Berliner Kämpfe*. Berlin und Stuttgart, 1901. Neudruck, Berne: Lang, 1971.

_____. *Neue Kunde zu Heinrich von Kleist*. Berlin: Reimer, 1902.

Stock, Fritjof. "August von Kotzebue." In *Deutsche Dichter des 18. Jahrhunderts*. Ed. Benno von Wiese. Berlin: Schmitt, 1977: 958–971.

Streller, Siegfried. *Das dramatische Werk Heinrich von Kleist*. Berlin: Rütten und Loening, 1966.

Szépe, Helen A. "Opfertod und Poesie: Zur Geschichte der Theodor Körner Legende." *Colloquia Germanica* 9 (1975): 291–304.

Tatar, Maria M. "Psychology and Poetics: J. C. Reil and Kleist's `Prinz Friedrich von Homburg´." *Germanic Review* 48 (1973): 21–43.

Taylor, Harley U. "The Dramas of August von Kotzebue on the New York and Philadelphia Stages from 1798 to 1805" *West Virginia University Philological Papers* 23 (1977): 47–58.

Thalheim, Heinz-Günther. "Kleist `Prinz Friedrich von Homburg´." *WB* 11 (1965): 483–550.

Überhorst, Horst, ed. *Friedrich Ludwig Jahn 1778/1978*. Bonn: Inter Nationes, 1978.

Unger, Rudolf. *Herder, Novalis, Kleist. Studien zum Todesproblem*. Berlin: Diesterweg, 1922.

Vierengel, Heinz. "Die `Geharnischten Sonette´ von Friedrich Rückert." *Rückert Studien* 1 (1963): 1–34.

Wachter, Karl. *Kleists `Michael Kohlhaas´*. Weimar: Duncker, 1918.

Wagner, Karl. "Die Flugschriftenliteratur des Krieges von 1809." *Anno Neun. Volkslieder und Flugschriften*. Bücherei des österr. Volksschriftenvereins, vol. 5. Brixen: Tyrolia Verlag, n. d. [1917]: 63–124.

Wagner, Richard. *Die Beziehungen Fichtes zu Süvern und die Entsendung der preußischen Eleven nach Yverdon*. Diss. Erlangen, 1914.

Weiss, Hermann F. *Funde und Studien zu Heinrich von Kleist*. Tübingen: Niemeyer, 1984.

Wierlacher, Alois. "August Wilhelm Iffland." In *Deutsche Dichter des 18. Jahrhunderts*, ed. Benno von Wiese. Berlin: Schmitt, 1977: 911–930.

Windemuth, Annemarie. *Ernst Moritz Arndts Napoleonbild*. Diss. Berlin, 1946.

Wittkowski, Wolfgang. "Schrieb Kleist regierungsfreundliche Artikel? Über den Umgang mit politischen Texten." *Jahrbuch der Görres Gesellschaft* 32 (1982): 95–116.

Wolff, Hans M. *Heinrich von Kleist als politischer Dichter*. University of California Publications in Modern Psychology, vol. 27, no. 6, Berkeley, 1947.

Wright, Walker, E., ed. *Idealistic Studies*. Worcester, Mass.: Clark University Press, vol. 6, no. 2 (May 1976).

———. "Existentialism, Idealism and Fichte's Concept of Coherence." *Journal of the History of Philosophy* 13 (1975): 37–42.

Wundt, Max. *Fichte*. Stuttgart: Frommann, 1947.

Zunker, Ernst. "Ernst Moritz Arndt und sein `Geist der Zeit´." *Baltische Studien* 55 (1969): 44–48.

Index

Abbt, Thomas (1738-1766) 131f., 139

Alexander I Paulowitsch, Czar of Russia (1777-1825) 2, 13, 110, 111, 125

Altenstein, Karl von (Prussian Finance Minister, Minister of State; 1808) (1770-1840) 26, 27, 31, 36, 37, 175

Ancillon, Johann Peter Friedrich (1767-1837) 98

Antommarchi, Francesco (1780-1838) 179

Archenholz, Johann Wilhelm (1743-1812) 79

Arledter, Carl 187

Arminius 2, 3, 13, 19, 37-47, 90, 93, 117, 123f., 127, 135, 137, 201

Arndt, Ernst Moritz (1769-1860) 2, 12, 35, 46f., 85-102, 103, 104, 107, 109, 125, 131, 133, 135, 137, 141, 151, 155, 156, 160f., 163, 166, 171, 173, 174, 175, 182, 197, 198, 200, 201, 202, 203

Arnim, (Ludwig Joachim) Achim von (1781-1831) 71

Aspern, battle of 36, 51

Auerstedt (Battle at Jena-Auerstedt; 1806) 1, 4, 11

August, Ferdinand (1795-1870) 160

Auguste, Sophia Dorothea (Princess of Württemberg, Czarina of Russia) (1759-1828) 86

Austria 35ff., 39, 40, 46, 48, 49, 50, 66, 68, 77f., 92, 116, 119, 125, 145, 146, 155f., 162, 168, 178, 190f., 195, 196

Baggesen, Jens (1764-1826) 23f.

Basedow, Johann Bernhard (1723-1790) 138

Beuchamp, Alphonse (1767-1832) 7, 9

Beauhàrnias, Eugène de (1781-1824) 120

Becker, Nikolaus (1809-1845) 189

Beitzke, Heinrich von (1798-1867) 152

Béranger, Pierre Jean de (1780-1857) 184f., 186, 192

Bergk, Johann Adam (1769-1834) 177

Bern, Dietrich von (Theodorich the Great) (456-526) 3

Bernadotte, Jean Baptiste Jules (1763-1844) 36

Bernhardi, Friedrich von (1849-1930) 202

Beurmann, Eduard Adolf von (1804-?) 130ff.

Beyer, Conrad (1834-1906) 166

Beyme, Karl Friedrich von (1765-1838) 24, 27, 81

Biester, Johann Erich (1749-1816) 10

Bismarck, Otto von (1815-1898) 85, 102, 141, 161, 192, 193, 194, 195, 200

Blücher, Gebhardt Leberecht (Prussian Fieldmarshal) (1742-1819) 39, 152, 173

Boeck, Joachim G. (1899-?) 201

Bonus, Arthur (1864-1941) 200

Börne, Ludwig (1786-1837) 177, 183

Boyen, Leopold Hermann Ludwig von (1771-1848) 109

Bran, Friedrich Alexander (1767-1831) 79

Braunschweig-Oels, Duke of (Black Duke) Friedrich Wilhelm (1771-1815) 156

Bredow, Gottfried Gabriel (1773-1814) 169

Brünn, (Brno, Czechoslovakia) 5ff., 13, 36

Brünn-Memorandum 5ff.

Bülow, Ernst Gottfried (1775-1851) 172

Buol-Mühlingen, Joseph von (Austrian Charge d'affairs at Dresden) (1773-1812) 35, 36, 37

Burke, Edmund (1729-1797) 12, 22

Burte, Hermann (1879-1960) 202

Canning, George (1770-1827) 1, 79

Carlowitz, Karl Adolf von (1774-1837) 36, 166

Castlereagh, Stewart (1769-1822) 168

Celtis, Conrad (1459-1508) 2

Chamisso, Adelbert von (1781-1838) 121

Champagny, Jean Baptiste (French Foreign Minister) (1756-1834) 170

Charles, Duke of Mecklenburg (1741-1816) 66

Charles, Archduke of Austria (1771-1847) 36, 48, 66, 145, 151

Charlottenburg Club (also Berlin Committee, Insurrectionist Committee of Berlin) 99, 109f., 173

Chasot, Ludwig August Friedrich Adolf von (Leader of Charlottenburg Club) (1763-1813) 99, 109, 125, 136

Chouans (province in France, last Royalist stronghold) 7f.

Christian German Table Society (Christlich-teutsche Tischgesellschaft) 68, 69

Collin, Heinrich Joseph von (1771-1811) 68

Confederation of the Rhine 34, 35, 39, 59, 99, 117, 162, 164, 166, 170, 191

Congress of Vienna 76, 141, 168, 175, 177

David, Jacques Louis (1748-1825) 178

Davout, Louis Nicolas (1770-1832) 111, 169

Delbrück, Johann Friedrich Ferdinand (1712-1848) 100, 101, 102

Dickens, Charles (1812-1870) 122

Dietrich von Bern (see Bern, Dietrich von)

Dohna, Count Friedrich Ferdinand Alexander (1771-1832) 24, 112, 114

Dörnberg, Wilhelm Caspar von (1768-1850) 56, 65

Droysen, Johann (1808-1884) 195

Dumouriez, Charles François (1739-1823) 125

Index

Dürre, Christian Eduard Leopold (1796-1879) 140

Eggers, Kurt (1905-1943) 202

Eichhorn, Johann Albrecht (1779-1856) 109, 174

Eiselin, Ernst (1793-1846) 139

Engels, Friedrich (1820-1895) 189

Enghien, Duke of, Louis Antoine Henri (1772-1804) 87

Euringer, Richard (1891-1953) 202

Eylert, Ruhlmann, Bishop of Potsdam (1770-1852) 172, 176

Fassbender, General 39

Fehrbellin, battle of (1675) 54, 67

Feuerbach, Paul Johannes, Anselm von (1775-1833) 162

Fichte, Johann Gottlieb (1762-1814) 2, 11, 12, 14, 15-28, 29ff., 37, 42f., 47, 49, 50, 51, 53, 62, 81, 88, 90, 91, 93, 95, 98, 102, 103, 104ff., 107, 108, 112, 113, 117, 131, 133, 137, 138, 139, 141, 146, 150, 151, 152, 155, 156, 172, 173, 197, 198, 200, 201, 202

Fouqué, Friedrich de la Motte (1777-1843) 136, 165, 166, 191

Franceschi, G. 187

Francis II (I), Emperor of Austria (last Holy Roman emperor) (1768-1835) 5, 34, 36, 48, 93, 119, 191

François, Carl von 54

Francoise, Luise von (1817-1893) 193

Frederick August I, King of Saxony (1750-1827) 36, 66

Frederick the Great (1712-1786) 3, 105, 106, 131, 132, 163

Frederick William II (1744-1797) 11

Frederick William III (1770-1840) 1, 4, 5, 11, 13, 24, 47, 50, 51, 55, 61, 62, 65, 66, 67, 76, 77, 78, 91, 92, 93, 98, 104, 110, 112, 117, 139, 152, 153, 156, 167, 169, 170, 171, 173, 175, 176

Frederick William IV (1795-1861) 67, 140, 192

Friedrich, Casper David (1774-1840) 64, 202

Friend of the People (see Der Volksfreund, journal of the Tugendbund)

Friesen, Friedrich (1785-1814) 140, 171

Gagern, Heinrich Christian Freiherr von (1799-1880) 166

Garlike, Benjamin (British envoy to Prussia; 1807) 13

Gaudy, Franz von (1800-1840) 186

Gentz, Friedrich (1764-1832) 22, 35, 36, 38, 68, 77, 115, 116

Germany in Her Low Abasement (anti-French pamphlet; 1806) 118-120

Gneisenau, August Wilhelm, Count Neidhardt von (1760-1831) 2, 34, 39, 75, 96, 98, 109f., 114, 138, 141, 152, 171, 173

Goethe, Johann Wolfgang (1749-1832) 121, 122, 130, 180, 182

Gottschall, Rudolf (1823-1909) 198

Götzen, Count Friedrich von (Governor of Silesia) (1767-1820) 47, 55

Grabbe, Christian Dietrich (1801-1836) 177, 183

Grenville, Thomas (1755-1846) 79

Grillparzer, Franz (1791-1872) 183

Grimm, Jacob (1785-1863) 137, 192

Grimm, Wilhelm (1786-1859) 137, 192

Gruner, Karl Justus (1777-1820) 71, 72, 74ff., 77-79, 80-83, 85, 98, 111, 118, 136

Gustav IV Adolphus, King of Sweden (1792-1809) 87

Guts-Muths, Johann (1759-1839) 138, 141

Gutzkow, Karl (1811-1878) 180

Hackländer, Friedrich Wilhelm (1816-1877) 187f.

Hanstein, Gottfried August Ludwig (1761-1821) 111

Hardenberg, Karl August von (1750-1822) 24, 26, 68, 75-79, 80, 82, 83, 98, 111, 117, 168, 171

Haugwitz, Christian von (1752-1832) 4

Hauff, Wilhelm (1802-1827) 178

Häußer, Ludwig (1818-1867) 193f., 195

Haydn, Joseph (1732-1809) 190, 191

Hegel, Georg Wilhelm Friedrich (1770--1831) 96, 180, 195 196

Heine, Heinrich (1797-1856) 130, 177, 178, 179, 180, 181, 182, 184f., 189, 192

Hely-Hutchinson, John (1787-1851) 1, 13

Hendel, Johann Christian (1742-1823) 161

Hentschel, Willibald (1858-1939) 200, 201

Herder, Johann Gottlieb (1744-1803) 3, 21, 87, 130, 132, 137, 202

Hermann der Cherusker (see Arminius)

Herwegh, Georg (1817-1875) 183

Herz, Henriette (1764-1847) 26

Heß, Rudolph (1894-1986) 203

Hesse-Homburg, Marianne von (Princess William) (1785-1846) 58

Himly, Karl Gustav (1772-1837) 75, 77

Hintze, Otto von (1861-1940) 196

Hitler, Adolf (1889-1945) 102, 129, 202, 203

Hitzig, Julius Edward (1780-1849) 69, 80

Hofer, Andreas (1767-1810) 125, 190f.

Hoffmann von Fallersleben, August Heinrich (1798-1874) 189f., 191

Holberg, Ludwig (1684-1754) 120

Hölty, Ludwig (1748-1776) 3

Hormayr, Joseph von (1782-1848) 13

Horn, Alexander 77

Humboldt, Wilhelm von (1767-1835) 24, 27, 28, 98, 112, 133, 134, 135

Hüser, Johann Hans Gustav Heinrich (1770?-1853) 34f., 53

Iffland, August Wilhelm (1759-1814) 67, 82, 104, 118, 126, 127, 128

Immermann, Karl (1796-1840) 130, 179, 180

Jacobs, Christian Friedrich Wilhelm (1764-1847) 162

Jahn, Friedrich Ludwig (1778-1852) 129-142, 153, 160, 171, 172, 173, 175, 176, 201, 202

Jancke, E. J. Th. (Hardenberg's spy 1812) 170f.

Jean Paul (Richter) (1763-1825) 130

Jena, battle of 1, 4, 11, 54, 85, 105, 119

John, Archduke of Austria (1782-1859) 13

Judenne, E. 187

Junker (East Elbian Nobility) 2, 4, 68, 70, 153

Kanikov (also Chanikoff), Vassily (1770?-1829) 36

Kant, Immanuel (1724-1804) 15, 17, 22, 29f., 50

Kapf, Karl Gottlieb (1772-1839) 131

Kathen, Charlotte von 177

Katte, Friedrich von (1770-1836) 56, 65

Kircheisen, Friedrich (1877-1933) 188f.

Kleist, Heinrich von (1777-1811) 2, 12, 20, 29-83, 85, 88, 89, 90, 93, 94, 95, 102, 103, 104, 107, 111, 123, 124, 131, 135, 137, 139, 141, 143, 144, 146, 151, 155, 156, 166, 173, 186, 198, 200, 201, 202, works by: Robert Guiskard 33; Die Familie Schroffenstein 33; Phöbus 31, 35, 36; Michael Kohlhaas 31f.; Die Hermannsschlacht 31, 33, 34, 35, 36, 37-47, 49, 50, 57, 67, 82, 90, 91, 95, 100, 124, 127, 135, 143, 144, 145, 146, 151, 197, 198; Das Käthchen von Heilbrunn 143; Prinz Friedrich von Homburg 31, 35, 47, 50-68, 93, 117, 126, 127, 198, 199; Germania 36; To Palafox 95; Catechism for the Germans 36, 47-49, 93; Aphorisms 49, 93, 144; Satirical Letters 49, 144; Textbook of French Journalism 49; Kriegslied der Deutschen 69; Berliner Abendblätter 68-83, 118; Die heilige Cäcilie oder die Gewalt der Musik 144

Kleist, Major Ludwig Leopold von (1780-1837) 79, 172, 173

Kleist von Nollendorf, Friedrich Count (1762-1823) 79

Klinger, Maximilian (1752-1831) 30

Klopstock, Friedrich (1724-1803) 3, 90, 137, 202

Koch, Max (1855-1931) 197

Köckritz, Karl Leopold von (1762-1821) 4

Korff, Hermann August (1882-1963)

Körner, Christian Gottfried (1756-1831) 143, 156

Körner, Karl Theodor (1791-1813) 12, 89, 93, 102, 117, 133, 135, 163, 167, 173, 191, 198, 199, 201, 202, 203

Kotzebue, August von (1761-1819) 82, 104, 115, 116, 118, 120-126, 128, 140, 161, 174

Kühne, Gustav (1806-1888) 180

Kunze, Julie Emma (1790?-1849) 143

Küster, Samuel Christian (1762-1838) 75, 77

Lannes, Jean L. (French Marshal) (1769-1809)

Las Cases, Emanuel de (Count) (1766-1842) 179, 187

Laube, Heinrich (1806-1884) 180

Lavalette, Jean de (1494-1568) 93, 145

Lehmann, Has Friedrich Gottlieb (1763-1821) 80

Lessing Gotthold Ephraim (1729-1781) 3, 22, 121, 130, 137, 202

Levison-Gower, George Granville (1758-1833) 13

Liberation, Wars of 163, 167, 169, 183, 191, 194, 199, 201

Liebenfels, Jörg Lanz (1872-1954) 202

Lilienstern, Otto Rühle von (1780-1847) 82

List, Friedrich (1789-1846) 192

Loeben, Count Otto Heinrich (1786-1825) 165

Louis Napoleon (III) (1852-1870) 184, 192

Louis, Prince of Prussia (1772-1806) 54

Lowe, Sir Hudson (1769-1844) 179

Ludens, Paul 140

Luther, Martin (1483-1546) 3, 89

Lützow, Ludwig Adolph Wilhelm (1782-1834) 110, 136, 139, 147, 152, 153, 154, 155, 156, 172

Maimburg, Lt. (Hanoverian officer) 79

Manzoni, Alessandro (1785-1873) 182

Maria Ludovica (wife of emperor Francis II) (1787-1816) 38, 39, 48

Maria Theresa (empress of Austria, 1740-1780) (1717-1780)

Marie-Luise (Archduchess of Austria, Empress of France) (1791-1847) 5, 59

Markwart, Christoph 201

Martini, Carl (?-1857) 161

Marwitz, Friedrich August Ludwig von der (1777-1837) 153

Massmann, Hans Ferdinand (1797-1874) 140

Massow, Friedrich von 11

Maximilian Josef I, (Elector of Bavaria, after 1806 king) (1756-1825) 166

Meinecke, Friedrich (1756-1825) 195

Menzel, Carl (1784-1855) 80

Methfessel, Albert Gottlieb (1785-1869) 99

Metternich, Clemens (Count) (1773-1859) 139, 140, 141, 183, 186

Miltitz, Dietrich von (1781-1853) 166

Mirabeau, Gabriel-Honre Riqueti, Count (First president of the National Assembly in France after the revolution) (1749-1791) 20

Montebello, battle of 146

Moreau, Achille 187

Index

Morhof, Daniel Georg (1639-1691) 3

Mühlbach, Louise (1814-1873) 188

Müller, Adam (1779-1829) 35, 53, 62, 63, 68, 71, 72, 78, 80-82, 118, 155, 166

Müller, Friedrich von 172

Mundt, Theodor (1808-1861) 180

Münster, Georg Graf zu (1776-1844) 2, 168

Murner, Thomas (1475-1537) 2

Musset, Louis Charles Alfred de (1810-1857) 189

Nagler, Karl Ferdinand Friedrich von (1770-1846) 58, 118

Napoleon Bonaparte (1769-1821) 5, 13, 16, 17, 26, 28, 33, 36, 39, 45, 48, 49, 50, 58, 59, 60, 72, 74, 75, 76, 77, 78, 81, 89, 91, 92, 93, 94, 95, 98, 99, 102, 110, 117, 119, 122, 125, 126, 128, 146, 154, 155, 156, 157, 159, 160f., 165, 166, 167, 170, 171, 172, 173, 174, 177, 178, 180, 181, 182, 183, 184, 185f., 187, 188, 189, 194, 195, 196, 197, 200

Napoleon III, Louis (see Louis Napoleon)

Nations, battle of (Leipzig) 99, 161, 162, 175

Nestroy, Johann (1801-1862) 122

Nicolovius, Georg Heinrich Ludwig (1767-1839) 112, 114

Niebuhr, Barthold Georg (1776-1839) 5, 109, 118, 170, 174

Nietzsche, Friedrich (1844-1900) 102, 200

Oehlke, Waldemar (1879-?) 198

O'Meara, Barry Edward (1786-1836) 179, 187

Ompteda, Christian Friedrich Wilhelm (1765-1815) 73f.

Opitz, Martin (1597-1639) 2f.

Osten-Sacken, Fabian Gottlieb von der (1752-1837) 159

Palafox, José de (1777-1847) 95

Palm, Johann Philipp, (Book dealer) (1768-1806) 28, 103, 118f., 125, 128

Parthey, Gustav Friedrich Constantin (1798-1872) 153

Passow, Franz Ludwig Karl Friedrich (1786-1833) 139

Pestalozzi, Johann Heinrich (1746-1827) 6, 20

Petersen, Julius (1878-1941) 201

Pflugk-Harttung, Julius von (1848-1919) 195

Pfuel, Ernst Heinrich Adolf (1779-1866) 94, 125, 156

Pölitz, Karl Heinrich Ludwig (1772-1838) 166

Pöschel, Thomas (1769-1837) 119

Public Opinion 80, 81, 82, 91, 96, 120, 127, 173

Prussian-Anhalt 46

Prutz, Robert (1816-1872) 183

Pufendorf, Samuel (1632-1694) 3

Radziwil, Prince Anton Heinrich (1775-1833) 66

Raimar, Freimund (pseud., see Friedrich Rückert)

Rambach, Friedrich Eberhard (1767-1826) 12

Raumer, Friedrich von (1781-1822) 78, 83

Reil, Johann Christian (1759-1813) 109

Reimer, Georg Andrea (1776-1842) 34f., 80, 88, 109, 110, 116, 139, 173, 174, 175

Rellstab, Ludwig (1799-1860) 186

Reventlow, Juliane von (Hardenberg's wife) 76f.

Riefenstahl, Leni 203

Rochau, August von (1810-1873) 195

Rousseau, Jean-Jacques (1712-1778) 132

Royalists 7, 20

Rückert, Friedrich (1788-1866) 163-167

Rühs, Christian Friedrich (1779-1820) 170f.

Sack, Johann August (1764-1833) 75, 81

Salzmann, Christian (1744-1811) 138

Sand, Karl (1795-1820) 174

Schall, Carl (1780-1833) 80

Scharnhorst, Gerhard (1755-1813) 2, 34, 75, 96, 109f., 114, 138, 141, 152, 167, 171

Schenkendorf, Max von (1783-1817) 191

Scherer, Wilhelm (1841-1886) 197

Schill, Major Ferdinand von (1776-1809) 50, 53, 54, 55, 56, 57, 59, 61, 65, 96, 110, 117, 118, 125, 156

Schlegel, August Wilhelm (1767-1845) 182

Schlegel, Friedrich (1772-1829) 31, 182

Schleiermacher, Friedrich Daniel (1768-1834) 12, 35, 88, 103, 104-112, 131, 137, 139, 141, 151, 152, 155, 173, 174, 175, 177, 198, 200, 202

Schmalz, Theodor (1760-1831) 108, 168-172, 176

Schmeller, Johann Andreas (1785-1852) 162f.

Schön, Theodor (1773-1856) 118

Schroetter, Karl Wilhelm (1748-1819)

Schubert, Gotthilf Heinrich von (1780--1860) 62, 63-65

Shaw, George Bernard (1856-1950) 122

Sheridan, Richard Brinsley (1757-1816) 122

Sohm, Peter (Swedish book dealer) 87

Sonnenfels, Joseph von (1733-1817) 131f.

Stadion, Friedrich Lothar, Count von (1761-1811) 35

Stadion, Johann Phillip (1763-1824) 35, 36, 38, 48

Stägemann, Friedrich August von (1763-1840) 72, 80, 81, 82, 103, 116-118, 156

Steffens, Heinrich (also Henrik) (1773-1845) 75, 110

Stein, Heinrich Friedrich Karl, Reichsfreiherr vom und zum (1757-1831) 1-14, 15, 19, 25, 27, 34, 37, 39, 40, 47f., 54, 58, 59, 61, 72, 75-82, 85, 91-92, 96, 98, 99, 103, 104, 105, 109f., 111, 112, 113, 114, 115, 116, 118, 123, 124, 129, 131, 133, 134, 135, 136, 138, 139, 142, 156, 167, 168, 171, 173, 176, 182

Stoecker, Adolf (1835-1904) 202

Stolberg, Friedrich (1750-1819) 3

Stolle, Ferdinand (1806-1872) 187

Süvern, Johann Wilhelm (1775-1829) 103, 112, 113-116, 136, 173

Sybel, Heinrich von (1817-1895) 195

Tacitus, Cornelius (55-116) 2

Teutoburg Forest (battle of, 9 A.D.) 2, 89, 91, 100

Theresa, Maria (see Maria Theresa)

Theodorich of Verona, Theodorich the Great, King of the Ostrogoths (see Bern, Dietrich von)

Thiers, Adolph (1797-1877) 189, 190, 191

Tieck, Ludwig (1773-1853) 38, 59

Tilsit (peace of, July 1807) 3, 4, 31, 87, 117, 119, 126, 138, 195

Treitschke, Heinrich von (1834-1896) 152, 194, 195

Tugendbund (League of Virtue, Moral Scientific Union) 55, 80, 168, 171, 173, 175, 187

Uhland, Ludwig (1787-1862) 198

Varnhagen von Ense, Karl August (1785-1858) 25f., 75, 87, 92, 152f.

Veit, Dorothea (1763-1824) 31

Vendee (province in France, last Royalist stronghold, propaganda) 7, 10, 12, 19, 20, 85, 91, 116

Venturini, Carl Heinrich (1768-1849) 169

Vieth, Gerhard Ulrich (1763-1836) 138

Vogt, Friedrich Hermann Traugott (1857-1923) 197

Volksfreund (Journal of the Tugendbund) 55, 108

Voss, Christian (1761-1821) 3

Voss, Otto Karl Frederick von (1755-1823) 4

Wagner, Richard (1813-1883) 101, 102

Wagram, battle of 37, 50, 145

Wahrlieb, Ernst (see Bergk, Johann)

Wallmoden, Adolf von 136, 156

Wars of Liberation (see Liberation, Wars of)

Waterloo, battle of 39

Weber, Carl Maria von (1786-1826) 152, 203

Westphalen, General 39

Wickende, Julius von (1814-1896) 188

Wieland, Christoph Martin (1733-1813) 170

Wieland, Ludwig (1777-1819) 170

Wienbarg, Ludof (1802-1872) 180

Willich, Henriette 109, 111f.

William, Prince of Prussia (1783-1846) 54, 58, 110, 167, 176

Wimpfeling, Jakob (1450-1528) 2

Winterfeld, Adolf von (1824-1888) 188

Wittgenstein-Sayn, Wilhelm Ludwig (1770-1851) 47, 114, 116, 170

Wohlfart, Karl 67, 127

Wünsch, Christian Ernst (1744-1828) 30

Zastrow, Frederick Wilhelm (1758-1830) 4

Zedlitz, Joseph Christian Freiherr von (1790-1862) 185f.

Zenge, Wilhelmine von (1780-1852) 29, 30

Zimmermann, Johann Georg (1728-1795) 12

Studies in German Literature, Language, and Culture

Vol. 1. Robert E. Cazden, *A History of the German Book Trade in America to the Civil War.* 1984. 801 pp.

Vol. 2. Christoph E. Schweitzer, ed., *Daniel Pastorius: Deliciæ Hortenses or Garden-Recreations (1711).* 1982. 102 pp.

Vol. 3. Lee B. Jennings, *Justinus Kerners Weg nach Weinsberg (1809-1819): Die Entpolitisierung eines Romantikers.* 1982. 136 pp.

Vol. 4. Christopher Dolmetsch, *The German Press in the Shenandoah Valley.* 1984. 180 pp.

Vol. 5. Valentine C. Hubbs, *Hessian Journals: Unpublished Documents of the American Revolution.* 1981. 127 pp.

Vol. 6. Ruth Gross, *PLAN and the Austrian Rebirth.* 1982. 157 pp.

Vol. 7. Christian Gellinek, ed. *Hugo Grotius: Drama Concordance.* 1983. 800 pp.

Vol. 8. Helene M. Kastinger Riley, *Die weibliche Muse: Sechs Essays über künstlerisch schaffende Frauen der Goethezeit.* 1986. 280 pp.

Vol. 9. Elizabeth C. Hesson, *Twentieth Century Odyssey—A Study of Heimito von Doderer's "Die Dämonen."* 1983. 158 pp.

Vol. 10. Alfons Paquet, *Prophecies.* Translated and with an introduction by H. M. Waidson. 1983. 140 pp.

Vol. 11. Donna L. Hoffmeister, *The Theater of Confinement: Language and Survival in the Milieu Plays of Marieluise Fleißer and Franz Xaver Kroetz.* 1983. 176 pp.

Vol. 12. Clifford Bernd, H. Günther Nerjes, Fritz R. Sammern-Frankenegg, and Peter Schäffer *Goethe Proceedings: Essays Commemorating the Goethe Sesquicentennial at the University of California, Davis.* 1984. 190 pp.

Vol. 13. David Scrase, *Wilhelm Lehmann: A Critical Biography.* Part I. 1984. 191 pp.

Vol. 14. Kathleen L. Komar, *Pattern and Chaos: Multilinear Novels by Dos Passos, Döblin, Faulkner, and Koeppen.* 1983. 150 pp.

Vol. 15. Albert E. Gurganus, *The Art of Revolution: Kurt Eisner's Agitprop.* 1986. 110 pp.

Vol. 16. M. S. Jones, *Der Sturm: A Focus of Expressionism.* 1984. 275 pp.

Vol. 17. J. W. Thomas, *The Best Novellas of Medieval Germany.* 1984. 104 pp.

Vol. 18. Ursula Mahlendorf, *The Wellsprings of Literary Creation: An Analysis of Male and Female "Artist Stories" from the German Romantics to American Writers of the Present.* 1985. 292 pp.

Vol. 19. Edson Chick, *Dances of Death: Wedekind, Brecht, Dürrenmatt, and the Satiric Tradition.* 1984. 181 pp.

Vol. 20. *The Correspondence of Stefan Zweig with Raoul Auernheimer and Richard Beer-Hoffmann.* Edited by Donald Daviau, Jeffrey Berlin, and Jorun Johns. 1983. 273 pp.

Vol. 21. Robert Harrison and Katharina Wilson, trans. *Three Viennese Comedies by Johann Nestroy.* 1986. 263 pp.

Vol. 22. Fritz G. Cohen, *The Poetry of Christian Hofmann von Hofmannswaldau: A New Reading.* 1985. 195 pp.

Vol. 23. J. W. Thomas, *Ortnit and Wolfdietrich: Two Medieval Romances.* 1985. xxviii + 97 pp.

Vol. 24. Richard E. Schade, *Studies in Early German Comedy 1500-1650.* 1988. 280 pp.

Vol. 25. Clifford Bernd, ed. *Franz Grillparzer's "Der arme Spielmann": New Critical Directions.* 1988. Circa 410 pp.

Vol. 26. *Seven Stories by Marie von Ebner-Eschenbach,* trans. by Helga H. Harriman. 1986. xli + 118 pp.

Vol. 27. Robert Spaethling, *Music and Mozart in the Life of Goethe.* 1987. 264 pp.

Vol. 28. Susan C. Anderson, *Grass and Grimmelshausen: Günter Grass's "Das Treffen in Telgte" and Rezeptionstheorie.* 1986. 107 pp.

Vol. 29. Hugo Bekker, *Gottfried's Tristan: Journey through the Realm of Eros.* 1988. 310 pp.

Vol. 30. Steve Dowden, ed. *Literature, Philosophy, Politics, and the Mind of Hermann Broch: Centenary Perspectives.* 1988. Circa 340 pp.

Vol. 31. John M. Grandin, *Kafka's Prussian Advocate: A Study of the Influence of Heinrich von Kleist on Franz Kafka.* 1987. 191 pp.

Vol. 32. Otto Johnston, *The Myth of a Nation: Literature and Politics in Prussia under Napoleon.* To appear 1988. Circa 250 pp.

Vol. 33. Edith Waldstein, *Bettine von Arnim and the Politics of Romantic Conversation.* 1988. Circa 150 pp.

Vol. 34. Richard Critchfield and Wulf Koepke, ed., *Eighteenth Century German Authors and their Aesthetic Theories: Literature and the other Arts.* 1988. Circa 270 pp.

Vol. 35. James C. O'Flaherty, *The Quarrel of Reason with Itself: Essays on Hamann, Nietzsche, Lessing, and Michaelis.* 1988. 248 pp.

Vol. 36. Thomas P. Saine, *Black Bread, White Bread: German Intellectuals and the French Revolution.* 1988. 440 pp.

Vol. 37. Robert Harrison and Katharina Wilson, trans. *Ad Absurdum: A Hans Weigel Anthology.* 1987. 157 pp.

Vol. 38. Jerry Glenn, Joachim Herrmann, and Rebecca S. Rodgers, ed. *Alfred Gong — Early Poems: A Selection from the Years 1941–1945.* 152 pp. 1987.

Goethe Yearbook

Yearbook of the North American Goethe Society, ed. Thomas P. Saine, vol. I. 1982. 196 pp. ISBN: 0-938100-18-1.

Vols. I-IV (1983–87) are available.